VISIT US AT

ESS®

Techno Security's™ Guide to Managing Risks

FOR IT MANAGERS, AUDITORS, AND INVESTIGATORS

Jack Wiles

Russ Rogers Technical Editor

**FOREWORD
BY DONALD WITHERS**
CEO AND COFOUNDER
OF THETRAININGCO.

KEY	SERIAL NUMBER
001	HJIRTCV764
002	PO9873D5FG
003	829KM8NJH2
004	GHJ923HJMN
005	CVPLQ6WQ23
006	VBP965T5T5
007	HJJJ863WD3E
008	2987GVTWMK
009	629MP5SDJT
010	IMWQ295T6T

PUBLISHED BY
Elsevier, Inc.
30 Corporate Drive
Burlington, MA 01803

Techno Security's Guide to Managing Risks for IT Managers, Auditors, and Investigators

Copyright © 2007 by Elsevier, Inc. All rights reserved. Printed in the United States of America. Except as permitted under the Copyright Act of 1976, no part of this publication may be reproduced or distributed in any form or by any means, or stored in a database or retrieval system, without the prior written permission of the publisher, with the exception that the program listings may be entered, stored, and executed in a computer system, but they may not be reproduced for publication.

Printed in the United States of America
1 2 3 4 5 6 7 8 9 0

ISBN-10: 1-59749-138-1
ISBN-13: 978-1-59749-138-9

Publisher: Andrew Williams
Acquisitions Editor: Gary Byrne
Technical Editor: Russ Rogers
Cover Designer: Michael Kavish

Page Layout and Art: Patricia Lupien
Copy Editors: Mike McGee, Adrienne Rebello
Indexer: Richard Carlson

For information on rights, translations, and bulk sales, contact Matt Pedersen, Commercial Sales Director, at m.pedersen@elsevier.com.

Acknowledgments

Syngress would like to acknowledge the following people for their kindness and support in making this book possible.

A million thanks to Jack Wiles and his partner, Don Withers, at The Training Co. They have been a good partner to Syngress, and we are delighted to bring this first Techno book to market.

Lead Author

Jack Wiles is a Security Professional with over 30 years' experience in security-related fields, including computer security, disaster recovery, and physical security. He is a professional speaker and has trained federal agents, corporate attorneys, and internal auditors on a number of computer crime-related topics. He is a pioneer in presenting on a number of subjects that are now being labeled "Homeland Security" topics. Well over 10,000 people have attended one or more of his presentations since 1988. Jack is also a cofounder and President of TheTrainingCo. and is in frequent contact with members of many state and local law enforcement agencies as well as Special Agents with the U.S. Secret Service, FBI, U.S. Customs, Department of Justice, the Department of Defense, and numerous members of High-Tech Crime units. He was also appointed as the first president of the North Carolina InfraGard chapter, which is now one of the largest chapters in the country. He is also a founding member and "official" MC of the U.S. Secret Service South Carolina Electronic Crimes Task Force.

Jack is also a Vietnam veteran who served with the 101st Airborne Division in Vietnam in 1967-68. He recently retired from the U.S. Army Reserves as a lieutenant colonel and was assigned directly to the Pentagon for the final seven years of his career. In his spare time, he has been a senior contributing editor for several local, national, and international magazines.

I really appreciate reading the comments written by my new friend Johnny Long as he first thanked his creator in his Penetration Tester's book by Syngress. I'm in Johnny's camp in acknowledging that I can do nothing without the help of my Lord and Savior, Jesus Christ. I dedicate my small part of this book to Him, my wonderful wife, Valerie, and my son, Tyler. My partner Don Withers is like a brother to me in every way. For eight years, we have been fortunate to produce our Techno Security and our new Techno Forensics conferences, which have had attendees register from over 40 coun-

tries around the world. I wish that I had space to thank all of the other authors of this book. I know them all well, and I have known some of them for more than two decades. These are some of the most respected and talented security minds in the world, and I am honored to have my work in the same book as theirs. And last but certainly not least, I'd like to thank my good friend Russ Rogers for his technical editing help and Amy Pedersen from Syngress Publishing for being so patient as I learned the ropes of getting a book ready to be published.

Jack wrote Chapter 1, "Social Engineering: Risks, Threats, Vulnerabilities, and Countermeasures.

Technical Editor

Russ Rogers (CISSP, CISM, IAM, IEM, HonScD) is author of the popular *Hacking a Terror Network* (Syngress Publishing, ISBN: 1928994989); coauthor on multiple other books, including the best selling *Stealing the Network: How to Own a Continent* (Syngress, ISBN: 1931836051) and *Network Security Evaluation Using the NSA IEM* (Syngress, ISBN: 1597490350); and Editor in Chief of *The Security Journal*. Russ is Cofounder, Chief Executive Officer, and Chief Technology Officer of Security Horizon, a veteran-owned small business based in Colorado Springs, CO. Russ has been involved in information technology since 1980 and has spent the last 15 years working professionally as both an IT and INFOSEC consultant. Russ has worked with the United States Air Force (USAF), National Security Agency (NSA), and the Defense Information Systems Agency (DISA). He is a globally renowned security expert, speaker, and author who has presented at conferences around the world, including Amsterdam, Tokyo, Singapore, Sao Paulo, and cities all around the United States.

Russ has an Honorary Doctorate of Science in Information Technology from the University of Advancing Technology, a Master's Degree in Computer Systems Management from the University of Maryland, a Bachelor of Science in Computer Information Systems from the University of Maryland, and an Associate Degree in Applied Communications Technology from the Community College of the Air Force. He is a member of both ISSA and ISACA and cofounded the Global Security Syndicate (gssyndi-cate.org) and the Security Tribe (securitytribe.com). He acts in the role of professor of network security for the University of Advancing Technology (uat.edu).

Russ would like to thank his father for his lifetime of guidance, his kids (Kynda and Brenden) for their understanding, and Michele for her constant support. A great deal of thanks go to Andrew Williams from Syngress Publishing for the abundant opportunities and trust he gives me. Shouts go out to UAT, Security Tribe, the GSS, the Defcon Groups, and the DC Forums. I'd like to also thank my friends, Chris, Greg, Michele, Ping, Pyr0, and everyone in #dc-forums that I don't have room to list here.

Russ wrote Chapter 9, "The Basics of Penetration Testing."

Contributors

Dr. Eric Cole is currently chief scientist for Lockheed Martin Information Technology (LMIT), specializing in advanced technology research. Eric is a highly sought-after network security consultant and speaker. Eric has consulted for international banks and Fortune 500 companies. He also has advised venture capitalist firms on what start-ups should be funded. He has in-depth knowledge of network security and has come up with creative ways to secure his clients' assets. He is the author of several books, including *Insider Threat: Protecting the Enterprise from Sabotage, Spying, and Theft* (Syngress Publishing, ISBN: 1597490482); *Cyber Spying: Tracking Your Family's (Sometimes) Secret Online Lives* (Syngress Publishing, ISBN: 1-931836-41-8); *Hackers Beware: Defending Your Network from the Wiley Hacker*; *Hiding in Plain Sight*; and *The Network Security Bible*. Eric holds several patents and has written numerous magazine and journal articles. Eric worked for the CIA for more than seven years and has created several successful network security practices. Eric is an invited keynote speaker at government and international conferences and has appeared in interviews on CBS News, "60 Minutes," and CNN.

Eric wrote Chapter 11, "Insider Threat."

Phil Drake is Communications Manager for the *Charlotte Observer* in Charlotte, N. C. *The Observer* is a daily newspaper that serves readers throughout North and South Carolina. In addition to the newspaper, the *Charlotte Observer* produces specialty magazines, voice information, and Internet services.

Phil is responsible for all aspects of communications at *Observer* operations in both Carolinas, including telephone and data communications, wireless systems, conventional and trunked two-way radio, and satellite systems. He is also responsible for business continuity and disaster response planning and related budgeting. He is responsible for providing emergency communications facilities for reporters and photographers covering breaking news stories.

His background includes photojournalism, mainframe computer support, network management, telecommunications planning and management, and business continuity planning. Phil is a former chairman of the Contingency Planning Association of the Carolinas and currently serves as a Board Advisor of the organization. He is a Certified Business Continuity Professional with the Disaster Recovery Institute International.

Phil speaks to public and private sector groups and has been interviewed by and written for a number of national publications on a wide range of emergency communication issues and business/homeland defense planning. He leads business continuity training seminars for both the public and private sectors. He also has provided project management in business continuity and has advised major national clients in emergency planning, workforce protection, threat assessment, and incident response.

He enjoys backpacking and spending time in the outdoors. He also has taught outdoor living skills to youth group leaders. He was appointed by the North Carolina Secretary of the Department of Environment and Natural Resources as a voting member of the NC Geological Survey Advisory Committee.

Phil wrote Chapter 2, "Personal, Workforce, and Family Preparedness."

Ron Green (CISSP, ISSMP), a Senior Vice President within the Information Security Business Continuity division of Bank of America, currently serves as an Information Security Business Continuity Officer supporting the Bank's Network Computing Group. He formerly managed a bank team dedicated to handling cyber investigations, computer forensics, and electronic discovery. Prior to joining Bank of America, Ron was a Secret Service Agent and part of the agency's Electronic Crimes Agent Program (ECSAP). In addition to the investigative and protection work all agents perform, ECSAP agents perform cyber investigations and computer forensics for the agency. Ron started with the Secret Service in its Phoenix Field Office and then transferred to the agency's headquarters to become part of the Electronic Crimes Branch (ECB). While part of ECB he provided support to the ECSAP agents in the field. He also worked on national and international cyber crimes cases, initiatives, and laws. He was the project manager for Forward Edge and the Best Practice Guides for Seizing Electronic Evidence, version 2.0.

Ron graduated from the United States Military Academy at West Point, earning a bachelor's degree in Mechanical Engineering, and he earned a Graduate Certificate from George Washington University on Computer Security and Information Assurance. Ron currently serves as the Treasurer/Secretary for the Financial Services Information Sharing and Analysis Center (FS/ISAC) and as a Board Member for the Institute for Computer Forensic Professionals. Ron currently lives in North Carolina with his wife, Cheryl, and their four children.

Ron wrote Chapter 6, "Open Source Intelligence."

Greg Kipper (CISSP) is a Senior Security Engineer with Tenacity Solutions Incorporated. Tenacity is a woman-owned, small business that is headquartered in Reston, VA, that specializes in information security and information assurance. Greg has been involved in the field of security and information assurance over the past 13 years. Through his experiences in the security sector as a systems engineer, security analyst, and consultant, he moved into the emerging field of digital forensics. The last seven years of his career have been spent on working on forensic investigations studying the future of technologies and their forensic impact of that data to the process of evidence. Some of his notable works include the books *Investigator's Guide to Steganography*, *Wireless Crime and Forensic Investigation*, and the upcoming *Proactive Forensics* as well as a Congressional report outlining technical methods of reducing the risk of insider threats. Greg continues to actively contribute to the fields of security and digital forensics by giving lectures annually at DoD Cybercrime, TechnoSecurity, and TechnoForensics.

Greg wrote Chapter 10, "What Is Steganography?"

Johnny Long is a Christian by grace, a family guy by choice, a professional hacker by trade, a pirate by blood, a ninja in training, a security researcher, and an author. My home on the Web is http://johnny.ihackstuff.com.

I would like to thank my wife and kids for their continuing support of yet another hobby (writing/editing) that has spun out of control just as all the others have. I love you guys.

I have many people to thank, but first, I would like to thank God for taking the time to pierce my way-logical mind with the unfathomable gifts of sight by faith and eternal life through the sacrifice of Jesus Christ. I would also like to thank Jack Wiles and Russ for bringing me on board with this project; the real Vince, who remains an inspiration; Adam Laurie (aka Major Malfunction); StankDawg (aka David Blake); Barry Wels of Toool; Malcolm Mead; Pablos Holman; Tim "Thor" Mulllen; Stephen King; Ted Dekker; Neil Stephenson; and the wealth of amazingly talented Christian rock artists whose music is present for every word I write. I would also like to thank the C.H.A.O.S. team (nudge, nudge) for being an important part of those early days. Thanks also to the moderators and members of my Web site for your constant support.

I had a great time with this chapter, and I look forward to expanding it to a full-blown book. No-tech hackers rejoice!

Johnny wrote Chapter 8, "No-Tech Hacking."

Dennis F. O'Brien is a private consultant having held senior IT security positions within Bell Laboratories, AT&T, Citigroup, and other Fortune 100 financial sector enterprises. Dennis, a well-known technical expert having more than 30 years' experience in the exploitation of controls, comes to us as a canary to discuss the kinds of "evil things" that can be done using well-intended, generally available tools and services such as RFID. Examining the big picture and then presenting realistic scenarios, such as destabilizing public faith in the financial services industry or corrupting an asset database through input data tampering, are examples of his work.

He is known for his annual predictions of possible mal-events that may occur in the near future and what the results may be.

Dennis wrote Chapter 5, "RFID: An Introduction to Security Issues, and Concerns."

Kevin O'Shea is a Homeland Security and Intelligence Specialist for the Technical Analysis Group in the Justiceworks program at the University of New Hampshire. Kevin assisted in the development of the NH Strategic Plan to Combat Cyber Crime and currently supports the implementation of the Strategic Plan. Kevin has authored and coauthored a number of high-tech training programs for the law enforcement community and has assisted in the development of a new digital forensics paradigm in use in N.H.

Prior to working at the University of New Hampshire, he was a Research Associate for Project Management within the Technical Analysis Group in the Institute for Security Technology Studies at Dartmouth College. He was a member of the research team and substantive author of three critical national reports to document and present the most pressing impediments facing the law-enforcement community when investigating and responding to cyber attacks: *Law Enforcement Tools and Technologies for Investigating Cyber Attacks: A National Needs Assessment, Gap Analysis, and the Research and Development Agenda.*

Kevin wrote Chapter 3, "Seizure of Digital Information." This chapter was taken from Cyber Crime Investigations: Bridging the Gaps between, Security Professionals, Law Enforcement, and Prosecutors (Syngress Publishing, ISBN: 1597491330).

Amber Schroader has been involved in the field of computer forensics for the past 17 years. Amber has developed and taught numerous training courses for the computer forensic arena, specializing in the field of wireless forensics as well as mobile technologies. Amber is the CEO of Paraben Corporation and continues to act as the driving force behind some of the most innovative forensic technologies. As a pioneer in the field, Amber has been key in developing new technology to help investigators with the extraction of digital evidence from hard drives, e-mail, and handheld and mobile devices. Amber has extensive experience in dealing with a wide array of forensic investigators ranging from federal, state, local, and foreign government as well as corporate investigators. With an aggressive development schedule, Amber continues to bring new and exciting technology to the computer forensic community worldwide and is dedicated to supporting the investigator through new technologies and training services that are being provided through Paraben Corporation. Amber is involved in many different computer investigation organizations, including The Institute of Computer Forensic Professionals (ICFP) as the chairman of the board, HTCIA, CFTT, and FLETC.

Amber currently resides in Utah and Virginia with her two children, Azure and McCoy.

Amber wrote Chapter 4, "Handheld Forensics."

Raymond Todd Blackwood is an IT Manager for a private university in Tempe, AZ, with over 12 years of experience in managing technology projects, teams, and systems. He currently oversees the development of technology projects at the university and provides lectures and training on leadership principles for technology geeks. Raymond teaches several courses that focus on thinking and brain performance, as well as managing technology, systems, and change.

Raymond started his career in digital film making, which took him from his southern roots to the Southwest, where he did his undergraduate studies and received his BA in Multimedia and Digital Animation and Production. Producing independent digital films led him into technology management as he began to design and implement technology for animation and multimedia applications. A series of events catalyzed by a passion for learning and working in all kinds of technology projects led Raymond to become a Manager of Information Technology in 2000 for the university. Soon thereafter Raymond began his graduate work and received his Master's of Business Administration and Technology Management in 2006.

Raymond is the comoderator of the Phoenix Future Salon through the Accelerated Studies Foundation. He also serves on the board of directors for the Greater Arizona eLearning Association and the Arizona Telecommunications and Information Council, and he is the faculty sponsor for DC480, the university's hacking club.

Raymond wrote Chapter 7, "Wireless Awareness: Increasing the Sophistication of Wireless Users."

Foreword Contributor

Donald P. Withers is the CEO and cofounder of TheTrainingCo., which produces the Annual International Techno Security & Techno Forensic Conferences each year. Don has an extensive background in Information Security and was a member of the management team at Ernst & Young's Information Security Services practice for the mid-Atlantic region. He also served as the Director of Information Security for Bell Atlantic, where he championed the development of a corporate incident response team and implemented their war room facility used for managing investigations, vulnerability testing, and forensic analysis.

He also served as a voting member of the American National Standards Institute Committee T1 for nine years developing and representing Bell Atlantic's positions on computer and network security. He was the Sub-working Group Secretary and Technical Editor for the committee that was instrumental in developing several of the first telecommunications standards in North America relating to network security.

Don was the cofounder and two-term president of the Maryland Chapter of InfraGard and is a member of the Secret Service's Electronic Crimes Task Force. He was the cofounder and two-term President of the mid-Atlantic Chapter of the High Technology Crime Investigation Association, and he has served as secretary for its National Board of Directors. He is a member of the

American Society for Industrial Security, the Association of Former Intelligence Officers, and the Academy of Security Educators and Trainers, where he earned the academy's designation of Certified Security Trainer. Don is also a member of the Nine Lives Associates and has earned its designation of Personal Protection Specialist from the Executive Protection Institute. He has attended the Federal Law Enforcement Training Center in Glenco, GA, and has a Bachelor's degree in Criminal Justice from the University of Maryland.

Contents

Introduction xxxiii

Foreword xxxvii

Chapter 1 Social Engineering: Risks,
Threats, Vulnerabilities, and Countermeasures 1

Introduction 2

How Easy Is It? 2

Human Nature: Human Weakness 3

Risk Management: Performing a Mini Risk Assessment 3

    What Do I Have at Risk? 4

    What Are Some Possible Threats? 4

    What Are Some of the Possible Vulnerabilities? 4

    What about My Countermeasures? 5

Outsider–Insider Threats 5

The Mind of a Social Engineer 6

The Mind of a Victim 7

Countermeasures: How Do Bad

Guys Target Us, and What Can We Do About It 8

    Key Control 8

    Dumpster Diving Still Works 10

    Employee Badges 12

    Shredder Technology Has Changed 13

    Keep an Eye on Corporate or Agency Phonebooks 15

    Tailgating 16

    Building Operations: Cleaning Crew Awareness 17

    Spot Check Those Drop Ceilings 20

    Check for Keystroke Readers 20

    Check Those Phone Closets 23

    Remove a Few Door Signs 23

    Review Video Security Logs 24

    Motion-Sensing Lights 25

    Check All Locks for Proper Operation 25

    The Elephant Burial Ground 26

    Internal Auditors Are Your Friend 31

Always Be Slightly Suspicious 31
Get Every Employee Involved 31
Social Engineering Awareness: A War Story 31
Answer to the Riddle 36
Summary 36

Chapter 2 Personal, Workforce,
and Family Preparedness 37
Introduction 38
Threats 38
Your Personal Preparedness Plan 41
The Escape Pack 43
Description of Kit Contents 44
Workforce Preparedness 45
Steps for Successful Workforce Preparedness 47
Get Out, Get Away, and Get in Touch 48
Family Preparedness Plan 50
Possible Meeting Points .51
Community Shelter 52
The Personal Evacuation Bag 52
Preparedness Pantry 53
Water 56
Cooking 57
Testing Your Home Preparedness Plan 58
Family Ready Kit 59
Family Ready Kit Contents 60
No Lights? No Problem! 61
Emergency Lighting 62
Handheld Lights 63
Headlamps 64
General Illumination Lamps 65
Spots and Floodlights 65
Emergency Power 66
UPS and Battery Backup 69
Portable 12-Volt Inverters 69
Alternative Power Sources 70
Staying in Touch 70

Dynamo Radios 72

FRS Radios 73

Ham Radio 73

The "POTS" Line 73

Summary 74

Chapter 3 Seizure of Digital Information 75

Introduction 76

Defining Digital Evidence 79

Digital Evidence Seizure Methodology 82

Seizure Methodology in Depth 84

Step 1: Digital Media Identification 86

Step 2: Minimizing the
Crime Scene by Prioritizing the Physical Media . . .86

Step 3: Seizure of Storage Devices and Media 87

To Pull the Plug or Not to
Pull the Plug, That Is the Question 88

Factors Limiting the Wholesale Seizure of Hardware 90

Size of Media 90

Disk Encryption 91

Privacy Concerns 92

Delays Related to Laboratory Analysis 93

Protecting the Time of the
Most Highly Trained Personnel 94

The Concept of the First Responder 96

Other Options for Seizing Digital Evidence 98

Responding to a Victim
of a Crime Where Digital Evidence Is Involved 100

Seizure Example 102

Previewing On-Scene Information to Determine the
Presence and Location of Evidentiary Data Objects . . .104

Obtaining Information from a Running Computer . . .105

Imaging Information On-Scene 107

Imaging Finite Data Objects On-Scene 108

Use of Tools for Digital Evidence Collection 111

Common Threads within Digital Evidence Seizure 112

Determining the Most Appropriate Seizure Method 115
Summary 117
Works Cited 119
    Additional Relevant Resources 121

Chapter 4 Handheld Forensics. 123
Digital Forensics 124
What Is the Handheld Forensic Impact? 125
    Digital Forensic Foundations 125
        File System Differences 126
        Static versus Active 127
        Storage Capacity Differences 128
        Imaging Techniques 129
    Evidence Collection 129
    First Responder 131
    Collection to Handling 133
    PDA Handling 133
Cellular Handling 135
Evidence Preservation 137
    Maintain the Device 138
Maintain a Forensic Data Connection 139
    Forensic Grade Tools 140
Analysis and Reporting 141
Summary 141
Bibliography 141

**Chapter 5 RFID: An Introduction
to Security Issues and Concerns 143**
Introduction 144
Background 144
    Early Implementations 145
        Manual Inventory 145
        Bar Codes 145
        Global Source Tagging 145
    Current RFID Implementations 146
        Unidirectional Information Flow 146
        Bidirectional Information Flow 146
    RFID Purposes 146
        Inventory Tracking 147

Where Does RFID fit in? 147
Technology Involved 148
  How RFID Works 148
    Parts of an RFID System 148
  RFID Security from a Functional Perspective 150
    Can RFID be used for Security? 150
    Can RFID, in and of Itself, Function Securely? 151
    Can Systems Implemented
    Using RFID Technology Be Secure? 151
  Spy Chips or Consumer Value Tags? 151
  The Electronic Product Code
  (EPC), an RFID Specification/Standard 152
    EPC Generation 1 152
    EPC Generation 2 152
    EPC Generation 3 152
  RFID Frequencies 152
    Low Frequency (LF) Band 153
    High Frequency (HF) Band 153
    Ultra High Frequency (UHF) Band 153
    Microwave Band 154
    Frequency-Based Information Protection Concerns   154
  Active and Passive RFID Comparison 155
    Characteristics of Active RFID systems 155
    Characteristics of Passive RFID systems 155
  Software RFID Tools 156
  New RFID Marketing Techniques 156
  Authorizing Access to Program an RFID Chip 156
  US Patent Application 20020165758 156
  Authority to Monitor RFID Transmissions? 157
  Providing Verifiable Protection 157
  RFID Chip Placement 158
  A Few RFID Uses 158
    Passports (Passive) 158
    Public Transportation Passess
    (Active, Battery Operated) 158
    Exxon Mobil SpeedPass (Active) 159

Conference Badges (Passive) 159
Tagging People as Resources (Passive) 159
Cow Chips (Passive) 159
Cadaver Chips (Passive) 159
Smart Shelves 159
Security TAG Concerns 159
Altering the Identity of Goods 159
RFID Money 160
Potentially Bad Uses 161
RFID Virus 162
The Future 162
Summary 163

Chapter 6 Open Source Intelligence 165
Introduction 166
Direction 166
Subcomponent: Purchase a Ticket 167
Subcomponent: Drive to the Stadium 167
Subcomponents: Purchase
Ticket and Drive to the Stadium 168
Concepts 168
Discovery 169
Sources of Information 169
Cyberthreats 169
Physical Threats 172
Financial Service Sector 172
Other Information Sharing and Analysis Centers . . .173
Search Engines 175
Fee-Based Services 177
Discrimination 178
Preliminary Assessment 178
Content Assessment 179
Advocacy Assessment 180
Business/Marketing Assessment 181
News Assessment 183
Informational Assessment .185
Personal Assessment 186

Collection Trade Craft 189
Distillation 191
Basic Analysis Support 192
Intermediate Analysis Support 192
Dissemination 194
Summary 195
Notes 196

Chapter 7 Wireless Awareness:
Increasing the Sophistication of Wireless Users 197
Introduction 198
Putting Together a War-Driving Team 200
Increasing User Sophistication 204
Frequency-Hopping Spread Spectrum
(FHSS) and Direct-Sequence Spread Spectrum (DSSS) 204
The 802.11 Alphabet 205
Unauthorized Access 206
Eavesdropping 207
Interference and Jamming 207
Physical Threats 208
802.11 Security 209
Confidentiality 209
Integrity 210
Availability 210
Goals of Network Security 211
Security Ramifications 212
Human Factors 213
Knowing Your Weaknesses 214
Limiting Access 214
Persistence Achieves Security 215
Physical Security 215
Perimeter Security 215
The Radiation Zone 216
Firewalls 217
Ad-Hoc and Infrastructure Modes 217
The SSID 218
Virtual Private Networks 219
Radius Servers 219

Configuration Weaknesses 221
Policy Weaknesses 222
Human Error 222
Legal Liability 223
Technology Weaknesses 224
802.11 Authentication 225
Open System Authentication 225
Shared Key Authentication .226
LEAP Point 227
SSL/TLS 227
Kerberos Authentication 228
802.11 Security (Encryption) 228
WPA 230
Intrusion Detection Systems 231
Access Point Spoofing 232
Summary 232

Chapter 8 No-Tech Hacking 233
Introduction: What Is "No-Tech Hacking?" 234
Physical Security 239
Tailgating 240
Where Are Your Badges? 243
Electronic Badge Authentication 248
Lock Bumping 250
Master Lock Brute Forcing .252
Picking Locks with Toilet Paper? 258
Electric Flossers: A Low-Tech Classic 260
Information Security 261
Shoulder Surfing 261
Dumpster Diving 271
Watching TV, Hacker Style .277
Checklist 285
Summary 287
Notes 287

Chapter 9 The Basics of Penetration Testing 289
Introduction 290
Know the Security Analysis Life Cycle 290

Programmatic Testing 292
Technical Testing 292
Customer Responsibilities 293
Penetration Testing 293
Know When to Deviate 293
Stick to the Life Cycle 294
Break Out of the Life Cycle .294
The Penetration Tester Mentality 295
Know the Core Processes 295
Think for Yourself 296
Ethical Conduct 297
Know When to Fold 297
Use the Right Tools 297
Build Your Own 298
The Penetration Methodology 298
Information Gathering 299
Search Engines 299
Newsgroup Searches 300
Forums and Blogs 300
DNS / WHOIS / ARIN 301
Web Site Mirroring 302
Financial Web Sites 302
Network Enumeration 303
Vulnerability Identification .303
Vulnerability Exploitation .303
Privilege Escalation 304
Expansion of Reach 305
Ensure Future Access 306
Compromise Information 307
The Cleanup 308
Summary 308

Chapter 10 What Is Steganography? 311
Introduction 312
Defining Steganography 312
Some Useful Definitions 312
The Differences between

Steganography and Watermarking 313
The Prisoners' Problem .313
History and Steganography 314
    The Greeks 315
    The Chinese 315
    Gaspar Schott 315
    Giovanni Porta 315
    Girolamo Cardano 316
The Culpers 316
Civil War Rugs 316
World War I 317
World War II 317
The Vietnam War 317
Analog Steganography 318
Microdots 318
One-Time Pads 318
Semagrams 318
Null Ciphers 319
    Type Spacing and Offsetting 319
    Invisible Ink 319
    Newspaper Code 319
    Jargon Code 320
Digital Steganography 320
Steganography Techniques 320
    Injection 320
    Substitution 321
    Generation of New Files 321
The Six Categories of Steganography 321
Substitution System 321
Transform Domain Techniques 322
Spread Spectrum Techniques 322
Statistical Methods 322
Distortion Techniques 323
Cover Generation Methods 323
Types of Steganography 323
Linguistic Steganography 323

Text Semagrams 323
Technical Steganography 323
Embedding Methods 324
Least Significant Bit (LSB) 324
Transform Techniques 324
Spread-Spectrum Encoding 324
Perceptual Masking 324
Steganography Applied to Different Media 325
Still Images: Pictures 325
Moving Images: Video 325
Audio Files 325
Text Files 326
Steganographic File Systems 326
Hiding in Disk Space 326
Unused Sectors 327
Hidden Partitions 327
Slack Space 327
Hiding in Network Packets 327
Issues in Information Hiding .328
Levels of Visibility 328
Robustness vs. Payload 328
File Format Dependence 328
Watermarking 328
Classification of Watermarks 329
Fragile 329
Robust 329
Steganography Tools 329
Still Images: Pictures 329
Moving Images: Video 330
Audio Files 330
Text Files 331
Steganographic File Systems 331
Real-World Uses 331
Detection and Attacks 332
Detection 332
Statistical Tests 332

Stegdetect 332
Stegbreak 332
Visible Noise 332
Appended Spaces and "Invisible" Characters 332
Color Palettes 333
Attack Types 333
Stego Only Attack 333
Known Cover Attack 333
Known Message Attack .333
Chosen Stego Attack 334
Chosen Message Attack .334
Disabling or Active Attacks .334
Blur 334
Noise 334
Noise Reduction 334
Sharpen 334
Rotate 334
Resample 334
Soften 334
Summary 335

Chapter 11 Insider Threat 337
Introduction 338
The Devil Inside 338
The Importance of Insider Threat 339
Insider Threat Defined 341
Authorized versus Unauthorized Insider 342
Categories of Insider Threat 344
Key Aspects of Insider Threat 347
Acceptable Level of Loss 348
Prevention versus Detection 349
Insider versus External Threat 350
Why the Insider Threat Has Been Ignored 351
Organizations Do Not Know It Is Happening 351
It Is Easy to Be in Denial .352
Fear of Bad Publicity 353
Why the Insider Threat Is Worse Than the External Threat 353

Easier 354
Current Solutions Do Not Scale 354
High Chance of Success .355
Less Chance of Being Caught 355
The Effect of Insider Threats on a Company 355
How Bad Is It—Statistics on What Is Happening 357
Insider Threat Study 357
Beware of Insider Threats to Your Security 365
Espionage: A Real Threat 367
Preliminary System Dynamics
Maps of the Insider Cyber-Threat Problem 367
Do You Really Know What
Your Programmers Are Doing? 368
How Much Is Too Much Data Loss? 368
Targets of Attack 369
The Threat Is Real 371
Profiling the Insider 374
Preventing Insider Threat 375
New World Order 376
Future Trends 377
Policies and Procedures .377
Access Controls 378
Miniaturization 378
Moles 378
Outsourcing 379
Porous Networks and Systems 379
Ease of Use of Tools 380
Relays on the Rise 380
Social Engineering 381
Plants 381
Tolerance Increasing 381
Framing 382
Lack of Cyber Respect .382
Summary 382

Index. 383

Introduction

Why a Book on Techno Security?

This book has been in the making for about 15 years. There are many ways to convey valuable information, but in my opinion, there is no better way than the printed word. It simply doesn't go away once the ink dries. That's a good thing. Many of the authors of this book have been asked to express their opinions in every way conceivable. They are the world's experts, and their opinions and suggestions can help save companies from a lot of headaches and even embarrassments.

I have personally been interviewed about a dozen times on television news broadcasts. The interview would typically take about 30 to 60 minutes. The footage of the interview that actually was transmitted over the airways was about 10 seconds. Did any of you see or remember any of these interviews? Most likely not, and there is no practical way to go back and see even the 10 seconds of information presented by an industry expert (their opinion) should you want to. It's just gone. Fortunately, the written word is here to stay. You can go back and reread any part of a book at your leisure.

This book is meant to be a reference full of lessons learned, war stories, and suggestions, all of which will help you improve your professional and personal Techno Security posture.

Our Authors' Writing Styles

We have intentionally not tried to limit how our authors share their information. Most of my writing is in the first person. I have been a professional speaker and trainer for over 20 years, and I put words on paper as if I were presenting them in person at one of my presentations. That's just my style, and it's very conversational. Some of our other writers will put their words on paper in different ways. For some of the authors, this will be their first published work by a major book publisher. Others are very well-known authors with several books of their own already in print.

One thing that all the authors do have in common, however, is their hard-earned knowledge in a variety of critical areas associated with Techno Security. The chapters addressing the various subjects covered in this first volume aren't compiled in any order of importance. Each one stands alone as a valuable reference for the area covered. Many of the chapters will address issues that could be considered a subchapter of that chapter.

Such critical countermeasures as physical security, employee awareness training, due diligence, risk mitigation, computer crimes, and working with law enforcement will be addressed as sidebars, tips, warnings, and suggestions in the respective chapters. Use them in whatever way you see fit. Many countermeasures discussed would make excellent subjects for monthly or at least quarterly security awareness training classes. If you find and react to even one small tip found in this book, that could be worth much more than the small cost to purchase this book full of hard-earned written experiences of these Techno Security pioneers.

Techno Security versus Computer Security

There is a reason why we have called our conferences and this book Techno Security and not simply Computer Security. When deciding to come up with a name for our company and our first conference, we thought long and hard about a name that would be meaningful, that would be relevant for a long time, and that would not sound worn out or overused.

As we all now know, technical security is so much more that just computer security. Just about everything that is important to every one of us now resides on some form of media in some database somewhere, and the ways of getting to that information are increasing every day.

Topics like RFID security didn't even exist as a major issue when we held our first Techno Security conference just eight years ago. Many of the topics addressed so well in other books published by Syngress weren't even issues back then. There is so much more to be aware of now, that getting and staying secure is more than a full-time proposition for most companies.

There is a lot more at risk as technology continues to advance beyond anything that we even considered just a few years ago. The threats targeting what we have at risk are increasing in sophistication each year. Our chances of being victims of these threats could grow simply because of a lack of knowledge of the new threats. The process of becoming aware of and implementing effective countermeasures is the name of the game in lowering your risk. This book is meant to help you do that.

Stay safe out there.

—Jack Wiles, Lead Author

Foreword

We're thrilled to be working on this book with the Syngress Publishing team, along with so many of our friends, colleagues, speakers, sponsors and exhibitors at our annual Techno conferences.

This book has been almost 10 years in the making. When my partner, Jack Wiles, and I started The Training Co. in 1999, we also started our first Techno Security Conference in Myrtle Beach, SC. We quickly realized that as we got older, a lot of our friends had made their way to the top of the very exciting worlds of information security, digital forensics, and risk management. Many of them became our keynote speakers, presenters, and trainers as we grew the conference business. We had tremendous respect for these industry pioneers, and the Techno Security landscape was growing rapidly, and so too was the popularity of our conferences. That was a very exciting period.

I remember meeting Jack in 1990 while we were on a train headed to Philadelphia. Jack and I quickly became good friends. We had similar values and a lot in common. We also shared a deep desire to help make a difference and give something back to the security community that we had been a part of for so long. As Jack took an early retirement offer and I moved on from the corporate world to a consulting firm, we began talking more intently about what we might like to do for our next steps in our professional lives. The more conversations we had, the more it became apparent to both of us that the training and conferences business was our choice. We both had prior experience and success in developing conferences and seminars. We also shared a real passion for wanting to create something new and innovative in the training conference business.

We both believed that the training and conference business followed a cookie-cutter model. We also thought it was too expensive and restrictive. We believed it needed a company with a new perspective and appreciation for those people who work in the trenches in law enforcement, government, and communities in the private sector. We also knew that those same technical people wanted and needed a place to go for excellent training and networking opportunities at a reasonable price. The rest is history. We have enjoyed more than eight years of successful conferences and have met thousands of wonderful new people whom we now call friends.

Once we started down the conference path, the thought of perhaps writing a book on the subject stayed in the back of our minds. We both had some writing experience, but taking on the task of a complete book was daunting. We did not consider writing a book as an undertaking in our immediate future. We did realize, however, that we had a lot of experiences and some terrific war stories to tell and share, and putting those words on paper was one of the best ways to make the thoughts come alive. We knew that we had some great content, and we had several wonderful friends and colleagues in the business who also had things to share, but we just didn't know the best way to get started.

Then one day out of the blue, one of our longtime friends, Russ Rogers, suggested that we get to know the team at Syngress. At first, we simply wanted to get to know the people at Syngress and invited them to our conference as our bookstore sponsors, since we had heard so many good things about them and the books they were creating. In 2005, our newest conference, Techno Forensics, was unveiled, and the Syngress team brought stacks of books to offer to our attendees who were interested in digital forensics and security. The books sold like hotcakes. As Jack, I, and the Syngress team got to know each other better, discussions about possibly publishing a book related to Techno Security began to be more frequent. As I said before, we had so many excellent writers as personal friends who were also considered industry icons that a special book written by these experts just needed to happen.

I believe you will find that this book contains some of the most up-to-date information available anywhere on a wide variety of topics related to Techno Security. As you read the book, you will notice that the authors took the approach of identifying some of the risks, threats, and vulnerabilities and then discussing the countermeasures to address them. Some of the topics and thoughts discussed here are as new as tomorrow's headlines, whereas others have been around for decades without being properly addressed.

I hope you enjoy this book as much as we have enjoyed working with the various authors and friends during its development.

—*Donald Withers*
CEO and Cofounder of The Training Co.

Chapter 1

Social Engineering: Risks, Threats, Vulnerabilities, and Countermeasures

by Jack Wiles

Jack Wiles is a security professional with over 30 years of experience in security-related fields, including computer security, disaster recovery, and physical security. He is a professional speaker and has trained federal agents, corporate attorneys, and internal auditors on many computer crime–related topics. He is a pioneer in presenting on subjects that are now being labeled "Homeland Security" topics. Jack is a co-founder and President of TheTrainingCo., which runs the well-known Techno Security and Techno Forensics trade shows. He is in frequent contact with members of many state and local law enforcement agencies as well as special agents with the U.S. Secret Service, FBI, U.S. Customs, the Department of Justice, and the Department of Defense. He was appointed the first President of the North Carolina InfraGard chapter, which is now one of the largest chapters in the country. He is also a founding member and "official" MC of the U.S. Secret Service South Carolina Electronic Crimes Task Force. Jack is also a Vietnam veteran who served with the 101st Airborne Division in Vietnam in 1967–68.

Introduction

Some of the things I will discuss in this chapter have been on my mind since the mid-1980s. I believe it's time I put them in writing and present my thoughts on what I believe could be the most effective and dangerous threat to any security plan: social engineering! This age-old threat has taken on a new meaning as what I collectively call "bad guys" have continued to use the art of the con to gain access to intellectual property and, if necessary, the buildings that house it.

This chapter isn't meant to be read as a complete story from beginning to end. Social engineering and ways to prevent it are subjects with many meanings. This will be more of a potpourri of tips, tricks, vulnerabilities, and lessons learned from 30-plus years of dealing with these issues. As an inside penetration team leader, I used every exploit I could to conduct a successful inside penetration test. It was during those years that I gained most of my social engineering experience. These skills helped me eventually hang up my dumpster-diving penetration team clothes and retire from the tiger team world UNDETECTED! Although I came close several times, I was never stopped or reported to security as a possible burglar or corporate espionage agent, even though that's what I effectively was while I had our teams inside their buildings.

If you think this chapter has a strong risk management flavor, it was intentional. Just about every area of concern with security today is a risk management issue. This chapter, and most of the others in this book, are chock full of what I like to call Techno Tidbits of useful risk management countermeasures. Hopefully, many of them will be topics you might not have considered in the past as you put together your security plan. External, internal, and information system auditors should pick up a few ideas for things that should be added to their audit process.

How Easy Is It?

Way back in 1988, I was part of an internal security team for a large corporation. On several occasions, I had the opportunity to hear some of the conversations that went on when a cracker (bad guy hacker) group targeted a victim by calling them on the phone. They were using social engineering skills to gain access to proprietary information, including passwords. I'll never forget what I heard one experienced cracker say to a cracker-in-training: "Social engineering is the easiest way to break into a system." He then followed up that comment by saying "The stupidity of the average system administrator amazes me."

That was almost 20 years ago and it was the first time I had heard the words social engineering. Why do I think of it as a tool that could be used by any "bad guy" from a cracker to a terrorist? Social engineering is what I believe could be the most effective and dangerous outsider–insider threat to any security plan.

Over the past 15 years, I have learned firsthand just how easy it is to be an effective con man as I lead several inside penetration teams into clients' buildings who hired us to test their vulnerabilities. Not one time did we fail or get caught as we roamed their buildings pretending to be employees. Everyone we encountered while doing our thing thought we belonged there.

Human Nature: Human Weakness

This is certainly not the first time anyone has written about the effects of social engineering. It doesn't take much searching on the Internet to find material on the subject, and in almost every article you will note a common thread. In each case, the social engineer turns our normal human nature of wanting to be kind, helpful, and sympathetic into a weakness they can exploit.

If we looked at this through the eyes of a risk manager performing a risk assessment, our untrained and unaware human nature could be considered a major vulnerability, threatening just about everything important to our company. We'll talk about possible countermeasures to these threats throughout of the rest of the chapter.

The reason I digressed into a full discussion about a risk assessment of the threat of social engineering is because I don't think many people have performed a detailed risk analysis. Since social engineering is a truly formidable threat, you need to know how vulnerable you are (at work and home) and what you can do to reduce those risks.

Any risk assessment needs to consider at least four things: risks, threats, vulnerabilities, and countermeasures.

Risk Management: Performing a Mini Risk Assessment

I recently had the opportunity to purchase my first boat. It's not huge, but it is just big enough for me to use as a floating mini-office a couple of days a week when the weather is nice. Just for fun, let's do a mini risk assessment of some of the risks, threats, vulnerabilities, and countermeasures associated with my new floating office. This isn't intended to be extensive (I'm sure you will think of things I didn't mention here). I just wanted to give us practice using terms most associated with risk assessments and risk management.

What Do I Have at Risk?

Being out on the water all day, my life is the first thing that comes to mind as a risk. The boat itself is also at risk, though I have passed some of the financial risk along to an insurance company, which is what we do with a lot of risks where it makes sense. Any equipment on the boat is at risk of not only sinking but of possibly being dropped overboard, or being soaked by a large wave. A sudden thunderstorm could cause problems. Depending on lake conditions, too many other boats could cause a problem. The battery in the boat could die causing me to lose all power and even strand me on the lake. As you can see, when you consider what you have a risk, you will immediately start to consider some of the threats that could possibly increase your risks. What I have at risk on the boat is everything I could lose if something bad happened. Let's call all the bad things that could happen "possible threats."

What Are Some Possible Threats?

We've already mentioned a few possible threats, which are different than those surrounding my home office. Weather could certainly be a threat, as could simply hitting something as I was moving from one place to another on the lake. The threat of a sudden thunderstorm, or of being hit by another boat, always exists. There isn't much risk of being hit by a car (hopefully), or suffering from a commercial power outage while I'm aboard. The possible threat of theft should be small as long as I keep an eye on my equipment while I'm launching the boat. Overall, the threats, which could possibly hinder my ability to conduct business from my boat, would be lower than most places. (Am I looking for reasons to work from my boat or what?)

What Are Some of the Possible Vulnerabilities?

I would be much more vulnerable to severe weather changes out on the lake than in my home office. I would also be vulnerable to lake conditions in general at any given time. (This is a large lake about 20 miles long.) For a few days following a heavy rain, hundreds of semi-submerged items float down stream. I would certainly be vulnerable to someone losing control of his or her boat and crashing into mine. If I didn't know the depth of the water I was in, I could possibly run aground or hit something in water that was shallower than I thought it was. It would most likely just be an inconvenience, but as in any vehicle, I could run out of fuel. I mentioned not being affected by commercial power failures, but I could easily run my only battery down to where I couldn't start the engine to return to the marina. In addition, though I am always very careful, I could possibly fall overboard—a difficult problem when you're on the water alone.

What about My Countermeasures?

I really enjoy talking about countermeasures. The word even sounds cool. You have all of these things that you have identified as yours and they could be at risk out there in the boat. You have considered the possible threats and how vulnerable you might be as you encounter them. Now, what can you do to lower your risk and decrease your vulnerability?

I've learned a lot during the few months I have had this new floating mini-office. Some of my newfound countermeasures are

- I only try to be on the lake when most other boaters aren't out there.
- I check the weather forecast every time before I head to the lake.
- I will install a second marine battery to insure I always have power.
- I have made sure special waterproof cases are used for my computer and cell phone.
- I carry a small inverter onboard to provide me with 110 volts AC from the boat battery.
- I make sure the marina and my family are always notified of where I will be, and when I expect to return.
- I always carry a small marina radio onboard.
- All data on my computer and cell phone have backup copies on shore.
- I wear a self-inflating life vest at all times.

I'm sure many more issues could be addressed in this mini-assessment, but the point is we all need to at least be familiar with, and understand, our risks at home and work. Included in this book is a detailed chapter titled "Personal, Workforce, and Family Preparedness," which contains a wealth of information for lowering your risk in some of the most important areas of your life.

Outsider–Insider Threats

For my definition here, let's consider the outside threats as those coming at you from the Internet or dial-up modem (You do know where all of your dial-up modems are; don't you?), or a simple phone call from a total stranger. The reason I mention dial-up modems is because there are still many of them out there. Many mainte-nance ports on older PBXs, building environmental controls, air handling systems, and access control systems still use them and probably will continue to rely on them well into the future.

I'm not considering insider (current employee) activity in this chapter. Even though malicious insiders can use social engineering in a number of ways, the coun-termeasures for that kind of activity can be much different. For this discussion, let's consider outsider–insider threats as people who never were employees and didn't belong in the building.

This would be the category my inside penetration team would fit into. When we roamed through buildings unchallenged, we definitely didn't belong there (other than being hired to try to get there). Someone checking out your building for pos-sible espionage or future terrorist activities would also fit in this category. In theory, some employee inside the building should eventually figure out that there is a "Trojan horse" in the camp. Someone who has gotten past whatever security there is at the perimeter where entry was gained. There is a good chance they used some form of social engineering to get there.

Here's why I keep preaching about this subject and the subject of knowing who is in your building at all times. For more than three decades now, I have observed what I believe is a lack of awareness of this concern. Over the years, I have seen comparatively few articles address this silent but formidable threat. Remember, when I spent those years doing this for a living, we were hired expecting to get caught in an attack that was designed to become bolder the longer I had the team in a building. Toward the end of just about every job, we were openly walking around like we worked there, almost hoping to get caught by someone. We never did!

We were good, but I suspect there are many "bad guys" out there who are much better at it than we were, and they won't try to get caught in the end like we did. We were also working under a few self-imposed rules that the real bad guys could care less about. Using forced entry, like a crow bar to get through doors or windows, was a no-no for us. Our main tools were a cool head and our social engineering skills whenever it made sense to use them.

The Mind of a Social Engineer

I'm not sure I'll do this part of the chapter justice, but I'll try. Although I've been involved with using and teaching about social engineering for almost two decades now, I didn't really understand why it works so well until about five years ago. When I was out in L.A. for a meeting on financial crimes security, I purchased a very inter-esting book titled *The Art of Deception* by Kevin Mitnick and William Simon.

Just above the title on the cover of the book in red letters are the words "Controlling the Human Element of Security." I have since read most of the book, as well as many of the reviews written about it on Amazon. I found it to be well written and full of many good examples of how social engineering works and how companies can try to defend against its use. I also learned quite a few new approaches to targeting potential victims I had never thought of before. A social engineer will continuously learn increasingly clever ways to take advantage of how our minds work. The perfection of these skills comes from what Kevin Mitnick mentions in the *The Art of Deception*: *practice, practice, and more practice*! That's what every good social engineer does a lot of.

The Mind of a Victim

Any one of us, at any time, could easily become the victim of some form of social engineering. I believe it isn't possible to completely eliminate all risk, but some things can and should be done to reduce the risk as much as possible. I'll address some of them throughout the rest of this chapter. Without some form of training and that same *practice, practice, and more practice* idea in learning how to prevent being a victim of social engineering, you could easily become a victim and not even know it.

Our minds work in very trusting and predictable ways, and that means exaggerated deviations from the norm might never be considered. This is what social engineers count on. Without awareness of the problem and without an understanding of how our minds can be fooled, there is little defense against social engineering. For this awareness training to be of any benefit for an organization, it must include every employee of every organization.

We see things all day long and we don't pay close attention to certain details because they are too familiar to us. That's exactly how the illusions that magicians call magic work. It's also why so many magic tricks are related to simple everyday things like a deck of cards. I use magic in much of my training and it really adds a lot to the attention span of the people in front of me. They are all so used to seeing those 52 cards that they don't think about how the different card gimmicks used in most card tricks work. Most of these illusions are self-working yet almost mind boggling to the unsuspecting mind.

Here's a quick example of a short riddle that catches many people off-guard because of the way our minds work:

I have two coins in my pocket that add up to 30 cents. One of them is not a nickel. What are the two coins?

I'll answer the riddle at the end of the chapter.

Countermeasures: How Do Bad Guys Target Us, and What Can We Do About It

As I mention some of the countermeasures I consider important, I'd like to do so in a more novel way. This list certainly doesn't include all of the possible countermeasures for trying to prevent a successful social engineering exploit. The Internet contains many other articles written by very experienced writers on the subject. I have read several of them and I agree with just about everything they suggest for countering social engineering.

The following is a list of some of the countermeasures I have recommended to companies we have performed penetration tests for over the years. Social engineering played a very important role in every test. In each case, it was the primary tool we used to perform the physical penetration of the client's building(s). Time after time, when we presented our after-action reports, most of the success of our penetration test was attributed to our inside team.

Most of our clients quickly reacted to attempts to gain access from the outside over the Internet. Their intrusion detection systems worked pretty well, and their incident response plans were effective. They were completely unprepared, however, for us simply walking into their buildings and acting like we belonged there. Once inside, we pretty much owned the building and everything in it. In the larger buildings, there were so many desks it didn't seem anyone knew everyone else. That was what we liked to see. Easy pickings.

What follows are some of the most important things for you to consider as you plan your defense against possible social engineering attacks.

Key Control

The types of keys used in most buildings have remained virtually unchanged since Linus Yale invented them in 1861. Just about all of our homes, and most businesses, still use his pin tumbler locks for their primary physical defense. I have no way of knowing how often the master, grand master, and possibly great-grand-master key systems in buildings are changed. I do suspect it's not very often. This can be an expensive process. Recently, I walked into a public restroom in a large office building and saw a full set of keys, including the building master key, hanging from the paper towel dispenser. I suspect the janitor had just filled the towel rack and left his keys hanging there. In the hands of the wrong person, that collection could prove devastating.

While using our social engineering skills during each penetration test, our team always tried to make friends with the cleaning crew. Sooner or later, we would need to ask a favor and borrow their keys for a few minutes. (Typically, their keys would open all of the doors on that floor and sometimes the entire building.) That was all it took for us to make a copy with the portable key machine we brought with us in a small bag. Very few people have any idea how keys and the locks they open work. This is another area of physical security that has changed greatly during the past few decades. I became a bonded locksmith back in the 1970s and found it fascinating. Back then, I couldn't even purchase lock picks or key blanks until I graduated from a credited locksmithing school and had proper identification. Now, about 30 years later, we have much more at risk in general, and anyone can purchase lock picks at several local hardware stores or from Internet-based stores with no questions asked.

Regarding the use of lock picks to get into buildings and rooms, I doubt many "casual" social engineers use them. They do require a lot of that "practice, practice, and more practice" stuff needed for any social engineering skills. The availability of these devices for anyone to purchase is something corporate security specialists need to consider as they plan their countermeasures.

TIP

Attempt to set up some form of key control if you don't already have a system in place. It is very important to know who has the keys to your kingdom as well as how many doors can be opened by each key. It is very seldom a good idea to have one key that opens everything in the building. It may be more convenient for certain things, but it does create the security concern of controlling who has those keys and how easily they can be duplicated.

Master keys are an additional concern if you rent space in a large building or office park. You might have a very strict policy of your own for your company, but if the management company that handles the building rentals isn't as careful with their master keys, the entire building is at risk. Unless the keys are of a high security design like the Medico line, they can be duplicated anywhere. Even if the disgruntled building maintenance person turns in his keys upon being fired, there is no way to be sure he didn't have copies made. You should ask the building manager about his policy regarding the issuing and security of the master keys. It will let them know you are aware there are keys to your office that are not under your control.

Install special locks on critical doors. Highly pick resistant Medeco locks are some of the most effective. In addition to providing additional security, they add another level of due diligence should you need to document your attempts to prevent intrusions.

Conduct special employee awareness training for everyone who works on the evening and night shift. That's when I took our team into their buildings most of the time. We used our social engineering skills to befriend these people and to the best of my knowledge, we were never reported by any of them.

Another prime target during our evening and night visits was the janitorial team. The main reason we always tried to befriend the people on the janitorial team is that they usually had those important keys we were trying to get our hands on. These are some of the most important people in your company when it comes to protecting your buildings when most employees are gone. They spend some time in just about every room in the building each week. If you don't train anyone else in your company, these people need to be well trained on how they can help. They should be made aware of your security policies and what they should do if they see anything suspicious. This would include strangers, suspicious packages, doors that are opened which should be locked, and so on. They are one of your most valuable resources. Tell them that, and teach them how they can help.

Dumpster Diving Still Works

"Dumpster diving" is one of the easiest ways to find out information about a company or its customers. This is sometimes referred to as "trashing," and there have been a number of articles discussing what worked and what didn't for some experienced "trashers." One article discussed "advanced trashing" and ways to talk yourself out of a confrontation if you get caught. I'd be willing to bet that only a very small percentage of "dumpster divers" ever gets caught. As simple as this problem seems, it isn't given much attention by most companies.

What kinds of things can you find in a company's dumpster? You would probably be shocked if you started looking through your own dumpster occasionally. (I highly encourage you to do just that.) There may be old company phone directories (still quite accurate and very valuable for use in social engineering), pieces of scrap paper with phone numbers and possibly passwords written on them, last month's customer lists that were discarded when the new list was printed this month, employee lists with home addresses and Social Security numbers, and so on.

It doesn't take much imagination to think of all of the potential problems that could have their beginnings right there in your trashcan. Someone who is trying to pretend that they work for your company can use the old company directories. Most names in the directory, their work locations and their titles remain the same from update to update. These discarded directories are some of the most prized finds of any "dumpster divers" looking to get information about your company. The discarded scraps of paper with the passwords on them are also prized finds. Many times, they are discarded just because they were no longer sticky enough to stay on the terminal they were attached to, so a new one was written and the old one thrown in the trash. Last month's customer list will probably wind up in the hands of your competitor if the wrong person gets his hands on it. The employee list with the home addresses and Social Security numbers on it will cause different problems if it winds up in the wrong hands.

What can you do about this problem? For one thing, we can all be a little more careful about what we throw in the trashcan. Management commitment to correct this problem, along with employee awareness of the problem will help solve it. This commitment usually involves the shredding or burning of all-important documents. If a company is going to invest in their own shredder, I always recommend a crosscut shredder over a strip cut shredder. Strip cutting is better than nothing, but crosscutting is much more secure. It turns the documents into small pieces of material instead of long strips that can be reassembled. I guess it's theoretically possible to reassemble a strip cut document, but if it falls into a bin with a large number of other strip cut documents, it will create the world's most difficult jigsaw puzzle.

Old habits die hard, and this one will probably be no exception. As a country, we have been throwing away just about everything since the end of World War II. During the war, security was on everybody's mind, and each person encouraged their friends and neighbors to be careful what they said and what they threw away. (I wasn't around during World War II, but I was the product of a happy homecoming after the war.) As individuals and companies, we need to bring back just a little bit of that way of thinking. We need to become aware of this problem and encourage each other to be more careful with assets by being more careful with our trash.

TIP

Many of the topics presented for thought in this chapter and throughout the entire book are just as appropriate in our homes as they are in our offices. This is especially true of our home office computers, networks, and trash!

Most of us are inundated with snail mail at home as well as at work. I have a policy in our home that nothing goes into our trashcan that has any family member's name on it. This requires a little extra effort to destroy a single page of a credit card offer each time I receive one. If it has a name and address on it (obviously everything that arrives at my home does), I destroy that part of the document. Every small thing I can do to protect my family against things like identity theft or credit card fraud helps me sleep at night.

Employee Badges

I know these can be faked, but I still think it's much better to have some form of visible identification worn by every employee at all times. Most of the companies that hired us did not have a policy requiring employees to wear their corporate ID badges all the time. This made our social engineering attempts much easier. Once we were inside the buildings, it was as if everyone just took it for granted we belonged there. Not only were we inside their buildings, but we had also breached their firewalls and intrusion detection systems.

Employees can be somewhat trained to even detect fake ID badges. I was working for a large company that did require employees to always wear their ID badges when they were on company property. This was back in the days when color printers were just starting to show up in homes and offices. I created a fake ID that was intentionally made without any thought of quality control. The first time I wore it into the building instead of my real ID, I suspected I would immediately be stopped and questioned about it. This was a security project, so I was prepared to explain myself. To my initial amazement, I never had to explain anything because it was never questioned. For the next three months, I wore it everywhere and not one person noticed. During one of our security meetings, I told everyone in our group about my little experiment and most people were quite surprised it was never detected.

Part two of my experiment held the most interesting results for me, however. I created a picture showing my two IDs side by side. The fake one was quite obvious when compared with the real one. We began to teach people how to take a closer look at the IDs others were wearing as they walked through our buildings. From that time forward, I only wore my fake ID when I was conducting security awareness training for a group of employees. I was amazed at how many of my friends (who had been through a version of the training) would spot the fake ID as I was walking past them on the way to the training class. Some would even spot it from ten feet away. These are the same people who (before the class) hadn't noticed it while sitting 3 feet from me in my office. The lesson here: AWARENESS TRAINING WORKS!

WARNING

Tailgating, frequently called piggybacking, is simply following someone into a building after they open the door with an access card or by entering a door code. The "bad guy" will often pretend to be searching for his or her access card while waiting for someone to enter with a legitimate card. If there is no guard at the entrance, the "bad guy" will probably go unchallenged and unnoticed. You really need to think about this one before you decide how you want to solve it. You can't place a legitimate employee in the position of having to challenge the "bad guy" about identification before letting them in.

The legitimate employee probably didn't come to work for you to be a security guard. On the other hand, you don't want "bad guys" just walking into your building. This problem is as old as dirt, but the solutions just keep getting more complex and expensive. Some companies employ cameras that photograph everyone who enters the building. Others are now using biometrics scanners and other high-tech devices. As with everything else in the security field, you need to get a system that is appropriate in cost for what you are trying to protect.

At a minimum, you can make your employees aware of this threat and have them notify their immediate superior that someone followed them in, and then note the time and date of the incident. This same employee awareness session should instruct all employees to display an ID so fellow employees who may not know them don't think they are "tailgating" as they walk in behind them.

Shredder Technology Has Changed

As with everything else these past few high-tech years, shredder technology has changed considerably. Our team had gotten really good at putting strip cut papers back together again. We used to take bags of it back to our office during the test.

Frequently, it was sitting outside in or near a dumpster where we simply picked it up and put it in our vehicle. Most of the time, documents that are strip cut shredded all fall neatly into place in the bag or box where they are stored, waiting to be disposed of. Our team was able to reassemble many of these documents within a few minutes. We would even take a document and paste the strips on a piece of cardboard in the shape of a Christmas tree, spreading the strips out as they were glued to the cardboard. Even with up to an inch between strips, the documents were still easily readable once reassembled. We never even attempted to reconstruct a document that had been sent through a cross cut shredder.

TIP

If you have too much invested in your strip cut shredders to replace them, at least consider purchasing some of the small cross cut shredders and place them directly in the offices of people who have especially sensitive documents that should be destroyed. These small cross cut shredders are very inexpensive and durable if you keep them oiled with the special oil available for shredders. I have a small one that cost $39 and it creates a very small particle that would be next to impossible to reassemble. I have tried to wear it out for about six months and it just keeps on working. I'd also recommend encouraging all employees to get one for home use. I believe it is a good policy to shred everything that comes to your home with any family member's name on it. Once you start doing this, it will become second nature and you will never need to wonder who might see your personal information once it leaves your home. After all, identity theft is on the rise as well.

Outdated but still sensitive documents should also be disposed of securely. When I worked at the Pentagon for the final seven years of my military career, we were required to place certain sensitive (not classified, simply sensitive) documents into a safe containing a burn bag. Burning them would then destroy these items. To this day, I still use a burn bag at home for documents that I need to destroy which are too bulky for my shredder. It's a great way to clean out the barbeque grill on a cold sunny day. I feel good every time I destroy sensitive personal documents rather than simply throwing them in a trashcan. Left unshredded or unburned, they become possible fuel for the most rapidly growing white-collar crime in the country: identity theft!

Keep an Eye on Corporate or Agency Phonebooks

When we were conducting a test, this was the first thing we went for. Once we got our hands on a corporate directory, the social engineering began. Most corporate phone books are laid out in a way that conveniently shows the entire corporate structure as well as the chain of command, building addresses, and department titles. That kind of information also lets us know the order in which to try entering the various buildings, if there were several. Wherever the Human Resources department was located was usually where we went last. Here's why. As we tried to enter all of the other buildings by simply walking in the door like we belonged there, we were frequently challenged by a receptionist and asked where we were going. Our social engineering answer was always the same. "We were told that this is where Human Resources is located, and we're here to fill out a job application." In every case, the receptionist simply sent us in the right direction. We thanked her or him and walked out the door and directly into the building next door to try the same con. The phonebook even gave us the Human Resources manager's name to drop if we needed to be a little more convincing that we belonged there but were simply lost. It also gave us the names and titles of the rest of the important people in the organization whose names we could drop if we needed to when challenged. In addition to the names in the directories, most contained the physical location and chain of command ranking for the most important person in each department. It was often their offices, file cabinets, and trashcans that we spent the most time in during our nightly visits.

Employee awareness of how important a corporate directory is will help greatly with this one. Old directories are still quite accurate especially regarding buildings and department locations. They should be burned or shredded rather than simply thrown into the dumpster.

If paper directories can be eliminated all together, that would even make our job a little tougher. Everything you do to make it a little harder for the bad guys will make you a less likely target—they're looking for an easy mark. Online directories are better only if you don't let the social engineers get into your building. Once we were inside, we began looking for a monitor with the infamous sticky pad note on the side listing the person's login ID and password. Once we logged on to the network as them, we could usually get to an online company directory if there was one.

Let me address one additional countermeasure while I'm on the subject of the login ID and password that's been written down and attached to the monitor or placed under the keyboard. Maybe that doesn't happen where you work, but we found at least one person who had done this on every job we were hired to do. There is another reason we like to use someone else's login ID and password to get onto their networks. If we are able to do that, not only are we on their network on the inside of any firewall, but everything we do will show up in some log as being done by the person who let us log in as them. Many larger companies now employ at least some form of two-part authentication using either biometrics or some type of handheld authenticating device to attain two-part authentication. Fortunately, some forms of biometric access control are becoming very reasonable in price. Everything you do in the way of authentication will greatly reduce your vulnerability in this form of instant identity theft.

Tailgating

This was one of our most successful entry techniques, regardless of the security procedures at the building. For some reason, people in the outside smoking areas didn't ever question our being there and eventually walking in right behind one of them as they went back to work. We found that many corporations had good security at their main entrance points, but were lacking at other entry and exit points. We were able to gain access on several occasions through parking deck or garage entry points that required card access. We would simply follow someone who was headed to the door and walk in behind him or her as we were pretending to search for our access cards that didn't exist.

WARNING

Here again, employee-wide awareness training and a strong security policy can go a long way in preventing this type of an entry. These outside break, lunch, and smoking areas are frequently places where there are no security guards or receptionists trained to ask for proper ID as someone passes through the door. As mentioned earlier, having every employee wear an ID badge would make this type of entry a little more difficult should someone try to walk in without an ID.

The countermeasures for this vulnerability really aren't as simple as we might think. Most employees entering a building aren't security people. They are simply trying to get back to work. Even though someone entering a building using the tailgating or piggyback method should be challenged, challenging them is an uncomfortable situation for most people. Unless there is a strong corporate policy requiring all employees to challenge anyone they can't identify, this is a difficult problem to deal with. At an absolute minimum, employees should be trained regarding when and how to notify security if they suspect an unauthorized person has followed them in.

Building Operations: Cleaning Crew Awareness

I can't emphasize enough the need to train all of your second- and third-shift employees, and especially your janitorial services people, about the threats of social engineering. Obviously, pre-employment screening, and possibly bonding, is essential for any outside firm you allow inside your buildings at any time. This is especially true for building access outside the normal 8 to 5 Monday through Friday standard work schedule. Frequently, these people have access to the master keys for a large section of the building and sometimes the entire building. They need awareness training to better prevent them from becoming victims of bad-guy social engineers who would like to borrow their keys for a minute or get them to open a certain room.

This team should also immediately know whom to contact should they see anything suspicious that should be reported. If there is no immediate supervisor on duty during the evening or night shifts, everyone on that shift should know how to quickly contact their security forces. It can be very dangerous for them to approach a stranger themselves in an attempt to get them to leave.

This suggestion may not seem to fit in the context of this book, but let me mention it anyway. There is another very good reason to train your janitorial team (at least the team supervisors) to be extra watchful during the evening and night shift work hours. I have been teaching bomb recognition classes for the past ten years. These same social engineering skills and physical building penetration methods could apply in any situation where the collective "bad guys" are trying to get into your building. The eyes and ears of the people who work in your building every day are critical when it comes to detecting anything, or anyone unusual in the vicinity of the building. Bomb recognition training for key individuals and as well as having an effective bomb incident plan are other countermeasures that can be employed to considerable effect.

Security Alert...

Bomb Threats in Chicago

This is a good time for a little side story that will let you see how the many risks, threats, vulnerabilities, and countermeasures overlay in the worlds of physical and technical security.

Several years ago, I received a call from a friend from the Chicago area asking for help. He said his company had office locations in several cities throughout the country, and one office out of the country. A series of bomb threats called into their corporate headquarters were causing them to lose sleep. They just wanted our team's suggestions regarding what they should do about it. This meant a trip to Chicago for us in February. (For the warm-blooded person from the sunny south that I am, it was like taking a trip to Iceland in mid-winter.) We went anyway.

Prior to going, I decided to look on the Internet to see if I could find out anything about the company. It could also provide a hint as to why someone would call in these bomb threats (that fortunately were only threats, so far).

The company flew in their senior managers from around the country and we suggested their corporate attorneys and risk managers attend the training as well. They would learn everything they wanted to know, but were afraid to ask about bombs and bomb threats.

We arrived a day early and asked if they would like for us to take a look around their corporate headquarters building to see if we saw any glaring physical vulnerabilities that might allow someone to easily place a bomb in their building, or in a spot nearby outside. The outer perimeter was about as close to perfect as I had ever seen in a building of that size. As we were looking at the various locations from the inside, my eyes kept being drawn to their newly installed access control system. Each employee had been issued an ID card that would allow him or her to enter certain doors at specific times of the day. The system also kept track of the times they entered and left the building. It was impressive.

My fellow team member gave me a strange "you've done it now" kind of look when I said that a simple metal coat hanger might be able to compromise the entire system. I was about to be put to the test as we approached the next set of outside access doors in that part of the building. The person who had hired us stood there with a metal coat hanger and handed it to me.

Keep in mind, we were walking around inside the nicely heated building without our coats. On the other side of the doors, which I would now attempt to open from the outside with the coat hanger, it was still Iceland in February.

Continued

I politely said I would go outside (without my coat) and try for a few minutes. All I asked was that if I started turning blue, to please "open the door from the inside and let me back in."

In the end, my request proved necessary. I was back inside in less than 30 seconds and everyone was standing there with a deer-in-the-headlights look as I calmly walked through the $250,000 security system with no indication I had ever been there. This was not the first time I had seen this issue with an improperly adjusted access control system. The system was one that detected motion from the inside, thus automatically unlocking the door as soon as it detected someone moving towards it. I noticed it detected us walking past the door from a considerable distance away. It was just too sensitive. I also noticed that the locking mechanism opened only one of a pair of double doors and that the motion sensor was mounted dead center between the double doors. The only thing protecting the opening between the double doors was a thin piece of weather-stripping. While I was standing outside, quickly freezing to death, it was a simple matter of taking my thin metal coat hanger and sliding it between the two doors while rapidly moving it up and down. Within seconds, I heard the familiar "click" I was hoping for. The security system thought I was inside because that's where it saw the motion of my coat hanger.

For another insight into this vulnerability, be sure to read Johnny Long's chapter as well.

All of the senior managers, attorneys, risk managers, and security team members were in a training room the following morning for their day of Bomb Threat Training. I opened the meeting by letting them know that this was most likely a low probability threat, but that they were smart to decide ahead of time to learn as much as they could about what they should do about these threats. We were going to spend the rest of the day learning about bombs, bomb threats, bombs in buildings, bombs outside of buildings, and all kinds of other scary things. It was going to be a fun day.

As I was finishing up my introduction, I walked around the room and placed a small packet of one to three pages in front of four of their most important people. As the four targeted people started to look through the papers placed in front of them, I simply stated that this was their high probability threat and something they needed to address immediately in our opinion. The papers contained just about everything we would ever need to know about these people. Where they lived, how they most likely traveled to work, where they went to college, where their children went to school, and much more. All of it was gained from a few social engineering phone calls and about an hour searching the Internet for information about them. Much of the information about these people (and possibly about you) was out on the Internet. It's not easy, but these people-type search engines all have an opt-out capability so you have your name and contact information removed from their databases. Just type the words "people search engines" into www.google.com for the most recent list of these services. You should input your name into

Continued

some of them to see what information is out there about you. You'll likely be surprised how many times your name pops up.

Spot Check Those Drop Ceilings

On several occasions, we used our social engineering skills to get into buildings and then install a sniffer in the telecommunications hub for that floor. I recommend all companies have their building maintenance teams perform a spot check above all suspended ceilings at least twice each year. We have been amazed at some of the things we found up there while we were conducting the penetration test. You may even stumble into a security vulnerability you weren't even aware of.

This suggestion would also be one I would make if considering places to hide things like bombs. We walk under drop ceilings day after day and normally have no reason to think about what might be up there. Usually, there is at least a foot of clearance between the grid work holding the drop ceiling in place and the ceiling itself. I have seen as much as three feet of clearance. You may be amazed at what you find hidden up there (hopefully, it isn't ticking).

Check for Keystroke Readers

Some of our favorite tools are the software, and newer hardware versions, for keystroke readers. These can make a good social engineer's job a lot easier. If we wanted to find out what a certain individual in the company was doing on their computer during a certain timeframe, we would install a keystroke reader on their workstation on one visit and retrieve the results on a second visit.

By far, the most effective keystroke loggers we have used are the Key Ghost hardware loggers being sold as security devices (www.keyghost.com). When these are installed between the keyboard of a workstation and the keyboard socket on the back of the computer, to the casual observer they look like they belong there. The one we used looked like the induction coils seen on some of the older parallel printer cables. It just doesn't look like anything you need to worry about.

However, if you didn't put it there, you better be worried! It's logging every single keystroke you type in.

The version we used would hold about 500,000 characters or half a megabyte. That might not sound like much, but just consider that the Word document that eventually became this entire chapter would take up about 20,000 characters (16,000 characters for the text and about 4,000 backspace key strokes to correct all of my typing errors). That would only be about 4 percent of its capability. By the way, those backspace keys would show up as ASCII characters (control H for you techies) as would any other non-printing character entered as part of a password or whatever. It only records keystrokes, so it holds a lot more than you might think. We've left them connected to target computers for up to three weeks and still only filled about 80 percent of their capacity.

Here's something else to consider if you feel safer entering information into your Web browser over a secure socket connection (https). The encryption happens between your browser and the server that is receiving your sensitive information over the Internet. That's a good thing if you're entering your credit card number or bank account access information. But here's the problem with that warm fuzzy. The keystroke reader is reading your keystrokes before they get to your browser. Everything will be in the clear when someone (hopefully only you) looks at the data your keystroke reader collected.

How do you know if you have one connected to your workstation or home computer? You don't unless you physically look back in the rat's nest behind most computers and see if anything looks strange. Unless you know what they look like, it probably won't appear strange to you even if you do see one. I pass one around for people to see at all of my security training classes. Statistically, I've read that people are 27 times more likely to remember something if they are able to see it and hold it. I usually ask my attendees to raise their hands if they've never seen one. Almost every time, more than half of the hands go up. How can you defend yourself against something you don't even know exists? (Another subtle hint for more awareness training.)

Here's a quick awareness training class using one of my workstations as the target computer. The picture in Figure 1.1 shows the workstation in a minimum configuration with only a monitor, mouse, power cord, and keyboard connected to the motherboard. Take a look at that little bulge about three inches from the end of the cable that goes to the monitor. It's the only cable that has a bulge of the four that you see. That's an induction coil and you may see one or more on cables found behind most workstations.

Figure 1.1 No Keylogger...

Let's take a look at this same workstation after I have installed my keystroke reader between the keyboard and the motherboard socket where the keyboard was connected (see Figure 1.2). Of the two cables in the center next to each other, the keyboard cable is the one on the right.

Figure 1.2 Keylogger...

Now what do we see when you look back there? The keystroke reader looks like a second induction coil and would be very hard to detect if you didn't know what one looked like. I didn't try very hard to hide it, and normally there are more wires back there than this. There is no way the computer would know it is there. It uses virtually no power, and doesn't require any software be installed to make it work. When I finally remove it and take it back to check out the internal log, the computer (or you) would never know it was gone again.

The keystroke reader is an excellent security device if you suspect someone is using your computer when you're not there, and is sold primarily for that purpose. It's a wonderful piece of equipment… as long as you know it's there.

Check Those Phone Closets

If your office is in a rented space, or in a multitenant building, it's a good idea to have someone perform a thorough check of your hardwiring for the phone lines. You don't know who was there before you were, and old wiring sometimes isn't removed when new tenants move in. On more than one occasion, our teams found old phone cable wiring still in place and being used in an inappropriate manner by inside employees. While we are on the subject, Techno Security also comes into play when considering the corporate PBX (or Private Branch Exchange), which is the internal phone company for larger corporations. It may still have a modem for remote maintenance needs, and the phone number for that modem may be written on the wall near the modem. We found many of the PBXs we "visited" to be very social engineering friendly.

Remove a Few Door Signs

It always amazed us to see rooms that had a sign over them saying *Computer Room* or *Phone Closet*. Obviously, the people who work there know where it is, and there is no reason for anyone else to know what's in there. It's all right for the room to have a number on the door that building maintenance would understand, but there is little reason to make it so easy for the bad guys to know where their best target is on that floor. This may sound like I'm getting a little too picky, but I'm not. The more difficult you make it for people who don't have a need to know about these critical rooms, the more secure you will be.

TIP

If you are going to have high-security locks on any doors in your building, dedicated computer rooms and phone closets would be high on my list of rooms needing the most secure locking mechanisms.

Review Video Security Logs

Normally, after we have completed our mission and have taken all of the "evidence that we have been there" out to our vehicle, we would reenter the building and try to be seen by the building security cameras we knew were there. Hopefully, there were some we didn't know about. We would even jump up and down waving our arms just to see if anyone would actually report us. As far as we know, we were never reported as being seen on the cameras' tapes. One of three things must have happened. Either the cameras weren't working (unlikely), or the people looking at the playback of the video missed seeing us on the tape (probably unlikely) or they were never looked at (most likely). I'd recommend that someone in the company periodically test this process. If there were internal auditors in the company, this would be a good audit step. That big expensive surveillance system is worthless if whatever is captured on tape is never seen by a human who can do something about it.

This is another area where I believe the people responsible for the systems' techno security need to talk with those responsible for physical security. Cameras and lights have always been excellent countermeasures in and around buildings and homes. They scream "go find an easier target" to the bad guys. Some areas may require additional cameras to help improve the security of critical areas or rooms. The team responsible for overall physical security might not know of these places unless you tell them. They may already be monitoring areas you aren't aware of, which could help you if an incident occurs.

The reason I mentioned homes several times throughout this chapter is because they are another soft spot when it comes to physical penetrations or social engineering. Many people now do much of their work from home on workstations using high-speed Internet connections. Personally, I employ as much physical security at my home office as at every other office I have worked. The technology associated with home security products has increased significantly, while the prices for that security have dropped, along with the cost of the latest computers.

I recently installed a number of digitally controlled security cameras around the perimeter of my home, as well as motion-activated security lights in all approach areas. This may sound a little paranoid, but I know that I am much more protected than most of my neighbors, and my family feels safe knowing it would be difficult to commit any crime on our property without someone knowing about it. The cameras are also motion activated, so the only thing I see is activity detected by the software. With the rapid advances in technology, these kinds of sophisticated security systems are very affordable and powerful.

Motion-Sensing Lights

Most of our social engineering–based inside penetration tests would have been much less successful if the companies that hired us had motion-sensing light controls installed in every office throughout their buildings. These same sensors then turn the lights off after a pre-set time once the last person leaves the room.

Every penetration test we were hired to conduct gave us several opportune buildings to enter, and every one had at least a few lights on all night long. While conducting our initial surveillance, that was one of the first things we noted. Are there lights left on at night, and if so, are they the same lights every night? In most cases, in a building with, say, 15 floors, six or eight lights would be left on. Our assumption was that whoever was assigned to that office was either still there, or they forgot to turn the light off when they left. Either way, it helped us significantly. If a random number of lights were left on each night, the security forces would not have an easy way of determining if everything was "normal" at any given time.

As they patrolled from the outside (we watched them do this from the outside, and also from the inside once we got into the building), they really had no reference for what was a normal building profile. As we became bolder towards the end of a penetration test, we would even turn certain lights on just to see if security would become suspicious of this activity. No one ever did.

Several of the buildings we penetrated didn't have anyone working in them at night. If motion-sensing lights had been used throughout these buildings, we would have looked for softer targets. If we had entered a room in a completely dark building, the light coming on would have been very abnormal for any security team member who saw it.

There is another good reason to install these sensors. Over time, the energy saved by having the lights automatically turn off when no one needed them could eventually pay for the cost of the sensor.

Check All Locks for Proper Operation

During each penetration test, we found at least one lock (either interior or exterior) in the building that wasn't functioning properly. This provided us with easy access to buildings and rooms that we shouldn't have been able to get through so easily. If employees are trained for just a few minutes on how to check if the locks on the doors they use every day are working properly, this vulnerability can be all but eliminated. Building maintenance teams should also take a close look at all locks at least twice each year. Slightly misaligned strikes on the doorframes are the most common problem found. This is a serious problem because it defeats the purpose of the lock's dead bolt. It takes me less than a second with my trusty finger nail file to see if a particular lock has this problem. If it does, I'll know (and have the door opened) instantly.

WARNING

Don't forget to check those locks and doors at home. We also recommend that lock combinations (keys) be changed immediately after occupying a new home, or after moving into a home that was owned by someone else. Keys are easy to duplicate, and you have no way of knowing how many copies are already out there, even for a brand new home. I'd also recommend changing the codes to your garage door openers as well, which is very easy to do with most modern openers.

If you have a garage door opener installed, do not leave it set to the default code (frequently 000000 or something very generic). This could make you vulnerable to another form of wardriving where the bad guys simply drive around neighborhoods with generic openers trying to see if any doors open as they drive past. This gives them a nice potential target for a future break-in. Also, many houses that have house alarms don't have an alarm on their garage door. Even worse, the keypad for turning the house alarm on or off is frequently located next to the garage entrance inside the house .

If you ever find your garage door opened and you didn't open it, I'd recommend immediately changing the door opener (and receiver) code.

The Elephant Burial Ground

I've been making a simple statement at presentations for the past ten years: "A new computer is a wonderful thing, but as soon as you buy it, it's already obsolete." Technology continues to change at a rate that few of us even notice. My statement isn't meant to be negative in any way. It's just that the computer is doing exactly what those new calculators did 35 years ago. They simply get faster, better, and cheaper as soon as you walk out the store's door. I'm not suggesting you don't buy the new (soon to be old) computer, you just must realize you will likely need a new one in two years.

What happens when that "elephant" you purchased a few years ago finally dies or becomes too old to do any work for you? I'll bet it gets moved to your elephant burial ground with the rest of the electronic equipment that still looks new and valuable but isn't fast enough to keep up anymore. You can't simply put it out for the trash man to pick up, so there it sits, sometimes for years.

This burial ground was a prime target for our penetration teams as we conducted vulnerability tests inside our clients' buildings. We frequently used our social engineering skills to find out where the old computers were stored. If it was in a locked room, we would find a way to either get someone to open the door for us, or we would use our lock picks or pick gun to open the door.

Figure 1.3 shows pick sets similar to the one I've owned for over 30 years, while Figure 1.4 shows a pick gun comparable to mine. It doesn't take a lot of practice to learn how to use the latter. If you are thinking about running out and buying some of these tools, please be sure to read the warning I have included below the pictures. I don't want to have to include you in a future war story about what NOT to do with lock picking equipment.

Figure 1.3 Examples of Lock Pick Sets

Figure 1.4 Example of a Pick Gun

Once we found a room that contained some outdated equipment, and so knew we were going to leave with some very valuable intellectual property. All we did was open a few computer cases, remove the hard drives, and neatly close the case back up. How valuable was the information on that drive, and how soon would you know it was missing from the elephant burial ground?

Most likely, you would never know the disk drives are gone. Our experience has been that these older computers are seldom powered on again by the organization that owned them. They may get powered on by whoever eventually winds up with them at some junk auction or thrift store where they were donated. If they sit in any onsite location for any length of time, the chances of anyone ever knowing that the entire computer is missing, much less the hard drive itself, are very slim. For the most part, it could remain an undetectable crime.

How valuable was the information on the old drive? Our experience has been that about 80 percent of the information on the old drive may still be of value to the "bad guys." If you think through the process of how that computer wound up in the burial ground, you will see what I mean. If the data on the old drive were properly backed up as a part of your disaster recovery plan, then it would most likely be restored to the new computer prior to retiring the old one. As soon as everything looked fine on the new computer, the old one may never be powered up again.

Technical issues are associated with each of the processes just described, but I didn't go into that detail here. Here's the bottom line from my experience with these old drives. If they weren't properly whipped clean, and if the drive itself was operational, we were able to get to the data on them with no problem.

TIP

Old disk drives will be an area of concern for years to come. Terabyte drives will soon be available at stores like Office Depot for anyone to purchase. Less than ten years ago, I was thrilled to be able to purchase a 200MB disk drive for $200. I was the first person in my circle of friends to own a drive of this size, and all for a mere $1 per megabyte. Today, 200GB disk drives can be found for as cheap as $50, after rebates. That's about 25 cents per gigabyte, which means that the same $1 per megabyte (actually worth less today) would buy me 4 GB, or 4,000 times as much storage space for the same dollar spent.

The tip here is to be careful with those old disk drives. This applies to the computers at home as well as at the office. Much valuable data is on them, and the risk escalates as the storage capacity of every drive climbs rapidly each year.

Figure 1.5 shows a destroyed disk drive, and Figure 1.6 shows the machine that destroyed it. The following is the URL of the only company I know that offers complete destruction of obsolete hard drives: www.edrsolutions.com.

Figure 1.5 A Destroyed Disk Drive

Figure 1.6 The Machine That Destroyed It…

Internal Auditors Are Your Friend

Just about everything I have mentioned in this chapter would make a good spot check audit point for an internal auditor. Someone on the good-guy side of the fence needs to check for these possible vulnerabilities and insure that the proper counter-measures are employed before they are exploited and become security incidents.

My experience with auditors over the years has been that things usually happen once they have made a suggestion to improve an area of concern. Many larger corporations have information system auditors who are primarily responsible for looking after the company's technical world. It's a lot to keep up with.

Most mid-sized corporations have internal auditors who are responsible for IS in addition to all their auditing tasks.

Always Be Slightly Suspicious

The number one countermeasure for social engineering is to be a little more suspicious than we normally are as friendly, trusting Americans. This holds true for social engineering attempts whether by way of a phone call or a visit from an amicable salesman. We all just need to be a little more aware of what is going on around us and those persons who might be pretending to be something they aren't.

Unfortunately, this is a difficult countermeasure to keep ongoing. Still, we should not become complacent in this area. If we do, it will make life much easier for future bad guys. This and most of the countermeasures suggested in this chapter will help mitigate all of these threats.

Get Every Employee Involved

I've been saying this over and over for close to two decades now. I don't care what kinds of sophisticated security devices are employed for physical access control or network access control with intrusion detection, firewalls, incident response, and so on, there will always be a large hole in a security plan if it doesn't get all of its employees involved with the protection process.

Social Engineering Awareness: A War Story

The phone rang at nine o'clock in the evening way back in the late 1980s. It was our national technical support group on the line. The caller said he had spoken to the day-shift supervisor, and that he needed to run a test by having us log in to our maintenance port while he was on the line. This was a UNIX-based operating system, and back then we always logged in as root. That was a very standard system administrator login ID and there was no need to guess it. What this social engineer needed was the password. In very official sounding language, he managed to convince our evening-shift computer operator that he was going to run a test to check the security of the password as the operator was entering it. The passwords themselves don't appear on the screen (echo is turned off, for you techies out there) but the characters are sent in the clear. The person on the other end of the line said that something wasn't working correctly. He couldn't see the password coming in to him (obviously, it wasn't really going in to him anyway). He then asked our operator to try again. The second time the operator had the same results. The pretend technical support group person began to sound a little frustrated. He finally said, "What password are you entering? I'll try it from this end." The unsuspecting social engineering victim was then told that this fake support person would get back to him when the problem was corrected. Obviously, he never heard from this person again.

Unfortunately, this was before our pre-awareness days, and the caller got what he was after. He had done his homework and come up with just enough information to sound "official" and catch our evening person off-guard. In a story with a happier ending, the same thing happened two years later, but we were completely ready for it this time. Our employee wide awareness program was paying off.

This process of calling and getting information from an unsuspecting victim over the phone is a form of remote "social engineering" in the "bad guy" circles. It's quite effective when used against an unsuspecting victim. Making sure every employee (especially everyone who answers the company phones) aware of this threat is your only defense against it. By asking questions back to any suspicious caller, you will drive away most of them. Ask for a number to call them back on. That doesn't guarantee anything, but I've heard a few clicks as the phone is hung up after I've asked for a number.

At a minimum, be aware of this highly probable threat and decide ahead of time what kinds of questions will, and will not, be answered about the company over the phone. This is an area where employees can get involved. At a monthly meeting, a "Social Engineering Attack Drill" can be staged. I've never been fond of role-playing sessions, but this is one area where it could be both fun and effective. The incoming caller can be engaged in industrial espionage, competitive spying, intentional destruction, just plain curiosity, or any number of things. If the team representing the company prepares for the questions that might be asked over the phone, there is a good chance they will hit on most of the questions the real social engineers will ask.

Once our employees were made aware of this threat, their antennas went up as soon as a call came in that was even the slightest bit strange. Yours will, too. You don't want to be insulting or rude to anyone who calls into your business. That's just not good for customer relations, and most businesses need customers to call them every now and then. You can be firm and alert sounding while still being nice to the caller. Gently let them know you are not about to give out any unnecessary information over the phone. If they are legitimate callers, they will come to appreciate your protection of company information. It may even be information about them, and who wouldn't want that protected?

Other good things start to happen as an awareness program filters through an organization. As employees learn more about the reasons for tighter security (such as keeping the company, and their jobs, from going down the tubes), they will tend to stop trying to circumvent existing security measures.

I learned something else from the seminars I gave years ago: employees are very much interested in helping with the overall security posture of their company. I started receiving copies of newspaper articles from former attendees, in case I hadn't seen them. I was starting to be made aware by my students, and it was rewarding for all of us. This internal network was starting to grow and security was becoming a challenge instead of a chore.

Something else I started took off as well as my homegrown awareness seminars: my security awareness posters. I wanted to make posters that were effective, eye catching, and cheap. My self-imposed criteria also demanded that they be easily reproducible on a standard copy machine. With those thoughts in mind, I sat down with a clipart book and let my imagination do the rest. After two hours, I had enough clipart drawings, and clever sayings to go with them, to design posters for the next two years. I sent out a new poster every three months to a select group of people. It didn't take long for others to call and want to be added to my list for receiving the next poster. Some people started to collect them and line them up along their walls.

After I spent six months sending these posters to whoever wanted one, a stranger I had never seen before in our building visited me. He came to my desk, said hello, and introduced himself as a corporate external auditor who was auditing a group in our building. I knew and worked with a number of our own internal auditors, but this was the first real live external auditor I had ever met. He made me feel at ease very quickly though by telling me he wanted to meet with the person who designed the posters. They were so simple, yet so effective, he wanted to take them back to *his* company. I said thanks and to help himself.

Here's a quick example of what I did for one of the posters. Using an interesting clipart picture of someone sitting in front of a computer, which included a caption that read "Take Advantage of Today's Technology," I simply added four words, creating what became my most popular poster. Below the phrase "Take Advantage of

Today's Technology" I added, in large print, "THE BAD GUYS WILL!" It was that simple.

With the clipart available today, you can come up with some excellent ideas very quickly. I even started a contest to see who could submit the most interesting poster suggestions for the following year's posters, even awarding prizes to the winners. All it takes is a little imagination and off you go. Have fun!

As the demand for my internal security awareness seminars increased, I was faced with an ever-growing problem. More and more groups wanted to see the presentation, and I couldn't possibly get to all of them. After all, giving these seminars wasn't even part of what my immediate group was supposed to do. My next step was to recommend a video be prepared and used by all of the groups that I couldn't get to. The initial reaction was that it could be too expensive. A studio quality video can cost over $1,000 per minute to create. Even a 30-minute video would be out of the operating budget for most groups at $30,000. That wasn't what I had in mind.

Something much less elaborate was what I was suggesting, and with the help of a friend with a video camera, it was created in less than two hours for just about zero cost. Just to see how it would look, we ran the camera during an entire 30-minute session that I presented to a small group. We then created a video of nothing but the slides that were used. The remaining hour was spent editing the two videos together. Our intent was to try this a few times until we got it right. We were trying to come up with something that would be cheap (the most important part at the time) and effective. We had no idea how successful our first attempt would become. Over 100 copies of it were sent all over the company, and most copies were shown a number of times throughout the next year to insure everyone had a chance to see it. As far as I know, it is still being shown.

I've shared all of this here for a reason. If I can do it, so can you or someone else in your company. I learned that homegrown videos are quite popular. In some ways, they gain a certain additional creditability if they are "real life" and not overly commercial. The equipment to create them is getting more sophisticated and less expensive all the time. If you try this yourself, I think you will be pleasantly surprised at the outcome.

There was someone else in the company that was pleasantly surprised by my seminars, posters, and videos: our internal auditors and attorneys. It was going a long way towards giving them plenty of good "Due Diligence" examples of what we as a company were doing to prevent computer security violations, both internal and external. Along those lines, I always encourage people who either attend a seminar, or view a video to make a note that they have had some security awareness training. As people all over the company do that, there will be an ever-growing population that is proof of the company's "Due Diligence" intent.

To help with this, I created a "Certificate of Attendance" that I send to everyone who attended one of my seminars. These are another low-cost and highly effective "Due Diligence" statement. Even though they are inexpensive to create, they are very nice and frameable. In fact, as I traveled around, I saw a number of them hanging near the desks of former attendees. You could create your own company certificate as easily as I did. All that you need is some good certificate stock (blank paper), a word processor, and a laser printer. After you experiment with the fonts and word sizes, you can keep a template that only needs to have the names mail-merged to create the documents. They will look as good as any you'll ever see, and you will have one more thing that the internal auditors will love to see hanging on the walls.

There is one final thing that an effective awareness program will help your company with, but I always dislike mentioning it. It will help deter "inside" activity. Unfortunately, every statistic I have ever read on the probability of security violations has pointed towards the "inside" of companies. (For more on this threat, read Dr. Eric Cole's book by Syngress titled *Insider Threat*.)

Security Alert...

Inside Threats

Experts estimate that over 80 percent of all breaches and problems come from someone inside the company. I never believed that until I started working with various law enforcement groups. Here's where awareness can even help deter that kind of activity. If your program is presented to all employees, obviously any potential inside "bad guys" will be sitting there as well. That's just fine. You won't be telling them anything they don't already know about how to get into your computers. You will be informing them that all the employees are now aware of a number of security issues and that their chances of getting caught in the act are far greater now that the corporate awareness level has been raised.

How long will you and your company have to continue your awareness campaign? Probably for as long as you continue to work, and computers continue to exist. I'm far from a doomsday person, but I do see this computer security issue as having the potential to be a major concern as we move deeper into the twenty-first century. There will always be those who find it an exciting challenge to see what they can get into in cyberspace.

Answer to the Riddle

The two coins are a nickel and a quarter. I know what you're thinking. I said that one of the coins was not a nickel. That's true. One of the coins is a quarter. The other one is a nickel.

Summary

I've thrown a lot at you in this combination of risks, threats, vulnerabilities, and countermeasures associated with social engineering. What I have tried to address in this brief chapter is what I consider the low-hanging fruit that the bad guys are very aware of. Most of the vulnerabilities mentioned are fairly easy to fix once you know about them. Most of you who read this book won't be responsible for correcting many of them, but you might be able to get this book to someone in your organization who can.

Security will always be a long-term team effort. This is true for every company and every home. If you have a computer in your home and you access the Internet to pay your bills or check your bank statement, you need to consider security every time you do so. Even though we live in a technical world that will do nothing but get more technical, we can't forget about physical security at home and work. If you become a victim of identity theft, you will spend about two years getting your financial life back in order. Prevention is your absolute best countermeasure for most, if not all, of these possible threats.

Thanks for reading all of my keystrokes as I put my 30 years of lessons learned on paper.

Stay safe out there!

Chapter 2

Personal, Workforce, and Family Preparedness
By Phil Drake

Phil Drake is Communications Manager for the *Charlotte Observer* in Charlotte, N. C. The *Observer* is a daily newspaper that serves readers throughout North and South Carolina. In addition to the newspaper, the *Charlotte Observer* produces specialty magazines, voice information, and Internet services.

Phil is responsible for all aspects of communications at *Observer* operations in both Carolinas, including telephone and data communications, wireless systems, conventional and trunked two-way radio, and satellite systems. He is also responsible for business continuity and disaster response planning and related budgeting. He is responsible for providing emergency communications facilities for reporters and photographers covering breaking news stories.

His background includes photojournalism, mainframe computer support, network management, telecommunications planning and management, and business continuity planning. Phil is a former chairman of the Contingency Planning Association of the Carolinas and currently serves as a Board Advisor of the organization. He is a Certified Business Continuity Professional with the Disaster Recovery Institute International.

Phil speaks to public and private sector groups and has been interviewed by and written for a number of national publications on a wide range of emergency communication issues and business/homeland defense planning. He leads business continuity training seminars for both the public and private sectors, and he has provided project management in business continuity. He has advised major national clients in emergency planning, workforce protection, threat assessment, and incident response for a number of large national corporations.

He enjoys backpacking and spending time in the outdoors. He also has taught outdoor living skills to youth group leaders. He was appointed by the North Carolina Secretary of the Department of Environment and Natural Resources as a voting member of the NC Geological Survey Advisory Committee.

Introduction

In this chapter, we'll discuss the need for a personal, workplace, and family emergency plan. We'll cover the basics of creating a plan for you and your family, identifying and obtaining the basic supplies you will need in an emergency, and why being prepared is so vitally important to you, your family, your community, and the nation. We'll also discuss workforce preparedness and the new urgency that applies to this important area in business continuity planning.

Threats

We live in a time and a nation where one can no longer take a "neutral position" regarding preparedness. As individuals, families, and workgroups, we are either an asset or a liability for our communities and nation when disaster strikes. To be an asset, we must be prepared.

You must be able to care for yourself and your family or you must depend on others to take care of you when disaster strikes. For too long, we have abandoned one of the founding principles that have made this nation great: self-reliance. "It's not my job" or "we have people to take care of that" when discussing preparedness is a far too common response.

Being prepared is having the ability to take care of yourself and your family at home, work, or school during an emergency situation. Likewise, business and government agencies must prepare to keep operating and supplying the goods and services that our communities need so as to return to normal life quicker.

NOTE

A family that has a disaster plan, supplies, and know-how in order to comfortably shelter in-place or evacuate during a severe storm, natural disaster, or other emergency will lessen the impact of whatever the emergency might bring.

Since September 11, 2001, our nation and the world have awakened to the very real threat of terrorism. While terrorist acts against the United States were not new, the scale of the coordinated attack of September 11 finally made even the most skeptical citizen realize we are a primary target for politically or religiously motivated acts of criminal violence.

While terrorism demands constant vigilance, so do the other threats that cause a tremendous loss in lives and dollars. Natural disasters, accidents, workplace violence, and crime also require our constant attention and preparedness.

While the average citizen can do little to stop these catastrophic events, they can prepare now to lessen the impact on themselves, their families, and their work environment. The first step in this preparedness process is to accept the fact that "it can happen to me" and "it can happen here."

Since Hurricane Katrina ravaged the Gulf Coast in 2005, FEMA and other government agencies have been clear in warning all who will listen that local state and federal government resources cannot save everyone. They cannot supply all the requested food, water, medical supplies, manpower, and infrastructure repairs requested in a widespread disaster in a matter of a few hours or days. With such things as the Katrina recovery, for example, we need to include months and years in our recovery projections.

For many years, the official recommendation was that you must be able to take care of yourself and your family for a minimum of at least 72 hours. Actually, two weeks is a more realistic estimate nowadays, given that the threat of a worldwide pandemic is a growing concern.

Public health experts are warning us that a major health crisis brewing in Asia will affect the entire world. We are being told that *when* a pandemic hits our nation (not if), it will be a very different disaster from any we have experienced in recent history. A pandemic will not only bring interruptions in key services and supply lines, but in the way we work and live for 12 to 18 months, perhaps longer. How can a business survive if the normally reliable electrical power, phone service, customers, suppliers, and workforce are missing?

How will our lives change when the schools and shopping malls close? In a highly contagious pandemic, few of us would want to find ourselves standing in a line to receive food or other basic supplies.

Our workplaces will change dramatically. The new terms of "social distancing," "lone worker," "virtual office," and "virtual workforce" will become commonplace. Not only must a workforce be prepared for power and communications outages, it must now be prepared to use new tactics, including social distancing, family preparedness, sheltering-in-place, and workforce continuity to reduce the impact of this new threat.

Preparing yourself and your family for emergencies requires more than just good intentions and a willingness to take care of yourself and your loved ones. Being prepared means much more than just having cash in your pocket and a "good" credit card ready to go. Preparedness means having a plan and the resources on hand to be totally self-sufficient during a natural disaster or other major emergency until normalcy is restored.

The Internet has made a wealth of family and workplace preparedness material available. "ready.gov," The American Red Cross, and other "official information" sites now offer information for a variety of age and reading levels. Official government pamphlets and booklets promote family preparedness and many commercial publications discuss this important topic. *Being informed is important, but being ready is absolutely imperative.*

"Workforce continuity" is defined as planning to have employees or contractors support the core business functions regardless of their work location. If the workplace is unreachable due to weather, road conditions, or some other workplace emergency, the employees can work from alternate locations or even from home. If an employee can't work for whatever reason, "workforce continuity" planning means training a backup to be ready to fill in for the missing worker. This may be other company employees or in some cases, outside contractors.

Workforce continuity also entails planning for a dramatic increase of absenteeism rates. If 40 or 50 percent of the workforce cannot or will not report for physical or virtual work, how does the enterprise survive?

It's smart to plan for the unexpected and use the Internet and wireless access to it to continue doing business. Virtual call centers and other technology depend heavily on the Internet and communications networks. What happens if those networks and other infrastructures are unavailable or so overtaxed that they become useless for mission critical use?

After all, what is the total capacity of the Internet? *Internet World Stats* reports that as of late 2006 there were 1,093 billion Internet users in the world. Now let's suppose that the majority of these users are currently working at home to support their employer's operations or are trying to keep abreast of the latest emergency information. At what point does the Internet cease to be a useful transport mechanism due to the demand for bandwidth? Probably long before the last user signs on.

A business that depends primarily on the Internet as a solution to a large-scale disaster or manmade crisis will be disappointed. Virtual office and a mobile workforce are ideal solutions to many of today's environmental and business scheduling problems. However, a solution that depends heavily on public infrastructure for success is doomed from the beginning. The only dependable solution is a reliable workforce willing to be there when needed to keep the business running.

Business leaders must understand that they we now face the very real possibility of not having enough employees to keep the business "in business."

Let's talk for a while about what's really important in your life, and what's really important in your family's life: YOU. Do you have a personal emergency plan? Does your family? Most individuals and families believe they will think about this when the time comes. Unfortunately, when a disaster strikes, there is little warning and the "planning" gets replaced by panic and uncoordinated responses to the event.

Your Personal Preparedness Plan

Let's start with that most valuable asset: "you." You need to have a plan, and you need to make sure your family and co-workers know what that plan is. If they are part of your plan, they surely need to know that now. And yes, just as with any plan, yours needs to be tested routinely.

We'll discuss workplace, home, and family preparedness a bit later in this chapter. It is vitally important to remember that personal, family, workplace, and community emergency preparedness complement each other.

Most of us spend the majority of our lives between home and work. If an emergency is preceded by a warning period (a winter storm or hurricane), you will have time to plan your response. In a winter storm, for instance, you'll probably stay at home or will be instructed to report later than usual by your employer. In the event of a fire, earthquake, or other unexpected emergency, your response must be immediate. You must act quickly to save your life and perhaps the lives of others.

TIP

Your personal goal is to make sure you survive and remain healthy, regardless of what the emergency situation may be. Getting out of a dangerous situation and staying out of the way are paramount. Being prepared will reduce your mental and physical stress levels and increase your ability to assist others.

The first step in your plan must be the protection of your own life. Personal safety experts will tell you to "always be aware of your surroundings." That's excellent advice. Look around; walk around your home and workplace. Where is trouble most likely to occur? Is flooding from a nearby creek or river possible? Are you near any major railroads or highways where transportation accidents may impact you?

Do the same "walkabout" inside, too. Are there dangers you've ignored in the past? Could any of these be used against you and/or your home or workplace? Be aware of unlocked exit doors, trip hazards, and blocked exits.

Wherever you work, know the environment, and if the situation requires, know how to get out quickly. Make sure you know where the emergency exits are, and if the one closest to you is blocked, where the next closest exit is located. How long does it take you to exit your facility? Do these exits have battery-operated escape lights? If not, provide your own with a small flashlight or chemical light sticks.

If you work in a multistory building, are you physically able to walk down the exit stairs? If not, make sure you can. Even if you are in good physical shape, stairs can be a challenge. If you are physically unable to walk down stairs because of medical reasons, find "escape buddies" to help you get down or check with your employer to determine the locations of any identified evacuation safe havens.

If you're shopping, at the movies, spending the night away from home, or conducting personal business in a building you're not familiar with, know how to get out.

Warning

Wherever you are, always know where the emergency exits are located. They are required by law to be clearly marked. In a hotel, I always find the exits before turning in for the evening.

Having a personal preparedness plan will make you and your loved ones safer. After all, they depend on you. A personal plan should include the following:

■ A commitment to be aware of your surroundings and current conditions

■ Alternate routes to and from home, work, or school

■ An emergency contact card with all family contact information

■ Knowing the locations of fire, police, and emergency medical facilities near your work, home, and routes of travel

■ If you commute, keep a spare car key hidden on the vehicle in case a building evacuation at work forces you to leave everything behind.

■ Everyone needs a few basic resources if circumstances strand you en route to home/work/school. (See the next section on the subject of escape packs.)

■ Always know the location of the nearest fire escape in your workplace, school, or hotel if traveling.

■ Familiarize yourself with the emergency exits and procedures on commercial buses, trains, and aircraft.

■ Remember my *3G rule*: "Get out, Get away, and Get in touch." Regardless of where you may be, always remember to get out of danger, get away from the danger, and let your family, friends, and employers know you are safe.

Don't get caught standing outside your workplace due to an evacuation and wondering "now what"? Your personal response plan must cover not only safely getting out, but safely getting away if necessary. If you drive to work, where are your vehicle keys? Can you get into your vehicle if your keys are in your coat, hanging beside your desk? Hide a key under, around, or near your vehicle. In the case of keyless entry, keep an ignition key hidden inside the vehicle. If you're carpooling, make sure everyone in the group knows how to get in, too.

One of the simplest ways to make sure you have basic items to help you respond in an emergency situation is to pack them now before you need them. This small "escape pack" is designed to help get you out of trouble if an emergency interrupts your normal routine. I'll also explain what these items are since I'm not a big believer in buying (or carrying) a bunch of "stuff" just for the sake of doing so. You can also purchase commercially available kits that provide some of the same items. However, if you assemble this kit yourself, you'll be more familiar with the contents and how to use them.

This is not a "survival kit" in the general context. It will supply your immediate needs in case you find yourself "on the street" unexpectedly due to an emergency in your workplace. All of these items can easily be packed in a small nylon pouch generally sold as "camera case."

The Escape Pack

■ Thirty-minute high intensity light sticks (two)

■ Compass (basic and small)

■ Metropolitan or area map

■ Disposable plastic rain poncho

■ Emergency contact card

■ Small note pad

■ Pencil

■ Matches (one book)

■ Aluminum foil (12 x 24 inches)

■ Important phone numbers

- Large handkerchief or bandana

- Change (quarters for payphone or newspaper racks)

- Extra cash (a $20 bill works nicely)

- Critical medication (one or two doses)

- Large 3 x 4 gauze pads and small roll of half-inch adhesive tape

- Four Large adhesive bandages (Band-Aids)

- Small pocketknife

- Energy bar or some hard candy

- Ziplock bags (two)

- Vehicle and/or home key if needed

- Bag to carry the above items

Description of Kit Contents

- **Light sticks** Used for escape illumination in office hallways and stairwells.

- **Map and compass** If you must walk home or to safety, you'll be able to navigate your way. Practice this important skill before you need it.

- **Plastic rain poncho** An inexpensive plastic poncho will keep you dry and help you retain body heat.

- **Emergency contact card** Keep those key emergency phone numbers, family, and out-of-area emergency contact numbers written down and handy. In a stressful situation, don't rely on your memory. Your cell phone or PDA may have been left behind, or might not be functioning.

- **Small note pad and pencil** Important for writing messages, notes, or observations. A pencil will not leak in the summer or stop working in cold or rain.

- **Matches (one book)** Can be used for starting a fire for warmth, or lighting up a cigarette if it will make you feel better.

- **Aluminum foil (12 x 24 inches)** Has a hundred uses. First aid, signaling, and food preparation are three that come to mind quickly.

- **Large handkerchief or bandana** For first aid, keeping your head warm, and cleaning glasses.

- **Change and extra cash** Quarters for payphones (if working) or news-paper racks. Newspapers provide a host of uses. Extra cash in case ATMs aren't working or merchants cannot use checks or read credit cards.

TIP

Your vehicle is an excellent place to store some emergency supplies, including your "escape pack." These items will be available in case of a workplace evacuation or other emergency away from home.

Workforce Preparedness

While the subject of workforce preparedness can fill an entire book, I want to devote some time to discuss its importance and offer some suggestions to help begin the planning process.

The most valuable asset any enterprise or organization has, regardless of its size, is its workforce. These are men and women who make a company run day-to-day and create ideas and products to serve its customers and communities. Until recently, the majority of business continuity efforts revolved around processes and systems that the company depends on to keep operating. Little attention has been paid to the most critical support process, those employees and their families who make the enterprise successful.

Throughout this section I use the descriptions of workplace, organization, agency, business, employer, and enterprise. These are generic terms of that place you call "work." I realize there are thousands of public and private sector operations and agencies that, while not motivated by profit, do have products, services, and delivery obligations.

The threat dynamics have changed dramatically in the twenty-first century and every aspect of our normal lives is now considered a possible target for terrorism. Senior managers must realize that interruptions to the normal flow of business may include community evacuations, workplace violence, lengthy supply chain interrup-tions, mass casualty situations, and direct attacks by individuals or groups using unconventional weapons. Do not assume your workplace is safe from these new threats, or old ones such as fire, natural disasters, or criminal activity.

An organization that only prepares for the occasional power failure, fire, hurri-cane, winter storm, or work stoppage is no longer exercising due diligence in the protection of the assets of that enterprise. Every organization, large or small, must have a *business defense plan* (business continuity plan) that includes protection and preparedness of the core operational functions, employees, and their families. In a community-wide emergency or disaster, companies and public agencies need their employees to return to work as quickly as possible to limit losses. A company or government agency may provide critical services that will be vitally necessary for the recovery of your community from the event. That company or agency *must* be prepared to continue operations. If an employee must choose between family and workplace, family will win every time. Senior executives, managers, and agency directors can no longer tell their employees that "we expect you to be here when we need you, under any circumstances" and be assured of a successful recovery.

Any organization that seeks to prepare their key processes for unexpected interruptions must maintain a prepared workforce to support those critical functions.

You may have heard the relatively new term *workforce continuity*. It's defined as having an uninterruptible and trained workforce that can continue the critical operations of the organization under any circumstances. Generally, this means planning to use virtual workers when weather or other conditions make travel to the primary work location hazardous. Cross-training employees to fill in for job functions that are not ordinarily their responsibilities is another workforce continuity tactic. Having contract employees on retainer is yet another.

TIP

Simply having a contingency plan *in case of trouble* is no longer adequate. For the foreseeable future, we must expect trouble and make sure each of us—as well as our families, workplaces, and communities— are at a higher level of readiness.

A well-developed business continuity plan that prepares the key businesses processes, employees, and employee families is no longer just smart planning. It is now critical to the survival of our economy (along with due diligence).

The most valuable asset your business, agency, organization, or home has is *you*. You, your family, co-workers, and stakeholders keep the enterprise running, and successful. What happens at home and in your personal life outside the workplace has a direct impact on how well you do your job. In an emergency situation, most people think of home and family first. Is everyone safe? If you are at home, will you report to work in a time of crisis? Will you leave your family to help your employer continue operations?

It's vitally important that every enterprise, regardless of whether it's a major corporation, small business, or government agency have plans to guarantee the safety of its employees. In fact, law in many instances requires it. However, don't assume that just because you participate in a "fire drill" that you are safe. Does your workplace have a safety committee? Are building evacuation plans documented? If an event happens in your community or workplace that places you in danger, how are you notified? Does your employer expect personnel to report to work under any conditions? If so, what are they doing to guarantee that?

The workplace that prepares employees and families by sharing preparedness information, plans, training, and support will have a workforce that is ready and willing to get things back to normal quicker than the unprepared. Replacing the fear and uncertainty in an emergency keeps the workforce, stakeholders, and families focused on recovery, not only in the enterprise but in the family unit and community as well.

Steps for Successful Workforce Preparedness

- Draw up a written business (or operations) continuity plan (BCP)

- Share the plan with employees and families as appropriate

- Exercise the BCP plan routinely

- Update building evacuation plans and practice carrying them out routinely

- Monitor local and national current events and share pertinent information with employees

- Conduct personal safety, first-aid, and CPR classes for employees

- Offer personal and family preparedness instruction and information

I've heard—and you probably have, too—the story about occupants in a multi-tenant building looking out of the windows to see a parking lot full of other building occupants. This usually means that the emergency alarm didn't sound or someone forgot to pass the word. Tragically, it can and does happen in real emergency situations generally related to workplace violence or bomb incidents.

An alerting system that can be used to quickly inform the entire population of a building, or an entire community for that matter, saves lives. This tends to be bells, horns, or sirens. However a building "enunciation" or public address system offers more control of the alerting process and evacuation. Electronic message boards, digital paging, and instant messaging to all LAN users are additional and highly effective ways of alerting and sharing emergency information quickly.

Get Out, Get Away, and Get in Touch

Federal, state, and local laws require that a workplace have an emergency evacuation plan (depending on the number of employees and the building structure) that must include an alerting system and annual exercises. Just getting everyone out, however, is not enough. For everyone's sake, you must prove it. That's not a new federal regulation; it's common sense. After all, would you want to be left behind and not be missed until it's too late?

In any emergency, remember the 3Gs rule of personal protection, which help remind you to get out, get away, and get in touch. Get out of danger—in this example, your workplace during an emergency. Get away—don't stand on the sidewalk in front of a building that may collapse or explode. And finally, get in touch with your supervisor, co-workers and family to let them know that you are accounted for.

First responders arriving on the scene at a fire, explosion, or building collapse will ask "is everyone out?" If you're the senior manager or building owner, you'll save time and precious resources by answering "everyone is accounted out" or be able to direct rescue teams to specific locations where missing workers were last seen.

If you cannot account for everyone, firefighters or search and rescue teams may have to search the building, and that puts lives at stake: those left behind and those searching.

In a large facility, your workplace evacuation plan should include "shelter locations." These assembly points inside the building—usually in fire escapes or other safe havens—offer shelter to injured or physically challenged employees. Such locations should be well marked and include some form of communication to a central emergency control point. Your local fire department can assist your efforts in identification and planning. Preparing a workplace evacuation plan includes the following.

- Senior management must make it clear to every employee that when told to evacuate, they should do so immediately, without hesitation, and in an orderly fashion.

- Permanent "meeting points" outside the building are identified and assigned by department or work location where a roll call is conducted. The results are communicated back to an evacuation control point by two-way radio or runners.

- A central permanent "evacuation control point" is established to collect and distribute information from the evacuation.

- Each department, section, or floor must have assigned "fire wardens" or "evacuation coordinators" who keep current rosters of all shifts and employees. These rosters are carried to, or stored at, the outdoor meeting points.

- The control point relays the roll call and any injury reports to emergency responders.

- The "all clear" signal to return to the facility (or other such information) can only be issued by the evacuation control point. All information or requests for assistance from the meeting points must go to the control point—no exceptions.

- Routinely exercise the plan.

The meeting points mentioned in the preceding list should be located as far from the building as practical. Just being out of the building does not mean the workforce is out of danger. Most buildings today are constructed with beautiful glass exteriors. An explosion can send glass shards and other debris flying hundreds of yards.

One general concern expressed to me by executives of several corporations is that "fire drills" reduce production time and that's why they are rarely done more than once a year—which, by the way, is not enough. I recently helped a large company redesign their evacuation plan based on the preceding information. Each evacuation coordinator was assigned not only rosters but an inexpensive two-way radio and a bright yellow bag to carry them in to the meeting point. That company now routinely evacuates 800 employees from a multistory building, conducts a roll call, reports results, and returns all employees to the building in 15 minutes during evacuation drills. The executives of that company are proud of this accomplishment and their employees are safer.

In the event of an actual emergency, a final evacuation responsibility that you have to your family is to let them know your condition and plans as soon as possible.

If your workplace does not have an updated building evacuation plan, inquire about starting one. Ask your supervisor, safety committee, or safety director. This would also be a good time to get involved by offering to help make it happen or to make an existing program better with your participation.

Some workplaces have well-documented evacuation plans, and area evacuation coordinators ensure that all employees in their respective areas understand the plan, have "escape buddies" to help them if necessary, and "sweep" their assigned areas in an emergency making sure everyone has left the area. This is excellent safety planning, but these plans must be practiced routinely. Unfortunately, far too many organizations pay too little attention to this vital preparedness planning. If you work in an organization that has not updated its evacuation planning or if you don't fully understand the plans, get involved and make your workplace and yourself safer.

Are first-aid kits distributed for emergency use in your workplace? If so, where are they and are they properly supplied? If they are not adequate, point this out to your safety director or supervisor. Know how to use the supplies in a first-aid kit. If you're unsure, enroll in a basic first-aid course. Such skills make you, your family, and co-workers safer in any circumstance. Your employer will probably be more than happy to arrange onsite classes through the local chapter of the American Red Cross.

Family Preparedness Plan

We create and work plans every day of our lives. We plan our days, what to wear, who to meet, where to go and how to get there, and what to eat. These are for the routine, good things in life. Why then don't we plan for the bad things that can sur- prise us and threaten our safety?

One of the most chilling memories of the 2005 hurricane season was the CNN coverage of the hundreds of cars running out of gas on streets and highways as Hurricane Wilma approached. These "average Americans" were stranded, hungry and scared. I could not help thinking that a bit of planning would have avoided most of this suffering. These families probably didn't have a family ready kit, a full gas tank, or extra cash on hand. They had not considered the possibility that another hurri- cane might strike so soon after Katrina. They aren't alone in their denial; most Americans believe that bad things happen to other people.

Every book on family preparedness includes a list describing items that should be kept ready for use in an emergency situation. I've included a list (the Family Ready Kit) later in this chapter, but the kit doesn't work by itself. It's more impor- tant for family members to know what to do than to count on a box or bag of "stuff." Family preparedness is a state of mind—it's planning, practicing, and working together as a team to thrive, not just survive, in emergency situations.

The most important point in family preparedness is family communication. Talk about what your family plans to do in the event of a major storm, natural disaster, or terrorist incident. Talking through what you expect, what might happen, and what "we as a family" will do removes a tremendous amount of stress and fear from any situation. Children especially need to know that the family has a plan for emergen- cies and that they are an important part of the plan.

A good way to begin your preparedness planning is to create a family fire plan.

- Check your smoke alarms for proper operation annually and change the batteries.

- Plan escape routes including those from second stories.

- Establish a family meeting point (more on this in the next subsection).

- Call for help once outside.

- Practice your plan until it works flawlessly.

Spend some time explaining that emergencies can happen anytime, and that if we're all home together, we'll be really lucky. In reality, that's not likely to happen and family members will probably be separated for a number of hours (or even longer) until they can be reunited. Mom and Dad may be at work, or the kids may be at school when a major disaster happens. Discuss, now, how best to get together following a major emergency.

Each family member should have assigned tasks and a procedure to follow in the event of an emergency situation. This emergency planning begins with how to get out of the house in case of a fire or other emergency, and establishing a meeting point afterward for all family members.

The 3Gs rule applies to the home as well as the workplace. If you need to leave due to an emergency in your home, "Get Out, Get Away, and Get in touch."

A key component in your family preparedness plan is to have several meeting points for various emergencies. These are locations the family identifies and where they agree to meet if separated due to a disaster or other emergency.

Possible Meeting Points

Here is a list of possible meeting points for your family following a disaster or emergency:

- A neighbor's home, the family swing set, the mailbox, bus stop, or tree in the yard where the family is to meet in case an emergency requires leaving the home on short notice

- A community shelter, relative's home, or neighborhood business in case a neighborhood requires evacuation

- A relative or friend's home or other location outside the community in case the family is separated in a wide-scale disaster

- A virtual meeting place such as an e-mail address or phone number outside the community so family members can check in if separated

Schools have very specific procedures for early dismissal situations. Releasing children to family members is usually an option, but this must be approved beforehand. Allowing the school system to transport your children home may be faster than you trying to pick them up. Find out what your children's school system policies are and discuss these policies with your children.

If students will be sheltered in-place (kept safe at school) how will they be released? Will students be transported to a community shelter? If so, where is that shelter located?

Community Shelter

Your local emergency management agency has designated certain facilities in your city or county as community shelters. These shelters are generally public high schools or other public buildings that can hold a large number of people for an extended period of time. Typically, the American Red Cross is the agency that manages these shelters and provides food services, cots, first aid, communications, and basic health care for individuals who may need it. Community shelters are a safe place to go when needed. In a dangerous situation—such as a tornado, hurricane, or other general emergency—many people will try to stay at home. If the order is given to evacuate, do not hesitate. Leave immediately and go to a shelter as directed.

It's important for you and your family to understand what to take and not take to a community shelter if you go to one of these facilities. You should bring pillows, blankets, toiletry items, prescription medications, games, snacks, and identification. Ask your local Red Cross or emergency management agency—before an emergency—what can and cannot be brought with you to a local shelter. If you're a pet owner, ask what arrangements will be in place for pet care.

TIP

Assemble a personal "evacuation bag" for each member of the family. This small duffel bag or day-pack can be packed with a change of clothing appropriate for the season, as well as other personal items, in case you are forced to leave home quickly.

The Personal Evacuation Bag

- Jeans or heavy pants/slacks with belt
- Two pairs of heavy socks
- Long-sleeved shirt/blouse

- T-shirt and change of underclothing
- One pair of shorts in warm weather
- Work gloves and winter mittens or gloves if appropriate
- Cap or hat with brim
- Sunglasses and sunscreen (regardless of temperature)
- Rain poncho or lightweight rain suit
- Personal hygiene items (comb, tooth brush, toothpaste, soap, razor, and towel)
- Sports/emergency or other lightweight blanket
- Copy of government-issued ID (driver?s license)
- Flashlight or headlamp
- Pocketknife, whistle, compass, and matches/lighter
- Other personal items as appropriate

Preparedness Pantry

Every home should maintain a supply of nonperishable food and water for the entire family. When asked "how do I buy and store two weeks worth of food?" My response is that you simply have to fill your pantry. Most of us never do that. Instead, we depend on stopping by the supermarket or carry-out on the way home to pick up dinner. Now is the time to change that behavior and it can be done easily (and affordably) over a period of several weeks.

I've mentioned being prepared for at least 72 hours and more realistically two weeks, earlier in this chapter. Over the next several trips to the supermarket, purchase extra cans or packages of the foods you most often use. Supplement these with additional canned meats, vegetables, and fruits. Plan and stock your "preparedness pantry" to provide a two-week supply of meals. Be realistic: In an emergency situation, you won't be entertaining, and in most cases "meals" will be simple and quick. Purchase additional items that store well and can be used in a wide variety of meal planning—rice, dried beans and pasta are ideal choices.

Simply add a few more items each time you grocery shop and plan to have your "preparedness pantry" completed in three trips. Shop with a list and buy shelf-stable items. Once your supply is purchased, date every item and rotate your supply by incorporating them into your normal menus. Always plan ahead by purchasing replacement items first before using anything from your "preparedness pantry."

Once your pantry is stocked, rotate that stock by using the food purchased first and then resupplying. I mark each can and package with its purchase date using a permanent marker. It's easy to use the first purchased items and then replace on the next trip to the supermarket. If you don't keep your preparedness pantry supplied with "rotated stock" you may find three-year-old tomato sauce that will add nothing but disappointment to your dinner plans.

I should at this point explain the term "shelf stable." Shelf-stable foods are prepared to be stored without refrigeration or any other special conditions for extended periods of time. Dried fruit and meat was the first "shelf-stable" food civilized man discovered. In fact, this food preservation method was used long before kitchens or shelves were invented.

While shelf-stable food purchased at the supermarket will easily last 12 to 18 months, I recommend a six-month storage/use/replacement routine. By incorporating your "emergency pantry" into your normal menus, you'll always have that two-week supply ready for use in an emergency.

Marking each container with the purchase date will help identify the "emergency pantry" items. Use these long-term storage items in normal weekly menus occasionally. You can purchase a replacement before it's actually used if you plan your menus a week beforehand. If you don't have a replacement before use, simply tear the label off and purchase a replacement on your next shopping trip.

An exception to this is MREs (Meals Ready to Eat) and dehydrated long-term storage foods that have a shelf life of six years and longer (depending on storage conditions). It's a good idea, however, to incorporate some of these occasionally into your regular meal planning, too, so family members know what these meals look and taste like. MREs (regardless of what you may hear) are tasty and nutritious.

"Soft pack canning" or MREs became the military standard in the 1960s. This process involves cooking the food in multilayer plastic envelopes that are impervious to the chemical action of the food or environment. This soft container maintains an airtight and almost indestructible "cocoon" for the fully cooked and "ready to eat food." This stuff stores for years and maintains flavor and nutritional benefits. Do not buy "military surplus" MREs; buy them fresh from local or online dealers.

MREs are a great choice for any organization or business that may need to feed employees and or family members in an emergency situation. They are packaged in complete meal servings. Each meal is unit packed in a plastic envelope that includes the entree, side items, drink, dessert, and accessories pack with salt, pepper, eating utensils, and napkin. All that is needed is a method for warming the food which, in a pinch, can be eaten at room temperature. One envelope contains a complete and balanced nutritious meal. This is especially important when mass feeding a large group without a large dining or food preparation facility.

Canned foods will easily store for 12 to 18 months. Some of the new microwave entrees are use-dated for generally a year. Look closely on your grocery store shelves (not freezer section) and you may be surprised at what you'll find that can be used in your emergency pantry. Along with canned vegetables and meats, you'll discover fully cooked meals ready to be warmed in the microwave, which include chicken, turkey, and beef entrees. You'll also find cooked pasta and rice dishes just waiting to be warmed and eaten.

Canning to preserve food and their flavors has been used for over two hundred years and is still the leading food preservation technology. Home canning remains popular especially when home gardens are producing more than we can use or give away.

NOTE

Napoleon offered a cash prize to anyone who could find a way to keep food from spoiling so that he could better feed his army on their long campaigns. In 1795, Nicolas Appert discovered that by placing food in sealed containers and cooking them in boiling water the food lasted for long periods of time. He won the prize, and his method of food preservation was declared a military secret. It wasn't long, however, before this new preservation method found its way to England where in 1810 Peter Durrand improved the process by using metal containers or "cans."

Home freezing and frozen foods (TV dinners) became popular in the 1950s. Today, refrigeration and freezing are the most popular forms of food preservation. By the way, if you have a freezer full of frozen food and no power, don't panic—and don't open the freezer door. A full freezer will keep frozen food "frozen" for around 48 hours *if* you avoid the urge to open the door.

Freeze-dried foods are very popular with backpackers. These foods are fully cooked and then flash frozen at temperatures around −125 degrees Fahrenheit. Water from the food is condensed and removed, leaving a dried food product, which is then packaged in an airtight (generally plastic/foil) package. All you need to do is add the water back, and heat the product when you're ready to eat.

Freeze-dried foods are very light and compact, and will store for many years. Complete freeze-dried meals are available in any outdoor supply or camping store. One small drawback is that they are a bit more expensive than hard or soft pack canned food items, you must have an ample supply of water to add to the contents, and they are not as easy to incorporate in a normal family menu for pantry stores rotation.

Irradiated food processing is still fairly new and in very limited distribution in the U.S. at the time of this writing. Irradiation offers some major food safety and preservation benefits. This technology uses a radioactive source to "sterilize" the food without cooking it. So, in theory, meat could be stored in a container without refrigeration for weeks and still be safe and favorable. Fruits and vegetables can be stored for months without loosing color, flavor, or food value. No radioactivity is transferred to the food, so your salad will not mutate into some giant walking green thing that chases you around the kitchen. The Food and Drug Administration reports that food irradiation is allowed in nearly 40 countries and is endorsed by the World Health Organization, the American Medical Association, and many other organizations. However, the percentage of food being irradiated is still very low due to the expense and lack of acceptance of this new process. Stay tuned, this process will be commonplace in a few years.

As you can see, we are blessed with an array of well-proven food preservation methods. You must keep a supply on hand and thus avoid the danger of going out to look for something to eat.

Water

Water is the most important item in your "preparedness pantry." Store one gallon of water for each family member for each day you plan to be self-sufficient. Generally plan on using a half-gallon of water per day for drinking, and a half-gallon per day for sanitation for each family member. Date each container and rotate your stock every six months. Most commercial water containers are dated, saving you from having to do it yourself. Most commercially bottled water is use-dated for at least a year or two.

I recommend several one-, two-, or five-gallon containers of water for cooking and sanitation, and smaller 8- or 12-ounce bottles for drinking and refilling.

What's the difference between distilled water, spring water, and drinking water? Generally, the price. Distilled water is of course distilled or boiled into steam, the steam is condensed back into liquid form and bottled. This process removes all of the minerals and impurities and in fact sterilizes the water. Spring water should come from a spring (no guarantees here) and is probably filtered.

Drinking water is just "tap water" from a municipal water supply that may or may not be filtered and then bottled. Most is filtered, but check the label. Do as you please, but I simply buy the cheapest "store brand" drinking water for less than 60 cents a gallon.

If you have a natural water source near your home (spring, stream, or lake), consider purchasing a water purification filter. These filters generally consist of a small hand pump and a high-efficiency carbon or ceramic element that will purify the most questionable water supply. Several new water purification products are on the market. These include filtering straws and even battery-operated ultra-violet systems. For now, these tend to be expensive and produce limited volume. Having access to a water source and the proper purification equipment will reduce the amount of stored water you may need.

Storing a supply of food and drinking water is not just for personal or family emergency planning. The workplace must be able to support employees who may be stranded or "sheltered" in the workplace. Every business continuity plan must address the likelihood of supporting employees who may be required to stay put in order to keep critical operations running if conditions warrant.

Cooking

Simple one-pot "camping" meals are best in an emergency situation. After all, you'll be concentrating on other important issues. Be extremely careful in how you prepare your meals, especially when operating gas or other open-flame stoves that should be used *outdoors*. Never use charcoal grills or other outdoor cooking "appliances" inside your home. *Use them outside where they belong.* The risk of fire (which is great) is overshadowed by the risk of carbon monoxide poisoning.

For one-pot meal suggestions, look no further than your "crock pot" recipe book. Search out recipes that use foods stored in your "preparedness pantry" and simply adjust cooking time from s-l-o-w to shorter times with higher heat.

Other good recipe resources are camping cookbooks and the official Boy Scout Field Book. *The Boy Scouts of America Field Book* is one of the best available manuals, not only for cooking but for general self-sufficiency as well.

Try the recipes that look interesting to you and your family. Tailor the ingredients to meet your specific tastes and portion requirements. The ones voted most enjoyable should be written on recipe cards and kept in your pantry.

I'm a lazy cook who loves to prepare and eat but hates to clean up. So after years of practice, I'm pretty good at whipping up some decent meals with little or no clean-up. Heating (see note that follows) foil packed meats, vegetables, and MREs in their packages in a single pot of boiling water allows you to use the water for hot drinks, rice, pasta, kitchen clean-up, and/or personal care. Cooking rice or pasta in "boiling bags" allows you to avoid more clean-up and requires less water, which may be in short supply. Of course, in an emergency, fuel may also be in short supply.

TIP

When you are heating food envelopes ("soft cans"), always tear a small "vent" opening in the envelope to eliminate any bursting hazard. If the contents start to boil and produce steam, the envelope may explode.

Most people have an outdoor gas grill, camping, or backpacking stove that will handle the cooking requirements just fine, just use them outside.

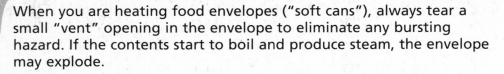

WARNING

Installed home gas appliances are properly vented and have low oxygen shutdown safety features. Any portable cooking stove brought into your home does not. So keep the disaster—and the portable cooking stoves—*outside* your home.

As with any new recipe or cooking technique, it's best to try these first yourself before serving them to others. And, of course, before a disaster; otherwise, you will very likely lose your cooking privileges!

Testing Your Home Preparedness Plan

Just like a business continuity plan, a family preparedness plan is not complete until it is routinely tested and updated. At work, you and your co-workers must be familiar with your employer's business continuity or emergency plan and understand your role in that plan. Semi-annual plan reviews and exercises are the best method of keeping the plan current and the recovery teams competent in their ability to successfully execute the plan.

This is true for your family preparedness plan, too. Family members (regardless of their age or physical abilities) must actively participate and thoroughly understand the purpose of the plan and the importance of their respective roles in making the plan work successfully.

In the business environment, our continuity or preparedness plans are concerned with the safety of the employees and the welfare of the enterprise. At home, our focus is on our loved ones and the survivability of our home and family.

I strongly suggest you use the same tactics for plan testing or exercising at home that you use (or should be using) at work. Tabletop emergency exercises at work can become a great rainy day "board game" at home. Plan "what if" and "how can our family handle an emergency" discussions, and include everyone's input. Hold a "walkthrough" of your plan to see if parts of it are unrealistic. Of course, scheduled exercises or even a few unannounced drills are the best method of keeping your family preparedness plan the best it can be, and as a result, your family will be safer.

One of the most enjoyable ways to test your preparedness plans is to have a "camp-in." Select a weekend evening and announce that you'll all meet in the living room or den and camp out for the night. Off go the lights and the entire family uses only the supplies on hand to "survive the disaster." Pretend there is no phone or power other than what you can supply with your own resources. Meals should be prepared using your "preparedness pantry" and alternate cooking methods.

We can promise three things if you follow our advice in this chapter. Your family will be better prepared for emergencies, you'll all have some fun, and you and your family will discover that doing something a bit unusual as a team brings you closer together and builds a stronger family bond.

Family Ready Kit

Designating a central point where special supplies and basic equipment will be stored saves valuable time in responding to an emergency. While there are a few "family emergency kits" now being marketed online and in some stores, I suggest you make your own. You probably already have many of the things you'll need, and by building the kit yourself and involving the entire family, everyone becomes familiar with the contents and the location of the kit.

Younger family members in particular feel more confident if mom and dad aren't around by knowing that the family ready kit has basic emergency supplies to help them until other family members arrive.

If the family can stay at home and shelter-in-place, the ready kit is "ready" to help the family stay safe and more comfortable. If the emergency requires evacuation to a safer location, the kit is easily carried with the family. Following are some suggested items; adjust as appropriate for your family. Keep your ready kit in a closed container and be sure everyone in the family understands its purpose and storage location.

While not part of the regular "family ready kit," don't forget pet food and pet medications. Your pets are an important part of the family, too.

Family Ready Kit Contents

- Water (one gallon per person per day)

- Maps (local and state) with compass

- Prescription and OTC medication; personal hygiene items

- Identification for each family member (copies of driver's licenses, other government-issued ID, and Social Security cards)

- Copies of financial records (bank and credit card account numbers, brokerage account numbers)

- Document copies (homeowners and other insurance policies, healthcare ID cards, and other important documents)

- Contact telephone numbers (family, relatives, friends, physicians, schools)

- Prepaid long-distance calling card

- Photos of home (exterior and interior), photos of family members, and pets

- Inventory of home contents

- Cash (including change) or traveler's checks

- Extra automobile and house keys

- Reading and religious materials, Boy Scout field book, other reference literature

- Inoculation records (children and adults, if warranted), other health records as needed

- Notepad and pens/pencils, permanent marker

- Board games, crayons, cards, and card games

- Disposable camera

- Shelf-stable foods: MREs, instant drink mixes, soups, energy bars, fruit, trail mix

- Special dietary supplements and/or infant formulas

- Salt, pepper, sugar, instant creamer/milk, hard candy, and other fun foods

- Camping or other small portable stove, extra fuel, and one-quart pot, matches, or lighter

- Paper plates, cups, and disposable eating utensils; manual can opener

- Sewing kit, nylon rope, repair tape, and wire ties
- Flashlight/battery lantern, chemical light sticks (do not use candles for emergency lighting)
- Extra batteries in plastic bag
- Pocket or other folding knife, whistle, and small mirror
- Rescue blanket for each family member and a group first-aid/medical kit
- Chlorine bleach (unscented, 24 ounce)
- Trash and plastic storage bags
- Plastic sheeting/drop cloth; trash and plastic storage bags
- Liquid soap, shampoo, and several small towels
- Multipurpose tool or pliers; screwdriver
- Plastic storage container or sturdy cardboard box to hold your "ready kit" items

No Lights? No Problem!

Lighting is a source of safety and comfort. Most of the conveniences in our homes and the tools in our workplaces are powered with electricity. When the power goes off, we suddenly find ourselves in an unfamiliar and sometimes scary environment. All the stuff we rely on to make us comfortable, help us do our jobs, and make us safe, stops working.

Let's get this out of the way right now: Candles are for birthday cakes, *not emergency lighting*. In an emergency situation, you'll have a tremendous number of things on your mind, stress will be affecting your ability to think clearly, and the fire department will probably be busy, so let's not complicate things by adding to whatever disaster you may be dealing with by burning your house down.

The major difference between candles and other sources of flame-dependent lighting is that candles provide little light, usually are not supplied with fire-resistant containers, and have an open flame. Coleman lanterns and the old reliable kerosene type lamps grandma used at least contain the flame in a fireproof enclosure. This enclosure (glass globe or chimney) generally prevents something from accidentally coming into contact with the flame and starting a fire. Generally, anything with a flame requires great caution when used, and can cause a fire or explosion if employed where natural gas pipes may be leaking.

Start with the safest form of auxiliary lighting, chemical light sticks, and then after making sure there is no danger of explosion (broken gas lines, leaking or damaged containers of gasoline or other volatile liquids) work into flashlights and battery-operated lamps. Pressurized gas camping lanterns are for outdoor use. Kerosene and other oil lamps, even the high-efficiency models, require extreme caution if used indoors. In an emergency, avoid any device that uses a flame for lighting—*especially candles*.

In the well-prepared workplace, emergency lighting and power must be provided so critical operations can continue and provide a safe and comfortable working environment. At home, these same reasons apply.

Power outages can be caused by storms, natural disasters, accidents, human error, equipment failure, and intentional acts. Blackouts and brownouts caused by a lack of generating capacity in some areas of the country are becoming a summer routine. Corporations and individuals are searching for ways to avoid the dangers, stress, and financial loss associated with power failures.

Emergency Lighting

"Where's the flashlight?" is the call of the unprepared when the lights go out. It's so simple, but few people know where it is or routinely check to see if the batteries are producing power and the bulb works. When you buy batteries, date them with a laundry marker, test them every three months, and change them at least once a year. By the way, standardize on the type of light—and for goodness sake, the battery size. Shopping for batteries will be much easier this way.

Since we mentioned chemical light sticks first (sometimes referred to as "snap lights"), it's only fitting to explain this safe light source first. My favorite is the Caylume 30-minute or one-hour high intensity white light stick. These six-inch long plastic tubes contain two *nontoxic* chemical agents that, when mixed, fluoresce with a bright white light. You simply bend the plastic tube at a sharp angle, which breaks (snaps) an inner capsule that starts the chemical process. Shaking the stick a couple of times completes the mixing process, and suddenly you have plenty of light to work with. There is no danger of heat, flame, fire, or explosion. These lights can be used safely in any environment, and they have a shelf life of approximately three years.

Light sticks can be purchased in a variety of colors and sizes. Buy high intensity where possible since these produce enough light to work and read by and will emit usable light for nearly an hour. The sticks will continue to glow for many hours, so they can be used to mark stairways, doors, or other locations. These light sticks have equal value as escape lights in both the workplace and home. They are a great source of comfort for children since they can be safely carried around, or even brought to bed.

Battery-operated lights, flashlights, and lanterns are the most common source of emergency lighting for most families.

While there are many flashlights and battery-operated lanterns on the market today, I want to discuss the four main categories of battery-operated lights.

WARNING

If you have gas appliances in your home, be extremely careful after any event (hurricane, tornado, or earthquake) that causes structural damage. Always check for gas leaks before switching on flashlights or anything else that may cause a spark resulting in an explosion.

Handheld Lights

These include the regular two-cell (three-cell, four-cell, and counting) flashlights. Types and prices run from as cheap as a dollar to several hundred dollars (no kidding). Avoid the cheap ones as they will break easily and the switching mechanism my not work more than a few times. Maglites are at the top of the scale in value. They are manufactured with aircraft aluminum, are water-resistant, come in many colors and battery-cell sizes, and contain a spare bulb. Several companies manufacture top of the line, expensive tactical flashlights designed for a military market that needs high intensity, indestructible combat-proven specialty lights. While these lights are bright, small, and indestructible, they are very expensive ($100.00 plus) and are designed more for target illumination than work area and general illumination.

A new family of flashlights has appeared on the market in the past several years and these lights use no batteries or bulbs. They are marketed as "everlasting" since there's nothing to replace. They produce power when the user shakes the light, which causes a magnet to slide back and forth through a coil of wire (generator), which charges an onboard capacitor, which then powers an LED (light-emitting diode). All of this is wrapped in a sealed water-tight plastic housing. These lights can be stored for many years, and when needed can be "charged" and used. A half minute of shaking will produce approximately 20 minutes of light.

Several models of "dynamo flashlights" are now available. These lights use a small hand-cranked dynamo to charge a battery to power the LEDs. Several models are available, including a camping lantern style.

When you purchase a flashlight, headlamp, battery lamp or spotlight, always buy extra bulbs and batteries (the exception of course being the LED models mentioned earlier, which last forever—almost). Remember to label the batteries with the purchase date. Yes, if you're using rechargeable batteries, you still need to date them since a two-year service life is average. After two years, rechargeable cells of all types become somewhat unreliable. OK, so you've had a set working for four years with no problems. I'm talking average commercial expectancy in critical situations.

NOTE

LED technology is advancing at a rapid rate, and soon filament-type incandescent bulbs will be completely replaced in the majority of low-voltage lighting applications. The major benefit is that less power is needed for an equivalent amount of light output, so fewer batteries and longer operation times result. Since these LEDs are solid-state devices, they aren't susceptible to filament breakage and burnout. Have you noticed that many commercial vehicles now use LEDs for brake and marker lights? Most new traffic lights now use LEDs instead of "bulbs."

Maglite and other manufacturers are marketing conversion kits to replace standard filament bulbs with LED modules. Generally, these aren't cheap. Nevertheless, they're worth the expense in my opinion due to the "lifetime" of service expected and the reduced battery replacement. You'll be impressed with the higher light levels produced by LEDs. In fact, the Maglite LED conversion kit for a two-cell Maglite appears to be brighter than the original standard bulb.

Headlamps

Headlamps (my personal favorite) can be worn on your head, leaving both hands free. The new ultra-light weight headlamps using LEDs are fantastic. They are small, lightweight, and produce good usable work light for any situation. The bonus, of course, is that these allow you to use your hands for something other than shining a light on your work. They work well for hiking, camping, or any other outdoor activity. Many search and rescue teams are converting to these lights. By the way, three AAA batteries will power an LED headlamp for 72 hours of *continuous* use.

A variety of larger headlamps are also available on the market. Some of these resemble miner lights, with various sizes of lamp heads, and many have external battery packs. They are, of course, heavier and tend to be more complicated to wear and maintain.

General Illumination Lamps

Illumination lamps are used to light a room or specific area. Battery-operated flores-cent lanterns or "pop-up" flashlights are the most popular. Many styles exist and some florescent lanterns are rechargeable. These offer good illumination for a room and usually have an option switch to choose between a "bright" setting (both flores-cent tubes on) for reading and critical work, and a "normal" position (one tube on) for navigating around the room and conserving battery power.

"Pop-up" flashlights are a terrific blending of a hand-carried flashlight (usually with a lanyard) and a general light source or "tent light" with frosted window that distributes light in a 360-degree manner. To convert from flashlight to "tent" or table light, simply pull on the front reflector, which exposes the frosted window. The front reflector serves as a base that stabilizes the light. These will illuminate a small room or your home office with enough light that you can move around safely. They gen-erally use four AA batteries and produce between five to seven hours of light.

A useful hybrid light is the "Syclone" made by Streamlight Inc. This small hand light has a tilting head and flat base that provides a good stable work light that can sit on a desk or work surface. The light has a dual position switch that selects either a regular tungsten bulb or an LED. The four AA batteries will power the LED continu-ously for 72 hours. This light has a high-impact plastic case, a rubber handgrip, and belt clip, and is supplied with a helmet bracket for fire/rescue or construction use. A bonus feature is that this light is rated for use in explosive atmospheres (this is impor-tant when around gasoline, natural gas leaks, or other hazardous environments).

Coleman-type camping lanterns (pressurized gasoline), butane or propane lanterns, kerosene table lamps, barn lanterns, and railroad lamps use combustible fuels. These light sources require extreme care in use. Even if you are familiar with the operation and maintenance of these lamps and lanterns, if they are accidentally knocked over, they can and probably will start a fire. Be careful, and never attempt to use or fuel a pressurized gas lantern inside your home. Flame-dependant lighting is strictly prohibited in commercial structures. You should have the same rule in your home as well.

Spots and Floodlights

Spots and floodlights are usually 6- or 12-volt lights used by fire departments, rail-roads, and utility crews. They tend to be heavy but very bright, and the batteries are long lasting. Some smaller versions of these "professional" lights are now showing up in the retail market. One of the best in the "professional" league is manufactured by Streamlight and sold by police/fire supply companies and larger hardware and out-door outlets. The Streamlight power fail model comes with a 110-volt charger base and a 12-volt DC mobile charger base. When using the 110-volt AC charger base, if the power goes off, the light comes on. These lights are an excellent choice for the workplace as power fail lights in critical areas. Plus, you can remove the light from the charger base and carry it with you. You have three lamp options, flood, spot, and a fairly new flood/spot combination model. They cost around $100, but if you need a tough dependable light, look no further.

Emergency Power

The subject of emergency power could itself fill an entire book. We'll spend a bit of time on portable electric generators because they are an emergency supply item that remains in high demand. As with any mechanical equipment, you must exercise good safety habits and understand the equipment, as well as potential risks from improper operation.

Whether your needs for a generator are of the "homeowners" variety with a capacity of one to five thousand watts, or a backup power plant with several million watts of capacity, some common decisions must be made before you go shopping. They are (1) What size do I need and what can I afford? (2) Will this be a portable or installed generator? (3) What fuel type do I plan to use? and (4) How can I get the emergency power to the devices I plan to operate?

All portable and backup generators have an engine, which requires fuel. This fuel can be gasoline, propane, natural gas, or diesel fuel. The vast majority of smaller gen-erators are gasoline powered, but propane and diesel are becoming more popular. The alternative "non-gasoline" fuels are safer to store, handle, and in the case of propane and natural gas, are cleaner burning.

WARNING

Never use a generator indoors, no matter how small it is. When using a generator outside of your home or office, be absolutely sure it is sit-ting well away from air intakes and any doors or windows that have been opened to permit the use of drop-cords or cables. Carbon monoxide, an invisible, odorless, and toxic gas, can seep indoors and cause illness or even death. Never operate a generator or other gas-powered engine under your home, in the basement, or in your garage. Carbon monoxide can easily fill an enclosed area. You'll nod off to sleep and very possibly die if carbon monoxide seeps into your home. Put generators outside!

The electrical output of most portable generators runs anywhere from 300 to 15,000 watts for generators sold through home improvement and hardware stores. Prices range from around $500 to a couple of thousand.

A relatively new entry in the portable generator market is the "inverter generator." These units combine the functionality of a portable generator and the "clean power" output of a UPS best. These hybrids generate AC voltage, which is then converted to DC, and then reconverted back into AC voltage by an onboard voltage inverter. The inverter generator is an excellent choice when using power-sensitive electronics such as servers, switches, routers, and communications equipment.

Regardless of the size or type of generator you purchase, always read the instruction manual and follow the manufacturer's operation recommendations. This includes grounding the generator before starting. This is probably one of the most overlooked safety steps by homeowners. Also protect the generator from flood water, rain, or other environmental hazards. Read the instruction manual.

Large commercial generators that can power an entire office complex or industrial operation, operate on the same basic principle as their smaller cousins (an engine turns an alternator to make electricity), but of course cost much more and require special engineering, installation, and maintenance. These larger generator installations generally use diesel fuel. Permanently installed generators for homes and small-to-medium businesses tend to use natural gas for simplicity of fuel delivery/storage issues. Prices including installation start around $4,000 for a home version up to many hundreds of thousands of dollars for a backup power plant with multiple generators and related equipment for commercial applications.

How much emergency power do you need? The simplest method is to use one of the many power sizing charts available online or at retail outlets. A portable generator in the range of 3,500 to 5,000 watts is a good fit for most homeowners to keep things running.

If you require a generator above 10,000 watts, will it be permanently installed or transportable? This certainly has a bearing on fuel type and the connection to your "load" (stuff to be powered). One of the most overlooked issues for generators (large or small) is how to get the electricity to the devices you want to power. In other words, where do you plug it in?

You have only two choices. First, and by far the best option, is an automatic or manual transfer switch. This device disconnects commercial power and easily (and safely) connects your "load" (home, office, or manufacturing facility) to the generator. Automatic switches sense when commercial power has stopped, starts the generator, and then switches the load to the generator. A manual switch requires human intervention to start the generator and then flip the switch to begin using the power. As you might expect, the automatic switches are expensive but worth the investment if power failure is not an option. All permanently installed generators require a transfer switch. Some small manual transfer switches are designed for residential use, allowing a single connection between the generator and the breaker panel. These cost a few hundred dollars and allow you to choose the area of the home to power while safely disconnecting from the commercial power supply.

TIP

Hire an electrician. A professional will be able to advise you on the best and safest method of installing a generator and power transfer switch for home or commercial use. This is serious stuff and mistakes can cost many more times the amount paid for professional consultation and installation.

The second option (and most used) is to utilize individual power cables or drop cords connected between the generator and your equipment or appliances. For smaller generators and home use for powering only a few items, the drop–cord solution is fine.

WARNING

Be extremely cautious when running drop cords into your home so that you do not allow carbon monoxide gas to enter as well. If using a window or door for cord entrance, be sure to make the access opening as small as possible and keep the generator well away. Use tape or weather stripping to make the entrance as air-tight as possible.

UPS and Battery Backup

An excellent way to keep critical equipment running during commercial power failures is a UPS power supply. These devices operate much like the automatic transfer switch and generator combination mentioned earlier except that they have no moving parts and are thus safe and simple to operate for indoor and home use. You'll probably find some of these near PCs and servers at the office.

The UPS contains one or more batteries that are kept charged by an onboard charging circuit that uses normal commercial power and an inverter to produce 110 volts of AC from battery power. A power sensing circuit monitors the commercial power source for quality and consistency. If the unit detects a low-/no power or high-voltage condition, (in the blink on an eye) it disconnects commercial power and supplies electricity to any equipment plugged into its outlets. These devices also filter the commercial power source and remove voltage spikes and ripples, which can damage sensitive equipment. They are available in various sizes depending on how much current you need and the length of time you want to operate the protected equipment when the commercial power goes away.

With a large UPS, the main consideration is how much time you need, want, or can afford before the batteries run out of power and no longer provide sufficient current to power the inverters. Most large commercial installations provide enough battery capacity to allow a generator sufficient time to start and rev up to operating speed to supply enough power to begin charging the batteries once again.

Portable 12-Volt Inverters

A reliable source of emergency power is sitting right out in your driveway. Your automobile and its 12-volt DC power system can provide plenty of power for charging cellular phones (you probably have a cigarette lighter adapter or "12-volt power cord" now anyway) and for producing limited (a couple of hundred watts) amounts of AC power with a DC inverter. As mentioned earlier, an inverter converts DC current into AC for the operation of lights, laptops, battery charging, and small power tools (this does not include hair dryers or toaster ovens). The inverters simply plug into the cigarette lighter socket of your automobile and provide a clean and quite safe source of voltage. They, however, cannot operate continuously and must be used intermittently. Larger inverters are available but require direct connection to the vehicle battery,

Solid-state inverter generators are marketed as "generators" but are in fact a large 12-volt battery or array of batteries, a DC inverter, and a container with 12-volt DC and 110 AC outlets. The smaller units work well for limited power use and for jump starting your vehicle if needed. Since there are no moving parts, they are quiet and can be safely used indoors. They can be recharged from a 12-volt DC power source or the supplied battery charger. These inverters are available in a number of sizes and weights (the batteries are heavy) from around 20 pounds up to several hundred pounds.

Larger permanently installed inverters can power an entire small business or home for extended periods of time. Many homeowners living in remote locations depend on large inverters with a battery array to supply AC voltage for some of their power needs. The batteries can be charged using one of the alternative power sources mentioned in the next section.

Alternative Power Sources

Wind, running water, and thermal and solar energy are all "alternative power" sources. While these may appear to be out of the financial reach of most homes and businesses, portable solar panels that can recharge cellular phones and laptops are becoming mainstream and affordable. As we move deeper into the twenty-first century, the "alternative" sources that become cost effective and dependable will find market share quickly. Portable solar cells in neat fold-up cases are available for $60 to $100 in many electronics and "road warrior" catalogs. Expect a good one to charge your cellular phone in several hours of bright sunlight. Larger "portable panels" can provide the power to charge and maintain satellite phones and other equipment requiring more current. Large solar panels for providing heat and electricity for homes is commonplace in many areas of the country, and these panels capable of supplying the needs of an entire home have dropped in price while gaining efficiency and market share. Solar-powered street lights, web cams, and traffic signs, while expensive, have an attractive return on investment.

Fuel cells are now finding their way into more common use. As environmental pressure increases, these "chemical generators" will become more cost-effective. While the technology is exciting, so is the cost. For the present, this technology is out of the reach of most individuals and companies for routine use.

Staying in Touch

I cannot overstate the importance of communications and how critical staying in touch will be for you and your family in a disaster or other crisis situation. (Under normal conditions, that's easy now since everyone has a cellular phone and "on-hip" Internet access and e-mail.) However, when the lights go out along with the infrastructure we depend on to make our normal communications effortless, we must have a "plan B."

Remember when there was no Internet? Close your eyes for a moment and pretend we've been transported back to a time when there is no e-mail and no browsing the World Wide Web for information and current updates on breaking news. There is no cellular service, no voice mail, fax, and no easy and reliable telephone service for that matter. It's a bit hard to imagine, isn't it? Really, it wasn't that long ago (about 50 years) that basic telephone service was considered a rare commodity. Even 15 years ago, the Internet was something that most people believed involved fishing.

Fifteen years ago, cellular phones were the size of bricks, service was limited to metropolitan areas, and the phones were used by the very few and the well-to-do.

Think back to those times and try to imagine how you would stay in touch with your family, customers, and the office. Your little investment in a daydream may pay big dividends in your future, for as soon as tomorrow, next week, or next month, we may be left without some, or most, of our modern communications infrastructure.

As a society, we are so dependant on our communications infrastructure that it makes a tempting (and sometimes very soft) target for those who would do our way-of-life harm. Turn off communications and you can no longer visit an ATM machine to withdraw cash. Businesses can't receive or fill orders; our transportation, finance, utilities, and even law enforcement depend on reliable and uninterruptible communications links to conduct normal operations.

Our communications infrastructure is designed for routine network capacity and normal traffic patterns. An event that destroys infrastructure and disrupts these "normal patterns" can overload surviving infrastructure and cause failures in communications networks. A "fast busy signal" is the first sign of trouble. How can you stay in touch when our normal communications services and systems fail or are taken away?

The first and most important radio you can own is a "SAME" all hazards alert radio. SAME is an acronym for "Specific Area Message Encoding." It naturally is a U.S. government term, but we can overlook that because the technology and system are so important. These radios, which can be purchased at any home electronics store or from numerous sources online, alert you to impending dangerous weather or other life-threatening incidents in your community. These include tornadoes, hurricanes, hazardous materials incidents, terrorism, and other civil emergencies.

The SAME alert radio has an audio alert tone, an alphanumeric display, and a speaker so you can receive audio information from your local NOAA (National Oceanic and Atmospheric Administration) office. Yes, this alerting service is provided by the National Weather Service but this is not just your old reliable weather forecast. NOAA has partnered with local, state, and national emergency management agencies and the Office of Homeland Security to provide emergency information for *any* emergency situation.

After purchasing, you simply program the SAME receiver with your community's unique alert code. Every city, county, and community has a unique code. When an emergency alert or warning is issued for your community, an alert tone sounds and the receiver's audio is turned on to inform you of what action is necessary. The alerts provided are *official information*, not someone's opinion based on second- or thirdhand reports.

Now, I'm sure you may be thinking that with CNN and the Internet, why bother? Unless you sleep with one eye on CNN or have someone at home or work monitoring local emergency response agencies around the clock, you need this radio. While CNN and other media reports are usually accurate, they are not "official" sources of information. The SAME all hazards radio is.

Several ideas and programs are in the works for an improved national alerting network, but for now the SAME radio is a dependable solution for quickly alerting the population of dangers at any time of the day or night. I urge you to purchase one for your home and workplace. Does your school have one of these? If not, make sure they do very soon. Cost varies from $30 to around $80. Most radios include a battery so the radio continues to work even if the power is off. By the way, once you purchase the radio, there is no monthly charge for this vital service

TIP

The SAME alert radio is as important to your safety as your smoke alarm, and just like your smoke alarm, it may save your life.

Dynamo Radios

Dynamo (emergency) radios are now marketed in numerous places and come in a variety of colors, including camouflage. I don't have a clue why, but they do look cool. They cover the AM, FM, shortwave, and/or weather bands. Most include a small light for finding your way, and some include an outlet for charging your cell phone.

An onboard dynamo or "generator" produces power by turning a small crank. This action produces direct current which charges an internal battery supplying power to the radio. You can store this radio for years and "crank it up" when you need it.

FRS Radios

FRS is yet another acronym, this one for "Family Radio Service." These two-way radios are the inexpensive pairs of "walkie-talkies" advertised in most of the sporting goods and electronics stores. They allow license-free family communication over distances of a half mile or so. They are extremely valuable for emergency communications in and around the neighborhood when nothing else works.

Ham Radio

When disaster strikes, ham (amateur) radio operators provide invaluable communications services to local, state, and federal authorities, the military, and the general public. These volunteer operators provide their own equipment, training, and electrical power to keep emergency information flowing when other communications facilities are out of service. It's their hobby, and they do this important service for free.

If you know a ham radio operator in your community, ask about his or her ability to get messages into and out of disaster areas. One day you may have need to get information about a loved one or family member in a disaster area, or you may need to send word that "we're OK." And while you're at it, you may just discover that you have an interest in getting involved in this fascinating hobby.

The "POTS" Line

We have access to so many cool communications technologies today that it's astounding. VoIP (Voice over Internet Protocol), personal satellite phones that fit into a coat pocket, cellular, and cordless phones with range that allows us to carry them with us when we visit neighbors. Remember that if the power goes off, so do most of our communications. While many cordless phones in our homes have backup batteries, the majority do not. However, the "Plain Old Telephone System" (POTS) operates on DC voltage supplied by the telephone company central office. Having a simple "plain old telephone" to plug in and use during these times will allow you to stay in touch.

Summary

In this chapter, we've covered a great deal of information related to your prepared-ness at work and at home for unexpected emergencies and disasters. If there is one single rule to remember, it is that all of us must be prepared mentally, physically, and emotionally for the next catastrophic event that may disrupt not only our lives, but also the lives of our family, friends, and coworkers. Having a plan, basic supplies, and the knowledge that we can and will get through it together will make us all stronger as individuals and as a nation.

Chapter 3

Seizure of Digital Information

By Kevin O'Shea

Kevin O'Shea is currently employed as a Homeland Security and Intelligence Specialist in the Justiceworks program at the University of New Hampshire. In this capacity, Mr. O'Shea supports the implementation of tools, technology, and training to assist law enforcement in the investigation of crimes with a cyber component. In one of Kevin's recent projects, he was a technical consultant and developer of a training program for a remote computer-forensics-viewing technology, which is now in use by the state of New Hampshire. He also has developed a computer-crime-investigative curriculum for the New Hampshire Police Standards and Training.

Introduction

Computers and digital devices are employed by the majority of people in the U.S. for myriad business and personal uses. Because of the wide acceptance of computers in our daily lives, it is reasonable to conclude that people will use a computer to assist them in the commission of crimes, record aspects of crimes on a computer, and use computers to store the fruits of their crimes or contraband.

Any of the computers involved in the situations just discussed will likely contain upwards of hundreds of thousands of pieces of information stored in a digital format, including operating system files, program files, user documents, and file fragments in drive free space. While the challenge for the laboratory examiner is to find the relevant *data objects* on a hard drive or other media, a greater challenge exists for the on-scene responders and investigators: How can the information be collected from the scene and brought to a location where it can be examined? Does all the hardware on-scene need to be seized as evidence, or will an exact copy of the information serve the purposes of an investigation? Are there other seizure options to be considered?

Notes from the Underground...

Data Objects

Throughout this chapter, the term "data object" will be used frequently to discuss information found on a storage device or a piece of storage media (SWGDE, 2000). The digital information on a piece of media is nothing more than a long string of 1s and 0s recorded on either magnetic, solid-state, or optical media. Hard drives and floppy disks are examples of magnetic media; USB thumb drives and flash memory cards are examples of solid-state media; and CDs and DVDs are types of optical media. Any number of digital devices, including computers, cell phones, and iPods, will have operating systems and programs that arrange the 1s and 0s into a particular order to create images, documents, spreadsheets, music, and so on. For the purposes of our discussion, each of these discrete arrangements of information that are logically organized into something meaningful will be called a *data object*. The choice to use the term "data object" instead of the more frequently used term "file" is based on the fact that not all organized digital information comes in the form of a file. Information attached to a file such as a file header and metadata are not technically separate files, but can be culled out from the file as separate

Continued

data objects. Other types of information found on storage media are not files, but fragments of files left by the constant write and overwrite of information caused by the deletion of existing files and the creation of new files. For example, a certain amount of an old file may be left behind when a new file is overwritten in the same space—so-called file slack space. Still other types of informational fragments may include files and commands temporarily stored in the swap file or within the RAM itself. For these reasons, I believe it is more appropriate to call these organized pieces of information "data objects."

What we consider to be evidence has a dramatic effect on how we view the electronic crime scene. The current model of digital evidence seizure is focused on physical hardware, which is appropriate in most situations. However, as we move forward from this point in time, factors such as the size of media and full-disk encryption will impact the ability to seize all the hardware on-scene for later analysis at a forensics laboratory. Other options besides wholesale hardware seizure—RAM recovery, on-scene imaging of hard drives, and imaging of select files—need to become part of the basic toolkit of on-scene responders.

But the acceptance of other options for digital evidence seizure will not be a spontaneous event. The legal framework, the established workflows of existing computer forensic best practices, and the fear of the unknown will all play a part in determining how quickly the digital evidence seizure methodologies are adjusted to accept other options besides wholesale hardware seizure. The community of people that respond to, investigate, and prosecute crimes that have a digital evidence component is a very diverse population with different frames of reference and different technical understanding. If one group decides to unilaterally implement a change in practices or policy, the ripple effect is felt across the entire system—which is what makes *bridging the gaps* such an important part of considering and implementing any change resulting from advances in technology. As the author and a member of the greater crime-with-a-cyber-component-community, I hope this work serves to create discussion between the disparate communities on the appropriateness of both the familiar and innovative methods to seize digital evidence.

To these ends, I have organized the following pages to guide the reader through a number of topics relating to both the existing method of digital seizure and the innovative options available for on-scene responders. First, we will examine some of the framework surrounding the legal view of evidence, then we will address how the current digital evidence seizure methodology evolved, and afterward we'll take a look at each of the seizure steps individually. This work is not intended to be a step-by-step guide for digital evidence seizure, but many of the current best practices are examined, and some common pitfalls are discussed. Following the discussion of the current method of seizure, we will explore some of the reasons why the wholesale seizure of hardware on-scene may become problematic in the future. Finally, we will discuss a number of options available for seizure of information, including the on-scene preview of information, the seizure of data held in the computer's RAM, on-scene imaging of entire hard drives, and the on-scene imaging of specific data objects.

WARNING

In the sections that follow, we will primarily be discussing criminal procedures, as I would hope that the civil procedures would follow the guidelines set forth by the criminal side of the house. Many civil procedures often turn into criminal events, and vice versa, so it's probably wise to be working each case as if it were destined for criminal court. Further, most of my work has been as a bridge between the technical community and that of law enforcement—and it is from this viewpoint that the chapter is written.

Obviously, criminals may actually steal a computer or other device directly—but the focus of this chapter is not on the physical theft of hardware. Instead, we target how information held within the storage medium can be processed into evidence.

Here, I will colloquially refer to computers and hard drives when discussing digital information. I do realize many types of digital devices and media contain data, but it is often too cumbersome to individually point out each item or specify each situation.

This chapter focuses more specifically on the seizure of digital evidence when that evidence relates to a static event, such as receiving a harassing e-mail or seizing a computer that contains child pornography. An analysis and discussion of recovering information and evidence from a more dynamic event, such as a Denial-of-Service attack or a network intrusion are covered in Chapter 5 of *Cyber Crime Investigations: Bridging the Gaps between Security Professionals, Law Enforcement, and Prosecutors* (Syngress Publishing, 2007). Although much of what is discussed in the following sections still apply to network forensics, please note that I am purposely minimizing the points that apply to it.

Finally, I am not a lawyer, nor do I play one on TV. The intent of this chapter is to provide investigators, prosecutors and private sector personnel with options and discussion topics related to the collection of digital evidence. **Any conclusions or recommendations in this chapter that may resemble legal advice should be vetted through**

legal counsel. Always check with your local jurisdiction, local prosecutors, and local forensics laboratory as to their preferred method(s) of digital evidence collection.

Defining Digital Evidence

Black's Law Dictionary—the Bible for legal definitions—provides several definitions for *evidence* (Nolan, 1990). One of the definitions reads "Testimony, writings, or material objects offered in proof of an alleged fact or proposition." I have to say it is rather refreshing to have a generally straightforward and concise legal definition; generally, I don't equate straightforward and concise with legal…well… anything. The definition does provide a good launching point for our discussions on how digital information is viewed in the criminal justice system.

Black's definition of evidence as applied to digital evidence can be viewed in two ways. First, we can examine the computer itself as the evidence. This is clearly the case when the computer is the actual instrument of the crime, such as when the physical parts of the computer are used to commit a crime—for example, I hit you over the head with a keyboard. Colloquially, most law enforcement investigators and prosecutors will call the computer itself evidence even in cases where information on the computer relates to a given crime. As one investigator told me: "Everything seized at a crime scene is evidence until someone tells me it's not." In this sense, when the computer itself is seized at a crime scene or through a warrant, it is considered by many to be evidence.

Building on the view of the computer as evidence, many assert that the information on the computer requires the original computer to view the contents. In other words, the original computer—along the lines of how the best evidence rule requires the "original" whenever possible—may have an impact on how the information on the computer was actually viewed by the suspect. This is a valid viewpoint because many forensic software packages will not provide a view that is exactly as the suspect would have seen it. Too many different programs may show a given file, image, movie, or e-mail in a particular manner. The computer forensic analysis programs will often use a generic viewer capable of displaying any number of different formats. For example, Access Data's FTK has a generic format in which all e-mails would be displayed regardless of the program in which they were created. The generic format provides all the same information that would have been shown in the original e-mail, but it clearly is shown in a very different format than what the suspect would have seen. An e-mail viewed through the AOL e-mail program will include all the banners, advertisements, and formatting that make up the AOL look and feel of the user's experience. The e-mail itself will contain a number of standard fields, such as the e-mail header and the body of the message. The AOL program places these fields in a particular "package." However, that same e-mail viewed in FTK, though containing the same content, would lack the AOL packaging. In court, the examiner may be asked "Is this exactly what the suspect saw?" and the obvious answer is "No—but…" And it is within this "but…" that the court may suggest that the evidence—the complete computer and information as a unified package—be brought forth in front of the court.

A second way to view *Black's* definition is that the information, or *data objects*, contained on the digital storage medium are the "testimony, writings, or material objects" offered in proof of an alleged fact. This viewpoint makes the computer nothing more than a device that is used to access the information, and the components of the computer that store digital information nothing more than mere physical containers that house information—similar to a file cabinet or briefcase. Arguments can be made that only the desired information can be seized as evidence. The ramifications of this change in focus from hardware-as-evidence to information-as-evidence are far reaching.

If we do propose there is a distinction between the data objects and the physical container, we need to examine the legal framework within which we operate and seize information to determine if it is permissible to seize either the physical hardware or the information, or both. Rule 41 of the Federal Rules of Criminal Procedure (FRCP), titled "Search and Seizure" provides a definition for property, stating that "'Property' includes documents, books, papers, any other tangible objects, and information" (FRCP, Rule 41(a)(2)(A)). Within this definition is our first inclination that, in fact, the legal system views both storage containers and information as property. When we move forward in the FRCP into the discussions on seizure, we see that persons or property are subject to search or seizure and that a warrant may be issued for any of the following: (1) evidence of a crime; (2) contraband, fruits of crime, or other items illegally possessed; (3) property designed for use, intended for use, or used in committing a crime; or (4) a person to be arrested, or a person who is unlawfully restrained (FRCP, Rule 41[c]).

TIP

A number of legal documents will prove helpful in the coming discussions. The *Federal Rules of Evidence* (FRE) addresses the manner in which evidence can be presented in a federal court. *The Federal Rules of Criminal Procedure* (FRCP) provides the guidance for bringing an accused through the process of arrest and trial. The Computer Crime and Intellectual Property Section within the Criminal Division of the United States Department of Justice publishes a document titled *Searching and Seizing Computers and Obtaining Electronic Evidence in Criminal Investigations* (Manual). The Manual provides a very thorough review of a number of issues related to working with digital evidence—particularly as it relates to federal case law. Obviously, the depth of the information contained in the FRE, FRCP, and the Manual is well beyond the scope of this chapter, but I recommend that anyone interested in this field become familiar with these documents. Absent from the following discussions is talk of state law. Although many states will retain the ability for their own courts to be the "final say" regarding procedural or evidentiary matters, many states have adopted rules very similar to the FRE and FRCP.

Of interest to our discussion here is that property includes information, and that search and seizure is authorized, with a warrant, for property that is evidence of a crime. The next logical conclusion being that warrants can be issued for information that is evidence of a crime—but do the courts interpret using specific files or data objects as evidence, or should the focus be on the physical storage devices? Here, we consult the United States Department of Justice's Computer Crime and Intellectual Property Section's document titled *Searching and Seizing Computers and Obtaining Electronic Evidence in Criminal Investigations* (Manual):

> "The most important decision agents must make when describing the property in the warrant is whether the sizable property according to Rule 41 is the computer hardware itself, or merely the information that the hardware contains (pg. 61). …if the probable cause relates in whole or in part to information stored on the computer, the warrant should focus on the content of the relevant files rather than on the storage devices which may happen to contain them." The Manual references *United States v. Gawrysiak* (972 F. Supp. 853, 860 [D.N.J. 1997], aff'd, 178 F.3d 1281 [3d Cir. 1999]) which upheld the seizure of "…records [that] include information and/or data stored in the form of magnetic or electronic coding on computer media . . . which constitute evidence" of enumerated federal crimes (Manual, pg. 62). …The physical equipment merely stores the information that the agents have probable cause to seize. Although the agents may

> need to seize the equipment in order to obtain the files it con-
> tains and computer files do not exist separate from some storage
> medium, the better practice is to describe the information rather
> than the equipment in the warrant itself (pg. 65)..."

The guidance from the Manual is that the Rules on Criminal Procedure, and the interpretation of the same in the courts, points to the difference between the information held in data objects and the physical container (hard drive, flash media) in/on which the data resides. This provides some positive reinforcement to those that make the claim that the data itself is the evidence and that the computer or storage device is merely a vessel.

The preceding discussions regarding the computer as the evidence versus the data as the evidence has a dramatic effect on how we "seize" or "collect" evidence both at the scene and in the forensics laboratory. If your viewpoint is that the computer is the evidence, then your seizure methodology will be focused on the collection of the computer itself at the scene of the crime. If your viewpoint is that the information is the evidence, then you may be more inclined to attempt to locate and retrieve the information-as-evidence, with less care as to the eventual fate of the hardware. Further, you may be more inclined to call your "computer forensic" efforts simple "evidence collection" and remove the requirement for expert classification at trial. The important point here is that there are options to be considered, examined, and discussed within the community—options that have the ability to significantly change the entire approach to computer seizure and analysis.

Digital Evidence Seizure Methodology

The proliferation of personal computers changed how computers were involved in criminal issues. In the past, computers were often used primarily as the attack plat-form or target of the attack—now the more personal use of computes creates a situation where the computer is the storehouse of evidence relating to almost every type of crime imaginable. The result is that more computers are involved in some manner in crime and that more computers need to be examined for information of evidentiary value. But before they can be examined, they must be seized.

Previously, the highly trained computer specialist would attend to each seizure personally; however, the proliferation of computers and their use in criminal endeavors made personal attention to each case impractical. In some areas of the country, one specialist may serve an entire region. It is clearly unreasonable to believe that one specialist will be able to perform each seizure and complete the examination of the digital evidence for every crime with a cyber component. To fill this apparent gap in need versus capability, state and local law enforcement agents have become involved in recovering digital evidence from a crime scene where a computer is directly involved. Not only are state and local investigators faced with dealing with a new type of crime, but they are also asked to perform the seizures of digital evidence.

The on-scene responders/investigators often know very little about computers and often have not been instructed on how to "properly" seize digital information. Existing seizure protocols for physical items are used, resulting in a focus on the seizure of the computer hardware—sometimes the entire computer, including the monitor, printers, keyboard, and so on are seized and packaged for delivery to the lab. Over time, it became accepted to use the seizure methods focused on the seizure of the *physical hardware* for the seizure of *digital information*. Let's take a look at the flow of a general seizure of a personal computer.

TIP

A number of other authors have nicely addressed the larger digital investigative model. Most notably, Carrier and Spafford present a "digital crime scene" model that exists within the physical crime scene (Carrier, 2003). Generally, these models present a complete framework for digital investigations, from incident response preparation right through to the examination and analysis of the seized information. Although this holistic viewpoint may be relevant to the administrator responsible for the entire operation, these models hold less applicability to the actual on-scene seizure of the relevant information, which is the focus of this chapter.

The current manner of seizure of computer hardware expects that the on-scene responder has a general knowledge about computers—to the level of "THIS is a keyboard, THIS is a mouse, THERE is no 'any' key," and so on. Better yet, the responder should have basic training on digital evidence collection, or, at the very minimum, be able to consult a guide on best practices, such as the *USSS Best Practices Guide* (USSS, 2006) or the *NIJ First Responder's Guide* (NIJ, 2001). Next, the responder would arrive at the scene, secure the scene physically, and begin to assess how the digital evidence is involved. The responder would take steps to secure the digital crime scene, which may include inspecting the devices for physical booby-traps and isolating the devices from any networks. The responder then seizes as many physical containers—physical media including hard drives, CDs, DVDs—as necessary to ensure the seized items reasonably include the information with probative value. The seizure of the hardware/physical containers involves labeling all wires connected to the computer or devices, and photographing the scene—paying specific attention to the labeled connectors. The physical items are seized, documented, packaged, and prepared for transport to an offsite facility for examination. At the offsite facility, possibly the local police agency or a state/regional forensic laboratory, the seized physical containers are examined for data objects with evidentiary value. If found, these data objects are usually included in a forensic findings report and are printed out or copied to other media and then provided to the investigator and prosecutors. Figure 3.1 outlines the steps of the traditional method for seizing computer hardware.

Figure 3.1 Traditional Seizure Methodology

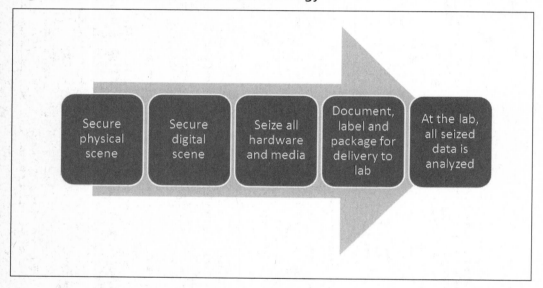

That sounds pretty straightforward, doesn't it? For the most part, the preceding reflects the general process that the wide majority of law enforcement agencies follow when it comes to the seizure of digital evidence. As you can see, the general methodology reflects a focus on the seizure of the physical items. Further, the preceding model shows that a division exists between the investigators / on-scene responders and the forensic laboratory/examiners.

Seizure Methodology in Depth

Unfortunately, current seizure methodology does not adequately prepare our investigators to respond to scenes that are more complicated than a single machine sitting alone in a bare room. The fact is that the world is a messy place. Our responders need to understand that they need to have a methodology in place that allows them to work through more complicated scenes, such as finding dozens of computers or dozens of pieces of removable media or hundreds of CDs. *The steps presented in Figure 3.2 are representative of current seizure methodology, but the steps have been crafted to provide a higher level guidance about approaching nonstandard seizure scenes.* Specifically, the "Seize All Hardware and Media" step shown in Figure 3.1 has been replaced by a series of three steps that help guide the responder through identifying all the digital media on-scene, minimizing the crime scene through prioritization, and then seizing the hardware and media that have the highest probability of containing the relevant evidence.

Figure 3.2 Seizure Methodology Featuring Minimization

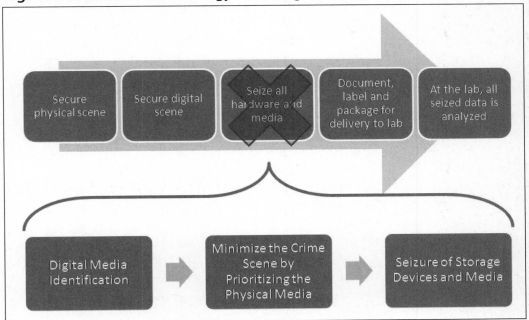

We begin our seizure methodology at the scene, where a warrant for digital evidence is being served. It is assumed in the following that the scene has been physically secured, and the responder has a safe working environment. It is also assumed that the responder has a properly drafted warrant that identifies the information to be seized and outlines that an offsite examination of the media may be required if the situation makes the on-scene seizure infeasible.

Step 1: Digital Media Identification

The first step is to begin to canvas the scene in an attempt to locate the digital media that you believe has the highest probability of containing the evidentiary information described in the warrant. If the suspect has one computer sitting in his bedroom and another in a box in the attic, I'd bet my money that the information I'm after is the one in his bedroom. Taking a step beyond the simple situations, one needs to also consider removable media such as flash drives and CDs or DVDs. Flash drives are often held as personal file cabinets and may contain information of a personal nature. Look for flash drives on key chains, watches, in cameras, and just about anywhere—flash media can be unbelievably small. Another strategy is to look for media that contains backups of files from on-scene computer(s). If the information is important, you can be sure it will be backed up somewhere.

Where can digital media be found? The answer is pretty much anywhere. Locating very small, but very large storage media could be a significant issue when conducting a search. Be sure to balance the perceived technical expertise of the suspect versus the type of crime versus where you expect to find the relevant information. For example, it is fairly well documented that obsessive collectors of child pornography will gather tens-of-thousands of pictures of children being victimized. In this type of case, it would be most logical to be looking for a hard-drive or optical disks, given the amount of storage required. At this point in time, obtaining such large amounts of storage on flash media would be difficult, however. On the other hand, the same collector may be accused of taking pictures of children being victimized, and in this case the search should definitely focus on small flash media–type storage cards that could be used in a digital camera and/or be used to store and hide coveted images.

Documentation is part of every step, so this won't be the last time you see it mentioned. Nevertheless, it's worth mentioning here as a reminder. While conducting the search for digital media, it may be appropriate to narrate your movements into a voice recorder and to photograph the found media in place before moving it.

Step 2: Minimizing the Crime
Scene by Prioritizing the Physical Media

After all the digital media is identified, an effort must be made to determine which storage devices or pieces of media have the highest probability of containing the information described in the warrant. Why? Because at some point it time, it will be impractical to seize all the digital devices, removable media, and storage media at a crime scene. At the current time, it may be possible to walk into a residence and only find one computer and maybe a few CDs. In this situation, the minimization of the physical media is all but done for you—you have in front of you only a few pieces of media that may contain the informational evidence. But technology is enabling homeowners to easily build rather complicated networks that may include wireless storage devices, multiple operating systems, shared Internet connections, integration with traditional entertainment media, and integration with home appliances and devices. Downloadable and burnable movies and music are generally an accepted technology, greatly increasing the amount of optical media found in homes. Based on the availability of technology, on-scene responders will be faced with multiple computers, storage devices, and dozens to hundreds of pieces of media—all adding up to terabytes of information.

The responder must make some tough decisions about where she believes the information will most likely be found. One suggestion is to prepare a prioritized ranking to help decide which storage devices and pieces of media should be seized for offsite review. The prioritized ranking is also critical in deciding which devices or pieces of media are previewed on-scene—one of the options we'll be discussing later in this chapter.

Step 3: Seizure of Storage Devices and Media

The seizure itself is rather straightforward. After the scene is secured and it is determined that the hardware must be seized, the investigator begins by labeling all the connections/wires attached to the computer. Be meticulous in the labeling of wires and thorough in your documentation. It's a good practice to label both the end of a cable and place a matching label where the cable connects—for instance, label a Monitor's VGA Cable B^1 and label the computer's VGA port as $B^{1'}$; label the monitor's power cable plug as B^2 and label the wall outlet as $B^{2'}$. Photograph as many relevant objects and seizure steps as you see fit—digital photos are basically free and can be burned to disk and added to the case file. Don't forget to remove the sticky labels from the power outlets once they have been photographed.

After the computer has been labeled, documented, and photographed, disassemble the components and prepare the computer case for shipment. Best practices state that an unformatted floppy disk should be placed in the floppy drive with a piece of evidence tape sticking out like a flag. The presence of the disk in the floppy drive may prevent an accidental boot to the hard drive—but the new trend from computer and laptop manufacturers is to omit the standard floppy drives entirely, so this recommendation may be deprecated over time. Other options available to prevent an accidental boot are to unplug the power to the hard drive in a desktop machine and remove the battery from a laptop. Some recommend placing evidence tape over the external drives, including the floppy drive and any CD/DVD drives. When transporting, be careful not to drop, or otherwise jar or shock, the computer, as this may result in damage to the hard drive and possibly the motherboard. When transporting, keep the storage devices away from heat and strong magnetic fields, such as high-powered radios and big trunk-thumping subwoofers.

WARNING

Regardless of what hardware seizure methodology is written here or contained in any of the other published guides, always check with the laboratory or department that is going to process the seized hardware. Most have preferred methods for hardware seizure and transportation.

To Pull the Plug or Not to Pull the Plug, That Is the Question

I always wondered where the phrase *pull the plug* originated. I can picture a stressed out, overworked computer forensic technician on the phone with an on-scene responder, attempting to guide them through a proper shutdown and then a controlled boot process—prompting the following exchange:

Responder: It says to hit any key.

Forensic Tech: Uh-huh.

Responder: Hang on.... Um... where is the any key?

Forensic Tech: You've got to be kidding me.... Just pull the @#$@#% plug, wrap it in tape, and bring it to me!

Since that first hypothetical exchange—which still gives me a chuckle when I think about it—the mantra from the forensic community has been to pull the plug from the back of the machine, regardless of the state of the machine—on, off, writing to the drives, or anything else. *I have no doubt that, across the board, the simplest most teachable method of seizure that will generally preserve most of the data and evidence is to pull the plug from the back of the machine.* Pulling the plug and prepping it for transfer to an examination lab is the only option that is reasonably teachable in a few hours to first responders of any skill level. But, surely, we need to be able to do something other than pull the plug. We cannot possibly make advances in this field if we limit all officers and agents to a methodology based on the lowest common denominator.

The most pressing issue relating to *pull-the-plug* is that some operating systems (OSes) really like to be shut down properly. Rapid power loss in some OSes can actually corrupt the operating system's kernel or the central module of the system. UNIX, Linux, and Macintosh operating systems are the most vulnerable, but some Windows-based OSes, such as a Windows 2000 server, should be shut down properly. Moore (2005) presents a good review of the proper shutdown method (shutdown versus pull-the-plug) for different operating systems based on the operating system's ability to recover from rapid power loss.

Obviously, if you intend to shut down the machine properly, you must determine the OS. To determine the OS and to initiate a proper shut down sequence, you need to manipulate the computer's mouse and/or keyboard, but manipulating the mouse/keyboard will change data on the suspect's machine. You say "But I'm not allowed to change data on the suspect's machine!" That may be the guidance given, but it is more appropriate to take the position: "I will do the most appropriate and reasonable actions during seizure to ensure I retain as much of the relevant information as possible. Here is the documentation of my actions." The focus here is on reasonableness and the documentation of actions. Also, it is important to key-in on the retention of the *relevant information*, which includes the information of potential evidentiary value and should not include the Registry changes made to indicate that a shutdown occurred. Simply put, moving the mouse to determine the OS and starting a shutdown sequence did not place 5,000 images of child pornography on the computer's hard drive. However, pulling the plug on a Linux system may actually impact the ability to recover those same images.

There is no one correct answer to the pull-the-plug question. If you have the skill and knowledge to determine the operating system of the suspect computer and you determine that the operating system and other data could be damaged by pulling the plug, then shut the machine down properly. Document your actions and explain clearly and knowledgeably how you prevented damage to the computer, and possibly to the evidentiary information, by following a shutdown procedure. Show how your actions preserved the evidence, as opposed to corrupting it. If you have the skill and document the steps you followed, you have solid footing on which to defend your actions. If you do not possess such skill, or if the more advanced techniques are not working in a given situation or on a particular piece of hardware, then by all means, pull the plug.

Factors Limiting the Wholesale Seizure of Hardware

Earlier we contrasted the historic seizure context versus the current context and discussed how the historic context placed a focus on the on-scene seizure of data objects, as compared to the current situation where the focus of the on-scene activities is to seize all the physical containers. The question I pose to you is this: Are we heading in the right direction by focusing on the seizure of the physical hardware (the container items) rather than focusing on the seizure of the relevant information (data objects)?

Earlier seizures of digital evidence focused on data objects because it was impractical to attempt to image an entire server, based on the high costs of storage media. I suggest we are heading toward a similar impracticality—although this time our inability to seize *all* the information is based on a number of different factors, including massively large storage arrays, whole disk encryption, the abundance of non-evidentiary information on media and related privacy concerns, and the time involved in laboratory forensic analysis. At some point in the future, the process by which we image entire pieces of media for forensic analysis will become obsolete (Hosmer, 2006).

I suggest we make the distinction that there other options beyond wholesale seizure available to our responders. We need to train our responders to have the ability to perform on-scene data preview, full data-image, and imaging of only the relevant data objects. Further, we need to begin to change the wholesale seizure paradigm now—for all responders not just the specialists—before we are faced with a greater volume of cases we are ill prepared to address.

Size of Media

Storage devices are getting big—very big. Now, at the end of 2006, it is quite common for a single hard drive to contain 100 gigabytes of information—roughly equivalent to a library floor of academic journals. It is very achievable for the home user, both technologically and financially, to put together a 2-terabyte storage array—an array that could house the complete works within an entire academic research library (SIMS, 2003). Storage is relatively cheap, and people are taking advantage of the extra space by storing music, movies, and creating mirrored backups (RAID 1 arrays). The typical crime that involves a computer won't include a multi-hundred terabyte server, but showing up at a crime scene with a 200-gigabyte destination drive and finding a 1.5-terabyte RAID will certainly have a negative impact on your ability to create an on-scene image of the data.

What exactly happens when the full 1.5 TB RAID and 200 DVDs are seized and brought back to the forensic laboratory for analysis. Do you actually have the hardware and software to acquire and process that much data? If the laboratory is not a regional or state lab, but a small laboratory set up at the local agency, the answer might be yes—but processing the case might use the entire budget set aside for target drives for the entire year for that one case. Once the data is examined, does the jurisdiction or local policy dictate that the imaged data be archived? At some point, the ability to seize and process *everything* will exceed the budget set aside for the purchase of forensic processing computers, target drives, and archival media and will also exceed the time available for forensic examiners to process the case.

Disk Encryption

A number of encryption programs exist now that provide whole disk encryption, a common one being PGP from pgp.com. These types of encryption programs encrypt all the data on the hard drive and are generally transparent to the user; meaning that one password in the startup sequence "unlocks" the contents for viewing and editing. Of course, looming on the horizon is the Windows Vista operating system, purported to incorporate BitLocker Drive Encryption tied to the Trusted Platform Module cryptographic chip in the higher-end versions of the operating system.

Whole disk encryption has some serious implications for law enforcement when performing seizures. First, if a whole disk encryption is enabled on a running computer, and the computer is shut down or the power is removed, there is a very good chance that the data on the drives will be unrecoverable without the proper key. Responders may need to determine if a whole disk encryption program is enabled before shutting down / pulling-the-plug on a computer during seizure. If one is present, bringing the computer back to the lab for analysis may be futile. One of the best chances to retrieve the evidentiary information is when the machine is running and the user has access to the files. Second, the implementation of the TPM chip may lock the drive so the data may only become available on a specific machine. This would prevent an image of the drive from being booted in another computer or viewed with a computer forensics program. The use of disk encryption is forcing law enforcement to have other data seizure options available beyond the seizure of physical hardware.

Privacy Concerns

Personal computers often contain myriad information about a person's life, including financial, medical, and other personal information, information related to their job (such as work products), and even information owned by several people, possibly a spouse, family member, or roommate. It's unclear how the criminal and civil courts would view a challenge from an impacted third party regarding the seizure of a common computer. However, if that third party maintained a blog or Web site, their information may be protected from seizure under the Privacy Protection Act (PPA) (42 U.S.C. § 2000aa). The PPA was specifically developed to provide journalists with protection from warrants issued to obtain information about sources or people addressed in their publications. The PPA reads "…it shall be unlawful for a government officer or employee, in connection with the investigation or prosecution of a criminal offense, to search for or seize any work product materials possessed by a person reasonably believed to have a purpose to disseminate to the public a newspaper, book, broadcast, or other similar form of public communication." The PPA may not protect the person that possesses the information if that person is suspected of committing the criminal offenses to which the materials are related. Simply put, if you committed a crime and you have publishable information related to that crime on your computer, that information most likely will not be protected under the PPA. However, the PPA may protect the interests of a third party that uses or stores data on a computer, and may possibly protect the information of the accused if the information does not relate to the crime being investigated.

The potential situations of co-mingled evidentiary data and publishable materials, each owned by a separate person do sound unlikely if you only consider a single computer. But what if you consider a network addressable storage device located in a home network? For example, let's say that such a storage device exists at the scene of a seizure. Every member of the household stores information on the device, and little Susie's unposted blog entries on her life-as-a-brainy-15-year-old-girl are located on the storage device commingled with the information described in the warrant. Although you may seize the storage device, you may also be involved with other court proceedings related to the violation of the PPA—civil, and possibly criminal, proceedings where you are the defendant!

The Secret Service ran across a similar situation in the case of *Steve Jackson Games, Inc. v. Secret Service* (*Steve Jackson Games, Inc. v. Secret Service*, 816 F. Supp. 432 [W.D. Tex. 1993]). The Secret Service seized two computers from the company, believing that the company's system administrator had stored evidence of a crime on company computers. The day after seizure, the Secret Service learned that the computers contained materials intended for publication; materials that belonged to the company. Regardless, the Secret Service did not return the computers until several months had passed. The district court ruled that the Secret Service had in fact violated the PPA and awarded Steve Jackson Games $50,000 in damages and $250,000 in attorney's fees. The story of this raid goes well beyond the short summary provided here. The raid and the trial play a significant role in hacker mythology and also played a part in the formation of the Electronic Frontier Foundation (Sterling, 1994). Nonetheless, the moral of the story is that the Secret Service was not prepared to seize the specific information described in the warrant when they learned of the to-be-published materials present on the seized hardware. It's not known how the Secret Service would have changed their seizure methodology if they knew about the publishable materials before they served the warrant—but, for example, if they didn't have the capability of solely seizing the relevant data objects, the Secret Service might have had no other option but to seize the hardware. This example goes to show that having other seizure options available may be a critical skill that determines the success of an investigation.

Delays Related to Laboratory Analysis

If investigators of crimes involving a computer rely completely and absolutely on their computer forensic laboratory for the processing of their seized hardware in search of evidence, they are at the mercy of the timing dictated by the laboratory. From my experience, a computer forensic laboratory can process anywhere from 30 to 60 cases per examiner per year; possibly more depending on the types of cases they work and their equipment, but considering most forensic laboratories are government agencies, I doubt they are operating year after year on the most current computers available. To make matters worse, the increase in the size of storage media has far outpaced the increases in processor power. The same $500 that could afford a 100MB drive in 1991 can now put a 750GB drive in your pocket. Compare that to a 50-MHz Intel from 1991, next to a 3-GHz processor in today's fastest computers, and you'll see that the cost effectiveness of hard drives grew 125 times faster than that of processors from 1991 to the present (Gilder, 2006). Depending on the backlog at the laboratory, investigators can be faced with waiting up to—and over—a year for the results of their examination to be returned from the lab.

I am unable to specifically quantify how delays in the forensic examination are impacting investigations and prosecutions, but I can offer my opinion that delays in the processing of digital evidence are one of the most significant impediments in investigations and prosecutions that have a digital-evidence nexus. Given the opportunity to perform an on-scene seizure of the relevant information versus being forced to wait one year for the results from the laboratory, the choice will be clear for many investigators. However, there are difficulties and challenges in seizing the information on-scene—but these challenges must be weighed against the time delay in receiving the processed evidence.

One investigator I interviewed about this type of situation described a child pornography possession case where there was a chance that the accused possessor was also creating and distributing images of child sexual abuse. Unfortunately, the investigator had no means to preview the digital information on-scene, nor back at the department, nor did the investigator have the ability to perform a digital information analysis in-house. The computer was sent off to a computer forensics laboratory, where it sat in the queue behind other just-as-important cases. Because the information could not be reviewed, the investigator had no evidence to substantiate the drafting of an arrest warrant for either the possession of child pornography or the child sexual abuse. In such cases, any delay caused by a backlog at a forensics laboratory not only impacts an investigation, but also has a direct effect on a (potential) victim and continued victimization.

Protecting the Time of the Most Highly Trained Personnel

Digital devices have become almost completely ubiquitous in our current society. The legends of "convergence" are slowly coming true, where the line between computers, cell pones, cameras, and so on is now fuzzy and may disappear altogether in the future. IPv6 looms on the horizon and promises to equip every device, from cars to toasters, with an IP address. How do we find the time to train our law enforcement community in an entirely new set of skills? What is the balance between knowing enough and making a specialist out of everyone?

Determining whether the individual data objects with evidentiary value are seized or the storage media is seized will likely depend on the technical prowess of the responding investigator. The best situation would be to have a team of highly trained digital evidence seizure specialists respond and then properly prepare a Windows computer for seizure. The reality is that there will never be enough computer specialists to respond to every crime scene—let alone a "team" of them—to seize every piece of information or computer involved either directly or peripherally in a crime.

Looking forward, we can anticipate that the number of computers and other electronic devices requiring seizure and examination to surely increase. Clearly, from all accounts of the situation, the current methodology has its flaws. Delays in the examination of seized digital media are frustrating investigators and are impacting prosecutions. Although we clearly need more computer forensic specialists, do we have the resources—specifically the personnel, time, and money—to train and equip enough specialists to meet the current demand for seizures and exams? What about future demands? From what I have observed, I don't believe we have anywhere near the number of qualified personnel to address the current issues, let alone what the future will hold. Nor do I believe that the existing infrastructure can support the required increase in the number of computer forensic examiners or specialists. Most agencies fight for the addition of a single position—so I'm doubtful that the system will suddenly change and begin hiring scores of new personnel.

The situation comes down to a simple law of economics: productivity will only be increased by adding more people or making existing people more efficient. We don't really have the ability to throw more people at the problem, so the only option is to do more with the people we have. As it pertains to cyber crimes and crimes with a high-technology component, this means we cannot continue to rely on computer specialists for every aspect of an investigation that involves a computer. Every law enforcement agent, from on-scene responders to detectives performing investigations, now have a duty to begin to pick up the slack that has created the conflict between the large—and growing—number of crimes with a high-technology component and the relatively small number of specialists available to work these types of cases. We need to consider the computer specialists and the computer forensic laboratories as a finite resource, and any constructive work performed in the field by patrol officers or detectives reduces the strain on the forensic system. *With this view, the most valued resource is the time of the highest-trained individuals.*

The general scenario of protecting the time of the most highly trained individuals so that they may focus on the most important issues is not a new concept. Those trained in hazardous material response work under a pyramid-like distribution of knowledge; the wide base of the pyramid consists of awareness-level trained people, while the small tip of the pyramid consists of highly trained specialists. Not only are these training levels generally accepted within the hazardous material response community, but they are codified in 29 CFR 1910.120(q)(6). The training code establishes the general level of knowledge, the hours of required training, and what can be expected from responders that have achieved each of the training levels. Because the different training levels are clearly defined, each responder on-scene understands their role and, more importantly, the role of other responders. Those with awareness-level training are taught to basically recognize that something bad has happened, call for help and watch from a distance with binoculars. Operations-level training prepares responders to respond in a defensive fashion, without attempting to stop the release. Technician-level responders are trained to attempt to stop hazardous material release, and specialist-level responders usually have specific knowledge pertaining to a particular chemical. At each level, the responder receives more training to be better prepared when responding to a scene.

At the current time, it would not be practical to attempt to regulate or codify the training requirements or duties of those involved in digital evidence seizure, but it is important to recognize that people of different training levels will likely approach seizure in different ways (see Figure 3.3).

The seizure methodology that is developed for the knowledge level of the non-technical responder is in direct conflict with the best possible seizure scenario. Any seizure methodology adopted by an agency must be fluid enough to allow a minimally trained responder and a highly trained responder to both seize the digital information in the manner most applicable to their knowledge level.

Figure 3.3 Digital Evidence Seizure

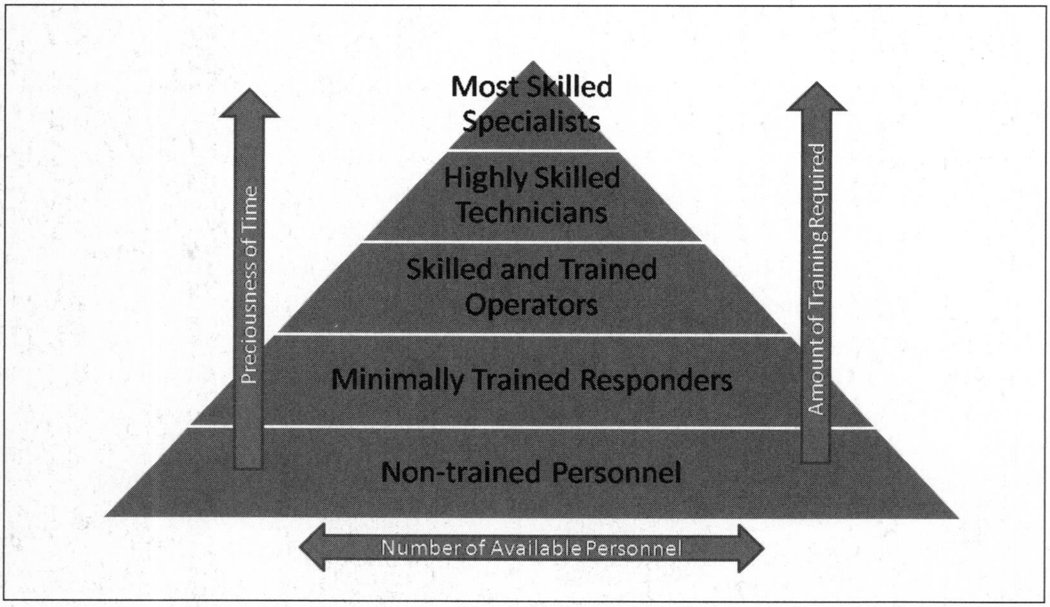

The Concept of the First Responder

Who exactly is the "First Responder" referenced in numerous digital evidence seizure guidelines and reports? Is the first responder simply the person that happens to be on-scene first? If yes, then the first responder could be any line officer. If every first responder needs to be trained to seize digital evidence, and we acknowledge that the seizure methodology will be necessarily fluid based on the responder's technical knowledge, you begin to see the problems involved with designing one particular training for first responders.

A second issue is the number of hours of training that could be allotted for first responder training. Will the administration of an organization allow their personnel to take a half-day course on digital evidence seizure? Probably. Realistically, though, what could you cover in four hours of instruction? I would guess the limit would be the recognition of digital evidence. So, would a two- or three-day training be sufficient to cover the recognition of digital evidence plus the seizure of digital information? Possibly, but would the people attending that training still be considered first responders or would the additional training necessitate they become specialists in this area? I am doubtful an agency's administration would agree to send every line officer to a three-day training to be first responders.

We are clearly caught in a catch-22. All line officers need to be able to seize digital evidence, but the first responder–level of training may not fully equip the officers to seize the evidence. The level of training required to more completely understand the digital evidence seizure process may involve multiple days of training, and multiple days of training on a single topic will most likely not be provided to all line officers. Unfortunately, it is not as simple as identifying one cadet in the academy that will specialize in investigating crimes with a cyber component, and putting this cadet through weeks of specialized training. The ubiquity of computers and digital evidence make the training of one single person insignificant—everyone's expertise needs to be raised to allow the specialists to focus on more technically challenging crimes.

There will be no clear-cut answer to this dilemma, but a number of factors could help mitigate the issue. First, law enforcement officers need more training in general computer skills. During a law enforcement officer's daily work, which is more likely? Arrest a suspect, be involved in a shooting, or spend some time working at a computer? The answer is a no-brainer—computers are an integral part of the law enforcement landscape and most officers cannot go a day without having some level of mission-critical interaction with a computer. However, the general level of computer knowledge among law enforcement personnel is low, and use of a computer is rarely a focus of academy setting. Providing law enforcement with basic, fundamental computer skills would not only impact their views toward digital evidence, but would also positively impact their daily work activities.

Second, all law enforcement personnel should receive basic awareness–level training on digital evidence. Awareness-level training need only cover the basics of a computer and where digital evidence may be stored. It is important for all officers to recognize that storage media, particularly flash-based media, may be no larger than a postage stamp, yet possibly contain several gigabytes of information. Understanding that many seemingly single-purpose devices, such as cell phones or mp3 players, may contain other types of information—for example, documents may be stored on an mp3 player—will have important investigative implications far beyond simple search and seizure concerns. Perhaps the next time a drug dealer is arrested with a PSP, you may want to search him for a small flash media card—as a dealer, his contact list might be accessed from the flash card on the PSP. Until a more uniform level of basic knowledge and awareness is reached among law enforcement, it is hard to speculate how the increased awareness will benefit investigations. But as the saying goes, you miss 100 percent of the shots you don't take, and more appropriately, you miss 100 percent of the evidence you don't look for.

Third, any seizure methodology developed and/or adopted by an agency must be fluid to allow for seizures to be conducted by both minimally trained individuals as well as highly trained specialists. Do you want to put your specialist on the spot when he breaks protocol to perform a function that is technically more appropriate? Conversely, do you want the specialist to be on-scene at every warrant service, arrest, or vehicle search? There must be options within the methodology that allow each officer to act reasonably according to their skill level.

Other Options for Seizing Digital Evidence

The wholesale seizure of the physical storage device/media is arguably the most common form of seizure practiced by law enforcement responders today. The question remains, are there other options besides the seizure of physical devices that are available to responders? If yes, are these methods of seizure within the reach of anyone but the most technical of responders?

For a long time, up to and including today, many in the forensics community place little faith in the ability for responders on-scene to deal appropriately with the computers they may encounter. The direction was simply "Don't touch the keyboard. Pull the plug and send everything to the lab." In many cases, the forensics side of the house is correct to protect against the possible corruption or destruction of data by taking this hard-line approach—particularly based on the technology of yesterday—but at what cost? Although the computer forensics community might have intended to do the most good by promulgating the pull-the-plug mantra, we need to examine how disempowering the on-scene responders may affect the overall forensic process, from seizure through analysis to investigation and ultimately prosecution.

The latest *Search and Seizure of Computers and Obtaining Digital Evidence* (Manual), published by the Department of Justice supports the proposition that the seizure of digital evidence should be an incremental process, based both on the situation and the training level of the responder. The Manual describes an incremental approach as a search strategy (pg. 221) for the seizure of digital evidence from a functioning company where the wholesale seizure of all the computers from the company would be impractical.

The Manual provides the following steps in its incremental approach:

1. After arriving on-scene, Agents will attempt to identify a systems administrator or similar person who would be willing to assist law enforcement in identifying, copying and/or printing out copies of the relevant files or data objects defined in the warrant.

2. If there are no company employees available to assist the Agent, the Agent will ask a computer expert to attempt to locate the computer files described in the warrant and will attempt to make electronic copies of those files. It is assumed that if the Agent is an expert, he/she would be able to proceed with the retrieval of the evidence.

3. If the Agent or expert are unable to retrieve the files, or if the onsite search proves infeasible for technical reasons, then the next option is to create an image of those parts of the computer that are likely to store the information described in the warrant.

4. If imaging proves impractical or impossible for technical reasons, then the Agent is to seize those components and storage media that the Agent reasonably believes includes the information described in the warrant.

The Manual has a focus on Federal law enforcement and the incremental search strategy is described in the context of responding to a functioning business where evidence of a crime may reside on the business's systems—hence, the focus in the Manual on gaining assistance from the business's systems administrator. Even though, realistically, you are not going to ask the suspect for help in retrieving the files of interest, there is good reason to expand this incremental search strategy to the search and seizure of digital information that resides on non-business systems. First, many home users set up networks similar to what would be present in a small business. Second, the amount of storage on a home network may exceed the amount of storage used for business purposes, as home users are more likely to possess large music and movie files. Lastly, current and impending technologies such as whole disk encryption make the offsite analysis of storage media impractical, if not impossible. A mechanism must be developed now that enables responders to pull evidence off of a running system before these types of systems are in widespread use. Otherwise, we may be changing the paradigm a few years too late.

Although the change in focus from hardware-as-evidence to information-as-evidence may be a radical departure from how many people currently view digital evidence, it is not exactly a new viewpoint. In fact, the change to a focus on the information as evidence may be a renaissance of sorts; the computer crime investigators of yesterday knew nothing other than the retrieval of relevant information from servers and networks. Much of the investigation of computer crime in a historic context related to examining events that occurred within a network infrastructure. In his book from the pre-World-Wide-Web year of 1990, *Spectacular Computer Crimes*, Buck Bloombecker discusses numerous computer crimes, most of which involve attacks on the network infrastructure (virus, worm) or schemes that were enabled by the presence of a network infrastructure, such as stealing unauthorized computer time or manipulating the wire transfer system to steal bank funds.

Crimes with a cyber component changed dramatically following the personal computing revolution, which was hand-in-hand with the rise of the World Wide Web. Prior to the 1990s, few people with personal computers used them solely for personal purposes. Prior to the 2000s, few people were providing personal information about themselves for the world to view. So it's not surprising that when we take a look backward, we see that the investigation of cyber crime involved incident response tasks, like pulling logs and records off of servers and other infrastructure-level digital devices, and less often concerned the seizure of a personal computer. Wholesale duplication of servers was impractical, storage costs were high, and so it was cost prohibitive to attempt to pull together the necessary equipment to image the entire server. Although the investigators of the time were breaking new ground, they knew enough to document their actions, make best efforts not to change the data objects with evidentiary value, and image the relevant data objects so they could be printed or referred to at a later date. Responders to network intrusion events were faced with no other option but to seize the relevant data objects—which is still the case today.

Responding to a Victim of a Crime Where Digital Evidence Is Involved

There is an old saying that all politics are local politics. Although I'm not quite convinced of the particular weight of that adage, I do believe that all crime is local crime. The Internet may have created a global community, but crime, even crimes committed over the Internet, will be reported to a local agency. It is imperative that local agencies have the ability to field a complaint regarding a crime with a cyber component and be able to respond appropriately. I have heard horror stories where complaints of e-mail harassment, auction fraud, and other crimes with a cyber component were just ignored by a local agency. Yes, a statement was taken and a report prepared, but no follow-up investigation was conducted. Worse, I have heard of agencies telling victims that the investigation of their complaint involved the seizure of their machine for forensic analysis, and that the analysis might take over a year to complete. I think it's pretty obvious why the complaint was dropped.

The unfortunate part of the situation is that the responding officer (or local agency) places an improper focus on the technology and loses sight of the crime that occurred. Often, the technology used is secondary and of little relevance. It could be quite possible that harassing statements in an e-mail might be coming from someone the victim already knew. If the harassment occurred through some other non-seize-able, non-virtual means (for example, spray paint on a car), the officer would most likely follow up with a knock-and-talk with the suspect. The follow-up on the e-mail harassment should use the same logic. Does the investigation need to be focused on tracing an e-mail to its source when you already have a good idea as to who sent the e-mail? It is important that investigators do not switch off their investigative skills because a computer is involved.

When responding to a victim, the focus must be on having the victim provide the law enforcement officer with something that substantiates their complaint—a print-out of the harassing e-mail with full header information, a cut-and-paste printout of the IM conversation where their child was sexually solicited, or a screen-print of a disturbing Web page. Any information that can be provided by the victim to a responding officer will increase efficiencies in the entire investigative process. The officer will be able to read the e-mail header and get preservation orders out to the ISPs; the detectives will be able to begin working the case, rather than securing another statement from the victim; and the computer forensics system won't be burdened by yet another machine requiring examination—particularly for data objects that could have reasonably been obtained on-scene.

Cases occur where the victim's computer must be seized. Harassments in e-mail or chat (when logging) that violate a protective order may have to be seized, depending on the situation. If a spouse or roommate finds child pornography on a computer, the computer should be seized since it contains contraband. But barring these unavoidable circumstances, the seizure of victim computers is often unnecessary and contributes to the logjam at the digital forensic laboratories.

When communicating with a victim, be sure you let them know to not delete anything on their system until their complaint has gone through the entire process. Also be quite sure to document the steps the victim took to provide you with the substantiating evidence. If you had to assist the victim in any way—maybe you showed them how to see full headers on an e-mail, for example—make sure those actions appear in the documentation. Make a note of the system time on the computer, and verify that the evidence contains a time and date stamp, and that the time and date make sense to the victim. Lastly, be responsive to the victim's needs. Many crimes with a cyber component—particularly frauds and thefts—will have an international component that makes the apprehension of a suspect and reimbursement to the victim nearly impossible. Be sympathetic and provide the victim with any resources that can assist them in dealing with banks, credit card companies, and creditors, such as a properly written police report. They have already been victimized; don't let your actions lead to a prolonging of the victimization.

Seizure Example

Here we will examine an example of a digital seizure to help explore the options available to on-scene responders. Let's start by saying that Sally receives a harassing e-mail from an anonymous sender. She believes it is a former co-worker named Sam, who has harassed Sally using non-computer-based methods before. The officer follows the guidance discussed in the "Responding to a Victim of a Crime Where Digital Evidence Is Involved" section and instructs Sally to print off a copy of the e-mail showing the full header information. Sally prints off the e-mail as substantiating proof to back up her complaint, and the officer leaves the scene with a statement from Sally and a copy of the harassing e-mail.

You notice that Sally was not told that her computer would need to be seized and held for a year—which would, in effect, cause Sally to drop her criminal complaint and also drop her opinion of the police. Instead, the officer leaves the victim scene with a statement, and some level of proof to back up the complaint, which allows the investigation to proceed without undue hardship to the victim.

The investigator then uses the information contained in the e-mail header to contact the e-mail provider, legal paperwork is sent to the provider looking for the account holder's information, and finally the e-mail is traced back to Sam's Internet service provider (ISP) account. We now have a general confirmation that the e-mail was sent from a computer connected to Sam's ISP account—although this could be any number of computers at Sam's house and possibly even be a neighbor using Sam's wireless access.

The investigator drafts a search warrant affidavit looking specifically for the information that is relevant to this case—specifically a preserved copy of the sent e-mail. The investigator is careful to focus the search warrant on the information to be seized, and does not focus on the containers or storage media in which the information may reside. The investigator further notes that an incremental approach will be used, which dictates that onsite seizures will occur when possible, but that factors yet to be determined may necessitate that all digital storage devices and media that may reasonably contain the sought after evidence may be seized for offsite review.

The investigator serves the warrant and finds a single computer at Sam's home. The system is on and, according to the suspect, has a Windows XP operating system. Based on the suspect's assertion that the computer is password-protected, and he has not given the password out to anyone, it is reasonable to believe that the computer is used solely by its owner. At this point, the on-scene investigator is staring at a glowing monitor with a happy desktop picture of calming fields and clouds, but the investigator is now faced with a few tough decisions. The computer appears to be running Windows XP, which corroborates the suspect's statement. Windows XP can survive a rapid power loss, so pulling the plug is an option, but pulling the plug means that the entire computer would need to be brought back to the computer forensics laboratory for examination. The investigator knows that the backlog at the computer forensics laboratory is approaching six months—way too long to determine if the suspect is stalking the victim. In six months, the stalking could escalate if there is no police intervention (depending on the type of stalker), and the victim could be physically assaulted. Further, the investigator knows that Windows XP is equipped with the Windows Encrypted File System, a seldom-used folder and file encryption system that, if enabled, would make the recovery of the information on the system very difficult without the suspect's cooperation.

The investigator thinks of other options at his disposal. The investigator could use a software preview tool in an attempt to locate the information stated in the warrant. In this case, Sam uses Microsoft Outlook as his local e-mail client, and a .pst file containing all the Outlook-related folders would exist on the system. This .pst should contain an e-mail in the sent items folder that matches the e-mail received by the victim. If the investigator had reason to believe there was information stored in the RAM that would be relevant to the case, the investigator could dump the RAM for later analysis. This might be the scenario if the investigator notices a draft of another e-mail currently on the screen. If the e-mail is found in the .pst during a preview, the entire drive could be imaged, or just the .pst could be imaged if the investigator has reason to believe that imaging the entire drive would be difficult.

In this example, maybe the investigator would decide to pull-the-plug and deliver it to the lab. Maybe the investigator believes there is enough evidence based on the victim's complaint to have the suspect come to the station for a talk about what is going on. But maybe the investigator's hair on the back of his neck rises up when talking to the suspect and the investigator gets a gut reaction about the level of urgency regarding the case. Maybe the on-scene preview and securing the .pst provides the investigator with enough evidence to take the suspect into custody. The important point is that without additional options to review the digital data, the investigator's hands are tied.

In line with the incremental approach described in the Manual, the investigator may have other options available besides wholesale seizure, such as:

- Previewing information on-scene

- Obtaining information from a running computer

- On-scene seizure of information through the complete imaging of the media

- On-scene seizure of information through the imaging of a specific data object

In the next section, we take a look at the preceding options and discuss how each fits into the larger picture of responding to and investigating crimes with digital evidence.

Previewing On-Scene Information to Determine the Presence and Location of Evidentiary Data Objects

The on-scene responder must make conclusions about where the information described in the warrant is most likely to be present on the storage device or media. In the case of a CD or DVD, the preview is much less complicated, as the chances of inadvertently writing to a piece of optical media are much lower than if they were working with magnetic-based media. With a CD or a DVD, the responder could use a forensics laptop running any number of computer forensic tools to quickly acquire and examine the contents of a CD or DVD for review. A similar process could be conducted for flash-based media, although a greater level of care may need to be taken to ensure the media is not changed. Here, flexibility is once again a critical characteristic. Previewing a few pieces of optical media on-scene may be appropriate, but greater numbers of media may need to be taken off-scene for review at the laboratory.

Technology exists that enables responders to preview the data on the storage media in an effort to locate the information described in the warrant. These "forensic preview software" packages, now in their infancy, are becoming more accepted within the community that investigates crimes involving a computer. The most common preview software packages come on CD and are essentially a Linux operating system that runs completely in the RAM and does not require any resources from the hard drive(s). Several of these disks are in current use by law enforcement, including Knoppix, Helix, and Spada. Several controlled boots will need to be performed to ensure the correct changes are made to the BIOS to direct the computer to boot from the CD. Although best practices should be determined locally, I recommend that the power to all the hard drives in desktop computers be disconnected and that laptop hard drives be removed while controlled boots are conducted to determine how to change the boot sequence in the BIOS. Further information on using controlled boots to examine and change BIOS and CMOS information can be found in the seizure procedures in the publication *Forensic Examination of Digital Evidence: A Guide for Law Enforcement* (NIJ, 2004).

Once the system is booted to the forensic preview software, the computer's hard drives can be mounted, or made available, in Linux as read-only. Once mounted, the preview software will provide the responder with an interface to either search for the desired information through keyword searches, or the responder can navigate through the directory tree in an attempt to locate a given file or directory. If the information described in the warrant is located during a preview, the responder may choose to image the specific data object, file, or folder where the information is located. The responder may also choose to seize the entire hard drive, now that the preview has provided him with a greater level of comfort that this particular "container" includes the desired information.

Over time, these forensic preview software packages will continue to evolve and develop as the problems with wholesale seizure become more evident and the need to focus the seizure of individual data objects from a digital crime scene becomes more apparent. It is hoped that the evolution of these tools will include the addition of features and special characteristics that make a tool "law enforcement specific." The lack of law enforcement specific features, such as intuitive interfaces, audit trail recordkeeping, and the production of evidence-quality data, are often an impediment to the adoption of commercial software by the law enforcement community (ISTS, 2004).

Obtaining Information from a Running Computer

If the investigator encounters a computer that is running, and the investigator believes there is information of evidentiary value stored in the computer's active memory, or RAM, there are options available that allow for the RAM to be recovered. For example, let's examine a situation where an investigator shows up on-scene at a location where a suspect has been chatting online with a minor or undercover officer. When the officers arrive at the scene, the suspect quickly closes the chat window. By default, many chat programs do not keep a log of the chat sessions and almost all of the actual chat activity happens in a portion of the program running in the computer's RAM. Without being able to obtain a *dump*, or download of the RAM, there would be little chance to obtain any information from the suspect's computer about the chat session that just occurred. Chatting is not the only type of data that would be held in RAM. Passwords, unsaved documents, unsaved drafts of e-mails, IM conversations, and so on could all be held in the RAM, and in no other place on the computer. The investigator needs to make a decision if the information described in the warrant would reasonably be found in the RAM of the computer. If the warrant describes information related to proof of embezzlement, there may be little reason to believe that the data held in the RAM would be relevant to the case. That is not to say that it isn't possible—but the responder needs to go through the process of determining the locations that have the highest probability of containing the information described in the warrant. Even if the suspect had worked on a relevant file and remnants of the same existed in the RAM, it would be logical to conclude that the file would be saved onto more permanent media, such as the hard drive. On the other hand, if the warrant detailed information related to inappropriate chat or instant messaging sessions, the RAM of the running computer would be the primary, and most likely the only, location where the information described in the warrant could exist. In this case, the use of a program such as Helix to "dump" the RAM to the responder's storage device would be a very high priority (Shipley, 2006).

Be careful about what you wish for, however, as the RAM dump could include several gigabytes of semi-random information. Pieces of documents, Registry keys, API calls, and a whole host of other garbage will be interwoven into a gigantic text file. Minimization still is a factor even when the RAM has been identified as being one of the locations where relevant data could exist—if the data might reside elsewhere, it may be more productive to go that route than to attempt to carve it from the RAM dump.

SEARCH, a national law enforcement training organization, recently published a primer on the collection of evidence from a running computer, which involves using preview software to obtain the contents of the RAM from a running machine before seizure (Shipley, 2006). SEARCH's article represents a departure from the norm in that the article recognizes that changes to the computer operating system will occur when a USB drive is inserted into the machine in order to receive the contents of the RAM. However, the important point highlighted by the SEARCH article is that the changes are known, explainable, and do not affect any information that has evidentiary value. "Hold on," you say, "moving the mouse and/or inserting a USB device will change the information on the suspect's drive, and that is strictly forbidden!" In response, I say that there are many in the investigative and legal communities that see little issue with a law enforcement agent performing operations that changed data on a suspect's hard drive or other media—as long as the agent acted in a reasonable manner and documented their actions appropriately. The firm and absolute stance that data cannot be changed needs to be examined to determine if our cases have been negatively affected by the promulgation of bad advice.

Imaging Information On-Scene

Imaging of an entire hard drive on-scene is fairly common among the more technically savvy digital crime scene responders—even more so for private sector investigators that often face cases where the hard drives need to be examined, but the business in question is not comfortable with letting the original drive out of their possession. In both of these cases, the analysis of the imaged drive usually occurs back at the laboratory. Rarely do you hear of a drive being both imaged and previewed on-scene—although such a process may actually address a number of concerns about the use of preview software to review the information on a drive while on-scene—specifically, performing a preview of the evidence on the original drive.

While the acquisition of an image of a drive on-scene may be fairly common among the more technically skilled, usually for corporate crimes, we find there is little use of this technique by less skilled personnel for low-level crimes. However, there are a number of good reasons to perform imaging on-scene for most computer crimes. First, as mentioned earlier, previews of the evidence can be performed on the imaged copy with less worry about the investigator inadvertently damaging information on the original hard drive. Second, in those instances where outside concerns prevent the seizure of the physical media, such as PPA concerns, third-party data, and multiple users of the computer, the imaging of the hard drive provides another option for the on-scene investigators.

Terminology Alert…

Imaging versus Copying and Hashes

It is important that the data on the suspect's hard drive be imaged to the destination drive/device rather than just copied. The process of imaging creates a bit-stream copy—or an exact copy of the 1s and 0s—of the information being copied. The regular copy function within the operating system will attempt to

Continued

write the file according to its logical programming—meaning that the file being written to the drive could be spread across numerous clusters on the target drive. The point of imaging the data is that an exact replica of the data as it appears on the source drive is created on the destination drive—specifically the exact order of the bits (the 1s and 0s) on the drive—hence, the term *bit stream copy*. Because imaging preserves the exact order of the bits from the original to the copy, hash functions are able to be run against the entire chunk of the source drive, which is then imaged and compared to the exact replica created on the destination drive. Image hashing allows the responder to mathematically prove that the data that exists on the source drive is exactly the same on the destination drive. Some claim that a few of the hash algorithms (like the MD5 hash algorithm) have been cracked. This is technically true; however, the circumstances for collisions—two different files that generate the same MD5 hash—were specifically created to prove that collisions can occur. The chances of an MD5 hash collision occurring during the comparison of a source drive and an improperly imaged drive would be unbelievably small. I would feel very confident that a hash match between two files/images that are supposed to match to be proof that the two files/images are in fact an exact copy. I feel even stronger about the validity of the next generation of hash algorithms, including SHA1, SHA-256, or SHA-512.

Imaging Finite Data Objects On-Scene

In the current law enforcement climate, there is little discussion of the seizure of particular pieces of information. Generally, the entire computer is seized—and the seized computer is usually called "evidence." The data contained within the computer are reviewed at a later date for any files or other pieces of information that can help prove or disprove a given premise. From an outsider's perspective, it would appear as if the seizure of the entire computer is the preferred method of obtaining the evidentiary information, but we've established that imaging on-scene is fairly well accepted within the digital investigative community. So, are there other options that include the seizure of a finite number of data objects as evidence?

If we can image the entire hard drive on-scene, there is an argument that we can image sections of it. We routinely ask companies and ISPs to do just that when we ask them to preserve evidence of a crime—rarely do we seize the ISP's servers, nor do we ask them to provide an image of the entire server so a computer forensics exam can be performed. Are there reasons why we can't use the same logic when responding to a suspect? The larger question is whether this type of seizure is appropriate. Are there circumstances when a finite amount of information is needed to prove guilt, and the seizure of the original hard drive is not an option? This discussion is very similar to the previous discussion regarding imaging the entire drive on-scene in situations where the physical media cannot be seized. There may also be situations where a finite piece of information would suffice to move the case forward. In these situations, the seizure of a finite number of data objects may be a viable option for responders.

In our case example discussed earlier, where Sam is accused of stalking Sally, let's assume that an arrest warrant hinged on the presence of the harassing e-mail on Sam's computer. If the preview of the computer showed that the e-mail in question existed on Sam's computer, and the investigator had the ability to image the .pst file that contained the e-mail, the investigator could take Sam into custody at this time and have all the evidence needed to wrap up the case. There would be no need to add yet another machine to the computer forensic backlog, and the investigation could be wrapped up immediately, rather than having to wait weeks to months for a completed forensic review.

NOTE

The focus on the seizure of data objects discussed within the other options section does not transfer well to the seizure of computers suspected of containing child pornography. It is strongly recommended that guidance on the seizure of computers containing child pornography be obtained from the Internet Crimes Against Children (ICAC) Task Forces. This network of 46+ law enforcement agencies specializes in the investigation and prosecution of crimes against children facilitated by computer. Additional information about ICAC can be found at www.icactraining.org.

I can hear you yelling "WAIT! What if I think he might have child pornography on his computer?" Good question. If the warrant for the case specifies that the investigator can search for and seize the sent e-mail in question, then it would be hard to justify why the investigator spent all day looking through the suspect's vacation pictures for possible images of child pornography. A warrant for the seizure of a given piece of information that results in the seizure of a computer, or other digital storage device, does not give the law enforcement agent carte blanche to look through every file on the computer. As it relates to the child pornography question, if the investigator believes there is evidence of child pornography on the computer, the investigator is better off obtaining a warrant for the suspected child pornography rather than to search for evidence of one crime under the pretenses of another crime.

That is not to say there aren't instances when you may stumble across evidence of a different crime when reviewing digital information. Should the occasion arise when you are looking for one type of information under a specific warrant, and inadvertently find evidence of another crime, the legal guidance is that you should immediately stop the review and obtain a second warrant to search for evidence of the second crime. It is theoretically possible that you could finish examining the computer under the first warrant, and not specifically search for items pertaining to the newly discovered crime. However, that strategy is not recommended.

But do we have the tools necessary to enable us to copy-off only the relevant data objects? Can this be done within a reasonable time frame? From a technologist's viewpoint, the technology is often more flexible than the legal framework within which the technology operates. The current technology allows us to search very rapidly through thousands of pages of information for keywords, a feat that would be all but impossible with paper records. But much of the specialized computer forensic tools are designed to be used in a forensic laboratory environment and not for on-scene response. These powerful forensic tools often require a fair amount of time to analyze and process the information on a target drive. Often, these laboratory examinations involve tools that may take hours to complete a given function, and the review of information often involves hours of pouring through documents and graphics. If we consider that "time" is one of the most limiting factors when conducting on-scene analysis, there is definitely a conflict between the best technical analysis that could be performed and the time frame in which a reasonable on-scene analysis should be completed.

The seizure of data objects from large servers while in the course of investigating network intrusion cases is fairly common and accepted, but it is difficult to tell if the seizure of data objects will become more common in the everyday investigator's response toolkit. Although there appears to be a general legal and technological framework within which data object seizure can occur, it is still difficult to swallow the fact that the original evidence will be left behind. The use of this technique on business computers and networks follows the argument that the business is a disinterested third party, and that if relevant data is missed, the investigator can go back and retrieve additional information because the business has no desire to interfere with the investigation. But would a spouse or roommate constitute a disinterested third party with regards to data on their computer? Can we develop tools that give the investigator a greater level of comfort regarding the thoroughness of the on-scene previewing/review? These questions, and others that will spring from discussions like this, will shape the way in which this technique, and the other options presented earlier, become accepted or rejected by the digital evidence response community.

Use of Tools for Digital Evidence Collection

Where the computer forensics of yesterday relied on vary basic tools that allowed manual manipulation of the seized data objects, we have since developed tools that assist in the acquisition, organization, and examination of the data. Both the ubiquity of electronic information and the sheer volume of seized digital information have necessitated the use of tools to assist in the investigative process. Hardware and software write blockers and hard-drive duplication devices have reduced the chances of damaging the information on source drives. Tools beyond simple hex editors and command-line scripts were developed to assist the examiner in performing keyword searches, sorting data objects by file type and category, and scouring the source disk for file remnants in file slack space and drive free space. Tools like Autopsy Browser, SMART, iLook, Encase, and Forensic Toolkit are dramatic departures from manual command-line searching and have had a significant impact on the efficiency in which large volumes of data are examined. These tools have also increased the accessibility of digital evidence to those outside of the closed circle of highly trained forensic examiners.

The way in which digital information is analyzed has changed over the years—obviously driven by the ever-increasing amount of information stored digitally. But other changes have been driven by the increase in our knowledge of how to work with digital evidence—most notably in the development of tools to assist in different phases of the investigative and forensic process. The use of software and hardware tools by on-scene responders can begin to address how we work toward achieving a greater level of data object seizure. Current tools, such as ImageMasster and Helix, begin to enable an on-scene responder to image an entire drive and to seize the contents of the RAM. Other tools in this domain provide some capacity to preview the contents of a suspect drive and to image only the necessary information, as has been the case for years in the incident response disciplines.

Some will argue that no one should use a tool if they cannot explain exactly what the tool is doing. In the computer forensics realm, this often translates to "no one should use a tool if they cannot perform, by hand, the operations that the tool is performing." There is a fair amount of disagreement on this position. The law enforcement community commonly uses tools where they can explain the basic principal, but not the exact manner in which the tool is accomplishing its task. For example, when an officer is trained on the use of the radar gun, she is taught the principals of the Doppler Effect and how the tool records the very precise timings between the sending of a radar impulse and the receipt of the reflected radar energy. The officer would also be shown how the unit is tested and calibrated to ensure reliability. In this way, the officer understands generally how the tool works—it is not reasonable to instruct them on how to construct the device, nor should the officer be required to manually calculate how the speed of a vehicle is determined from recorded radar signals in order to be a proficient operator of the tool.

That is not to say that we should be able to use any tool without accountability. Tools that are used in the seizure or analysis of digital evidence must be tested. This testing is commonly performed by the organization using the tool—since the tool must be tested within the parameters of the agency's protocols—but larger tool verification efforts are underway at the National Institute for Standards and Technology (NIST). NIST has created tool testing specifications for disk imaging tools, physical and software write blockers, and deleted file recovery programs. A number of products have been tested under this program, and the results look very promising. Almost all of the programs or devices tested actually work as purported. That's not to say there are not issues with the NIST program. Technology changes faster than the standards development and tool testing processes, and the overall number of standards developed through the NIST program has been, unfortunately, small.

However, placing tools at the disposal of the greater law enforcement community has some significant impacts related to the overall model that we follow when working with digital evidence: If we are able to train officers/investigators on the proper use of a given tool, and the tool has passed muster through testing under a given protocol, whether at their local agency or at the NIST, then the officer/investigator is empowered to take an active role in the recovery of digital evidence and in the investigation on the whole.

It is clear that we do not have all the answers to the technological hurdles worked out, but the technology is often not the limited factor, as was discussed earlier. Understanding that the technology will forever be changing and advancing, the legal community must begin to play an active role in providing the technologists with direction and boundaries. The technologists need to heed the legal guidance, examine how future issues will affect law enforcement, and begin designing tools that will provide a critical edge to the good guys.

Common Threads within Digital Evidence Seizure

The landscape of potential seizure environments is complicated and variations are nearly infinite. The level of knowledge of the on-scene responders includes a wide range of skills and abilities. Because the seizure process will be greatly impacted by the particular hardware and software arrangements and knowledge of the on-scene responder, it is not possible to present one correct way to seize digital evidence, unfortunately. What does exist is a continuum of methods mapped against the complexity of the scene versus the skill of the responders.

There are, however, basic threads that tie any seizure process together. The first thread is that you must be able to explain what steps you took to arrive at a particular destination. It does not matter if you come out of a building with a floppy disk or an entire network, you should be able to replicate each step in the process. If you were presented with an exact replica of the scene, you should be able to refer to your notes and do everything exactly the same from arriving on-scene, to collecting the evidence, to walking out the door. In order to achieve this level of enlightenment, there are two sub-threads: (1) Document everything—and I mean everything. Have one person process the scene while the other one writes down every single, mind-numbing step. The documentation should be as complete as practically possible. If one is working alone in the seizure process, consider using a voice recorder and narrate each step for later transcription. The exact steps taken in the process become doubly important if and when the target computer is manipulated in any way—for instance, moving the mouse to deactivate the screen-saver, or initiating a shutdown sequence. (2) Confucius is attributed to saying: "To know that you know what you know, and that you do not know what you do not know, that is true knowledge." Translated for relevance for the second sub-thread here, it means that if you don't know what you are doing (or worse, what you just did…), or aren't really comfortable with determining the next steps, *stop*, and revert to a less technical seizure method, or seek assistance from someone more qualified. Your knowledge will be judged by your ability to know what you don't know—when to stop—over the knowledge you do possess.

The second thread is that you should seek the seizure method that best minimizes the digital crime scene. If you can reasonably come up with an "area"—meaning drive, directory, file, and so on—where you believe the evidence will be located, it makes the most sense to look in that specific location for the digital evidence. Limiting or minimizing the crime scene has different implications based on whether the search for digital evidence is occurring on-scene, at the station, or back at the forensic laboratory. On-scene, minimization may include excluding professionally produced and labeled CDs from the seizure. Minimization may also include the use of software tools to preview the contents of a computer for a specific data object. Offsite minimization efforts may include searching only certain keywords or examining only a given file type. Even given our ability to search for and find most anything on a computer, we must remember that not every fact is relevant, and analyses that are 100-percent comprehensive do not exist. At the heart of minimization is the ability to know when to stop while looking for digital evidence.

The third thread is that whatever is seized as having potential evidentiary value must be authenticated by the court before it can be admitted into the case. The ability for the court to authenticate the evidence is a significant issue related to digital evidence. Authentication is governed by the Federal Rules of Evidence Rule 901 (28 U.S.C.), which states "The requirement of authentication or identification as a condition precedent to admissibility is satisfied by evidence sufficient to support a finding that the matter in question is what its proponent claims." The salient point of the definition for our discussions is that digital evidence can be authenticated by providing evidence that shows that it is in fact what it is purported to be. I realize that is a bit of cyclical logic—so let's break down the authentication process further for clarification.

Evidence presented to the court can be authenticated a number of ways, including the identification of distinctive characteristics or by merely what type of evidence it is, as is the case for public records. Evidence may also be authenticated by way of testimony to the fact that the matter in question is what it is claimed to be. Courts have upheld the authentication of documents based on testimony (U.S. v. Long, C.A.8 [Minn.] 1988, 857 F.2d 436, habeas corpus denied 928 F.2d 245, certiorari denied 112 S.Ct. 98, 502 U.S. 828, 116 L.Ed.2d 69).

However, in the past, computer forensics has relied less on the testimony of those performing the on-scene seizure and more on the testimony of the computer forensic technician. Where the on-scene responder would be able to testify as to where the hardware was located before seizure, the computer forensic technician would take the position to defend their laboratory techniques. The computer forensics community chose to address the authentication issue by creating exact duplicates of the seized digital information and proving mathematically that the copied information was an exact copy of the seized information—and the courts have supported the position that a duplicate of the information can be submitted in lieu of the original when it can be proved that the duplicate is the same extant as the original (U.S. v. Stephenson, C.A.5 [Tex.] 1989, 887 F.2d 57, certiorari denied 110 S.Ct. 1151, 493 U.S. 1086, 107 L.Ed.2d 1054).

As it relates to our options for seizure discussed earlier, there are two salient points for discussion. The first is that the seized data—whether from a RAM dump or as a result of the creation of an image of the drive or file—may be authenticated by the testimony of the investigator that retrieved the evidence from the suspect machine. If the case involved a child pornography photograph, and the investigator saw the photograph during a preview, the investigator may be able to assert that the recovered photograph is the same photograph he saw during a preview. The second point is that the creation and matching of mathematical hashes provides a very high level of proof that the recovered data is an exact copy of the original. Although the best evidence rule states that the original should be provided whenever possible, *U.S. v. Stephenson*, noted earlier, shows that an exact duplicate is satisfactory when circumstances limit the production of the original evidence in court. Hard drives, the most commonly encountered type of storage media, are mechanical devices, and all mechanical devices will fail at some point—perhaps after days, months, or decades—but they will fail. By working off of a copy of the seized drive, and presenting the same in court, the investigator is reducing the chances of completely losing all of the data on the seized drive. Taking steps to reduce the complete loss of the digital information relating to the case is but one of the reasons to justify the use of exact copies over the original data.

The final thread is the admissibility of the evidence. The admissibility of evidence is based on the authentication, and the authentication is based on the proof that the seized object is materially unchanged—proof that can be accomplished by showing a complete chain of custody (*U. S. v. Zink*, C.A.10 [Colo.] 1980, 612 F.2d 511). For digital evidence, the proof that the data is what it purports to be and is unchanged has been accomplished by both testimony and use of the cryptographic hash algorithms. Similar to how the forensic laboratory technician uses the hash function to show that the entire seized drive was copied accurately, the on-scene responder can refer to their detailed notes to testify as to the location of the seized information and show that the hash functions proved that the integrity of the data was not compromised during imaging.

Determining the Most Appropriate Seizure Method

Clearly, there will be cases where the most appropriate action is to seize all the physical hardware at a suspect's location. Perhaps it is the only option that the minimally trained responder has at their disposal. Maybe the forensic preview software didn't support the graphics card for the computer. It's possible that additional keyword searches need to be performed or items need to be carved from drive free space, and both would be better performed in a controlled laboratory environment. There are any number of reasons why the on-scene responder will choose to seize the physical container, and that's ok! The important point is that the most appropriate method of seizure is chosen to match the responder's skill level, and that it appropriately addresses the type of crime.

The minimization stage may provide the investigator with the places—computers, storage media, and so on—that have the highest probability of containing the desired information. A preview on-scene may verify that the information exists. In cases of child pornography possession, the on-scene preview may allow the investi-gator to take the suspect into custody right at that moment—or at least have some very frank discussions about the material found on the computer. The case may be provided to a prosecutor with just the previewed images, and discussions of sentences and pleas can occur immediately, instead of having to wait for a complete forensics examination. If the case is referred to trial, the full forensic analysis of the seized computer can be conducted at that time. On the other hand, maybe a full examina-tion of the data should be conducted to determine if the suspect has produced any new images of child pornography—information that is critical in determining if an active victimization is occurring and is critical to the overall fight against this type of crime. *This simple scenario shows how the incremental approach and the seizure options dis-cussed earlier are needed so as to even begin to get a foothold on crimes with a cyber compo-nent, but that circumstances may force investigators to throw out the incremental approach in favor of a complete examination.*

There are a few other key points relating to physical seizure. The first is that the entire computer will be needed by the laboratory to determine the system time and other settings related to the motherboard. If you plan on only seizing the hard drive, imaging the hard drive on-scene, or only imaging relevant information, follow the methodology outlined by NIJ in the *Forensic Examination of Digital Evidence* (NIJ, 2004) to use controlled boots to record the system time versus a trusted time source.

The second key point is that there are many computers and laptops that do not allow for easy access to the hard drives—which would make any attempts to image on-scene impractical and, as a result, require seizure of the hardware. For example, some laptop designs require the majority of the laptop to be disassembled to gain access to the hard drive. I strongly recommend that the disassembly of laptops or other hardware take place in a controlled laboratory or shop environment—there are just way too many little pieces and screws, often with unusual head designs, to be attempting a disassembly on-scene. In these cases, the physical seizure of the com-puter itself may be required even if you came prepared to image on-scene.

The third key point is that there may be other nondigital evidence that could reside with the physical computer. Items such as sticky notes can be found stuck to a monitor; passwords or Web addresses can be written in pencil or marker on the computer enclosure; or items may be taped to the bottom of a keyboard or hidden inside the computer itself. I remember one story of a criminal that hid his marijuana stash inside the computer; the wife asserted that he had child pornography on the computer and the computer examiner—and wife—were amazed when bags of mar-ijuana were found inside the computer enclosure.

One last note: Don't turn off the investigative part of your brain while con-ducting the seizure. Use all the investigative techniques you learned in the academy and employ during the execution of physical search warrants. You will get much further in the case if you use information from one source (computer/suspect) to gain more information from the other source (suspect/computer)—but remember that Miranda rights may be applicable when having discussions with the suspect.

Summary

There is no doubt that the investigators of tomorrow will be faced with more digital information present in greater numbers and types of devices. Seizing the relevant evidentiary information is, and will continue to be, a critical step in the overall computer forensics process. The current view that the physical hardware is the evidence has now been joined by a different view that the information can be regarded as evidence—whether the hardware or information is viewed as evidence has a dramatic effect on how we "seize" or "collect" evidence both at the scene and in the forensics laboratory.

A number of factors may limit the continued wholesale seizure of the physical hardware. The storage size of the suspect's computer hard drive or storage network may exceed an investigator's ability to take everything back to the forensics laboratory. Full disk encryption, now released as part of the Windows Vista operating system, may foil an investigator's ability to recover any data without the proper encryption key. Further, concerns over commingled and third-party data, covered by the Privacy Protection Act, may impact the ability of an investigator to seize more data than specified in the warrant. Lastly, the increasing amount of seized digital evidence is having an effect on the ability of many of the computer forensics laboratories to complete forensic analyses in a timely manner. Both investigations and prosecutions may be suffering because of delays in the processing of digital evidence.

While the existing seizure methodology is focused on the seizure of hardware, investigators need to be able to select the most appropriate option for seizure according to the situation and their level of technical expertise. There are other seizure options that could be considered by the digital evidence response community. On-site previews using Linux- or Windows-based bootable CDs allow an investigator to review the contents of a suspect's computer in a relatively forensically sound manner. Techniques exist to dump the RAM of a suspect's computer to attempt to recover any information that may be stored in RAM but not written to disk, such as passwords, chat sessions, and unsaved documents. Imaging on-scene is yet another option available to investigators. Full disk imaging—where a complete bit-by-bit copy of a hard drive is created on a black drive—is more common and is currently used by a fair number of investigators. Less common is the imaging of select data objects that have evidentiary value. While still controversial, there appears to be a legal and technological framework that makes the imaging of data objects a viable option.

Clearly, there will always be more digital evidence than we can process within our existing organizational and governmental structures. More trained examiners in the field does not always equate to more trained examiners in the understaffed laboratories nor out in the field. The *time* of the most highly trained personnel is one of our most precious resources. There is no possible way that the limited number of specialists can process electronic evidence at every scene. Not only would they not be able to cover every scene, the laboratory work would undoubtedly suffer. In order to protect the time of the most highly trained and specialized people, those with less technical knowledge need to receive some level of training that allows them to perform a number of duties normally performed by the specialist. In this way, knowledge and high-technology investigative skills are pushed-down to all levels of responder. That is not to say that *training for first responder* isn't plagued with problems—the knowledge required to properly deploy advanced tools often exceeds the amount of time allotted for such training. We're caught in a Catch-22: all line officers need to be able to seize digital evidence, but the first responder level of training may not fully equip the officers to seize the evidence, and the level of training required to more completely understand the digital evidence seizure process may involve multiple days of training, and multiple days of training on a single topic will most likely not be provided to all line officers.

The level of training will affect the responder's use of technology, and the technology encountered will dictate whether the responder's level of training is appropriate in a given situation. There will be cases where the most appropriate action is to seize all the physical hardware at a suspect location. Perhaps it is the only option that the minimally trained responder has at their disposal, or maybe the technology encountered is so complex that none of the responders know exactly how to handle the seizure.

As it stands now, the forensic collection and analysis system works—sometimes tenuously, and frequently at a snail's pace—however, we will undoubtedly continue to face more change: change coming in the way of new devices, higher levels of inter-connectivity, and the ever-increasing amounts of data storage requiring examination. Will the existing manner in which we go about seizing and examining digital information be sufficient in five years? Ten years? Are there changes we can institute now in the way we address digital evidence that will better position us to face the coming changes?

I hope throughout this chapter that I made myself clear that I am not advocating any one seizure methodology over another—the critical take-away point is that we need to provide our responders with options to choose the appropriate seizure method based on their level of technical skill and the situation at hand. I have found in my work with law enforcement in New Hamphire, as well as throughout the nation, that crimes that involve a computer closely map to crimes that do not involve a computer—all of it part of the migration of traditional crime into the digital medium. If we expect our law enforcement agents to be responsive to traditional crimes with a high-technology component, we must provide them with the appropriate tools and procedures to enable them to actually investigate and close a case. Asking investigators to send each and every case that involves a computer to a forensic laboratory for review is not a sustainable option. If we don't "push down" technical knowledge to investigators and line officers, the specialists will quickly become overwhelmed and investigations will grind to a halt—a situation that has already begun to occur across the country.

The volume of computer forensic exams is only one factor that is driving us toward changing our approach to digital evidence seizure. As outlined in the previous pages, whole disk encryption, personal data and Privacy Protection Act concerns, and massively large storage arrays are all playing a part in the move to minimize the amount of information seized from a suspect machine. The landscape is quickly changing, and designing solutions to problems of today will not prepare us for the challenges of tomorrow. It is hoped that the change in focus away from the wholesale seizure of digital storage devices and media, in the appropriate situations, will better prepare our law enforcement agents and private sector investigators for the new technologies and coming legal concerns that the future holds.

Works Cited

Association of Chief Police Officers and National High Tech Crime Unit. 2004. Good Practice Guide for Computer based Electronic Evidence, Version 3.0. Available on the Internet at www.acpo.police.uk/asp/policies/Data/gpg_computer_based_evidence_v3.pdf (12/2006).

Bloombecker, Buck. *Spectacular Computer Crimes: What They Are and How They Cost American Business Half a Billion Dollars a Year.* 1990. Homewood, IL: Dow-Jones Irwin.

Carrier, B. and E. Spafford. "Getting Physical with the Digital Investigation Process." *International Journal of Digital Evidence.* Volume 2, Issue 2, 2003. Available at www.ijde.org (12/2006).

Computer Crime and Intellectual Property Section (CCIPS), Criminal Division. "Searching and Seizing Computers and Obtaining Electronic Evidence in Criminal Investigations." United States Department of Justice. Washington, DC. 2002.

Gilder, G. "The Information Factories." *Wired Magazine*. Volume 14, Number 10, 2006.

ISTS. "Law Enforcement Tools and Technologies for Investigating Cyber Attacks: Gap Analysis Report." Institute for Security Technology Studies, Dartmouth College. Hanover, NH. 2004.

ISTS. "Law Enforcement Tools and Technologies for Investigating Cyber Attacks: A National Research and Development Agenda." Institute for Security Technology Studies, Dartmouth College. Hanover, NH. 2004.

Meyers, M. and Rogers, M. "Computer Forensics: The Need for Standardization and Certification." *International Journal of Digital Evidence*. Volume 3, Issue 2, 2004. Available at www.ijde.org (12/2006).

Moore, Robert. *Cybercrime: Investigating High-Technology Computer Crime*. Anderson Publishing, LexisNexis Group. 2005.

National Institute of Justice (NIJ). *Forensic Examination of Digital Evidence: A Guide for Law Enforcement*. Office of Justice Programs, U.S. Department of Justice, Washington, DC. 2004.

National Institute of Justice. *Electronic Crime Scene Investigation: A Guide for First Responders*. Office of Justice Programs. U.S. Department of Justice. NIJ Guide Series. Washington, DC. 2001.

National Security Agency Information Assurance Solutions Technical Directors. *Information Assurance Technical Framework*, Release 3.1. 2002. Available at www.iatf.net/framework_docs/version-3_1/index.cfm.

Nolan, Joseph R. and Jacqueline Nolan-Haley. *Black's Law Dictionary*, Sixth ed. St. Paul, MN: West Publishing Company. 1990.

School of Information Management Systems (SIMS). "How Much Information?" University of California Berkeley. 2003. Available on the Internet at www2.sims.berkeley.edu/research/projects/how-much-info-2003.

Shipley, T. and H. Reeve. *Collecting Evidence from a Running Computer: A Technical and Legal Primer for the Justice Community*. SEARCH, The National Consortium for Justice Information and Statistics. Sacramento, CA. 2006.

Available on the Internet at www.search.org/files/pdf/ CollectEvidenceRunComputer.pdf (12/06).

"Scientific Working Group on Digital Evidence (SWGDE) and International Organization on Digital Evidence. Digital Evidence Standards and Principles." *Forensic Science Communications*. Volume 2, Number 2, 2000. Federal Bureau of Investigation. U.S. Department of Justice. Washington, DC.

Sterling, Bruce. "Hacker Crackdown." *Project Gutenburg*. Champaign, IL. 1992. Available on the Web at www.gutenberg.org/etext/101.

Technical Working Group for Electronic Crime Scene Investigation, Office of Justice Programs. *Electronic Crime Scene Investigation: A Guide for First Responders*. U.S. Department of Justice, National Institute of Justice. NIJ Guide series, NCJ 187736. Washington, DC. 2001.

United States Secret Service (USSS). "Best Practices for Seizing Electronic Evidence." 2006. Available on the Internet at www.secretservice.gov/electronic_evidence.shtml (12/2006).

United States Department of Justice. *Federal Guidelines for Searching and Seizing Computers*. United States Department of Justice. Washington, DC. 1994.

Federal Rules of Evidence (FRE) are available at judiciary.house.gov/media/pdfs/printers/108th/evid2004.pdf.

Federal Rules of Criminal Procedure (FRCP) are available at judiciary.house.gov/media/pdfs/printers/108th/crim2004.pdf.

Additional Relevant Resources

Daubert v. Merrell Dow Pharmaceuticals, Inc., 509 US, 579 (1993).

Noblett, M., M. Pollit, and L. Presley. "Recovering and Examining Computer Forensic Evidence." *October Forensic Science Communications*. Volume 2, Number 4, 2000. Federal Bureau of Investigation. U.S. Department of Justice. Washington, DC.

Duerr, T., N. Beser, and G. Staisiunas. "Information Assurance Applied to Authentication of Digital Evidence." *Forensic Science Communications*. Volume 6, Number 4, 2004. Federal Bureau of Investigation. U.S. Department of Justice. Washington, DC.

Brown, C. and E. Kenneally. "Risk Sensitive Digital Evidence Collection." *Digital Investigation*. Volume 2, Issue 2, 2005. Elsevier Ltd. Available on the Internet at www.sciencedirect.com/science/journal/17422876.

Brenner, S.W. and B.A. Frederiksen. "Computer Searches and Seizures: Some Unresolved Issues." *Michigan Telecommunications Technical Law Review*. Volume 8, Number 39, 2002.

Joint Administrative Office/Department of Justice Working Group on Electronic Technology in the Criminal Justice System. "Report and Recommendations." 2003. Available on the Internet at www.fjc.gov/public/pdf.nsf/lookup/CompInDr.pdf/$file/CompInDr.pdf (12/06).

Wright, T. *The Field Guide for Investigating Computer Crime: Parts 1–8. 2000–2001*. Available on the Internet at www.securityfocus.com/infocus/1244 (12/2006).

Chapter 4

Handheld Forensics
by Amber Schroader

Amber Schroader is the CEO of Paraben Corporation; she continues to act as the driving force behind some of the most innovative forensic technologies. As a pioneer in the field, Amber has been key in developing new technology to help investigators with the extraction of digital evidence from hard drives, e-mail, and handheld and mobile devices. Amber has extensive experience in dealing with a wide array of forensic investigators ranging from federal, state, local, and foreign government as well as corporate investigators. Amber is involved in many different computer investigation organizations, including The Institute of Computer Forensic Professionals (ICFP) as the chairman of the board, HTCIA, CFTT, and FLETC.

Digital Forensics

The field of digital forensics has long been centered on traditional media like hard drives. Being the most common digital storage device in distribution it is easy to see how they had become a primary point of evidence. However, as technology brings digital storage to more and more devices, forensic examiners have needed to prepare for a change in what types of devices hold a digital fingerprint. Cell phones and PDA (Personal Digital Assistant) devices are so common that they have become standard in today's digital examinations.

Security Alert...

What Is Digital Forensics?

Digital forensics is the examination of hardware or software in the pursuit of evidence to disprove or prove an allegation.

Handheld forensics is the examination of hardware and software that are typically an integrated unit in the pursuit of evidence to disprove or prove an allegation.

However, as you can see from these definitions, the scope of how they impact forensics is one that is very new and very different. These small devices carry a large burden for the forensic examiner, with different handling rules from scene to lab and with the type of data being as diverse as the suspects they come from.

Handheld devices are rooted in their own operating systems, file systems, file formats, and methods of communication. Dealing with this creates unique problems for examiners. Performing a forensic exam on a cell phone or PDA takes special software and special knowledge of the way these devices work, as well as where possible evidence could be stored. Having a basis of knowledge to build on in order to start adding these types of devices into your forensic examination will help you not only be more comprehensive in your methods, but also gain new insight to your suspect.

What Is the Handheld Forensic Impact?

Many people have asked me, Why is the handheld device so important in my forensic processing?

My answer is somewhat simple. They are the only devices that your suspect can have with them at all times based on their size, and they have immediate access to them 24?7 because they are immediate boot cycle devices. In addition, these are the devices that typically hold all our dirty little secrets with colorful pictures and descriptive text messages. They are a vault of evidence for the forensic examiner. A lot of handheld devices are traded on popular auction sites online as people are always looking for the latest gadget they can show off. We gathered a variety of these devices for testing purposes and found that 80 percent of them retained the user's information on the device. The information ranged from complete address books, work related e-mails, to pictures that were of intimate moments. Surprisingly as we contacted the people who belonged to the devices most of them had no idea that the data was retained on the device, let alone recoverable. Dirty little secrets were ripe for the taking for a trained forensic examiner.

These things make it so the handheld devices can carry some of the most crucial pieces of evidence in your forensic examination. The digital fingerprint on a handheld device is much larger than most assume.

So now that we know how important a device can be in forensic processing, it is important to have a good understanding of how handheld forensics impacts the four main foundations of digital forensics.

Digital Forensic Foundations

A sound forensic foundation is no different than other forensic foundations when dealing with handheld devices:

1. Evidence Collection

2. Evidence Preservation

3. Analysis

4. Reporting

These foundations are the core to dealing with all types of traditional digital devices. However, when it comes to the nontraditional devices like handhelds, these foundations change regarding how a forensic examiner would apply them.

There are certain levels of groundwork that have to be put into play to establish these foundations. The easiest way to understand and bring handheld forensics into your examination process is to compare and contrast what digital forensics has been dealing with for years in regard to hard drives and media, and show how handheld forensics are different. Table 4.1 breaks down each area of traditional forensics vs. the nontraditional in the areas of storage through examination.

Table 4.1 Comparison Table Traditional and Nontraditional Forensics

	Hard Drive and Media Forensics (Traditional)	Handheld Forensics (Nontraditional)
1.	Storage device requiring file system	Embedded system device
2.	Device is static	Device is active
3.	Larger built-in storage capacity	Smaller on-board storage capacity
4.	Forensic acquisition: bit stream imaging	Forensic: active memory imaging

File System Differences

- Hard Drive and Media Forensics—Storage device requiring a file system
- Handheld Forensics—Embedded system device

As you can see, data on a handheld device is stored and handled differently from that on a hard drive. A hard drive has static memory, but a handheld device has active memory; a hard drive has large storage capacity, but a handheld device has very limited storage capacity; and so on. Because of this, the forensic processing of the data must be handled differently. Typically you will seize a hard drive or other piece of media and you know it will contain data associated with one of a few different file systems. These file systems can range from FAT, NTFS, to EXT2, but the base principle is the same; a file system manages the data.

Handheld devices are designed differently. They might have items associated or attached to them that have file systems, like media cards. But overall the data itself is bound to the actual device to gain its structure. To clarify, according to whatis.com, an embedded system is some combination of computer hardware and software, either fixed in its capability or programmable. It is specifically designed for a particular type of application device. The impact of this design in forensics is dramatic because the tools the examiner uses must understand not only the operating system on the device that chooses how the data is stored, but also the design of the device to the chip set level to gauge how much storage is available on the device. Beyond this, the tool must understand how to communicate with the device in order to gain access at a low enough level to acquire all data available on that device for evaluation.

An excellent example of this can be found in the earlier Palm OS PDA devices. These devices typically used a type of Dragonball processor as one of the main components on the device. This processor would determine the true capacity of the ROM (Read Only Memory) section of the device. The operating system would see a size that was reflected as smaller than what was actually writable to the device by the processor. The processor would set the size of memory allocation for the operating system to see, when in fact the device had more usable space that could be used by the savvy user. For the forensic examiner, it was crucial they used tools that would be able to communicate to the processor itself as opposed to the OS on the device in order to get all the potential evidence from the unit. The embedded nature of the device is what causes the extra steps to go into effect with the forensic processing.

Static versus Active

- Hard Drive and Media Forensics—Device is static
- Handheld Forensics—Device is active

When we say a device is static we do not mean that the device does not have the ability to change. Static means that, after the proper forensic procedure has been per-formed and followed, the device itself has no risk of changing while seized. In hard drive and media forensic a variety of different write protection devices are used to prevent this static state from changing. However, with a handheld device it is active even after proper seizure protocols have been followed.

To best understand the handheld device, I have always compared it to a very popular game, Tetris. The object of the game is to match up blocks into a solid line design that then disappears from the display. The handheld device is somewhat sim-ilar as it is actively moving around data on the device to form solid lines of storage to ensure optimal use of its limited storage capabilities. This active system is part of what makes the handheld devices harder to deal with in forensics.

In addition, a vast majority of handheld devices are also active wireless points ranging from the different cellular communication networks, to Bluetooth, to 802.11. They are all actively receiving some type of data. This makes the preservation foundation of forensics increasingly difficult, but not impossible as we will see walking through the seizure of these devices later.

Tools & Traps…

Preservation of Evidence

A basic rule in digital forensics is the preservation rule. Unlike other disciplines in forensics where small amounts of biological evidence must be destroyed to establish blood type, finger print, or even DNA matches, digital evidence must be preserved to the last bit or byte. This verification method typically is done through a computation of a mathematical hash value such as a MD5 or SHA1. If one single byte of data has changed the hash value will also change. The hash of digital evidence typically is done after the acquisition stage of the digital forensic process.

Storage Capacity Differences

- Hard Drive and Media Forensics—Large built-in capacity
- Handheld Forensics—Smaller on-board capacity

If there is one thing that has impacted the field of digital forensics more than anything else, it would have to be the dramatic change in cost and capacity of storage. It used to be that a gigabyte of storage would have cost around $5.00 per gigabyte. Now, at times, it is under $1.00 per gigabyte. The average consumer has gone from a standard hard drive of 8 gigabytes in size to not being able to find a drive under 80 gigabytes. This is 10 times the growth that was expected, and has made some paradigm shifts occur with hard drive and media processing. Besides the processing power needed to create a forensic image of the staggering amounts of hard drive space available to the average consumer, the man hours and ability to sift through the mountains of data associated with this much storage has become almost impossible to combat.

Handheld devices also have changed in their capacity, but not at the same dramatic rates as hard drives. Their on-board capacities have increase from 8 megabytes to over a gigabyte based on the storage structure of the device, which has had a huge impact on these small devices. Don't heave a sigh of relief with these small capacities, however. The counter to this is that the handheld systems require less space for one file than a hard drive would. The change is back to the core with the file systems on the devices and how they function. If you are never given a large space to live in you will find the most efficient method of using it. Since hard drives have always been larger, they have never had to account for their data as closely as that on the handheld device. Storage may be a race to see who can store what in a certain size, but the power will still remain in how the data will be put to this storage.

Imaging Techniques

- Hard Drive and Media Forensics—Forensic acquisition: Bitstream image
- Handheld Forensics—Forensic acquisition: Active memory image

This is probably the largest point of comparison and the one that is the hardest to comprehend for the seasoned forensic examiner.

Bitstream image is considered to be a bit-for-bit copy of all data associated with the media device, including all allocated and unallocated data.[1] This is a fundamental difference between a forensic image and a backup image that might be made using conventional software. The other fundamental difference is that a forensic image is verifiable and can be rechecked for accuracy.

Active memory image is similar to a bitstream image as it is copying allocated and unallocated data. Where it differs from a traditional bitstream image is that there is more data available on the device either reserved by the manufacturer or encrypted and locked from access, making it inaccessible to the examiner. These unique characteristics are where you see the properties associated with imaging the devices change. Another reason it is referred to as an active memory image is based on the fact the data itself is constantly moving and being reallocated. This prevents the verification step of the hash value from serving the same purpose. It is still verification to an image; however, it is a verification of an image at just one point and time. Another way to think of this type of image is through the term *snapshot forensics*. A snapshot of the device is taken and that is the point of verification for the examiner. This is discussed further later in the chapter.

Evidence Collection

Collection is a very sensitive area for forensics because if this stage is not handled properly the rest of the forensic process is not needed. Good collection tools and techniques are crucial to having good viable forensic evidence.

The basic rules of collection are somewhat simple in regards to handhelds:

1. Always know what you are looking for. This comes to point a lot with handheld devices. There is a very diverse range of devices that can easily blend into the environment. Cell/mobile phones in particular are designed

to be almost a digital chameleon. Devices are now starting to look like everyday items such as pens, watches, and even makeup cases. The potential is endless and with so many different things to look for, our digital collection process just has gotten harder.

The phone shown in Figure 4.1 is a good an example of how modular devices have become: a multiposition camera was a major selling point for this particular device.

Figure 4.1 An Example of How Modular Devices Have Become

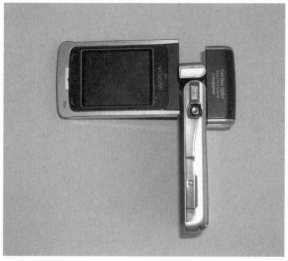

2. Always remember, multiple points of evidence are available. Handheld devices are rarely seen alone. Most of the time they will be seized as accessories to larger desktop or laptop systems. However, we now even accessorize our accessories. Figure 4.2 shows an example of a standard handheld media card. Notice the form factor being smaller then a fingerprint. However, the fingerprint it holds can make or break a case.

Figure 4.2 An Illustration of How Small the Media Associated with Handhelds Have Become

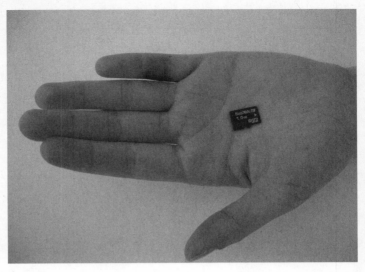

In addition to the digital points of evidence, it is important to remember that biological evidence also exists. With handheld devices, especially with the excessive contact, they have the suspects biological "ports," imprints of the suspect's person can still be found on the devices. Always handle with care and consult a specialist in the appropriate forensic discipline for forensic advice associated with the collection and handling.

Taking these somewhat simple collection principles and applying them for everyone that gets involved in the collection process can be very difficult. Most of the time, digital evidence is now collected in the field by what have come to be known as first responders.

First Responder

Typically, first responders are not directly trained in the field of digital evidence, so it is important to get them the basic procedures and protocols to best provide a forensic lab with the most viable evidence. However, doing so in a manner that is applicable to their skills and interests is somewhat difficult. To make things easier for most first examiners when dealing with handheld evidence, the handling and collection process has been broken down by device type. This is a very general method but has been found to be helpful to make sure the proper handling is done.

NOTE

A first responder is an individual first in contact with a forensic scene.

Simple cards, like the ones shown in Figures 4.3 to 4.6, have been designed so that the first responder can carry them on their person. Each card is separated by the type of handheld device.

Figure 4.3 PDA Devices: The Front of the First Response Card

Figure 4.4 PDA Devices: The Back of the First Response Card

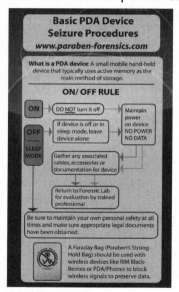

Figure 4.5 Cell/Mobile Devices: The Front of the First Response Card

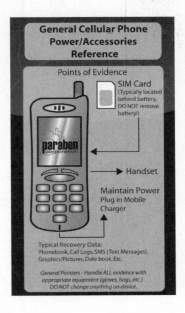

Figure 4.6 Cell/Mobile Devices: The Back of the First Response Card

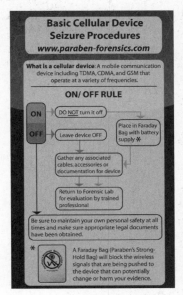

These evidence-handling cards are provided free by Paraben Corporation to departments or organizations to help them educate and facilitate the proper evidence handling of handheld devices.

Requests should be sent to cards@paraben.com.

Collection to Handling

With handheld devices, the first interaction with the device can be the most crucial. To understand the crucial points of handling associated with each handheld device, they have been broken down here into step-by-step instructions.

PDA Handling

1. Maintain the power on the device. The power on the device is what allows the device to maintain the data associated with it. Most of the PDA devices maintain potential evidence in RAM (random access memory) and, without power, this memory is cleared on the device. There are a variety of devices that are now designed to help maintain power to a handheld device

without a physical power supply. Most of these devices are battery powered and can be purchased through a forensic software provider or through a retail store.

Figure 4.7 shows an example of one of the commercially available power supplies for phones and PDA devices. The different tips can be attached based on the model.

Figure 4.7 A Commercially Available Power Supply for Phones and PDA Devices

2. Gather all accessories, manuals, cables, and such. Remember that even our accessories have accessories nowadays, and it is important that all items that can potentially be associated with the devices are gathered as well. There are a lot of accessories that will affect the device's ability to run without them being present. It is important to remember that when in doubt you should take it with you.

3. Wireless devices need special handling. With all wireless devices, it is important to remember that you have to do your best to block the wireless signal from connecting to the device. This is discussed more in the cellular

evidence handling section. However, some PDA devices do have the ability to turn the wireless functionality off through a simple switch or through the device interface. Depending on what type of device you are working with, this does have a risk of changing data on the device; it is recommended to follow the Faraday rules that are associated with cellular device handling as the best practice.

Cellular Handling

1. Maintain power on the device. Most cellular devices are not as power dependent as the PDA device is, however they can also be sensitive to power. Power helps the device maintain the last state it was left in by your suspect, so for example if your suspect has entered a PIN code into the cell phone, the device will remain authenticated as long as you maintain the same state on the device.

2. Control the wireless to the device. Wireless access of a cellular device can create a rather tricky situation when dealing with it in the field. If the device is still actively receiving signals from the tower, there is a risk that additional phone calls, text messages, or even damaging applications from another source involved could be received by the phone, which all could ruin your potential evidence. To protect the device from these types of risks, the use of Faraday technology typically is deployed. The principle of a Faraday device is to act as a cage for wireless signals. The Faraday cage will cause the signals from the device to bounce back onto the device, preventing it from escaping. Figure 4.8 is an example of a first responder bag for handheld devices that acts as a Faraday cage.

3. There are other options besides commercial bags that can be used as a Faraday cage by first responders, but depending on the type of materials used and the type of device it is enclosing, you will receive varying results.

Figure 4.8 An Example of a Wireless Protection Bag for Cell and PDA Devices

4. Gather all potential accessories. When in doubt, teach first responders to take anything and everything. There are a large variety of accessories that are designed to connect or communicate with a cell phone When in doubt, it is always better to seize the device and sort through these accessories in a controlled lab environment to determine their forensic viability.

5. Cellular devices have a very unique seizure issue associated with their cables. Each cellular cable can be proprietary or unique to the device. So, if the cable is available on scene it is strongly recommended that it be seized. There are excellent third-party cable kits (see Figures 4.9 and 4.10) that have been put together by forensic as well as commercial companies that are also recommended to be part of your standard lab equipment.

Figure 4.9 An Example of a Comprehensive Cable Kit (Device Seizure Toolbox) for PDA and Cell Devices

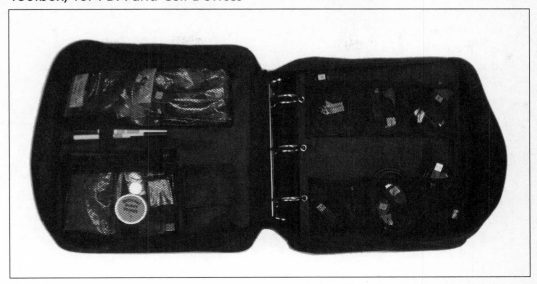

Figure 4.10 An Example of a Cable Provided with the DataPilot Cable Kit

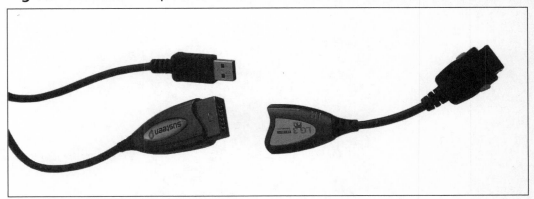

The preceding guidelines are based on available testing and devices that were available when this publication was put together. As technology evolves, so will the techniques required to deal with that technology in forensics.

Evidence Preservation

Typically, the preservation stage is associated with the actual processing of the evidence. Each forensic examiner will process evidence in a different manner since they were taught or based on their own organization's associated standard operating procedures. Following is a list of guidelines to follow in evidence preservation to aid in the proper process despite the type of tool that is used.

Preservation is based primarily on retaining consistent results that are verifiable through method and end content. This part of processing is what makes digital forensics more than just the use of software but the formulation of a process. The following are recommendations for establishing a proper preservation process in a lab environment.

Maintain the Device

The device will always be in an active, volatile state and it is important that as little information as possible change on that device. Once a device arrives in a lab, it is important that it be checked for power and to make sure the wireless signal, if applicable, is still being blocked. For most lab environments, it would be difficult to make the entire lab a Faraday cage so smaller Faraday devices typically are used—see Figure 4.11.

Figure 4.11 The StrongHold Box Is an Excellent Lab Tool for Processing Cell and PDA Devices

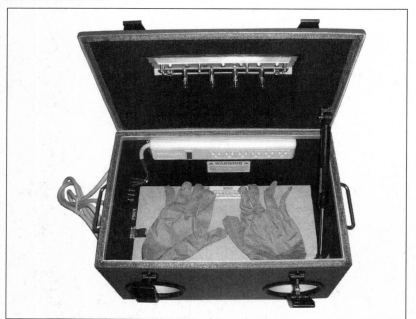

These types of devices are more convenient than using a bag system once the device itself is required to interact with a computer system for a forensic acquisition.

Part of maintaining a device is also having a realistic expectation of what can be maintained. One of the differences between processing a static digital evidence item such as a hard drive and processing an active item such as a handheld device is that the active item will have the risk of the hash verification changing. The hash verification that typically is done at the end of the acquisition process is used to prove that the process is repeatable and to mathematically prove that the data has not changed. However, with handheld devices the system is constantly actively processing data and there is a risk that the data itself might change. This change would then also affect the hash value. This is where the step of maintaining the device comes into play. Once an acquisition is completed, the device acquisition file can be verified and the analysis stage can begin. At the end of the analysis stage, a reverification of the data that has already been acquired can be performed and then that can be used to show that the analysis process did not affect the acquisition file. This is commonly referred to as snapshot forensics. Imagine the shift in paradigms that would need to take place for the traditional hard drive forensic examiner who has always based examinations on the basis that data is static and does not change without being altered by an outside force.

Maintain a Forensic Data Connection

There are a lot of different methods by which a handheld device can talk to another device. Cables, Bluetooth, IrDA are a few, but a lot of these connection options also hold pitfalls for the forensic examiner. Sometimes the easiest option for connection to a device can be a Bluetooth or IrDA connection; however, these connections are not considered to be traditionally forensic either. Both of these types of connections allow for an open communication port on the evidence device. Once this port is open, a variety of things can happen to the device. An example of this is with a typical Bluetooth connection on a phone (see Figure 4.12). The connection opens the device to be modified by programs that call through that communication port. The write protection through some of the wireless options is not available, forcing a hard position for a forensic examiner. Can they verify with absolute certainty that no one else utilized that open communication method to alter the evidence? For some devices, this is the only communication method available and this acts as a short level justification. Most devices, however, have other options that are considered to be more forensically sound. Cable communication is always best for connection in a forensic acquisition with a handheld device because it maintains the device better. It also is verifiable in court based on the communication protocols written for the device and cable.

Figure 4.12 An Example of the Proprietary Connections That Are Found for Cell and PDA Devices

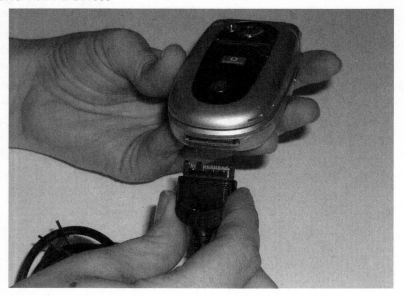

Forensic Grade Tools

There are many tools that are available in the commercial market for handheld data use. These tools vary in function from phone book downloads to ring tone transfer tools and each have their place in consumers' toolkits. However, the use of commercial tools that have not been forensically validated in handheld forensics can be a dangerous game.

1. Always test your tool and make sure you have a verification method in place for the data it provides.

2. Check the source of your tool; make sure it comes from a provider that is willing to support you in court.

3. Understand your tool's limits and what it was designed to do. Never rely on just one tool for all your examinations. The use of a primary and secondary tool is always recommended to make sure you receive the best evidence possible.

Preservation is about a process and a process is simply thinking through what you need to accomplish and making sure the road you take is the best one. With all handheld devices, there will be many deviants in the road that will frustrate and annoy any examiner, but the evidence they provide can make or break a case with something as simple as a text message.

Analysis and Reporting

Analysis and reporting is based primarily on the tools that are used by your particular lab. Before starting any examination process, I always have recommended to find out as much as possible about what you are about to examine. When dealing with handheld devices, there are a couple very good Web resources that will allow you to look up information on the particular devices so you will have a better understanding of what you can expect in your evidence:

> www.phonescoop.com
>
> www.wireless-forensics.com
>
> www.phonefinder.com

Details on particular tools can be found in other manuscripts or from the manufacturers themselves.

Summary

Handheld forensics is more than just a new forensic discipline; it is a new lifestyle choice for the field of digital forensics. With new devices coming out every day and more and more of the population switching to the handheld addiction, this area of digital evidence will only grow and expand with time.

Bibliography

Kovacich, Dr. Gerald L. and William C. Boni. *High-Technology-Crime Investigators Handbook Working in the Global Information Environment*. Butterworth Heinemann, 2000.

Chapter 5

RFID: An Introduction to Security Issues and Concerns

by Dennis F. O'Brien

Dennis F. O'Brien is a private consultant, having held senior IT security positions within Bell Laboratories, AT&T, Citigroup, and other Fortune 100 financial sector enterprises. Mr. O'Brien, a well-known technical expert with more than 30 years of experience in the exploitation of controls, comes to us as a canary to discuss the kinds of "evil things" that can be done using well-intended, generally available tools and services such as radio frequency identification (RFID). Examining the big picture and then presenting realistic scenarios, such as destabilizing public faith in the financial services industry or corrupting an asset database through input data tampering, are examples of his work. He is known for his annual predictions of possible mal-events that may occur in the near future and what the results might be.

Introduction

The year was 1949 and the author George Orwell presented a chilling view of a future society, one where the *Ministry of Truth* works in the service of Big Brother, the ruler of a society not all that unfamiliar to people today. This chapter will focus on RFID technology and discuss the adoption of this well-intended technology, and the gradual eroding of acceptable usage until undesirable fringe implementations are possible.

RFID technology offers a method for a unique identifier or other prepro-grammed information to be transmitted to a receiving station upon request.

Background

Radio frequency identification (RFID) has been with us for quite a while. Airplanes are monitored and can be controlled through the use of RFID technology. Electronic door locks have been available for many years implementing RFID tech-nology, either alone or in a multifactor implementation. Although RFID technology was initially about inventory control, its functionality and applications have expanded significantly. And though the initial effort was to develop a cost-effective technology to allow for the tracking of a resource or inventory, current implementations go much further.

Early computer systems were designed to do a particular task. The UNIX system evolved through the concept that applications can be built using tools, with each tool designed to optimally perform a specific function. As the list of available tools grew, even greater efficiencies occurred. One of the results is that UNIX systems eventually were constructed using tools, such as the *C language*, which was designed on other UNIX systems.

The Internet was not designed by a central committee. It evolved—mutated may be a more appropriate term—by separate people and organizations building on the ideas of each other. The more it grew, the more evident the need for standards became. To influence standards, companies contributed resources to solving chal-lenges in areas that best suited their needs. As with most other evolution processes, the stronger implementations survived and the weaker ones were cannibalized or fell to the forgotten sidelines.

For the purposes of this document, the term *resource* will be used when referring to anything being tracked, animate or inanimate. Resources may include objects or people. An *interrogator* is a device having the minimal function to query a resource for some sort of message designed for further processing.

Early Implementations

Success or failure in business can be tied to the ability to control costs. Fixed costs are those over which there is little control. Discretionary costs are those that can be controlled in such a way as to affect the bottom line. Unsold product represents a cost that has not yet created a return in the investment. Therefore, the ideal situation has a company position sufficient product in the distribution chain so that it is available for timely customer distribution, while minimizing the amount of product in the same supply chain. In order to accomplish this, accurate counts of product are necessary. Throughout history, product counts frequently became less accurate as time passed, necessitating periodic recounts. In many cases, this inventory process would have to be performed outside the scope of the normal business day, and frequently occurred at a time when the enterprise was entirely shut down.

Manual Inventory

Manual inventory is a time- and effort-intensive process where the number of resources are counted manually so that an assessment can be made for a number of reasons, to include financial investment in "on hand stock."

Bar Codes

This method uses a system where a code, using magnetic ink, scannable characters, or an optically recognizable code, is printed on a resource. A typical function for this coding method allows for item counts to be decremented and for restocking of the items sold upon sale. Disadvantages of this method of control are that:

- Much of the process is still manual.
- It is easy to bypass.
- It provides one way, *write-once* transfer of information.

Global Source Tagging

This method uses an inventory control system where Electronic Article Surveillance (EAS) devices are attached to a resource with a purpose of reducing the risk of shoplifting. Tags frequently are attached to the internal package as part of the assembly process. These tags typically are located within a sealed product, typically directly behind the UPC barcode and parallel to the UPC bars. The tag is designed to activate a sensor when it passes within close proximity of the scanning device. These tags typically are disabled at the point of sale by use of a magnetic field.

Current RFID Implementations

As the technology improves, a wide variety of challenges are being dealt with using vastly differing methods, all centering on a *resource-interrogator* design to query the resource. Beyond that, vastly differing solution features and enhancements were made to suit individual project requirements, as shown by the following examples.

All airplanes use a transponder, designed to transmit an identification code to a receiver for resource management purposes, in this case, air traffic management and control. High technology traffic management signs are being installed in many metropolitan areas. If you look close, you will see both an observation camera and a RFID sensor used. This is done by reading a vehicle's *EasyPASS* or similar type device.

Unidirectional Information Flow

The air traffic transponder system, as just mentioned, is an example of a resource transmitting either fundamentally fixed, but ultimately changeable information.

Air Force One

An example of a need for a plane to change its transponder identification code occurs with Air Force One (AF1), the plane used by the President of the United States.

In this case, the identification of AF1 moves to whatever plane the president happens to be traveling on, superseding its own code; therefore the code sent can be manually adjusted.

Bidirectional Information Flow

Since RFID chips are full computers, including storage, the information stored within these tiny devices can be changed as the resource flows through the system. As with any other computer providing services, proper care should be exercised in providing the data. Whether provided by a mainframe or an RFID device, the same controls should be in place for accessing the data.

RFID Purposes

RFID systems support the tracking of resources. The purpose is to instantly see what is occurring in your supply chain, be it inventory or people, and empower you to make smarter decisions.

Major industry players such as Wal-Mart, the U.S. Department of Defense (DOD), and the North Atlantic Treaty Organization (NATO) strongly encourage top suppliers to implement RFID technology within delivered products. This technology allows for tracking of *resources* throughout all or part of their lifecycle.

The fundamental purpose of an RFID system is to enable data to be transmitted upon interrogation. The data typically is used to track the location of a resource as it moves through its lifecycle. Its movement during the lifecycle will have a direct impact on a wide variety of management systems such as resource location, and financial control systems. Every resource that is part of an RFID system has an entire computer, though very small, attached to it.

History tends to repeat itself. As we examine RFID, we will examine it through adherence to *best security practices* and *generally accepted industry standards* as applied to the seven layers of the OSI model.

Inventory Tracking

It is said that money is power, and those investing the money are currently controlling the direction in which RFID is going. RFID is not being implemented because companies want to incur the additional expense of tagging each item at a cost upward of one dollar per item tagged. It is viewed as a way to manage cost through managing resources.

Where Does RFID Fit In?

RFID is the key to comprehensive resource tracking and management. The financial advantages are becoming more evident with significant increases in the number of uses for the technology. As the technology grows, the need for international standards and guidance will become increasingly more evident in much the same way as the Internet grew as a critical resource. What the Internet did to packet transit, RFID will do to resource management and tracking. Systems that provide RFID-based services will be integrated to provide a worldwide linkage of just about every resource or asset on the planet. As we move forward, extreme care should be taken because this can be a double-edged sword along the lines of Orwell's timelessly written 1949 book, occurring just a little later than its title *1984*, and unfolding today.

Technology Involved

How RFID Works

The simplest description of how RFID works is that a radio transmitter sends a message to a radio receiver. These two radios communicate on an agreed-to frequency within the spectrum of all wavelengths. The following paragraphs provide a functional overview of the parts within a typical implementation of RFID.

NOTE

Remember that RFID technology will likely be a part of a more expansive system, which will interconnect with further reaching systems and clients in many cases.

Parts of an RFID System

An RFID system is made of the same parts as most other information technology systems. In this chapter, we will be focusing on the part of the system that:

- Stores the initial information to be passed
- Uses a radio as the information transport medium

A typical RFID system includes much the same as most other IT systems, especially since it frequently interfaces with many other applications and systems. The typical RFID system includes:

- TAG (Proximity Chip)
- Tag Reader
- Server
- Middleware
- Application software

The TAG

The TAG is composed of a microcomputer attached to an antenna. All input/output (IO) is performed through the antenna. RFID antennas relay the Electronic Product Code (EPC) information from cases and pallets to RFID readers.

Various models are available to meet portal, conveyor, and shelf installations. TAGs are designed so that they can be deactivated. This is intended to be done at a point of sale or equivalent. Compromised tags have been known to be deactivated prior to the end of their lifecycle.

Tags can be:

- Sewn into clothes
- Integrated within product labels
- ID cards
- Money
- Implanted within animals and people

TAG Readers

RFID readers provide exceptional flexibility in RFID design:

- High read rates
- Multiprotocol
- Multifrequency capabilities

They are useful in a wide variety of environments including dock doors, conveyor systems, stock rooms, smart shelf applications.

Server

The server is a device that the tag reader passes the received information to for processing by software.

Middleware

This typically *canned* software prepares the received messages for downstream processing.

Application Software

This is where most of the actual work is performed. It is at this layer where most controls should be in place to validate the information received. The application may include many other tools such as databases for preparation for the primary purpose to be achieved.

RFID Security from a Functional Perspective

Securing RFID should be similar to securing almost any other platform or technology, new or old. Guarding an asset starts with designing the protection in with the system as it is built. Unfortunately, in a desire to showcase functionality and additional features, controls are not implemented until after the project or technology is up and running. This results in piecemeal efforts being applied, as opposed to a comprehensive protection initiative being incorporated right from the start.

Can RFID Be Used for Security?

RFID technology can be used for security in a number of ways. For example, RFID badges can be used for access to unlock a door.

Advantages of this technology are:

- Ease of use
- Tacking based on something you have
- Event logging can be enabled

Disadvantages are:

- One factor authentication
- Can't tell who really accessed, unless accompanied with video surveillance
- Doors typically are managed by a non-IT department called building management.

Although the overall system should be under the control of building management, seldom is direct access allowed to the organization responsible for security.

WARNING

The son of the chairman of a corporation owned the franchise to the office cafeteria. The son had both a global access card key and a master key for the building. Since electronic locks are expensive, there are frequently doors that have only traditional mechanical keys for access accompanied by a sign that says "Do Not Use This Door." The cafeteria manager, having the master keys to the multitenant building, reassigned the location of over a million dollars of assets for his own personal ventures. He used the unmonitored, unlogged, back door to *relocate* the assets.

Can RFID, in and of Itself, Function Securely?

The answer is yes, but with a number of caveats. If your RFID implementation is nothing more than a chip responding with a value when in the presence of an induction field (for power), you have large areas for concern. The answer is the same as if you can secure an environment by providing a layer 3 solution. The time has come for more global standards and independent certification of the specific product used.

> **NOTE**
>
> What if a radio transmitter either resends the same message, or worse, sends multiple deceptive messages? Ah, the simple elegance of electronic warfare!

Can Systems Implemented Using RFID Technology Be Secure?

The answer is yes. Again, the answer comes with the caveat that the system is only as secure as the sum of its parts. No wait, it is much easier than that—the system can be secure if the protection is end-to-end and does not lose integrity or is not subject to tampering while in transit over any and all transports used. Therefore the answer is that, as with many other information protection solutions, strong *originator-to-application authentication* is necessary to establish the validity of the sender, and an appropriate level of encryption is necessary to safeguard that being sent or stored.

Spy Chips or Consumer Value Tags?

Is it a bug or is it a feature? Is Internet SPAM unwanted junk or is it of great value to someone? Who is empowered to make those decisions?

On one hand, it may be convenient just to grab a product off the shelf and walk out the door. On the other hand, how do you feel about advertising being targeted to you and your "E-profile as you walk through a store"? What would you think if, as you walk through with your new date, most of your targeted ads were for bail bond services?

The Electronic Product Code (EPC), an RFID Specification/Standard

The AutoID Center, having performed much of the original work, closed its doors in September 2003 with EPCGlobal being set up to continue its work of commercializing EPC technology. EPC Class RFID labels offer long read ranges and are suitable for supply chain environments. Data can be written to Class 1 labels, whereas Class 0 labels are read-only.

EPC Generation 1

This early generation is basically the equivalent of a wireless barcode. It is easily spoofable and replayable. Systems implementing this standard appear to be susceptible to the greatest number of attacks, from replay through spoofing and high power radio transmission.

EPC Generation 2

This is the current standard, with features that are believed to cause increased risk.

EPC Generation 3

This is a significantly improved standard, adding authentication and encryption to the TAG-Inquisitor data path.

RFID Frequencies

Each RFID implementation runs on a specific frequency that was specifically selected based on the optimum characteristics of that frequency. These are typically short-range, low-powered TAG-Inquisitor pairs that tend to operate on frequency bandwidth *chunks* reserved for research. Many governments have regulated frequency allocation with vast differences existing. The result is that worldwide, a wide variety of standards and implementations currently exist, resulting in compatibility issues at the heart of a technology designed to seamlessly integrate resource movements.

On a special note, since all frequencies can be disrupted through sending interference (jamming), the reliability of the messages can be affected. A good application can frequently determine that an error has occurred in processing and reinterrogate. This functionality is typically an application layer function.

Low Frequency (LF) Band

Characteristics of a LF band include the following:

- Frequency Bandwidth: 30–300 Kilohertz
- Most common RFID range: 125–134 Kilohertz
- Operating distance: < 3 feet

Typical uses are for access control and payments. LF devices work well when implanted in humans and animals because LF RFID TAGS in many ways are resistant to shielding. They are not typically used for tagging objects (resources) for movement.

High Frequency (HF) Band

Characteristics of a HF band include the following:

- Frequency Bandwidth: 3–30 Megahertz
- Most common RFID range: 13.56 Megahertz
- Operating distance: < 3 feet

Typical uses of a HF band are, for example, when many items are in close proximity. It works well with liquids and metals.

Ultra High Frequency (UHF) Band

Characteristics of UHF bands include:

- Frequency Bandwidthn   860 to 960 Megahertz
- Most common US RFID range: 902 to 928 Megahertz
- Operating distance: 30 to 40+ feet
- Typical uses: access control and payments—frequently used for access
- Divided into 124 channels
- Ideal for reading every resource going through a door, accurately
- Has trouble working through liquids and metals
- Great for supply chain management
- Frequency range is easily reflected and absorbed

Table 5.1 lists UHF requirements by region.

Table 5.1 UHF Band Requirements by Region

	UHF Frequency	Power	Comment
AU	918–926 Megahertz	1 Watt	
China	915 Megahertz		Conflicts with GSM
Europe	865.6–867.6 Megahertz	2 Watt	
Japan	952–964 Megahertz		New
US	902–928 Megahertz	4Watt Shared between 128 channels	Shared – 20% import

Microwave Band

Characteristics of the microwave band include:

- Frequency Bandwidth: Above 415 megahertz
- Most common RFID range: 2.45 gigahertz
- Operating distance: Up to 30 foot range

Frequency–Based Information Protection Concerns

Radio frequencies are subject to jamming, where another signal appears on the same frequency or bandwidth specifically designed to disable communications. Interference caused by any one of a number of possible means can also provide disruption of transmission if some sort of error correction methodology is not in place. The lack of international standards keeps a uniform solution from being recommended at the present time. Summing up frequency concerns, there are three main factors—speed, accuracy, and distance. You can have only two out of the three in most implementations.

Active and Passive RFID Comparison

In this section we compare the requirements for active and passive RFID systems (see Table 5.2).

Table 5.2 Active and Passive RFID Comparison

	Active RFID	Passive RFID
TAG power source	Internal to TAG	RF from reader
TAG battery	Yes, possibly line voltage source	No
Availability of TAG power	Continuous	Only within field of the reader
Required signal strength from reader to TAG	Low	High; must power the TAG
Required signal strength from TAG to reader	High—Can do 100 meters or more; 100 MPH or more reliably	Low; typically under 3 meters, less than 3 MPH

Characteristics of Active RFID Systems

Basically, active RFID systems involve tags that transmit at all times, typically because they operate on their own power. Active systems frequently transmit greater distances and at all times.

Characteristics of Passive RFID Systems

Passive RFID implementations involve a TAG that typically receives its power through induction. Since power is received in this manner from the inquisitor, the response will typically be one designed for short distance reception, based on the characteristics of the radio spectrum (frequency) used.

Table 5.3 compares the characteristics of active and passive RFID systems.

Table 5.3 Characteristics of Active and Passive RFID Systems

	Active RFID	Passive RFID
Effective range	Long range (100+ meters)	Short or very short range (3m or less)
Multitag collection	Collects 1000s of tags over a 7 acre region from a single reader Collects 20 tags moving at > 100 MPH	Collects hundreds of tags within 3 meters from a single reader. Collects 20 tags moving at 3 MPH or slower
Sensor capability	Can continually monitor and record sensor input, data/time stamp for sensor events	Ability to read and transfer sensor values only when tag is powered by reader No date/time stamp
Data storage	Large read/write data storage (128KB) with sophisticated data search and access capabilities available	Small read/write data storage (e.g., 128 bytes)

Software RFID Tools

In 2004, Lukas Grunwald released a software tool called *RFDump*, which allows a user to rewrite the data stored within an RFID chip. This tool requires an RFID reader and a PC. Retail fraud is a concern for the misuse of this tool. Additional information on this tool can be found at www.rf-dump.org.

New RFID Marketing Techniques

One European producer has RFID tags for inclusion hidden within the labels of clothing.

Authorizing Access to Program an RFID Chip

An RFID chip is similar to any other computer and as such warrants the use of identification using strong one-time password technology. Like any other access control process, the entire data path used within the authentication process should be encrypted.

US Patent Application 20020165758

Identification and tracking of persons using RFID-tagged items

Abstract:

A method and system for identifying and tracking persons using RFID-tagged items carried on the persons.

Previous purchase records for each person who shops at a retail store are collected by POS terminals and stored in transaction database. When a person *carrying or wearing* items having RFID tags enters the store or other designated area, a RFID tag scanner located therein scans the RFID tags on that person and reads the RFID tag information. The RFID tag information collected from the person is correlated with transaction records stored in the transaction database according to known correlation algorithms.

Based on the results of the correlation, *the exact identity of the person or certain characteristics about the person can be determined.* This information is used to monitor the movement of the person through the store or other areas.

Authority to Monitor RFID Transmissions

Only the future will give the answer to these questions, typically through challenges to lawful use. Who of the following will gain authority to monitor RFID transmissions?

■ Justice department (Title 5, 18, 20, 50)

■ Courts (phone, Internet, RFID)

■ Intelligence groups

■ Lawyers

■ Stalkers

Providing Verifiable Protection

In order to protect any asset, you must view it from all applicable layers of the OSI model, both while in static storage and while in transit. Failure to do so, for whatever reason, might yield unplanned results.

- Exploit the weakest OSI layer.

- In-transit versus in-storage

- *Integrity* belongs at the application layer, whereas *reliability* can be implemented at all other layers.

- What about dishonest insiders?

RFID Chip Placement

The RFID chip typically is placed in close proximity to the bar code on the package. When attached as a labeled barcode, it can most frequently be found on the underside of the barcode label.

A Few RFID Uses

The following items outline just a few of the uses for this exciting technology. Additional uses will be referenced elsewhere within this chapter.

Passports (Passive)

Effective October 2006, all U.S. passports will include a RFID chip including, but not necessarily limited to name, nationality, sex, date of birth, place of birth, and digitized photograph of the passport holder.

Public Transportation Passes (Active, battery operated)

A common use is a public transportation pass system (e.g., EZ-Pass, FasTrak, etc.), where an RFID transmitter typically is located on the windshield of a vehicle. As the vehicle passes a toll scanner, the toll amount is deducted from the users account automatically. Look to see tokens of this type being used at commercial fast food establishments in the near future.

> **WARNING**
>
> Be aware that these cards are monitored without prior warning at many other locations, such as traffic management sites along the highway. Next time you are a passenger under a high tech traffic sign, examine it for cameras, RFID readers, and so on. It is likely just a matter of time until tickets are generated based on RFID technology calculations

Exxon Mobil SpeedPass (Active)

This is an RFID implementation initially used for paying for gas services. You will see its technology used in a variety of additional devices in the future, such as bank cards.

Conference Badges (Passive)

Many conferences now issue you an ID badge equipped with RFID technology. This badge may include lots of information at the discretion of the conference provider. Each time you move by a vendor booth, your information is passed to their scanner to become part of their database.

Tagging People as Resources (Passive)

One planned place for tagging people with an RFID chip is on their hands (the chip would be place in between the person's thumb and index finger).

Cow Chips (Passive)

Help track the origins and path the product has taken to slaughter. This technology has proven very useful in tracking problems with the food supply.

Cadaver Chips (Passive)

Cadaver chips are gaining popularity in that a chip can be placed with each resource so that in the event that a need exists to identify the cadaver at a later time, it can be done. At some future time, this may be the chip that contains the person's history.

Smart Shelves

The use of smart shelves will allow you to take an item off the shelf and walk out the store exit with it. Billing is automatic, and the item is automatically reordered.

Security TAG Concerns

Altering the Identity of Goods

Although shoplifting has been a concern throughout history, advances in technology lead people to rely more on the technology and less on the item being stolen. In many cases tags can be moved from one item to another so that the item being scanned will identify as a less costly item, therefore allowing the item to be removed while appearing to be legitimately purchased. The buyer can deny all if detected because they were unaware.

Another type of attack is to steal a controlled resource, while leaving the TAG behind either by itself or as a second tag on another item.

RFID Money

There are a wide variety of items that have an equivalency of currency in the world today:

- Two-way radio resort RFID *wristbands* (passive) are being issued to all guests that have either an established cash amount or the equivalent of the magnetic strip of one of your personal credit cards stored on them. These bands serve as your passport during your stay, and are intended to make you and your children's stay more seamless.

- Many banks and credit card providers have started sending updated credit cards (passive), each containing an RFID chip so that the customer can just wave the card in close proximity at the point of purchase, where you formerly needed to produce two-factor authentication, a card and a signature. Challenging a purchase may become harder unless more point of purchase video is also implemented.

- Poker chips (passive) are in use today to distinguish legitimate from counterfeit chips. With all the controls in a casino, tracking who has how much will be easier. The appropriate controls will be at the discretion of the chip provider.

- Taking money between countries using resort bands or casino chips is a concern.

NOTE

That $20 bill contains an RFID chip implanted near Andrew Jackson's eye. The myth claims that microwaving the bill three minutes will result in the chip burning. There are no RFID chips in either U.S. or European currency at this time.

Potentially Bad Uses

RFID as a technology is neither good nor bad. It is how the technology is used or misused that will determine whether the general public feels that it is good or bad. Experience has shown that the intentions for adopting widespread use of the technology are perfectly honorable and therefore should proceed. On the other hand, as with audio and video capture and duplication devices, there are vast areas for inappropriate uses, which even vary from country to country. The following is a listing of some potentially undesirable uses for the technology:

- Traversing a subway car or football game capturing passive data from credit or debit cards and such. A problem in early generations of the technology, but will hopefully someday no longer be a concern any more than interception of home walk-around phones.

- Retransmitting (active and passive) data using a more powerful transmitter. If the receiving application or service does not have the appropriate controls in place to evaluate overloads and inappropriate data patterns, this could cause massive disruption of service. How massive is a function of the criticality and interconnected systems.

- Reading all sorts of assets while in transit, and replaying the data elsewhere. Can data appear in two places at once? Can the data just pop in and out as it is used for fraudulent purposes?

- Electronic warfare applications. Let's leave that realm of possibilities to those specializing in that area.

- Detonators, remotely powered, can wait for their targets indefinitely.

- Wreaking havoc with DOD and NATO supply chain management. Possible disruption of accuracies within the supply chain have been known to alter the course of history.

- Remote disabling of a vehicle. (Out of one episode of Star Trek.) Of course this would all be done with *Big Brother* being the only one in possession of the digital certificate allowing this to happen.

- Terrorist activities.

An opposing view includes some items that may or may not be good based on your own values, such as:

- Significantly reduced underground economy.

- Significantly less hard-to-track political payoffs.

- Reduced bribes, at least cash ones.

- Tracked money; you will no longer be able to hide cash from Big Brother.

- Cash flow audit trails may be easier to follow once government cash flow databases are implemented.

- Cash payments to your home and lawn help will now be available for review.

- Every financial transaction verified through the OCC clearinghouse.

RFID Virus

It has been reported that an RFID buffer overflow bug could infect RFID databases at airports for baggage, and possibly passport databases to compromise confidential information.

- Attacks have been predicted to come in the form of a SQL injection or a buffer overflow attack.

- For demonstration purposes, researchers have created a proof-of-concept, self-replicating RFID virus.

The Future

RFID chips are being placed everywhere, maybe even on your person, without your knowledge or approval, having possible ramifications that you never intended.

WARNING

"Warning Will Robinson... Big Brother has determined that you should maintain a 50-foot buffer with the person you are with. Failure to do so may produce children that cause a burden on society."

Privacy vs. the government protecting us? What is the answer to the question of how much of each is reasonable?

How will it impact your life? Will the world be better for it or not?

RFID tracking information in the hands of lawyers? Imagine if RFID inquisitors are placed in public places, like motel rooms by owners seeking to protect themselves by providing a more comprehensive audit trail.

> **NOTE**
>
> Big Brother is analyzing your life through your purchases. For example, a high school student recently purchased nitric acid, glycerin, and a container of baking soda at different stores. Should he or she be placed on a watch list?

Summary

In summary, the use of RFID technology has definite pros and cons. The debate on the use of the technology will likely go on for many years to come and new unintended results of the technology will likely appear in the media on a regular basis. With that in mind, do the benefits overshadow the risks? It will depend on which group you are speaking with. The use of this technology will likely become more of a moral or privacy issue as it rolls out further. I predict one thing though, and that is the technology and infrastructure will be pretty much in place before the general public knows what is happening. Then comes the use or misuse of the technology, depending on your perspective. Luckily each country has legal systems to resolve any issues and take corrective action. Simply put, if you think you may be doing something wrong, don't do it, because Big Brother may be watching...

Chapter 6

Open Source Intelligence
by Ron Green

Ron Green (CISSP, ISSMP) a Senior Vice President within the Information Security Business Continuity division of Bank of America, currently serves as an Information Security Business Continuity Officer supporting the Bank's Network Computing Group. He formerly managed a bank team dedicated handling cyber investigations, computer forensics, and Electronic Discovery. Prior to Bank of America, Ron was a Secret Service Agent and part of the agency's Electronic Crimes Agent Program (ECSAP). In addition to the investigative and protection work all agents perform ECSAP agents perform cyber investigations and computer forensics for the agency. Ron started with the Secret Service in its Phoenix Field Office, and then transferred to the agency's Headquarter to become part of the Electronic Crimes Branch (ECB). While part of ECB he provided support to the ECSAP agents in the field, worked on National and International cyber crimes cases, initiatives, and laws. He was the project manager for Forward Edge, and the Best Practice Guides for Seizing Electronic Evidence, version 2.0.

Ron graduated from the United States Military Academy at West Point earning a bachelor's degree in Mechanical Engineering, and he further earned a Graduate Certificate from George Washington University on Computer Security and Information Assurance. Ron currently serves as the Treasurer/Secretary for the Financial Services Information Sharing and Analysis Center (FS/ISAC), and a Board Member for the Institute for Computer Forensic Professionals. Ron currently lives in North Carolina with his wife, Cheryl. and their four children.

Introduction

Open Source Intelligence (OSINT) has a nice ring to its name. What *is* Open Source Intelligence? Simply put, it's the gathering of information from publicly available sources in order to develop a greater level of awareness or understanding. The Department of Defense more precisely defines OSINT as "intelligence that is produced from publicly available information and is collected, exploited, and disseminated in a timely manner to an appropriate audience for the purpose of addressing a specific intelligence requirement."[1] A good Open Source Intelligence program can provide a great deal of knowledge, create leverage in negotiations, enable smarter decisions regarding the selection of goods and services, help avoid pitfalls and hazards, and generate many other advantages useful in giving one group an edge over another. While there are many uses for Open Source Intelligence programs, the focus of this chapter is on the use of Open Source Intelligence to identify and help mitigate risks to security—particularly information security.

Open Source Intelligence is far from a new concept. Many states, businesses, academics, and individuals have always found uses for public information. Clearly, national intelligence services the world over have uncovered useful information by reading newspapers, listening to the airwaves of their adversaries, or looking up vital facts about their counterparts in encyclopedias and atlases. Businesses have learned from rival companies by following patents, reading product information, or reviewing public financial filings. What's different in the twenty-first century, and what makes Open Source Intelligence a great part of the whole package of intelligence gathering? The answer is the pervasiveness of the Internet and its use as a tool. This has been helped along by the explosion of information available today, much of it from sources where access was once denied. These key dynamics make Open Source Intelligence a truly relevant information gathering technique for both nation states and everyday citizens.

Given all this, in order to develop useful information products, it's important to bear in mind that the basic tenets of the intelligence process can be explained with five Ds.

Direction

It's hard to begin anything without having an idea of why you are doing it. Direction provides that guidance to move forward in order to deliver or meet a certain goal or objective. To be successful, an OSINT program must deliver expected information at appropriate times so as to support decision makers. But in order to deliver the right information to your client, you must know what their expectations are. Time must be set aside to work with those decision makers that receive the OSINT products. Gaining an understanding of key elements of the decision maker's process will help formulate the direction or mission for the OSINT function. From the decision maker, a clearly defined "Mission Statement" or goal for the decision maker can be used to set the stage for information collection and analysis.

Once the objective of the group has been identified, the goal of its information collection and analysis can be derived. What steps must be taken to complete the goal? As a simple example, let's establish that our aim is to go to a baseball game today. The subcomponents that must be accomplished to make this goal a reality are to (1) purchase a ticket, and (2) drive to the stadium. Thus, we've identified two simple subcomponents that must be achieved.

Next, review the subcomponents individually. Determine what might affect each subcomponent, or what information needs to be known to support the subcomponent. Going back to our example:

Subcomponent: Purchase a Ticket

- What are ticket prices?
- When are the games?
- Where are the games?
- Who is playing?

Rethink the subcomponents. Analyzing a subcomponent may reveal other views or contingencies that were not originally part of the stated goal, but that may help reach it. Try paraphrasing or broadening the scope of the subcomponent.

Subcomponent: Drive to the Stadium

- Can we walk to the stadium?
- Can we catch a bus to the stadium?
- Can we take a boat to the stadium?
- Should we take a taxi to the stadium?
- Can we watch the game on TV at home?

Provide counter views and identify both positive and negative potential impacts for each subcomponent. In looking at the subcomponents, review them for best- and worst-case scenarios, along with other things that might affect the success or failure of the subcomponent. For more complex subcomponents, it may be necessary to contact experts in those fields to flesh out a full set of focus areas. Continuing with our baseball game example:

Subcomponents: Purchase Ticket and Drive to the Stadium

- Would a traffic accident make it difficult to drive to the stadium?
- Can other major events cause congestion on the roads to the stadium?
- Are major celebrities or political figures going to attend the games?
- Could I be defrauded when I purchase the tickets?
- What will happen if there is heavy rain or a thunderstorm?

Once the analysis of the goal is complete, it is possible to develop key concepts or areas of focus. With the concepts and an understanding from the decision maker about time tables, it is possible to begin collecting information, and then process that information to develop the Open Source Intelligence products. From the example we started, we can derive the following concepts that would be of interest to the decision makers.

Concepts

- Pricing baseball tickets to include deals and plans that affect the price
- The scheduling of baseball games at local stadiums
- Directions and routes to the stadium
- Major local events scheduled during baseball games
- Frauds related to baseball tickets sales

Now that we have key concepts that will support the decision makers and provide them with information that is relevant, it is necessary to determine the appropriate intervals to provide reports and information to the decision makers. Too frequent reports will generate noise and take away focus. It will also produce a heavy burden on the collection and analysis efforts of the OSINT team. Too few reports and information that was once relevant may have expired or been rendered useless by the time it is given to the decision makers. Urgent updates may need immediate dissemination, while routine updates may come on a daily, weekly, or monthly schedule, as well as another that is relevant.

Also keep in mind that there are times when information is provided to a member of the organization that cannot be shared. This information could be provided as a classified briefing or come from a source that prefers anonymity. While the information provided may be too sensitive to share directly, it's possible the information (or something sufficiently close) exists in open-source information. Or, if too sensitive, the concept may be given, but not sources and details. Such directed collection efforts often results in a single special OSINT product that can be used to share relevant information.

Discovery

The second D is for Discovery: "Knowing who knows." This is the first step in the process, and is of vital importance. Knowing what sources of information exist to support the effort is critical. No program should confine itself to using only online sources, limiting the sources in this manner makes the program little more than a treasure hunt. Thankfully, some partnerships and forums exist that have common interests. The following are some groupings by area that may be of interest if you are in the discovery process yourself.

Sources of Information

In this section, we list various sources of information pertaining to Open Source Intelligence.

Cyberthreats

- **United States Secret Service, Electronic Crimes Task Force (www.ectf.usss.gov)** On October 26, 2001, President Bush signed into law H.R. 3162, the USA PATRIOT Act. The U.S. Secret Service was mandated by this act to establish a nationwide network of Electronic Crimes Task Forces. The concept of the ECTF network is to bring together not only federal, state, and local law enforcement, but also prosecutors, private industry, and academia. The common purpose is the prevention, detection, mitigation, and aggressive investigation of attacks on our nation's financial and critical infrastructure. The task forces exist in numerous Secret Service field offices, and each provides regional support to assist and gain the help of individuals and institutions in a geographic area.

NOTE

Of the cyberthreat information sharing groups, I find the USSS ECTFs the most open to sharing and to developing open partnerships. I believe their ability to forge these relationships is founded on their need to collaborate with state and local police and community businesses to be successful in their protection work... Or maybe I'm just biased since I was once a USSS agent.

- **Federal Bureau of Investigation, InfraGard (www.infragard.net)** InfraGard is a Federal Bureau of Investigation (FBI) program that seeks to gain support from the information technology industry and academia for the FBI's investigative efforts in the cyber arena. This program exists in many FBI field offices, and the national program is assigned to the FBI Cyber Division. InfraGard and the FBI have developed a relationship of trust and credibility in the exchange of information concerning various terrorism, intelligence, criminal, and security matters.

- **High Tech Crime Consortium (www.hightechcrimecops.org)** The High Tech Crime Consortium is a pool of experts in diverse professions such as intelligence analysis, investigation management, computer forensics investigation, crime analysis and research, computer programming, and software development, whose goal is to proactively respond to the need for developing high-tech investigative systems and software, and to increase awareness through the exchange of information and the sharing of knowledge and resources.

- **International High Tech Crime Investigation Association (www.htcia.org)** The High Technology Crime Investigation Association (HTCIA) is a group whose purpose is to encourage, promote, aid, and affect the voluntary interchange of data, information, experience, ideas, and knowledge about methods, processes, and techniques relating to investigations and security in advanced technologies among its membership.

- **Computer Crime and Intellectual Property Section (www.cybercrime.gov)** The Computer Crime and Intellectual Property Section (CCIPS) is an organization within the Department of Justice responsible for implementing the Department's national strategies in combating computer and intellectual property crimes worldwide. The group's Computer

Crime Initiative is a comprehensive program designed to combat electronic penetrations, data thefts, and cyber attacks on critical information systems. CCIPS attorneys aid in the prevention, investigation, and prosecution of computer crimes by working with other government agencies, the private sector, academic institutions, and foreign counterparts. These attorneys work to improve the domestic and international infrastructure—legal, technological, and operational—to pursue network criminals most effectively.

- **Forum for Incident Response Security Teams (www.first.org)** FIRST is an organization that has provided global leadership in incident response. Membership in FIRST enables incident response teams to more effectively respond to security incidents, both reactive and proactive. FIRST brings together a variety of computer security incident response teams from government, commercial, and educational organizations. FIRST aims to foster cooperation and coordination in incident prevention, to stimulate rapid reaction to incidents, and to promote information sharing among members and the community at large.

- **National Vulnerability Database (www.nvd.nist.org)** NVD is a comprehensive cyber security vulnerability database that integrates all publicly available U.S. government vulnerability resources and provides references to industry resources. It is based on, and synchronized with, the Common Vulnerabilities and Exposures (CVE) vulnerability naming standard.

- **CERT CC (www.cert.org)** CERT is a center of Internet security expertise, located at the Software Engineering Institute, a federally funded research and development center operated by Carnegie Mellon University. CERT studies Internet security vulnerabilities, researches long-term changes in networked systems, and develops information and training to improve security. CERT once meant Computer Emergency Response Team, but the organization has chosen to forgo this acronym and simply retain the name CERT.

- **US-CERT (www.us–cert.gov)** The United States Computer Emergency Readiness Team (US-CERT) is a partnership between the Department of Homeland Security and the public and private sectors. US-CERT was established in 2003 to protect the nation's Internet infrastructure. It coordinates the defenses against, and responses to, cyber attacks across the nation. US-CERT is also responsible for analyzing and reducing cyber threats and vulnerabilities, disseminating cyber threat warning information, and coordinating incident response activities. US-CERT interacts with federal agencies, industry, the research community, state and local governments, and others to disseminate reasoned and actionable cyber security information to the public.

Physical Threats

- **ASIS International (www.asisonline.org)** Formerly the American Society for Industrial Security (ASIS), ASIS International is one of the largest organizations for security professionals, with more than 33,000 members worldwide. ASIS was established in 1955, and it is dedicated to increasing the effectiveness and productivity of security professionals by developing educational programs and materials that address broad security interests.

- **Overseas Security Advisory Council (www.ds-osac.org)** The Overseas Security Advisory Council (OSAC) is a federal advisory committee with a U.S. government charter to promote security cooperation between American business and private sector interests worldwide and the U.S. Department of State.

Financial Service Sector

- **Financial Services / Information Sharing and Analysis Center (www.fsisac.com)** Created in 1999, the Financial Services Information Sharing and Analysis Center (FS/ISAC) was established by the financial services sector in response to 1998's Presidential Directive 63. That directive—later updated by 2003's Homeland Security Presidential Directive 7—mandated that the public and private sectors share information about physical and cyber security threats and vulnerabilities to help protect the U.S. critical infrastructure. The FS/ISAC gathers reliable and timely information from financial services providers, commercial security firms, federal, state, and local government agencies, law enforcement, and other trusted resources. From these sources, the FS/ISAC is positioned to disseminate physical and cyber-threat alerts and other critical information to the financial services sector. This information includes analysis and recommended solutions from leading industry experts.

- **BITS (www.bitsinfo.org)** At one time, BITS stood for the Banking Industry Technology Secretariat like CERT CC, but BITS is no longer an acronym. It is a nonprofit, industry consortium whose members are 100 of the largest financial institutions in the United States. BITS was formed by the CEOs of these institutions to serve as the strategic "brain trust" for the financial services industry in the e-commerce, risk management, payments, and technology arenas. BITS addresses emerging issues where financial services, technology, and commerce intersect, acting quickly to address problems and galvanize the industry. BITS goals are to identify issues and develop strategic recommendations. Additionally, BITS facilitates cooperation between the financial services industry and other sectors of the nation's critical infrastructure, government organizations, technology providers, and third-party service providers.

Other Information Sharing and Analysis Centers

- **Communications ISAC (www.ncs.gov/ncc)** In January 2000, the NCC was designated an ISAC for telecommunications in accordance with PDD-63. The NCC-ISAC will facilitate the exchange among government and industry participants regarding vulnerability, threat, intrusion, and anomaly information affecting the telecommunications infrastructure.

- **Electricity Sector ISAC (www.esisac.com)** The Electricity Sector Information Sharing and Analysis Center (ESISAC) serves the electricity sector by facilitating communications between electricity sector participants, federal governments, and other critical infrastructures. It is the job of the ESISAC to promptly disseminate threat indications, analyses, and warnings, together with interpretations, to assist electricity sector participants in taking protective actions.

- **Emergency Management and Response ISAC (www.usfa.dhs.gov/fireservice/subjects/emr-isac)** Emergency Management and Response - Information Sharing and Analysis Center (EMR-ISAC) was established by the U.S. Fire Administration to collect, analyze, and disseminate Critical Infrastructure Protection (CIP) information in support of federal government initiatives, and encourage the leaders, owners, and operators of the ESS throughout the nation to practice CIP.

- **Highway ISAC (www.highwayisac.org)** The Highway Information Sharing and Analysis Center (ISAC) is operated by the American Trucking Associations (ATA), in partnership with the state and national trucking associations and conferences of the ATA Federation, numerous other national highway transportation organizations in the Highway Watch

Coalition in cooperation with the Department of Homeland Security, for the benefit of the entire highway transportation sector.

- **Information Technology – ISAC (www.it-isac.org)** The Information Technology – Information Sharing and Analysis Center (IT-ISAC) is a trusted community of security specialists from companies across the Information Technology industry dedicated to protecting the Information Technology infrastructure that propels today's global economy by identifying threats and vulnerabilities to the infrastructure, and sharing best practices on how to quickly and properly address them. The IT-ISAC also communicates with other sector-specific ISACs, enabling members to understand physical threats, in addition to cyber-based threats. Taken together, these services provide members with a current and coherent picture of the security of the IT infrastructure.

- **Multi-State ISAC (www.msisac.org)** The MS-ISAC is a voluntary and collaborative organization with participation from all 50 states and the District of Columbia. The mission of the MS-ISAC, consistent with the objectives of the National Strategy to Secure Cyberspace, is to provide a common mechanism for raising the level of cyber-security readiness and response in each state and with local governments. The MS-ISAC offers a central resource for gathering information on cyber threats to critical infrastructure from the states and provides two-way sharing of information between the states, as well as with local government.

- **Surface Transportation ISAC & Public Transportation ISAC (www.surfacetransportationisac.org)** Ninety-five percent of the U.S.'s critical infrastructures are privately owned. Originally detailed in Presidential Decision Directive (PDD-63), Homeland Security Presidential Directive (HSPD-7) encourages the creation of private sector Information Sharing and Analysis Centers (ISACs) to protect this infrastructure from attack. At the request of the U.S. Department of Transportation, this ST-ISAC was formed. The PT-ISAC has since become an "ISAC within an ISAC," to take advantage of the overarching ST-ISAC to realize increased economies of scale.

- **Supply Chain ISAC (https://secure.sc-investigate.net/SC-ISAC/)** The Supply Chain Information Sharing and Analysis Center (SC-ISAC) collects, analyzes, and disseminates integrity and security threat information across the supply chain industry.

- **Water ISAC (www.waterisac.org)** The Water Information Sharing and Analysis Center (WaterISAC) is a comprehensive and up-to-the-minute online resource of security information for America's drinking water and wastewater utilities. It provides a unique link between the water sector and federal environmental, homeland security, law enforcement, intelligence, and public health agencies.

WARNING

The online contact information has been provided for each information sharing group listed. Don't depend solely on those links to keep yourself informed, however. Much of the true information sharing takes place in face-to-face meetings, over a meal or drinks. To get the most out of a group, you will need to join them and support some of the initiatives that don't directly affect you. As you get to know them and they get to know you, they will come to confide in you and share some of the real details of what they encounter.

Search Engines

Search engines are extremely useful tools that can provide users with access to information. Knowing how to effectively use a search utility is important in increasing the likelihood that the results provided will be relevant to your collection effort. A number of good search engines are available. Most are free, but all have their own nuances. Understanding the proper syntax for searching and having a basic understanding of how the tools work will help ensure they provide the needed information.

Individual Search Engines

Individual search engines are systems that compile their own searchable database of the Web. These systems catalogue or index the site by using Web crawlers, spiders, or robots that roam the Web looking for new information to index. When a user searches with an engine, the search criteria or terms are checked against the index, and based on the terms' frequency in the document and their location in relation to each other, a relevancy number is provided. The actual working processes that establish what is indexed, how a search is executed, and how the relevancy rating is assigned differ greatly from search engine to search engine.

Examples of individual search engines include:

- Google (www.google.com)

- Yahoo (www.yahoo.com)

- Alta Vista (www.altavista.com)

- Lycos (www.lycos.com)

Meta Search Engines

Meta Search Engines do not have their own individual database to search. Nor do they search the Internet to find a page of relevancy. Instead, they capitalize on querying other search databases. The results they provide cover the use of a number of individual search utilities. The results are then blended together, which should yield a cross-spectrum search and should theoretically produce a list of results with greater relevancy.

Examples of meta search engines include:

- Dogpile (www.dogpile.com)

- Vivisimo (http://vivisimo.com)

- Kartoo (www.kartoo.com)

- Mamma (www.mamma.com)

Deep Web Search Utilities

The deep Web is primarily information that is stored information on databases. The reason it is called the "deep Web" or "Invisible Web" is because it consists of data on the Internet that cannot be indexed by individual search utilities. The deep Web is estimated to be 500 times the size of the known Web. Most of this information is housed on databases. These are databases that cannot be scanned or accessed by the individual search utilities. Nevertheless, tools exist that allow users to search these databases and receive relevancy information as well as notices of updates.

Examples of deep Web search utilities include:

- Search Systems (www.searchsystems.net)

- Genius Find (www.geniusfind.com)

- Infomine (http://infomine.ucr.edu)

- Direct Search (www.freepint.com/gary/direct.htm)

- Invisible Web (www.invisible-web.net)

- Complete Planet (www.completeplanet.com)

Fee-Based Services

Fee-based sources allow for the recovery of very useful information and research, but of course there is the caveat that it costs money. With other Internet-based utilities, there is the ability to remain somewhat anonymous. A greater discussion of why you may wish to keep some anonymity when conducting your collection efforts is detailed in the section titled "Collection Trade Craft." In using a fee-based service, the ability to remain anonymous disappears, so when using the service, realize that your actions may be logged. The logging should not be a problem, but know that the potential exists for someone to review your actions.

> **NOTE**
>
> Using fee services can be very helpful. The information they provide can be crucial, and much of the information they possess is not, nor can it be, provided by free solutions. Generally, no concerns exist about the logging or the potential for log analysis, but when forming collection plans and executing them, a little paranoia can do you good.

Another consideration when using fee-based services is that some skill or essential knowledge may be required to use them effectively to obtain information relevant to a particular issue or collection tactic. Without the necessary level of understanding, the information collected may be completely irrelevant. The service may charge for the results obtained, so collecting useless info may become a very costly endeavor. The following are examples of fee-based services that may be supportive of your collection efforts.

- Factiva (www.factiva.com)

- Lexis-Nexis (www.lexis-nexis.com)

- Dialog (www.dialog.com)

- I-Defense (http://labs.idefense.com/bs.idefense.com)

- Cyviellance (www.cyveillance.com)

While many potential sources of information have been identified in this section, this is far from a comprehensive list. The information provided is intended to offer a starting point, and although the Web site of the sources are identified, true understanding and capabilities assessment requires personal contact with the groups. Personal knowledge and assessment will help identify those products, services, or contacts produced by these groups that are relevant, reliable, and useful. This candid understanding of sources makes up the third D of Open Source Intelligence, the "D" of Discrimination.

Discrimination

In OSINT, "discrimination" is the art of "Knowing What's What." Numerous sources of information exist to tap into. Many contacts are freely available, while many are fee-based vendors. Having a wide base of information is a necessary component of the program, but just as elsewhere in life, you can have too much of a good thing. For instance, having too much information that does not correlate easily can end up burning more of your time and resources than can be justified. Too much unfocused info coming in can be described as noise. Resources tied up trying to identify golden nuggets of info from noise ends up delaying analysis and thus crippling the development of useable intelligence estimates.

Bias is another consideration within the discrimination phase. Knowing why a source is willing to provide you with information is critical in assessing the value of the information provided. Everyone has a bias, it is sometimes obvious, but more often than not predispositions are subtle and not readily evident. A way to identify some of a source's bias is to review the source's history, objectively read works produced by the source, and review critiques, evaluations or directly ask for feedback from others who have previously engaged the source. Of course, with the latter analysis, keep in mind that those providing feedback also have their own bias. These are parts of effective source evaluation. Remember that you have your own bias as well, which may affect your interpretation of the source material and perhaps slant your analysis. Looking at source evaluation a bit more holistically, it would be fair to make the evaluation in two phases. Phase 1 is the Preliminary Assessment, while the second phase is the Content Assessment.

Preliminary Assessment

In the preliminary assessment, the evaluation that you make is based on secondary information. More precisely, it's information not directly derived from the source content. Assess the individual—know the writer or interviewee's credentials. It is helpful to know the source's background. If they have a long and credible history working directly in the field they are providing information for, there is a good chance they are knowledgeable in the subject. Look for the source's biography if it's available.

As an additional consideration for the preliminary assessment, determine if the source has ever been cited in other material. If the source is respected in the subject area, they are often cited in other works. Look for the association or institution to which the source is a member. If there is a group the source is affiliated with, gaining an understanding of that group by identifying the group's goals and values would be helpful in assessing the knowledge, and even the bias, of the source.

Timeliness is also a factor in making a preliminary assessment. In most cases, the more current the date, the better the chance the information includes the latest data on a topic. Publishing dates are normally found on or near the title page of a work. On Web pages, especially news services, the date of publication may be listed down to the exact time of day the information was posted to the Internet.

Who is the publisher? Knowing a bit about the publisher can provide some insight regarding their consideration for the source. A well-known publisher may engage in a great deal of discrimination considering it must invest lots of time and resources into the works it supports. A university press may be more scholarly and less likely to create a popular work. This insight may provide a view into the respect afforded a writer, but it does not guarantee the work's quality.

Content Assessment

After you complete the initial assessment, the true work begins on analyzing the source. Content assessment deals with getting into the substance of the source. It begins by reading the preface of the work to gain an understanding of the source's intent. Review tables of contents to identify areas of interest within the work.

When reading the work, keep in mind that identifying the intended audience for the author will help in understanding the usefulness of the information. Is the author trying to educate the public, or is the author focused on providing material to experts in a particular focus area? The information may be too general or too detailed depending on the intended audience of the author.

Is the author's bias reasonable? Is the information the author is presenting the facts, their opinion, or is the material propaganda? If the information is factual, it can be corroborated through another source. Validating information across several sources assists in validating several works in parallel. Without validation, a writer can generate opinions that resemble fact but are not. In reading the material, it is vital to look for new ideas or concepts not consistent with other material previously reviewed that is related to the subject.

Understanding the scope of the work in relation to other material already analyzed helps to further provide greater knowledge of an area, or validate other facts currently known. More views of a subject ensure that the resulting analysis takes into consideration other thoughts on a particular issue. If the material is a primary source, the factual information is directly collected through this work and is considered original. A secondary source uses primary sources to deliver these thoughts.

It should also be possible to categorize the sources into several groups; Advocacy, Business/Marketing, News, Informational, and Personal. You may find additional categories useful, but these should offer a good start. Each category has traits particular to it and all provide valuable information if analyzed appropriately.

Advocacy Assessment

Advocacy sources have a goal of influencing public opinion or drawing attention to a particular cause. They frequently use ".org" as the extension of their Uniform Resource Link (URL) address. Influencing is a direct goal of their existence; thus, the information provided is generally very supportive of their cause. The following is a checklist[2] that can be useful in assessing an advocacy source.

Criterion #1: Authority

1. Is it clear what organization is responsible for the content?

2. Is there information describing the goals of the organization?

3. Is there a way to verify the legitimacy of this organization? In other words, is there a phone number or postal address for more information? (A simple e-mail address is not enough.)

4. Is there a statement that the content has been officially approved by the organization?

5. Is the content from the national head of the organization, or a local chapter?

6. Is there a statement that indicates the named organization is the copyright holder?

Criterion #2: Accuracy

1. Are the sources for any factual information clearly listed so they can be verified in another source? (If not, the page may still be useful as an example of the organization's ideas, but not as a source of factual information.)

2. Is the information free of grammatical, spelling, and typographical errors? (These kinds of errors indicate a lack of quality control, thoroughness, and professionalism. They also can actually produce inaccuracies in the information.)

Criterion #3: Objectivity

1. Are the organization's biases clearly stated?
2. If there is any advertising on the page, is it clearly differentiated from the informational center?

Criterion #4: Currency

1. Are there dates that indicate:

   When the content was written?

   When the content was first placed on the Web?

   When the content was last revised?

2. Is there any indication the information has been kept current?

Criterion #5: Coverage

1. Is there any indication that the document or content is complete, and that it's not a draft or currently under construction?
2. Is it clear what topic the work is intended to address?
3. Does the page succeed in addressing the topics, or has something significant been omitted?
4. Is the organization's point of view presented clearly, with its arguments well supported?

The greater the number of questions answered "yes," the more likely the source is of high information quality as an advocacy page.

Business/Marketing Assessment

Business and Marketing materials are just that. Designed to promote or sell a company's goods or services. These pages can be very useful in learning details about a product of interest, or learning particular details of an incident being handled by a company. The following is an evaluation checklist for business/marketing sources.[3]

Criterion #1: Authority

1. Is it clear that the company is responsible for the material?

2. Is there information describing the nature of the company, who owns it, and the types of products the company sells?

3. Is there a way of verifying the legitimacy of this company? In other words, is there a phone number or postal address for more information?

4. Is there a way of determining the stability of the company?

5. Is there a statement that the material has the official approval of the company?

6. Is there a statement giving the company's name as copyright holder?

Criterion #2: Accuracy

1. Has the company provided sources for outside reviews of its products, and have reports been filed by regulatory agencies that can verify company claims?

2. Are the sources of factual information clearly listed so they can be verified through another source?

3. Is the information free of grammatical, spelling, and typographical errors?

Criterion #3: Objectivity

1. For any given piece of information, is it clear what the company's motivation is for providing it?

2. If there is any advertising on the page, is it clearly differentiated from the informational content?

Criterion #4: Currency

1. Are there dates that indicate:

    When the content was written?

    When the content was first placed on the Web?

    When the content was last revised?

2. Is there any indication the information was kept current?

3. For financial information, is there any indication it was filed with regulatory agencies like the SEC, and is the filing date listed? For material from the company's annual report, is the date of the report listed?

Criterion #5: Coverage

1. Is there any indication that the document or content is complete, and that it's not a draft or currently under construction?

2. If describing a product, does the page include an adequate description of the product?

3. Are all of the company's products described with an adequate level of detail?

4. Is the same level of information provided for all sections or divisions of the company?

The greater the number of questions answered "yes," the more likely you are to determine if the source is of high information quality as a business/marketing page.

News Assessment

Internet news is a primary way to gain up-to-date information. This channel of information sharing also provides access to news outlets from other countries, as well as news assembled at local levels. Examples of news sources are www.cnn.com and www.news.bbc.co.uk. The following is an evaluation checklist for news sources.[4]

Criterion #1: Authority

1. Is it clear what company or individual is responsible for the contents of the page?

2. Is there a link to a page describing the goals of the company?

3. Is there a way of verifying the legitimacy of the company? Is there a postal address or phone number to contact for more information?

4. Is there a non-Web equivalent version of this material that would provide a way of verifying its legitimacy?

5. If the page contains an individual article, do you know who wrote the article, and his or her qualifications for writing on this topic?

6. Is it clear who is ultimately responsible for the material's content?

7. Is there a statement giving the company's name as copyright holder?

Criterion #2: Accuracy

1. Are sources for the factual information clearly listed so they can be verified in another source?

2. Are there editors monitoring the accuracy of the information article being published?

3. Is the information free of grammatical, spelling, and typographic errors?

Criterion #3: Objectivity

1. Is the informational content clearly separated from the advertising and opinion content?

2. Are the editorial and opinion pieces clearly labeled?

Criterion #4: Currency

1. Is there a link to an informational page that describes how frequently the material is updated?

2. Is there an indication of when the page was placed on the Web?

3. If it's a newspaper, does it indicate to which edition of the paper the page belongs?

4. If it's a broadcast, does it indicate the date and time the information on the page was originally broadcast?

Criterion #5: Coverage

1. Is there a link to an informational page that describes the coverage of the source?

2. If you are evaluating a newspaper and there is a print equivalent, is there an indication of whether the Web coverage is more or less extensive than the print version?

Informational Assessment

Informational sources are established for the purpose of providing factual information. These sources are usually provided by educational institutions or governmental agencies. They offer access to information such as calendars, services, statistics, and dictionaries. The following is an evaluation checklist for informational sources.[5]

Criterion #1: Authority

1. Is it clear who is responsible for the material's content?

2. Is there a page describing the purpose of the sponsoring organization?

3. Is there a way of verifying the legitimacy of the content developer?

4. Is it clear who wrote the material, and are the author's qualifications for writing on this topic clearly stated?

Criterion #2: Accuracy

1. Are the sources for any factual information clearly listed so they can be verified in another source?

2. Is the information free of grammatical, spelling, and typographical errors?

3. Is it clear as to who is ultimately responsible for the accuracy of the material's content?

4. If there are charts and/or graphs containing statistical data, are the charts and/or graphs clearly labeled and easy to read?

Criterion #3: Objectivity

1. Is the information provided as a public service?

2. Is the information free of advertising?

3. If any advertising exists on the page, is it clearly differentiated from the informational content?

Criterion #4: Currency

1. Are there dates that indicate:

    When the material was written?

When the information was first published?

When the material was last revised?

2. Are there any other indications that the material has been kept current?

3. If material is presented in graphs and/or charts, is it clearly stated when the data was gathered?

4. If the information is published in different editions, is it clearly labeled which edition the material is from?

Criterion #5: Coverage

1. Is there any indication that the page has been completed and is not currently under construction?

2. Is there a clear indication of whether the entire work is available on the Web, or only parts of it?

Personal Assessment

Materials from personal sources are often the most difficult to evaluate because the information needed to validate them may be difficult to find. Information from personal sources are published or made available by individuals that may not have an affiliation with any organization or group. The following is an evaluation checklist[6] for personal Web pages.

Criterion #1: Authority

1. Is it clear which individual is responsible for the contents of the page?

2. Does the individual responsible for the page indicate his or her qualifications for writing on this topic?

3. Is there a way of verifying the legitimacy of this individual?

Criterion #2: Accuracy

1. Are the sources for any factual information clearly listed so they can be verified in other sources? (If not, the page may still be useful as an example of the ideas of the individual, but not as a source of factual information.)

2. Is the information free of grammatical, spelling, and typographical errors? (These kinds of errors not only indicate a lack of quality control, thoroughness, and professionalism, but can actually produce inaccuracies in the information.)

Criterion #3: Objectivity

1. Are the person's biases clearly stated?

Criterion #4: Currency

1. Are there dates in the material to indicate:

When the material was written?

When the information was first published?

When the material was last revised?

2. Are there any indications that the material has been kept current?

Criterion #5: Coverage

1. Is there any indication that the page is complete, and not currently under construction?

2. If there is a print equivalent of the Web page, is there a clear indication of whether the entire work is available on the Web, or only parts of it?

This preliminary assessment affords some discrimination to hopefully reduce and even eliminate investing effort in analyzing works that are not worthwhile.

After you develop your key concepts and assessing the sources to draw from, it's possible to build the collection plans to support the OSINT process. Collection plans establish the process workings for the OSINT team. The collection plan needs to include the name of the source, who is responsible, the concepts being researched, any key search terms or focuses, any necessary information required to access the source, and the appropriate time interval associated with the collection. A simple chart can help manage the collection effort for the team. So, continuing with our baseball game intelligence requirements, an example chart may look like that shown in Table 6.1.

Table 6.1 Baseball Game Requirements

Task #	Concept	Source	Terms and Access	Responsible	Interval
1	Ticket Pricing for Games	www.example eventtickting.com, www.example ticketdeals.com	example team home games.com	John Public	Monthly
2	Baseball Game Scheduling	www.localteam.com	schedule	John Public	Monthly
3	Major Local Events	www.localcity events.com	dates of baseball schedule	John Public	Weekly
4	Frauds Related to Ticket Sales	www.google.com; Fraud magazine	online ticketing fraud, event ticket scams	John Public	Weekly

Collection Trade Craft

Knowing what you will collect is critical in ensuring you get the information you require to support the decision maker's goals and meet the task requirements assigned to you. You must also consider that there are adversaries and competitors formulating strategies and tactics similar in nature to yours, and as a part of that they may have an Open Source Intelligence program of their own. Even if they don't, plenty of others like to observe, and they are often more than happy to share their findings to further a cause that interests them, to provide the same to your competitors for a fee, to happily sell their findings back to you so you can prevent disclosure, or they may simply disclose information just for the sake of doing so. Thus, Operational Security (OPSEC) comes into play when considering the actions you intend to take.

NOTE

OPSEC becomes important in your collection effort in that an adversary may be able to identify your direction and intentions by understanding what you are looking for. If you overhear me ask someone: "Do you know when the next baseball game is?", "How much are the tickets?", and "How long does it take to drive to the baseball stadium?" You learn something about me and my direction. You could think of strategies that would make my quest to see a baseball game more difficult if you were so inclined, and had the resources available to be successful.

In addition to OPSEC concerns, methods of collection may be potentially hazardous to the health of your computer systems or supporting networks. Going to sites that are unknown to you may lead you to Web sites containing code that takes advantage of vulnerabilities existing in your system. Collections systems should be used for just collecting information. There should be no other information contained on the device should the system become compromised and exploited by an adversary.

Employ discretion, not deception. In being discrete, you choose not to provide information, thus concealing data that may be used to piece together your identity and direction. In being deceptive, you choose to give information, but the information you provide is false or misdirecting. This may be dismissible in many instances, but it only takes one bad incident to make a very painful or embarrassing mark. It is very hard to get a full understanding of a person without spending a good deal of time observing their behavior and working closely alongside them. Most of the relationships forged using Internet-based systems results in the issue of engaging and collecting information from people who are unknown. Providing misleading information to the wrong person can lead to digging that will unravel the lie and create an unfortunate situation.

WARNING

Consider that your operations may be disclosed. If they are, given the two directions available to you, what choice would you make? "We chose not to disclose information because we did not feel such disclosure was necessary," or "We chose to lie because... er... ah..." As you can see, the latter choice has the potential of becoming very embarrassing.

In establishing your connectivity to the Internet, try to keep it as anonymous as possible. Do not use a company or agency proxy for your connection. Internet Proxy (IP) addresses for an individual require court subpoenas in order for a requestor to identify the customer using the IP address. While for many, mid-sized or larger companies are issued IP address blocks. A "whois" look up of the IP address may yield the company of origination. If you cannot obtain a personal account to access the Internet, use a "legitimate" anonymous proxy. Fee-based services for anonymous surfing are available. The following vendors provide such service:

- Anonymizer (www.anonymizer.com)
- Find Not (www.findnot.com)
- Anonybrowser (https://anonybrowser.com)
- Public Server (www.publicserver.com)

Refrain from entering identifying information to initialize your hardware or software. Registered user names exist within the system almost permanently, in one form or another, as resident information on the device. Leave the information blank, or enter a couple characters to have the field accept the entered information.

Keep the browsing system clean, do not develop intelligence reports, handle personal e-mail, write memos, or check personal bank accounts. Use the browsing system only for browsing and move collected and useful info to external media, or a prepared shareable media. Keep a pristine original of your browsing system so you can restore your machine to its day-one status in case things go bad. Schedule to wipe and restore your system at a time period you determine, and then do so at the appointed time.

> **NOTE**
>
> You address two concerns with wiping. One destroys the collections you've already made. If those weren't eliminated, a person gaining access to those may be able to determine past collection direction and possibly uncover your current interests. Again, a touch of paranoia is good. The second worry is that your system may pick up code "cooties" or viruses along the way; thus, wiping and restoring brings back a certain level of confidence in your system.

Work safely. Maintain a fairly high security posture, keep up with your system updates, implement firewalls correctly, maintain up-to-date antivirus and spyware applications. Reduce exposures by working in text, limiting many Web content supporting applications, and removing applications that are outdated or unused.

Distillation

The fourth D is for Distillation—"Knowing What's Hot" is probably the hardest part of the process. The challenge of analyzing open-source information is that the readers can potentially miss the biases inherent in such sources. The nature of the material also exposes readers to the risk of outright deception. Therefore, before the analysis can occur, considerable time must be spent detailing the validity of the source and having a firm understanding of the biases that exist with the source. Even if the source is deceptive, knowing this up-front, the reader should still be able to gain valuable knowledge despite the façade.

Providing the right kind of support to meet the expectations of the client (the decision maker) is very important. In analyzing the data, does the client expect to receive information without too much analysis? Does the client expect the information to forecast possible future actions or events? Or does the client expect a level of effort that provides options to remedy possible events, and then forecasts the effects of the decisions made by the client? Expectations cause varying degrees of stress to the process and require different skill levels to meet the demands effectively. Clearly understanding the expected level of effort will help ensure the client's expectations are met when the final product is delivered.

Basic Analysis Support

Basic analysis support is only slightly more work than the information collection effort. In collecting the information, the collection effort is centered on searching assessed sources for concepts that support or detract from the team goal. In providing this level of support, the analysis is fairly simple. To be successful, the concepts that affect the outcome of the team goals must be well laid out and addressed with the collection effort. The analyst must understand the concepts, and then use that knowledge when reviewing the collection material to ensure that the information not only meets the needs of the decision maker but fulfills the requirements outlined by the decision maker's parties as well as others who have been impacted.

So the analysis is a review of the information and confirms that the information directly ties into the concepts previously identified in the direction phase. While this may seem like an easy task, even if the team only matures to provide basic analysis support, getting the resources to drive even this level of support is a daunting task. The goal should be to deliver the information as quickly and concisely as possible.

Consider including a validations step. Confirm the findings you intend to present from another source. It will add time, but this step may save countless explanations should you report on something inaccurate, absolutely wrong, or that is a complete fabrication. It may not be necessary to validate the info before dissemination if the proper expectation has been set.

Warning

Carefully consider who you will be providing the information to. If they cannot handle stress well, and can't quite see the big picture, you may be about to set their hair on fire and prompt them to ignite additional issues. It is far better to simply validate and inform people who have a low threshold for stressful problems.

Intermediate Analysis Support

In an intermediate analysis support function, the goal is to offer predictive information as well as provide the decision maker with relevant information that supports the team's goal. Considerations must be made about the skill sets of the analysts achieving this level of support. Having people with an understanding of how to think analytically would be a major benefit to support this activity.

NOTE

Thinking without adding personal biases becomes fairly difficult. Everyone has a bias. Whether or not they admit it or actually know it's a real problem, is the question. Know yourself.

When reviewing the collection material, remain objective. Do not make assumptions. Simply look at what the data provides. As a first step, review the concepts identified for the team to meet its needed goals. When analyzing the collected information, you can focus on it in three ways to yield information that is supportive of your effort. Look for emergence, trends, and aberrations of trends.

When considering emergence, know what the assumptions are and list them if possible. When reviewing collected information, look for messages or information that contradicts the expected norm. Take that emerging issue, revisit your concepts, and ask what effect the change would make, and what else is impacted. Conduct research in these areas to help form a better picture of the future for the decision maker.

Identifying trends allows you to forecast normal events. When reviewing the collected information, look for any messages or themes that repeat themselves over time. Understanding the consistent themes will provide a baseline from which to operate. Knowing what is expected not only provides predictive information, it also helps identify aberrations.

NOTE

Don't become complacent knowing the trends and perceiving them to be the only way for events to unfold. Failure to remain current will create a bias toward the way things have worked in the past. Someone may eventually say, "Well that's the way we've always done it," but that doesn't mean it's the right course of action now.

Knowing the trends will highlight concerns that violate the status quo. Aberrations of trends speak to how a change affects the business as usual trends, while emergence looks for something that is unexpected from the outset.

Dissemination

The final D is for Dissemination, "Knowing Who's Who." When the information is collected to help provide direction, one of the most important issues is to tackle just who the decision makers are and what information they need to be successful. These are the individuals that the intelligence products are being created for and delivered to. Also, understand how they would like the material presented to them. In addition, the information should contain a subject line, source of information, the concept impacted, the information itself, and a validation source. Table 6.2 shows an example of a simple report.

Table 6.2 A Report Example

Intel Update	
Subject	The Circus Is in Town
Source	Today's Paper
Concept	Major local events scheduled during baseball games
Info	Today, the annual circus is performing at the town center. There are animal cages and habitats set up in a number of places in town. The train and subway lines into town are expected to be flooded with children and their parents. The circus will be in town for six days.
Validation	Evening News on Local Channel
Potential Issue/ Response	Potential Issue: The circus will be impacting surface traffic and train lines into town. High traffic is expected. Possible Response: Do not go to the game.

Summary

To be useful in a business setting, intelligence gathering must have a purpose. The collection of information for the sake of knowing as much as you possibly can is hard to justify to a company carefully monitoring its expenditures. Depending on the type and size of the business, there may be many business partners struggling with how exactly they may scope the risk. A physical security detachment may be concerned about the safety, health, and welfare of the company's employees. A fraud loss protection group may be attempting to shield the company from sustaining financial losses due to fraud, or may be seeking to gain assistance from law enforcement in an attempt to recover lost funds. Information security teams worry about threats both external and internal to a company that may cause a loss of availability, reliability, or confidentiality of their information resources. Each partner may have at its disposal many sources of information particular to its needs. A truly effective plan would cut across the silos of information to develop a more detailed understanding of threats, and how those threats would manifest themselves to the risk partners and company. Each partner will have reservations about sharing, and resistance will naturally be demonstrated. Think about it: the type of people that usually work in these areas are skeptical by nature, so presenting them with the concept of sharing info would be fairly hard met.

In order to be effective in developing a program for a company, the facilitator leading the charge must have buy-in from executive management, spend time understanding the needs of all the potential customers and stakeholders of the intelligence products, clearly identify the requirements needed to be successful for the customer, do an inventory of the information sources already available within the organization and learn what sources are needed to complete the program. Develop clear collection plans and sensible analysis techniques. Deliver clear reporting that is timely and meets the expectations of the clients.

Completing all those tasks should create a perfect opportunity for an OSINT team to exist and excel in a business environment.

Notes

1. Definition in Section 931 of Public Law 109-163, "National Defense Authorization Act for Fiscal Year 2006."

2. Evaluation Checklist for an Advocacy Web Page, North Atlantic Treaty Organization (NATO) Intelligence Exploitation of the Internet, October 2002.

3. Evaluation Checklist for a Business/Marketing Web Page, North Atlantic Treaty Organization (NATO) Intelligence Exploitation of the Internet, October 2002.

4. Evaluation Checklist for a News Web Page, North Atlantic Treaty Organization (NATO) Intelligence Exploitation of the Internet, October 2002.

5. Evaluation Checklist for an Informational Web Page, North Atlantic Treaty Organization (NATO) Intelligence Exploitation of the Internet, October 2002.

6. Evaluation Checklist for a Personal Web Page, North Atlantic Treaty Organization (NATO) Intelligence Exploitation of the Internet, October 2002.

Chapter 7

Wireless Awareness: Increasing the Sophistication of Wireless Users

by Raymond Todd

Raymond Todd is an IT manager for a private university in Tempe, Arizona. He has over 12 years of experience in managing technology projects, teams, and systems. Raymond teaches several courses that focus on thinking and brain performance, as well as managing technology, systems, and change. He is the comoderator of the Phoenix Future Salon through the Accelerated Studies Foundation and serves on the board of directors for the Greater Arizona eLearning Association and the Arizona Telecommunications and Information Council. In addition, he is the faculty sponsor for DC480, the university's hacking club.

Introduction

For the past few years I have been passionate about increasing the sophistication of wireless users through ethical war driving and the development of grass roots educational programs. It all started back in the fall of 2004 when I and a group of colleagues sat around a table to discuss ideas we could implement in our area with limited funding but that would have maximum impact on the community. Collectively, we came up with the idea of conducting a war driving research project to assess the growth of wireless networks over a 12-month period in a major metropolitan area—specifically the Phoenix, Arizona area.

Phoenix is a large metropolitan city with a representative population that is ideal for collecting demographic data. Covering over 9200 square miles, the Phoenix Valley metroplex is the sixth largest city in the U.S., and as the population of the valley grows, so does the widespread use of the Internet, with the addition of many wireless access points within network infrastructures. These networks are incorporated within businesses, schools, government offices, and private homes. The convenience of wireless networks has driven their phenomenal growth within the last few years. This has exposed a large amount of corporate and personal data to outside individuals, leading to the possible theft of this information, which can include trade secrets, financial data, and individual identities. Our 12-month study was designed to evaluate the growth of wireless network presence and the various wireless security protocols used. The results of the study were intended to be compared to census data to support or disprove assumptions made regarding the proliferation of wireless and the use of wireless security standards.

With the idea in place, my role in the project was to supply the resources to implement the project both from a human and technological standpoint. My first order of business was to get the technology in place. I knew I had a very limited budget and that most of that would have to be allocated to gas for the drivers. I would have loved to have had unlimited funds or even grant money to purchase all kinds of equipment. As I sat and thought about it, I really wanted to purchase a fleet of Scion XBs and turn them into the ultimate war-driving vehicles, complete with omnidirectional antennas and built-in Linux boxes that booted up when the car was turned on so that data was collected every time they ran, and then they uploaded the information to a secure database as soon as they parked on campus. In reality, however, all I had to work with was eight IBM A22m laptops that were fully depreciated and due for sale at the next liquidation date. But at least I had eight working laptops with PCIMCA slots.

I knew I needed working computers, a reliable operating system that allowed for the most stable build of Kismet, GPS devices, power for the machines in the vehicles, drivers, a database programmer, and a project champion. I was fortunate enough to have access to faculty and students at the university so after casually interviewing a few interested faculty members, I recruited Al Kelly to assist me in leading the group of students. Overall, I had a budget of $5,000 to complete the entire project, and I knew I was going to be hard pressed to complete the project for that amount of money.

My next task was to design a War Driving Kit. The kit needed to be a plug-and-play unit that any student group or volunteer could use with little expertise or set-up time. I worked with Professor Kelly on this as well as one of my IT comrades who is excellent at finding and negotiating hardware deals. As mentioned before, we knew what computers we were using and were fortunate enough to have eight machines with the exact same configurations that were all in working order. We decided on using the Garmin eTrek handheld GPS with serial adapter, a 5db magnetic mount antenna, Orinoco Gold cards with the antenna input, a car power adapter specifically made for the IBM computers, a map of Phoenix and a laptop bag to hold all the goodies. When all was said and done, we spent a total of $2,190 on the war driving kits.

Once the initial kits were put together, it was time to assemble the team. We put some fliers up around the University campus attracting students that would be interested in receiving college credit for participation in the program. To no one's surprise, we assembled a team in no time at all. There were six teams of two, consisting of a driver and a computer operator. The teams were given specific areas around the valley from which they would collect data. We let the teams go, and when the data began streaming in, we were surprised what we found.

After the first round of data came in, I had a sneaking suspicion that the use of wireless networks was not so much a growing trend, but had already penetrated the market. Researching its growth was not going to be useful information. From the data we had collected, it was clear that wireless coverage was dense, even in the lower economic levels where we assumed there could be some disparity in the number of wireless access points. The reality was that in some places wireless network coverage was better than cell phone coverage. This was disappointing to some who thought this would become an economic study. But what the data showed was that while the use of wireless networks was clearly adopted in the residential areas of the city, security of those networks was not. This is where we began to get excited about making a difference.

I hate to admit this as an educator, but generally I find research projects like the one we were working on quite useless to the average person. Who really cares about the growth of wireless networks in a metropolitan area? Maybe some entrepreneurs seeking to capitalize on a new market might be interested, but for the average person the data is dull. I like working on projects that make a difference. I am a technologist and a futurist; I like being a part of changing the way people interact with technology more than observing how technology is being adopted. I have to say, when we saw the overwhelming numbers of access points that had no security on them whatsoever, I felt like we could actually take action and demonstrate how our data collection could lead to a more secure Internet, make users more aware of these technologies, and change the security posture of our society. That excited me.

I began thinking about what it would take to actually change the security posture of Phoenix. Then it hit me. What was it that made America start locking their cars and homes? When I grew up in the 1980s, hardly anyone where I lived locked their homes or cars. Yet now, everyone does it. It isn't as if we expect to have our vehicle stolen or house broken into every time we leave, but just to be safe, because it is a good practice, we all do it. I felt we needed to achieve the same with wireless networks. Here was the issue, though: I wanted to secure our wireless nation without instilling fear into every wireless user. It's fear that has made America a paranoid society—fear brought into our homes each night on the local news, on CNN, in the paper, all of which has been sensationalized in movies and television dramas. People were already afraid of hackers and it seemed like every time you turned around someone's identity was being stolen.

The other major obstacle I found was that many people just didn't care about securing their wireless networks. The more people I spoke to that were inherently nontechnical immediately lost interest as soon as I mentioned the phrase 802.11, drop in a couple more terms like packets, DHCP (Dynamic Host Configuration Protocol), WEP (Wired Equivalent Privacy), or WPA (Wi-Fi Protected Access) and it was like their brain began to shut down. It was almost as if they were afraid of even learning how the technology worked. This was the most frustrating discovery—and it seemed that unless you did use fear tactics, there was no incentive for people to take the few minutes necessary to configure their network devices to communicate in a more secure fashion. In order to reach the people I wanted to help, I couldn't assume it was help they wanted. I needed to do that dreaded thing all network and systems administrators fear: I needed to think like a user and, thus, lead by example.

Putting Together a War-Driving Team

The term *ethical war driver* has come up recently, and I know we used it extensively when discussing the project. But what does it mean to be an ethical war driver? Technically, it means that as you are scanning wireless networks, you make sure your wireless card is set to not automatically accept every DHCP address in your area. It also means you are not going to use the data you collect to harm the networks you detect. Instilling this message into savvy technical users is harder than it sounds. The reality is that to lead by example means you must adhere to these rules yourself. It was then I realized how often I could open my laptop and "hop online" wherever I was. If there was information I needed, I undertook to get it instantly. Now, however, I am responsible for not only securing all of the networks that make "hopping on" so easy, but taking a group of people out to gather data and dump it into a database that maps out the nearest wireless access point and all of its security information. I think ethical war driver means that as you learn more and more about wireless security there is an internal struggle as to how to use that information. As long as this internal struggle exists, you're all right.

Putting a team of people together that collectively goes out and scans for wireless networks with the aligned goal of bettering the community is fun. Discovering the information in your area is fun. Driving around in your car, hearing the laptop beep every time a new network is discovered, reading the clever SSID (Service Set Identifier) that people use is exciting—it feels like you're hunting for treasure. With honest up-front communication in the beginning, partnered with reliable technology, you can assemble a team that can collect a lot of data in a short period of time.

The following guidelines apply if you are putting a team of one or more people together for war driving, with idea of increasing the sophistication of wireless network users. First, *all members must be committed to behaving ethically*. It is imperative that when you embark on your journey of increasing the security posture of an area that the people in front of the community are above reproach. This means that no member of your team will connect to networks in which data is being collected. No information that is collected while war driving is published in any way that could potentially harm the users of these networks. Your role is to gather data to make a difference in a positive way, and your community should see you as a hero, not a criminal mastermind. Finally, in terms of ethical behavior, each member of your team should display that they have some level of internal struggle with the balance of knowledge, and the application of such. Just because you know how the technology works and how to circumvent most security measures does not give anyone the right to use that knowledge for personal gain or exploit the naïve.

The second trait you look for in assembling a war-driving team is *technical proficiency*. Each member of your team should be familiar with the tools they are using. You don't need a team of Linux gurus. In fact, it is best to have a well-rounded team of people with knowledge in OSX and Windows, as well as the suite of open-source tools available. In reality, it doesn't take much to assess the security posture in your immediate area. Almost all wireless devices will tell you what networks are visible— the ones you can connect to without any form of authentication are essentially unsecured. The more knowledge you can draw from within your team, the better your educational programs will be and the more impact you'll have on local networks. Technical proficiency really comes into play during data collection. There is nothing worse than using an entire tank of gas collecting data only to find that none of the data was logged. Understanding what information is streaming in during the data collection process allows your team to better understand the security posture of the area. Hitting a neighborhood with a large number of access points displaying default settings is a clear indicator that you are in a place that needs education.

The last skill set you are looking for when assembling a team is *the ability to speak the user's language*. This may even take longer than training people to uses the technical tools. I have found in most cases that those interested in assisting you are interested in the technology. Having your team learn to look at the technology from the point of view of the users can be difficult. Users in most cases just don't understand the technology, the vocabulary, how it works, or why it works. Your team must unlearn their lingo and speak in terms and metaphors users can relate to and understand.

Security Alert...

Assembling a War-Driving Team
The following points should be imperative for your team.

1. All members must behave ethically.
2. All members should demonstrate technical proficiency.
3. All members should be able to speak the language of the users.

Whether you have a team of 1 or 20, it is important to remember your goal, which is to increase the sophistication of wireless network users. If everyone who understood the technology did his best to affect all of the networks he comes in contact with, eventually, every network would, at a minimum, have some level of encryption or some authentication method in place. Not everyone needs to have multiple layers of security, especially home users who use their laptops to check e-mail and surf the Web. Nevertheless, it can start in your home. When you connect to your home network, do you see your neighbor's wireless network? Is it open? Does your computer at times connect to a network other than your own? If so, then you can start with that network. Our team actually developed a way to continually collect data and extract information from the database that told us what areas had the greatest need for awareness programs.

During the project, we had each member of our team submit the raw Kismet logs to the professor. From there, the teams' Database Administrator uploaded the information into a Microsoft SQL 2000 database. Once the information was in SQL, we were able to use Map Point 2000 to generate maps with color-coded dots to represent access points, and the security level of those access points. Security levels were assigned to each access point with a value of 0 to 3. Security Values were defined as follows:

- 0 = Default Settings
- 1 = Unsecured
- 2 = WEP or WPA
- 3 = WEP or WPA + no broadcast of SSID

By assigning these values to each access point, we were able to then leverage the tools within Map Point 2000 to discover areas that needed training. We developed an algorithm that queries the information in the database to determine potential target access points. A target access point (TAP) is an access point in the database that has the following characteristics:

- Seventy percent of the access points within a half mile radius have a security value of 0 or 1.
- More than 50 percent of the adjacent access points must be of the same access point type.
- The TAP must be in a residential area.

Implementing this algorithm was slightly more complicated than designed on paper, but in the end we were able to get the information we needed from the database in order to see areas that needed training or awareness programs the most. Now that we knew where to go to evangelize users on the ease and importance of wireless security, we needed to make sure we all understood the technology in case we got some really good questions. The following information on wireless technology was compiled in cooperation with students from the University of Advancing Technology involved in the Phoenix War Driving Project from the fall of 2004 through April of 2006.

Increasing User Sophistication

Making a difference in the security posture of a city or neighborhood takes more than just an idea. To truly make a difference, you need to have the knowledge of an expert and the patience and sensitivity of an elementary school teacher. It is essential for those of us out there that want to make a difference to fully understand the technology and take that knowledge to the people in a language they can understand. In this section, we shall cover the technical terms and functionality of wireless technology.

Wireless networks use radio frequency (RF) to transfer data from wireless access points. The Federal Communications Commission (FCC) and a common international agreement set aside the radio frequencies that can be used for unlicensed commercial use. The Industrial Scientific and Medical (ISM) bands include the 900-MHz, 2.4-MHz, and 5-GHz bands. When those frequencies become overcrowded, higher frequencies may be released.

Wireless access points use 2.4 GHz and 5 GHz to transmit data. This frequency is called Spread Spectrum—meaning it traverses the frequency band to reliably transmit data. Spread Spectrum was originally designed by the military (just like most wireless technology). Spread spectrum distributes its signal over a wide range of frequencies uniformly, thus consuming more bandwidth in exchange for reliability, integrity, and security of communications. This wideband lets your wireless access point avoid interference and other signal noise. Wideband communications are nosier and easier to detect.

You can think of it this way: the radio frequency used for wireless networks is able to find your wireless device and communicate with it using the best signal it can find based on its location. In your car, when you tune into a radio station and the channel gets fuzzy, your radio and the station do not change frequencies to provide a better listening experience for you, but your laptop and access point do.

Frequency-Hopping Spread Spectrum (FHSS) and Direct-Sequence Spread Spectrum (DSSS)

Two different versions of spread spectrum are available: Frequency-Hopping Spread Spectrum (FHSS) and Direct-Sequence Spread Spectrum (DSSS). DSSS has higher data rates, and a better range and error correction, while FHSS is easier to deploy because the equipment is less expensive. Wireless access systems use this Spread-Spectrum technology to transmit data, typically over the 2.4-GHz range. Unfortunately, Spread Spectrum is easy to detect if the attacker knows its signal since the receiver uses the same spreader code by the transmitter to be able to communicate. The FCC-released frequency of 2.4 GHz is divided into 75 1-MHz channels with a code sequence known to both the transmitter and receiver. DSSS on the other hand uses spread spectrum but breaks each bit in the signal into 11 sub-bits that are converted into waves over a wide range of frequencies. The receiver then spreads the chirp to decode the message. In 802.11, DSSS uses 64 8-bit code words to spread the signal, which to an eavesdropper just looks like random characters.

From a security standpoint, an eavesdropper must know the hopping pattern of the Spread Spectrum in FHSS, and in DSSS the eavesdropper must know the code or code words, despite having to know the frequency band and modulation. Also they must know the scrambling pattern of the radio signal. DSSS and FHSS, and vice versa, are not interoperable, and can't communicate, and they would have to use entirely different techniques to intercept one another. The strengths of Spread-Spectrum technology are sufficient enough to defeat most eavesdroppers and contribute to the security of wireless networks.

You can think of the information traveling on the FHSS as like the classic video game *Frogger*. The player moves from the bottom of the screen to the top, jumping into open spaces on a moving road, or on objects that can transport the data safely across the spectrum. The data is like the frog, making its way across the lanes of traffic and objects in the water, where each level represents a frequency. An observer watching the game can see how many spectrums can be traveled and the various ways to cross, but cannot reliably predict how the player will time the moves across the level.

The 802.11 Alphabet

One of the most talked about confusions in the world of wireless networking is that of the 802.11 alphabet. 802.11 operates in an unlicensed spectrum, where a license from the FCC is not required. Though there are some differences between the IEEE (Institute of Electrical and Electronics Engineers) who drafted the 802.11 protocol in 1997, these 802.11 signals a, b, and g (the most commonly used) employ DSSS, although 802.11a uses something called Orthogonal Frequency Division Multiplexing as a modulation technique in the 5-GHz spectrum. 802.11b is currently the most popular form of Wi-Fi. It uses frequencies in the 2.4-GHz range (2.400 to 2.485) and has 11 channels. Only three of these channels are nonoverlapping: channels 1, 6, and 11. This is only a guideline in reality, because if you begin to transmit too close to the range of the channels, you will get degradation of signal quality and throughput. I have seen this demonstrated in southern Arizona during the implementation of a Municipal Area Network. The top speed for 802.11b is 11 Mbps, but typically wireless networks work at about 50 percent their stated throughput, or around 6.5 megabits per second. The upside is that 802.11b is the most popular, widely available, and least expensive—and it offers decent coverage.

802.11a is less common and never achieved the same acceptance as 802.11b. It operates in the 5-GHz spectrum and has 12 nonoverlapping channels instead of 3. As a result, it can't penetrate obstacles as well, and has a shorter range but higher speed. It is also less prone to interference because of the fact it is used on a frequency that is not clouded by other cordless devices such as phones and microwaves and is relatively unused— however, this is changing.

Finally, 802.11g was released in 2003 and took the speed of 802.11a at 54 Mbps (although there are faster techniques, such as frame bursting or packet bursting). It supports the OFDM and DSSS modulation. From a security standpoint, most wireless network cards are compatible with 802.11b and g, and this is what's typically used in consumer devices. As a result, fewer cards can jump onto your 802.11a frequency because it can't operate at 5 GHz. This is quickly changing due to the 802.11g standard, which is now able to operate at the 5-GHz frequency, meaning most wireless network cards are now compatible with 802.11a. However, relying on this mechanism alone is a poor method of keeping your wireless network secure.

The 802.11n standard has been recently released to consumers (as of April 2006) and has speeds in excess of 300 Mbps. There are also others, such as 802.11h–w, that have specific functionality. However, unless you are out there designing complicated networks for multiple users on encrypted channels what you really need to understand in order to change the world is an understanding of a, b, and g, but mostly just b and g.

Unauthorized Access

Unauthorized access is a term used commonly in conjunction with wireless security and networking. It basically means that someone other than the owner and specified users of a network have been granted access. When it comes to basic users of wireless devices, unauthorized access means that somehow a user has access to the Internet. The issue surrounding unauthorized access lies in the inherent flaws in the open licensing of the frequency itself. In order for companies to make devices that allowed regular people to connect their laptops and personal data assistants (PDAs) to the Internet, the process had to be as simple as possible. How simple? Automatic. The default settings on most wireless devices are to automatically connect when a network is present. This is usually true for wireless transmitters as well; their default setting is to give out connections. In the most basic terms, all wireless devices are made to connect to each other without interference from a human. This makes enforcing unauthorized access the responsibility of the installer or administrator of the wireless network.

Social etiquette among wireless users is that if you did not set up the network or get explicit permission to access it—like a sign outside that says "Free Wireless"— then do not connect. But not all owners of wireless devices are knowledgeable of the social norms of the computer geek. The best way to explain this is to let everyone know that unless they explicitly want to keep people out, they have given them an open door to the network and, essentially, authorized access.

There are very simple steps anyone can take to lock down their network. The first is to understand what the wireless transmitter, wireless router, or access point does to grant connectivity. This is usually done by assigning the device an IP address. Turn this feature off and no one gets access. Putting in place some kind of authorization, whether a pass phrase or device filter is another way to do this. All of these measures can be done with little to no understanding of the technical workings of the technology because the manufacturers have created user interfaces that allow configuration with simple clicks.

Eavesdropping

Eavesdropping, sometimes referred to as a man-in-the-middle attack, is a big problem due to attackers being able to intercept RF communications between the transmitter and the wireless network card. This in turn could compromise the confidentiality or integrity of data. Eavesdropping is typically passive since you would never notice if someone was intercepting your traffic—until, that is, you find illicit charges on your credit card for the local Starbucks wireless network. For example, a common form of eavesdropping is packet sniffing. This typically transverses on a wired LAN and is easily readable with messages in clear text. Now the medium has changed and this can easily be done over a wireless network.

Eavesdropping is essentially hacking (or in the perspective of a network administrator "monitoring"). The reality is that because of the nature of the technology, devices are able to listen to the traffic on a network. There is hope for the security of wireless networking, but it comes from understanding the technical specifications, and balancing user experience, cost, and administration. The technology was built to be mobile and quickly used; it wasn't designed for security.

Interference and Jamming

Another major threat to your wireless network is interference. By their very nature, most wireless access points work on the 2.4-GHz RF signal (802.11b, 802.11g), and thus has to collaborate with many other devices. Whenever this happens—

unfortunately because this is unlicensed by the FCC—many other devices can overlap on the channels your wireless access point is using. This is called interference. Most of the time it's unintentional, and this interference can be caused by high-power amateur, industrial, scientific, and military transmitters, microwave ovens, and more recently, your neighbor's wireless network. Ever experience a faint conversation going on in the background of your wireless telephone conversation? This is the same principle, except instead of your ear hearing the interference your wireless card is getting jumbled data.

Though this connection may gain interference from intentional sources, in which they can jam the frequency range of the access point by either using a single channel or all of the channels. This jamming equipment is easily accessible to attackers on the Internet, although their use is typically illegal. Jamming occurs in high-density Wi-Fi areas like apartment complexes—for instance, a building may be three stories tall, with nearly everyone having a wireless access point of their own, resulting in many bad connections. If the wireless access points are open for anyone to connect to them, the wireless device will continuously hop around seeking the best connection. This results in poor network connectivity.

Physical Threats

Currently, the BBC airs a show called *The IT Crowd*. In this sitcom about two guys in an IT department, the running joke is that when anyone calls they ask if the user has turned the system off and then back on again just before they hang up the phone or slam the door. The sad reality is that in so many cases when troubleshooting problems, the solution is to make sure the device is plugged in.

A wireless network uses a wired network as its backbone. Thus, a disconnect of the physical wiring could render the wireless network useless. Also, wireless network infrastructure hardware relies on many things such as access points, the cabling to them, antennas that provide the coverage, and adapters of some sort. If any of these components are damaged, the wireless network will not operate effectively. Also, wireless infrastructure is susceptible to weather conditions, especially when wireless access points are outdoors. Other environmental factors are lightning strikes or water intrusion. Attackers can physically attack the access points by cutting its wires, power cables, or destroying its antennas. An attacker may also try to steal or compromise the wireless access point to gain access to the network. It is important to realize that attackers may be able to reset the access point to default settings and easily access the network since most access points are unsecured out of the box. At the university, I submitted a challenge to a group of network security students to hack a wireless video projector we had installed in the ceiling. The projector was to display information to students about projects that had been completed on campus the previous semester. The next day when I arrived on campus, the projector showed an image of the students on a ladder hitting the reset button on the back of the device. Sometimes it's that easy.

802.11 Security

Information security is the process by which digital information assets are protected, whether wireless or wired. Confidentiality, integrity, and availability are the guidelines typically used in the information security field as baselines for security threats. These are the basic three, but more can be defined depending on what is important to the organization. Therefore, the goal of wireless network security is to keep the confidentiality, integrity, and availability of information on the wireless network.

Confidentiality

Confidentiality is the projection of data from unauthorized disclosure to a third party. Whether it is customer data or internal company information, confidentiality must be protected. Majority of company's intellectual property and information needs to remain confidential from other competitors. Only authorized persons should have access to this information. For example, if you have an unsecured wireless access point and you are a medical billing facility, you would have to adhere to the Health Insurance Portability and Accountability Act (HIPPAA) that establishes national standards for health care information. If the company failed to provide confidentiality for customers' health records, then it could be subject to stiff penalties under U.S. law. You could be in violation of this if an attacker was easily able to connect to a wireless access point and read clear data containing this information. Some other federal requirements that companies have to adhere to are Sarbanes-Oxley, the Federal Information Security Management Act, and the Family Educational Rights and Privacy Act. All require information technology controls, and, typically, unsecured wireless networks violate these controls.

Keeping information confidential is always difficult when working with humans and open technology. Humans like to talk; they love to be helpful, so if asked a question about anything they have knowledge about the chances of them telling you are high. The best practice for organizations that have sensitive data is to not allow that traffic to be sent over a wireless network. However, I am finding that many organizations feel that being mobile is more important than being secure. Take our university, for example—we have all of our administrators on a wireless network. This network uses encryption keys, MAC filtering, monitoring, static addressing, and various other methods of security, but that doesn't mean the traffic is completely secure. It's difficult to gain access to it, but difficult does not mean impossible. For our users, the ability to be mobile is important to the culture and environment, but we are not working with anything other than grades and student numbers. Imagine if we were working on patented secrets. Is difficult enough to allow mobility?

Integrity

Integrity refers to the assurance that data isn't alerted or destroyed, whether this is in transit at the starting or ending point. Integrity is maintained when the message sent is identical to the message received. For example, you wouldn't care if someone could view the e-mail you were sending to your colleague, but if a third party changed this e-mail you might be upset. An example of this is a man-in-the-middle attack. The good news for home users is that attacks like these cannot happen accidentally. They are generated using sophisticated software and hardware by people who are patient and have the time and willpower to go through the trouble of intercepting your communications. If you are the type of neighbor who has brought this type of attack upon yourself, you are lucky that is all they are doing.

All joking aside, this is a real threat to organizations transmitting information in public places. For example, I have seen groups of people in the hotel lobby bar checking important e-mails, sending directions to subordinates, and negotiating land deals. Think about the kind of information that passes through the radio frequencies with every type of conference in hotels. Interception is possible and could be dangerous. It is important when using and administering wireless connectivity to users that they be aware of the potential risks when outside the confines of the office and be sensitive of what information is sent, and how.

Availability

Availability is defined as the continuous operation of information technology systems. An IT system should always be available to the user, and security controls must always adhere to making the service available. A common opposite of availability is a Denial-of-Service attack. Different services or applications have different availability levels according to how critical the business process is. In order to be available, the application must have continuous service when it is needed. This is important because if these systems are down it can cost business valuable revenue. It may also result in a lack of credibility and low customer satisfaction. Think about when your cell phone loses it signal. What if it was your wireless access points that kept dropping out on you?

As mentioned before, methods exist for decreasing the availability of a wireless network through interference and loss of connectivity to the physical network. Environmental factors may also hinder service in outdoor wireless networks, and it is the goal of the network administrator to take these factors into account and monitor the conditions. Going back to the real purpose of this information, which is to increase the sophistication of wireless users, how do we talk about "availability" to average nontechnical users? I have found over the last few years that listening to the language of the layperson can reveal symptoms that lead to fundamental problems. The following are some terms I often hear from nontechnical consumers to describe inconsistent availability in wireless networks.

"My Internet" is down. In this case, "My Internet" usually refers to the browser not loading Web pages. As avid computer users, we instantly begin troubleshooting this in our minds, but to a nontechnical user this is baffling. However, this is different from when the same person says "My Wireless" is down. Nontechnical users that have a wireless network in their homes can usually tell when their computer has not acquired an IP address. In nine cases out of ten, it is because in newer laptops they have a switch for the wireless network card on the machine and this has been turned off. Other times it's usually caused by overload on the access point or router, which simply needs to be rebooted. Oh, if managing an enterprise network were easy, life would be grand.

The point here is that knowing the terms and technical specifications of a technology does not make you helpful to users that need your expertise. We, too, must be sensitive to their language and understanding of how the technology works so we can praise, redirect, and reprimand their understanding of wireless technology to make everyone more secure and yet do so with increased availability.

Goals of Network Security

One of the most important goals of network security is to achieve a state where any action not expressly permitted is prohibited. We can accomplish this by understanding the expectations of our organizational leaders and users, developing communications that clearly explain desired performance, and show how to prevent and respond to incidents that occur. As security professionals, we want to ensure that the devices on our network are operated by authorized personnel, that the data is secure, and that all of it is invisible and effortless to the users. Typing a 24-character password versus four characters every time a user needs to access a different data system or access point will, over time, deter the user from using that system. It will also greatly decrease productivity. The cost for stronger authentication or encryption mechanisms is high and perceived as a hassle, such as using passwords and tokens simultaneously. The support involved in troubleshooting users with hardware- and software-based tokens on a wireless network requires a full-time helpdesk at many organizations. Most companies and consumers aren't able to afford the expertise, software, and long-term maintenance costs of keeping a secure wireless network available 24 hours a day.

An information security program is based on experienced staff, good policies, procedures, training, awareness, management support, and its implementation from the highest level of the organization. This is typically called the top-down approach. Good information security is also based on a sound technical information security architecture utilizing the correct products in the correct locations on the network. Senior leadership is one of the most effective tools in preventing security chaos in an organization. A good CIO responsible for implementing an effective organizational information security program that propagates to all individuals can be the best investment an organization with mobile users can make.

Having an organizational hierarchy is immensely effective in improving the information security posture of the corporation. Having a hierarchy allows senior management to effectively enforce policies and procedures, which in turn spreads throughout the entire organization. Policies and procedures typically make up 85 percent of the security posture of an organization. Effectively enforcing these policies and procedures of the organizational information security program greatly disseminates risk to an organization's information assets and lowers their overall information security posture, thus decreasing the risk of wireless network security fallibilities.

I have to admit that the preceding paragraph is the standard model of good practice. Personally, I do not like hierarchies and believe in flat organizations that are managed by a discipline of skill sets that are natural to the leaders in the organization, and that technology should be coddled and promoted as an enhancement to life, work, and freedom. In our organization, everyone is responsible for making good decisions about security and we are not driven by a hierarchy of policies and procedures that flow from the top down, but practices that are constantly evolving based on the need of the users and organizational goals. Our security administrator has the final say in information security, but with input from many divisions to balance usability and risk.

Security Ramifications

When the confidentiality, integrity, and availability of a business, organization, or consumer are compromised, they usually must incur some costs to mitigate the consequences of the attack. The basics are simple: if there is a problem, it is due to weaknesses in the technology, configuration, or policy, or is a result of human error. This is typically when authors will begin unleashing the terror and instill fear into users employing every worst-case scenario ever told about identity theft, bandwidth loss, and holding companies hostage over their critical information. While there *are* risks and the stories are true, our goal is to increase the sophistication of wireless users at the residential and consumer level, not necessarily the corporate and organizational level. They have resources to mitigate risk, but what about your neighbor?

The real threat to the average home wireless user is that they will make themselves vulnerable to having their financial data exposed and will have to go through the pain and hassle of clearing that data up. I had my identity compromised and it was a nightmare getting all of my bank accounts and bills back in order. I can empathize, but that does not deter me from being mobile or having a wireless network at home. It makes me check my accounts more often and set up alerts where available, but I do not fear the technology or the people out there. That is our role in communicating security ramifications.

Several times since working with this initiative, I have talked about incentives: both for wireless users and for hackers. There is no real incentive for hackers to hack into home networks because there is no real value there. The value that an open network of a residential home has is bandwidth, a gateway to get to the real information. Stealing the account information of a person in suburbia usually doesn't result in a worthwhile payoff to the criminal.

Human Factors

Keeping with the idea of incentives, humans are the reason technology continually evolves. The idea is that the more we integrate our lives with technology, the more human we want to be. We want to be able to meet face to face at a coffee shop or book store and build relationships and still be connected, to the phone, to e-mail, and to information. Humans will drive technology and I find it comical when technology tries to dictate how people will use it. We see this with the Internet, wireless devices, TiVo, and all kinds of technologies that people have taken a liking to. Technology gets in the hands of people and they use it, but the administrators and engineers sometimes interfere by saying, "You can't use this wireless network; you can't record a movie and watch it as many times as you want; you can't make that information available to people; and you surely cannot download it without my permission." All of these actions show technology trying to dictate human behavior instead of realizing that humans create technology to make life the way they want it, and not to be controlled by technology.

So what do we do as security professionals, technology innovators, and administrators to ensure that humans can have access to these networks while at the same time protecting the information that travels across such technologies?

The human factor must be considered when implementing a wireless network at home and in the workplace. Security that *forces* people into a policy, and procedures that create environments of fear also create a breeding ground for revolt. Balance, training, and communication are the key to managing the human factor of your wireless network

Knowing Your Weaknesses

No matter how secure your system is, it will always have weaknesses. The radio frequency technology we are using is weak, which is why it is unlicensed. You should attack your own system to determine where your weaknesses are located. Of course, if you do not know how to hack or you don't understand the technology, how can you do this? Know the areas that offer the largest threat to your system and mitigate that risk. Determine the level of security for the level risk, and then develop or use a methodology for testing to ensure your system remains safe. For example, if your wireless access point handles credit card transactions, make sure you have made every opportunity to mitigate all risk to them system instead of focusing on a public Internet computer.

When working with people with little knowledge of the technology, understand that their lack of knowledge is a weakness. In organizations, we protect critical data, our products, and our services against competitors. For residential users, we simply ask them to protect their network like they do their house or car—you lock it to deter people from entering. Locks can be broken, cars can be stolen, and wireless traffic can be intercepted—thus, due diligence is the key. For houses and cars, industries have risen to mitigate risk. They are called insurance companies. Even now, identity theft insurance is available because of inherent flaws in the technology.

Limiting Access

Not everyone needs access to the wireless access point in your network, and some may need more access than others. Public users don't need to access your network! Take the necessary steps to make it as difficult as possible for outsiders to gain access, and as simple as possible for permitted users to work without being tethered to the wall.

Persistence Achieves Security

A persistent, well-documented chain management process is important. Whenever there is a network upgrade, whether patches, new users, firewall updates, or new access control lists, they should be well documented. Methodically written processes are best. Be persistent with your users so that they are well informed of the information security policies. Add banners to wireless network connectivity with a legal disclaimer "for authorized use only," and give a link to your information security policy. Make it a point to patch systems and devices as often as possible and communicate all changes as best you can in terms that users can understand. Remember, information technology is not taught as part of our required education. It is unrealistic to expect all users to understand the language and architecture of network technology.

Physical Security

One of the most basic and overlooked ways of securing a wireless network is to physically secure the access point (AP). This can be done by placing the access point in a secure location, such as a locked room, that has limited access. By preventing unauthorized personnel from reaching the access point, a layer of security is created.

Another basic approach to securing a wireless local area network (WLAN) is to ensure that no additional unauthorized access points are added to the network. This is to prevent unauthorized access to the network through an AP that is not configured securely. In a corporate setting, employees should be notified of this practice. Once the AP has been physically secured, it is important to configure it properly. Configuring it includes the process of setting authentication/encryption measures. By preventing unauthorized personnel from reaching the access point, a layer of security is created. When doing so, it is also important to set a secure password for the access point so it cannot be logged into remotely by unauthorized individuals.

The reality is that in homes and many small business offices, the access point is sitting out in the open, on a desk, or near the Internet connection. There are usually one or two access points to provide better coverage or to support more users, and focus is given to protecting the data in the air and not at the AP. Nevertheless, protecting the access point should be considered.

Perimeter Security

A critical starting point in implementing network security is to create a strong network perimeter that protects internal resources from threats outside the organization. These threats can come from the Internet, external businesses, or users connecting to your network. Anything that connects to your network is a risk. To alleviate many of these risks, a strong network perimeter must be created to block out undesirable traffic, especially on your wireless access point. For example, a wireless network point should never access a network backbone directly, or any place that is transferring a heavy amount of confidential data, or that has access to important servers, data, and so on. In this case, an excellent example of good perimeter security is that when a user authenticates to the access point, he can only access things like the Internet, and nothing internally. Then, once he wants to access business critical servers or data, he could then use a virtual private network to successfully log into the critical network in which the connection could then be entirely encrypted and secured by multiple authentication algorithms. Also, this should be used with a three-tiered architecture that's located in a semi-trusted network and then VPN into the trusted network. It shouldn't be placed in an untrusted network since it could be susceptible to Internet attacks.

The Radiation Zone

Unlike a traditional wired network in a corporation or home where a security team or locked door can prevent access to the system, a wireless network has the access pointability to extend its range outside the walls of the building. This creates the potential risk of unauthorized access to the network from outside the building (such as in an alley or parking lot).

The area in which the radio signals from an access point are usable is known as the radiation zone. When a wireless network transmits data, it does so over a radio frequency. Many things can obstruct the radio frequencies, such as steel, walls, and other devices in the area. A number of steps can be taken to lower the risk. Many access points allow their antenna to be positioned. This can be done to direct the signal from the access point away from unused areas. This may contribute to reducing the visibility of the network, but some security experts still warn against using this as a form of security.

There are companies that have designed products to stop a wireless signal from radiating outside of a building. Force Field Wireless of Sunnyvale, California sells DefendAir paint, which contains copper filings as well as aluminum. The company claims that the paint will greatly reduce the emission of wireless signals. The company also sells "Window Shield," which is attached to windows and serves roughly the same purpose. A significant problem with both of these methods is that it also blocks other radio signals, including those of broadcast radio, cell phones, and television.

While physically securing the network is an important step to enforcing the security of the overall network, it is still only a single step towards fully securing the network. For any network that will be transmitting sensitive data, including home networks that transmit credit and banking information, it is still important to utilize some form of authentication and encryption.

Firewalls

A firewall is a hardware or software solution that contains programs designed to enforce an organization's security polices by restricting access to specific network resources. The firewall creates a protective layer between the network and the external networks. It is used in the three-tier layer and replicates the network at the point of entry so it can receive and transmit authorized data without much delay. Its filters either allow or deny data from entering, and firewalls log any attempted intrusions and alarm the owner.

Outside of securing the access point, another important part of securing a network is to have a firewall. Those packets or bits of data that do not meet the security policy are discarded and aren't allowed into the internal network. A firewall serves as yet another method of preventing unauthorized access to an internal network. Additionally, if the sole purpose of an access point is to allow wireless Internet connectivity, with no need for access to the internal network, then the access point can be installed on the outside of the network, with a firewall between it and the internal network. Demilitarized zones, or DMZs, are areas that allow access typically to external networks without sacrificing unauthorized access to its private network. This is typically in the semi-trusted layer. Typically, a DMZ contains Web servers, mail servers, and so on. It is known as the neutral zone between a private network and an outside network and keeps outside users from getting direct access to an important server on a private network. This further helps to protect the network and can be used with a virtual private network.

Ad-Hoc and Infrastructure Modes

Two modes can be used to operate in a wireless connection in 802.11: ad-hoc mode and infrastructure mode (also called an IBSS, where the network's card works peer-to-peer and no wireless access points are used in the topology—for example, two computers directly communicating with each other over 802.11b). From a security aspect, ad-hoc mode can be a security problem because if they were simultaneously hooked up using a wired connection, then at any time they could be considered a wireless access point and give anyone unsecured access unknowingly.

In infrastructure mode, a wireless user is always connected to a wireless access point and a wireless provider with a direct connection to a wired infrastructure such as Ethernet. All communication occurs through the access point—never through any peers. Multiple wireless network access points that work together are typically called a Basic Service Set (BSS), while a multiple BSS is called an ESS. This is typically a security problem, because if one access point gets compromised, a whole basic service set or extended service set can be compromised, which will give the attacker an even greater range to access the network. Whenever a client connects to an access point, it has to know the Service Set Identifier (SSID) of the network and then authenticate and associate in whichever of three relationships exist: unauthenticated and unassociated, authenticated and unassociated, or authenticated and associated. In security, 100 percent of the time we want to make sure the client is successfully authenticated and associated.

The SSID

The SSID is essentially the name of the access point or wireless network seen by the user. There are only two ways a client can know their SSID: it can be told by the access point actively, or you can passively put it in the client's configuration. When it is given out automatically, it is called Open Network mode, but is known as Closed Network mode when "cloaking," meaning the SSID is not broadcast over the radio frequency. The automatic giving out of the SSID occurs typically every 100 milliseconds and is called a beacon, within which is contained synchronization information such as channel, speeds, timestamps, encryption status, and other information.

In Closed Network mode, the SSID is not broadcast out to the user or administrator programs. Thus, the client must probe the access point, and if the SSID matches, it will synchronize and go through the authentication process. Authentication can occur using an open system or shared key authentication. An open system does not need any credentials supplied. The SSID is used in wireless networks to identify the wireless access point and its associated network. It can be up to 32 alphanumeric characters long and is attached to all packets sent over the wireless connection. Additional access points in the area can broadcast the same SSID, so its use as a security or authentication method is negligible. However, the SSID may be changed and cloaked (meaning it is not set to be broadcast by the AP) in an attempt to minimize the visibility of the network. By default, most APs broadcast their SSIDs to the surrounding area. This beacon method occurs roughly every 0.1 seconds. Most APs ship with a default SSID (see Table 7.1). These defaults are widely known and can be found on a number of Internet sites. Using a default SSID may draw malicious users who suspect that additional settings on the AP are set to default settings as well (such as the administrative password). From a security stand-point, changing the SSID may cause some possible attackers to choose a wireless network that uses default settings. Changing the SSID is reasonably simple for a nontechnical user, and though minor, is a step toward securing the AP. It is important to note that disabling the broadcast of the SSID does not completely cloak the AP. It simply makes it less visible. Nevertheless, it is still an important step in lowering the risk of unauthorized access by reducing the visible footprint of the network.

Table 7.1 Default SSIDs on Several Access Points

3com AirConnect 2.4-GHz DS	Comcomcom
Apple Airport	Air Port Network
Compaq WL-100	Compaq
Dlink DL-713	WLAN
Linksys	Linksys
Netgear	Wireless

Virtual Private Networks

A virtual private network (VPN) is a method of creating a secure network connection between two devices through a nonsecure network. This can often be found on the Internet when an individual at their home connects to the corporate network at their job site. By using encryption, the communication remains secure, even though it is being sent over an insecure network. It is important to note that by using a VPN an individual may connect to the main network over an unsecured wireless connection and is secure in the fact that any data they may transfer is indeed safe over an encrypted session.

Radius Servers

Remote Authentication Dial-In User Service (RADIUS) provides a client/server security system. Any communications server or network hardware that supports the RADIUS client protocols can communicate with the server. RADIUS is a system of distributed security. It includes two pieces: an authentication server and client protocols. The server is typically on the corporate LAN and is designed to simplify the security process by separating security technology from communications technology. The information is forwarded to a RADIUS authentication server that validates the user and returns the information necessary for the access server to initiate a session with the user. In 1997, the RADIUS protocol was designed by Livingston Enterprises, Inc. When connecting to an ISP or other network that utilizes RADIUS, the connecting point is known as a network access server (NAS). The device wishing to be authenticated sends its authenticating information to the NAS via PPP (point-to-point protocol). Then, the authentication request is forwarded to the RADIUS server using the RADIUS protocol. After attempting authentication, the RADIUS server either grants or denies the connection. If the authentication is successful, then the authenticated device is granted access to the greater network, which is typically the corporate local area network.

The RADIUS packet is encapsulated in a stateless UDP data stream that is addressed with the destination ports 1812, 1813, and 1814 representing access, accounting, and proxying, respectively. Packets consist of multiple elements, code, identifiers, length, and authenticator and attribute elements.

In a RADIUS packet, the code element identifies the type of the RADIUS packet. The different packet types are shown next. The identifier element allows the client to match a RADIUS server response with the correct request. The length element indicates the length of the RADIUS message. It also represents the corresponding sum of the code, identifier, length, authenticator, and attribute fields. The authenticator element is used to authenticate and verify replies from the RADIUS server. It also serves to hide the password. The two values that can be found in the authenticator element are *request* and *response*. The final element of a RADIUS packet is the attribute element. Six of them classify the characteristics and behavior patterns of the service.

Further details on the process of RADIUS authentication are warranted. When a user attempts to obtain authentication, the query sent from the NAS to the RADIUS server is an Access-Request packet. The corresponding response will either be an Access-Accept or Access-Reject packet. To decide whether to accept, and choose how to respond to, the Access-Request packet, the RADIUS server searches a database for the supplied credentials. If it does not find that account, then an Access-Reject packet is sent. This will often be accompanied by a text message to explain the reason for the authentication failing. If the credentials exist in the database, then an Access-Accept response is sent. Included in that response is a list of attribute values that describe the parameters of the session. This typically includes the service type, protocol type, and IP address assigned to that user.

RADIUS authentication allows for a number of different mechanisms to be used in authentication. These methods include varying protocols, such as PAP (Password Authentication Protocol), CHAP (Challenge Handshake Authentication protocol), as well as other authentication methods like PAMs (Pluggable Authentication

Modules), LDAP (Lightweight Directory Access Protocol), and SQL (Structured Query Language).

The authentication protocols and methods previously given deserve further analysis. CHAP is a procedure similar to Shared key Authentication, which is detailed within this CHAP pointer. Password Authentication Protocol (PAP) is a simple authentication protocol, which as a security measure performs poorly because it transmits the password information in unencrypted ASCII format over the network. Pluggable Authentication Protocol (PAM) has the ability to integrate login capabilities of different authentication mechanisms through the same framework, thus providing greater compatibility with authentication methods. The method used in the ISP example can be extended to a wireless network. In this case, the access point is connected to a RADIUS server. The access point forwards authentication requests to the RADIUS server to obtain authentication. If authentication is granted, then the wireless device is allowed access to the network.

Configuration Weaknesses

Many security problems are often caused by configuration weaknesses, especially in access points. A common problem in misconfiguration is unsecured accounts. User accounts may sometimes be transmitted insecurely if the wireless access point is not set up right, therefore exposing usernames and passwords to attackers. In addition, these system accounts typically have weak passwords, or passwords that can be broken or guessed with ease. Very unsecure passwords are those that are easy to crack. It is recommended you use an alphanumeric password with capital letters and special characters, and that it be at least 16 characters. The longer the password, the better the protection. Another thing that is common is misconfiguration of services on the access point. A common problem is to allow for remote administration through a Web browser. This should only be activated if necessary; otherwise, it should be deactivated. In residential areas that have dense wireless populations, users that are connected to a nearby access point of the same make and type can be accessed using the same credentials, and the users may not realize they are not even accessing their personal access point. An access point should never use the default password since it is a simple process to find the default password for an access point online. When doing so, it is also important to set a secure password for the access point so it cannot be logged into remotely by unauthorized individuals.

Some wireless access points also have default passwords or no passwords at all. This should be changed immediately, as soon as you configure them. These are known as default settings, and these default settings typically permit security holes such as an access point that does not secure itself. Another common problem of configuration weaknesses is misconfigured network services. For example, you should not start Telnet on your wireless access point since all information is sent in clear text and a hacker could easily intercept the password when an administrator logs into it.

In our study of the Phoenix area, we found nearly 80,000 access points using their default configurations.

Policy Weaknesses

Many security problems exist because there is a lack of policy. If there is a lack of a written security policy, security cannot be consistently applied or enforced. Office politics can play a big roll in this issue—for instance, if you do not have management support of the policy from the top down, your policy can't be enforced and will be ineffective. Businesses that lack continuity cannot implement policy evenly, and frequently replacing personnel leads to difficulty in enforcing security. Many policies have concise access controls that are not applied, are poorly chosen, easily cracked, or that use default passwords that could allow unauthorized access to your wireless access point. For example, if your policy is to use a minimum four-character password, it will be overwhelmingly ineffective as a network security policy. Your software and hardware changes should always follow policy and there should be no exceptions. If your information security policy is enforced, unauthorized changes to the wireless access point should not be an issue, and security holes will not be created.

Finally, always have a disaster recovery plan. If the plan is nonexistent, it can lead to chaos, panic, and confusion if an attack or outage occurs. Always have a backup plan. Wireless networks are increasingly being used in disaster areas due to their tremendous scalability and feasibility. This does not just apply to businesses but residential users as well. If your only access to the Internet is your laptop and wireless router, then a loss to either can be painful, difficult, and expensive to recover from. A good rule to follow is that 100 percent of all technology will fail. Keep that in mind when investing and relying on wireless network technology.

Human Error

Lastly, as with everything, human error is a major cause of information security breaches. Well-intentioned users can cause great harm to information technology systems without even knowing it. Unfortunately, hackers and criminals prey on unsuspecting users and typically use social engineering tactics to gain information to access networks. Excessive IT workload is another problem many companies face that helps bring down their corporate guard. Dishonesty is also an issue, due to humans wanting to commit fraud, theft, or sell intellectual property. A major cause of hacking or attacks is disgruntled employees. Those who have been fired, laid off, or reprimanded may intentionally infect the network or hack it, or release confidential information—for example, giving out the wireless access code to people so they can enter the company network and steal information.

The reality is that people are generally trusting, and if asked a question that they have the answer to, they will give it up, especially over the phone or in casual conversation. This is why communication and education to users is essential. In addition, the communication and training must be geared to the language and skill set of the user, and not use the nomenclature of the technologically proficient.

Legal Liability

As with many things, there are some downsides to wireless access points, especially if they are freely open to the public. Typically, they can be used for illegal or immoral activities, and as stated earlier, this is one of the main reasons for a hacker to attack your wireless access point. If a perpetrator is doing illegal things on your network, such as hacking, launching viruses, e-mail fraud, and stealing credit cards, chances are law enforcement can easily track it back to the originating access point. All that stands in the way is a subpoena to an Internet service provider to obtain all log information on the victim's account activity. Any good forensic work will typically tell if you are the culprit or not. Many consumers and businesses would rather not deal with this hassle, so it's important they have a secure network. Also, there can be some liability involved. For example, if you are running a community free wireless network and a person downloads a lot of illegal music, and so forth, you could have a lawsuit waiting at your door from the Recording Industry Association of America or the Business Software Alliance, demanding you repay them for lost revenue since you were providing the Internet access to the perpetrators and were neglectful to monitor the content. To protect an open public network, you could implement a term of service agreement where the user would have to agree to abide by these terms in order to use the Internet. That would at least cover some of your legal liability. But once the damage is done and the actions are in the hands of lawyers, a term of service agreement will not do you much good.

It is best that when investing in, and implementing, a wireless network that is open to the public that steps be taken to mitigate risk to the owners, and yet have usability be considered for the clients. We can not go through life fearing the information on the Net, or the cases on the docket for review. Instead, we must educate, inform, and behave above reproach at all times, while expecting nothing less from our users.

Technology Weaknesses

Wireless access points have intrinsic security weaknesses in the following areas.

Hardware and MAC Addresses

With few exceptions, network devices contain a physically unique burned-in Media Access Control address (MAC address). The purpose of this is to give a unique identifier to that piece of equipment. It is pre-assigned to the devices by its manufacturer, and in theory is completely unique. In most cases, the MAC address is 48 bits long. A standard format exists for writing MAC addresses, which consist of three groups of four hexadecimal digits separated by dots. The more common method of writing is to use six groups of two hexadecimal digits, which are in turn separated by colons or hyphens—for example, 00-07-E9-E3-84-F9.

Since each MAC address is unique, it can be used to limit network access. The steps to do so will vary by access point, but will always involve the following:

- Finding the MAC address for the devices that will be allowed to access the network (this can be found either by looking on the actual device itself, or by using the *ipconfig /all* command in the Windows command console, and *ifconfig – a* for Linux and OSX consoles).
- Entering the MAC address into the configuration for the access point (this will vary by device).

In theory, once the MAC addresses are entered into the access point, they will be the only devices allowed to access the network. In practice, a number of issues can come up, including, but not limited to, the fact that any time a new system is used in conjunction with the access point (such as a visiting client who needs to connect to the network), its MAC address must be entered individually into the access point. This can pull the network administrator away from other tasks of monitoring the network. The administrator must also periodically remove the information for devices that are no longer being used.

Another problem that exists is that of MAC address spoofing. While the address is typically encoded to the physical medium of the network device, software exists that can make a device access point have a different MAC address than it actually does. While this does have legitimate and useful purposes, including privacy and interoperability, it can also be changed to access a system illegally. Because of this large security hole, MAC address filtering should not be used by itself, and should instead be included in a wider security policy involving encryption and other authentication methods.

802.11 Authentication

Authentication is the process of determining whether someone using the wireless network is who or what they declare to be. This is typically done with a technical mechanism.

The basic requirements for authentication in a wireless LAN are

- A robust method providing identity that cannot be spoofed
- A method of preserving the identity of subsequent transactions that cannot be transferred
- Mutual authentication
- Authentication keys independent from encryption (and other) keys

Ideally, an authentication system for a wireless network should encompass all of the preceding ideas. Unfortunately, a method of this type has yet to be successfully implemented. It is also important for the authentication process to be repeated on a regular basis to ensure that the correct devices are still communicating.

There are several methods of authentication available for 802.11 networks. While they vary in their methods and effectiveness, the 802.1x standard has helped improve the security of Ethernet networks by requiring that network devices be authenticated before opening a communications port. Regardless of the method of authentication, its type is always transmitted in the frame body of the 802.11 media access control frame, and when sending frames to the access point to request authentication, the frames will almost always follow the same format.

Algorithm Number, Transaction Sequence, Status Code, and Challenge Text

The algorithm number simply indicates the form of authentication. A 0 is sent when Open System Authentication is used, and a 1 is sent when Shared Key Authentication is used. The transaction sequence number simply indicates the current step. The status code shows the final status of the authentication request, and the pass-phrase text is only sent when using a shared key.

Open System Authentication

The first and simplest method is known as Open System Authentication, and is the default method of authentication for the 802.11 standard. It essentially authenticates anyone who requests to be authenticated, which makes it a weak security method. It involves a two-step process of authentication. First, the device that wishes to associate with an access point sends a frame to the AP, giving its station ID and making a request for authentication. Once the authenticating device receives this request, it does one of two things. It either authenticates the device and sends a success message back to the point of origination, thus causing both stations to be mutually authenticated, or it sends a failure response and the authentication fails.

Open System Authentication provides little in the way of security. But it is not entirely without use, it does let two devices connect easily to each other. Additionally, it can be used with other authentication methods, such as MAC filtering.

Shared Key Authentication

Shared Key Authentication provides a more secure method of authenticating a device before it gains access to the network. It is built on the assumption that the devices authenticating each other share a common key. This key is either a 40-bit or 104-bit key in the form of 10 or 26 hex characters. The key is distributed to each station individually and not over the network. In WEP networks, the key is entered manually at each station, at the access point, and the client device.

The authentication process that follows is quite similar to that of Open System Authentication. Its differences are best demonstrated visually using a picture.

Once the access point receives an authentication request, it responds with a passphrase text, which is sent in plaintext format and is created using the WEP Pseudo Random Number Generator. The station requesting authentication then encrypts the challenge text using the key assigned to it, and sends the encrypted response back to the access point. Upon receiving the response, the access point decrypts the message and compares it to the original challenge text. If they match, it responds to the client acknowledging that it has been authenticated. Otherwise, the access point responds by rejecting authentication. This method of authentication is also known as CHaccess point (Challenge-Handshake Authentication Protocol). This is the method of authentication used in networks that utilize WEP, which is further discussed later in this chapter.

802.1x was originally designed for *wired* networks. The methods were implemented into the wireless standard with the introduction of 802.11i Like RADIUS, EAP point is not an actual authentication method. Instead, it supplies a framework in which to perform authentication. It is often found in wireless networks.

There are three significant benefits to using EAP point over standard 802.11 security methods. With EAP point, both the client and the server authenticate each other, removing the problem of what is known as a man-in-the-middle attack. Another benefit is that EAP point provides for centralized management and distribution of encryption keys—thus, saving time and effort if a device is lost. Yet another benefit is that EAP point allows centralized policy control, providing for re-authentication any time a session times out.

According to the 802.1x standard, the network is broken into three separate entities.

■ The supplicant, which is the device wishing to access the network

■ The authenticator, which controls access

■ The Authentication server, which makes authorization decisions

Because EAP point is only a framework, a multitude of methods for using EAP point exist. Among them are LEAP point (Lightweight Extensible Authentication Protocol), EAP point-TLS (Transportation Layer Security), PEAP point (Protected EAP point), and EAP point-TTLS (Tunneled Transportation Layer Security). While each version uses slightly different methods, the overall process remains roughly the same.

LEAP Point

The Lightweight Extensible Authentication Protocol (LEAP) is a proprietary version of EAP point developed by Cisco Systems. Cisco LEAP point is the widely deployed EAP point type in use today in WLANs. LEAP point supports all three of the 802.1X and EAP point elements mentioned previously. With LEAP point, mutual authentication relies on a shared secret, the user's logon password, which is known by the client and the network. The RADIUS server sends an authentication challenge to the client. The client uses a one-way hash of the user-supplied password to fashion a response to the challenge and sends that response to the RADIUS server. Using information from its user database, the RADIUS server creates its own response and compares that to the response from the client. When the RADIUS server authenticates the client, the process repeats in reverse, enabling the client to authenticate the RADIUS server. When this is complete, an EAP point-Success message is sent to the client, and both the client and the RADIUS server derive the dynamic WEP key.

SSL/TLS

Transport Security Layer (TLS) is the successor to the Secure Socket Layer protocol (SSL), which has become a standard for Internet-based transactions. SSL was originally designed by Netscape Corporation as a method of authenticating a Web site so a user could perform a secure transaction. Based on the use of digital certificates, SSL allows for both the client computer and the host Web site to authenticate each other using digital certificates. Often times, however, only the Web server has a digital certificate, relying on the user to instead authenticate themselves via use of a password or with credit card information. SSL was designed as a proprietary technology, even though it was also licensed to other browsers. As a result of the desire to have an open version of SSL, TLS is a standardized nonproprietary version of SSL, but unlike SSL it does not deal with browser security. Instead, it builds on the TCP/IP and transport layers of the OSI model.

The structure of the Transport Layer Security protocol is split into two protocol groups: the TLS Record Protocol and the TLS Handshake protocol. To briefly summarize them, the Record Protocol is a layered protocol that includes fields for length description and content. Messages to be transmitted are fragmented by the Record Protocol into smaller, more manageable blocks. The data is then compressed (if so desired), given a message authentication code (MAC), and then encrypted and sent. Once the message is received, the opposite process occurs and the data is delivered to the layers above the Transport layer.

Some of the information needed for the Record Protocol is received through the TLS Handshake protocol. Through the handshake protocol, the rules of the connection are decided upon by the communicating systems. Another important action performed by the Handshake protocol is to decide which form of encryption will be used.

Kerberos Authentication

Kerberos is another available authentication method. Evolving continuously from its original version, it was designed by the Massachusetts Institute of Technology. It allows for credential information to be embedded into a "ticket" that can then be used to access services over the network. Additionally, it can encrypt the authentication information within the ticket, preventing a number of possible attacks, as well as ensuring data integrity. Though not directly specified in the 802.11 protocol, Kerberos can be utilized over a wireless network using EAP point.

One security weakness in Kerberos is the fact that the point of access to the network must share a secret with the Key Distribution Center. Additionally, the method of sending the encrypted password with some fields in plain text allows for the possibility of a dictionary-based brute-force attack.

802.11 Security (Encryption)

Wired Equivalent Privacy (WEP) is an optional security feature that was specified by the 802.11 protocol to provide authentication and confidentiality in a wireless access point. It was one of the original methods of sending secure information using a wireless network. When the IEEE committee recommended WEP be used as a mechanism, it also said that WEP should not be considered an adequate security and strongly recommended that it not be used without an authentication process for key management. WEP employs a symmetric key to authenticate wireless devices and guarantee the integrity of the data by encrypting the transmissions. Each wireless access point and client must share the same key in order for authentication to take place. Once WEP has been enabled, it then begins a challenge and response authentication process. WEP encrypts data before it is sent from the system, and then decrypts it at the access point. It has been shown to be severely inadequate in its security methods, and as such was replaced as the wireless encryption method of choice in 2003. It uses the stream cipher RC4 (Rivest Cipher). Its method of authentication is essentially that of Shared Key Authentication since both the access point and the wireless device possess the same key. WEP keys are always either 40 bit or 104 bit. The advertised 64-bit and 128-bit encryption results from the fact that the Initialization Vector (IV) is 24 bits.

The IV is sent openly in every transmission and changes with every frame to assist in providing security. With a 24-bit key there are almost 17 million possible values for the IV. Yet with a moderately busy wireless network, that number of IVs is reached in only hours and in some cases minutes. This represents a major flaw in WEP. As IVs are reused, an attacker can employ them to decipher the WEP key.

WEP has a number of security issues involved with it. The first is that of authentication. As mentioned earlier in this access point, the four basic requirements for authentication in a wireless LAN are

- A robust method providing identity that cannot be spoofed

- A method of preserving the identity of subsequent transactions that cannot be transferred

- Mutual authentication

- Authentication keys independent from encryption (and other) keys

As mentioned in a number of sources, WEP fails on all these points. Its authentication key is the same one it uses for encryption. Additionally, no further authentication is performed after the initial authentication, meaning that after authentication occurs, another device could potentially infiltrate the network; also, the wireless device never authenticates the access point itself, leaving the possibility open that a rogue access point could spoof the wireless device into sending additional information that could help crack the key.

With the encryption method used by WEP, an attacker with enough IVs can crack the key used and gain full access to the network. In studies, WEP networks have been broken into extremely quickly. Recently, at an information security conference, the Federal Bureau of Investigation demonstrated how to crack WEP—and they did it in three minutes.

Overall, the use of WEP can create in the casual user a false sense of security. In the worst-case scenario, an attacker can gain full access to the network extremely quickly—as such, this should not be used to secure a sensitive network. In today's access points, WEP is not considered a secured method of securing a wireless access point. Be careful of out-of-the-box encryption using WEP.

With all of that said, WEP is better than the default settings. It should not be used to secure company information or trade secrets, but for regular home use. It is the equivalent of locking your front door when it is made of glass windows. It will not keep a focused attacker out, but it is more complicated than just walking in.

WPA

WPA resolves the issue of weak WEP headers as explained earlier, or the IVs, and provides a way of insuring the integrity of the messages that passed the integrity check using TKIP (the Temporal Key Integrity Protocol) to enhance data encryption. WPA-PSK is a special mode of WPA for home users without an enterprise authentication server and provides the same strong encryption protection. In simple terms, WPA-PSK is extra-strong encryption where encryption keys are automatically changed (called rekeying) and authenticated between devices after a specified period of time, or after a specified number of packets has been transmitted. This is called the rekey interval. WPA-PSK is far superior to WEP and provides stronger protection for the home/SOHO user for two reasons. The process used to generate the encryption key is very rigorous, and the rekeying (or key changing) is done very quickly.

WPA improves over WEP because it uses a per session encryption key. Every time a station associates, a new encryption key is generated based on randomization and the media access control addresses of the wireless access point.

Unfortunately, though, the easiest way to use WPA actually makes it easier to crack than WEP. When 802.1X authentication is not used in WPA, a simpler system called Pre-Shared Key (PSK) is. A pre-shared key is a password that all clients need to be configured with in order to access the access point. Most consumer routers have the capability of using the WPA with the PSK preshared key.

With WPA-PSK, and almost all passwords, if you make a short character password, then you are susceptible to an offline dictionary attack where an attacker grabs a few packets at the time a legitimate station joins the wireless network, and then can take those packets and recover the PSK used. An attacker can get what he needs in order to guess the PSK and get out without anyone noticing. This can occur because the attacker doesn't have to be near the WLAN for more than a few seconds, and the LAN doesn't have to be very busy. This attack depends on the choice of a password, although cracking techniques get better and better. Thus, WPA has been defeated. Most wireless access points have a mechanism built into WPA, which converts an 8- to 63-character string you type in to the 64-digit or 128-digit key (as used with WEP). Although most wireless access points won't be able to use the whole 64-bit key with pass phrase mode.

The innate problem is that a pass phrase is easy to guess. The IEEE committee that wrote 802.11i pointed out that an eight- to ten-character pass phrase actually has less than the 40 bits of security that the most basic version of WEP offers, and said that a pass phrase of less than about 20 characters is unlikely to deter attacks. As with WEP, wireless cracking tools exist that are specifically designed to recover the PSK from a WPA-protected network (such as Kismet) which are easily available to download.

WPA with 802.1X authentication (sometimes called WPA-Enterprise) makes for a much more secure network. 802.1X offers strong positive authentication for both the station and the WLAN infrastructure, while deriving a secure, per-session encryption key that is not vulnerable to any casual attack. This is typically used with a RADIUS server as explained earlier regarding authentication. The best wireless security mechanism out there with most access points is 802.1X authentication, combined with WPA's improved encryption.

But instead of pointing out all of the inherent flaws with passing data over unlicensed radio frequencies, WPA, which comes with most new consumer routers, is an excellent way to keep your Internet surfing and home network as safe as it can be. Add VPN connections and MAC filtering and you basically have the same security as you do with an alarm system on your home. It deters people from getting access without considerable resolve.

Intrusion Detection Systems

Intrusion detection systems (IDSes) are monitoring devices on the network that help security administrators identify attacks in progress, stop them, and conduct forensic analysis after the attack is over. These can either be network-based or software-based and can be used with wireless network points to determine if a wireless access point is being attacked and perhaps compromised. Intrusion detection tools assist organizations by expanding options available to manage the risk from threats and vulnerabilities. They gather useful information that can not only be used to detect an attacker but also to identify and stop him, support investigations as to the attacker's strategy, and prevent his strategy from being used in the future.

Access Point Spoofing

Sometimes hackers can imitate an existing access point. By doing this, they change the SSID and MAC address to totally imitate a wireless access point already in existence. Then, for example, when you unsuspectingly connect, the attacker will be able to intercept all confidential information and much more. In order to thwart this wireless access point, audits should be done periodically to make sure there aren't unsuspected rogue access points.

Many off-the-shelf access points allow you to see all of the devices connected to the network or that have connected to the network in the past. This is how you are able to see if an unsuspecting neighbor has accessed your network by accident or on purpose. If your network was accessed by a real intruder, more than likely the tracks will have been covered. But someone active on their network will tend to see unfamiliar peers through the access point, or on their network.

Summary

Over the last few years wireless has become integrated into the computer user's life. The technology has allowed us to get out of the home and office, or off the desk, and let us seek and send information where and when we want. This is a great leap in communications and lifestyle. With all such things, there are risks, however, and people who are out to take advantage of the openness of the technology. It is our responsibility as those that administer and understand the technology to educate, communicate, and support our users despite their lack of interest in understanding how it works.

We could go about preaching policy, firewall rules, and access control lists to help limit the connectivity of our users, but this would go against the very reason the license was granted to use the radio frequency in the first place. We are here to increase the sophistication of our users through patience and communication. At the same time, we have an obligation to protect our data systems and promote the use of new technologies that make us more mobile and more human. The key is to pay attention, to look for bad practices, and take the initiative to improve them. More importantly, it is to let users know why we are taking action, and spreading such news for the sake of security. It took years for the American people to lock their homes and cars; it took massive crime waves and news casts to get people to take action to protect their valuables. We should do our best to ensure that we relay these same messages in order to secure not only data but the access to bandwidth and private information.

Chapter 8

No-Tech Hacking
by Johnny Long

Johnny Long is the author of the bestselling *Google Hacking for Penetration Testers*, as well as a contributing author to *Stealing the Network: How to Own a Shadow* in the popular "Stealing" series. He is a professional hacker by trade and a security researcher and author. His home on the Web is http://johnny.ihackstuff.com. His popular "Death by a Thousand Cuts" presentation was one of the most-talked-about sessions at conferences this past year.

Introduction: What Is "No-Tech Hacking?"

When I got into this field, I knew I would have to stay ahead of the tech curve. I spent many sleepless nights worming through my home network trying to learn the ropes. My practice paid off. After years of hard work and dedicated study, I founded a small but elite pen testing team. I was good, my *foo* strong. Networks fell prostrate before me. My co-workers looked up to me, and I thought I was The Man. Then I met Vince.

In his mid-40s, hawk-eyed, and vaguely European looking, Vince blended in with the corporate crowd. His usual attire consisted of a pair of black wing tips, a nice dress shirt, a black leather trench coat, and every now and then, he topped it all off with a black fedora. He had a definite aura. Tales of his exploits were legendary. Some said he had been a fed, working deep-black projects for the government. Other insisted he was some kind of mercenary genius, selling his dark secrets to the highest bidder.

Vince was brilliant. In fact, brilliant was an understatement. He held several college degrees—or so I heard—but it wasn't his academic knowledge that people talked about. He could do interesting and seemingly impossible things. He could pick locks, short-circuit electronic systems, and pluck information out of the air with fancy electronic gear. He once showed me a system he built called a "van Eck" something-or-other.[1] It could sniff the electromagnetic radiation coming from a CRT and reassemble it, allowing him to eavesdrop on someone's computer monitor from a quarter mile away. He taught me that a black-and-white TV could be used to monitor 900MHz cellular phone conversations. I still remember hunching over a table in my basement going at the UHF tuner post of an old black-and-white TV with a pair of needle-nosed pliers. When I heard a cellular phone conversation coming through that old TV's speaker, I decided then and there I would learn everything I could from Vince.

I was incredibly intimidated before our first gig. Fortunately, we had different roles. I was to perform an internal assessment, which emulated an insider threat. If an employee went rogue, he could do unspeakable damage to a network. In order to properly emulate this, our clients provided us a workspace, a network jack, and the username and password of a legitimate, non-administrative user. I was tasked with leveraging those credentials to gain administrative control of critical network systems. If I gained access to confidential records stored within a corporate database, for example, my efforts were considered successful. I had a near-perfect record with internal assessments and was confident in my abilities.

Vince was to perform a physical assessment that emulated an external physical threat. The facility had top-notch physical security. They had poured a ton of money into expensive locks, sensors, and surveillance gear. I knew Vince would obliterate them all with his high-tech superpowers. The gig looked to be a real slam-dunk with him working the physical and me working the internal. We were the "dream team" of security geeks.

When Vince insisted I help him with the physical part of the assessment, I just about fell over. I imagined a James Bond movie, with Vince as "Q" and myself (of course) as James Bond in ninja assault gear. Vince would supply the gadgets, like the van Eck thingamabob and I would infiltrate the perimeter and spy on their surveillance monitors or something. I giggled to myself about the unnatural things we would do to the electronic keypad systems or the proximity locks. I imagined the looks on the guard's faces when we duct-taped them to their chairs after silently rappelling down from the ceiling of the surveillance room.

I couldn't wait to get started. I told Vince to hand over the alien gadgets we would use to pop the security. When he told me he hadn't brought any gadgets, I laughed and poked him. I never knew Vince was a kidder. When he told me he really didn't bring any gear, I briefly considered pushing him over, but I had heard he was a black belt in like six different martial arts, so I just politely asked him what the heck he was thinking. He said we were going to be creative. The mercenary genius, the storm center of all the swirling rumors, hadn't brought any gear. I asked him how creative a person could be when attacking a highly secured building without any gear. He just looked at me and gave me this goofy grin. I'll never forget that grin.

We spent the morning checking out the site. It consisted of several multistory buildings and a few employee parking lots, all enclosed by protective fencing. Everyone came and went through a front gate. Fortunately, the gate was open and unguarded. With Vince driving, we rounded one building and parked behind it, in view of the loading docks.

"There," he said.

"Where?" I asked.

"There," he repeated.

Vince's sense of humor sucked sometimes. I could never quite tell when he was giving me crap. I followed the finger and saw a loading dock. Just past the bay doors, several workers carried packages around. "The loading dock?" I asked.

"That's your way in."

I made a "Pffft" sound.

"Exactly. Easy." he said.

"I didn't mean 'Pffft' as in *easy*. I meant 'Pffft' as in *there's people there* and you said *I* was going in."

"There are, and you are," he said. Vince was helpful that way. "Just look like you belong. Say hello to the employees. Be friendly. Comment on the weather."

I did, and I did. Then I did, and I did and I found myself inside. I walked around, picked up some blueprints of tanks and military-looking stuff, photocopied them and left. Just like that. I'm skipping the description of my heart pounding at 400 beats per minute and the thoughts of what military prison would be like and whether or not the rumors about Bubba were true, but I did it. And it was an incredible rush. It was social engineering at its simplest, and it worked wonders. No one questioned me. I suppose it was just too awkward for them. I couldn't hide my grin as I walked to the car. Vince was nowhere to be found. He emerged from the building a few minutes later, carrying a small stack of letter-sized paper.

"How did you get in?" I asked.

"Same way you did."

"So why didn't you just do it yourself?" I asked.

"I had to make sure it would work first."

I was Vince's guinea pig but it didn't really matter. I was thrilled and ready for more. The next building we targeted looked like an absolute fortress. There were no loading docks and the only visible entrance was the front door. It was wood and steel—too much like a castle door for my taste—and approximately six inches thick, sporting a proximity card-reader device. We watched as employees swiped a badge, pulled open the doors and walked in. I suggested we tailgate. I was on a roll. Vince shook his head. He obviously had other plans. He walked towards the building and slowed as we approached the front door. Six feet from the door, he stopped. I walked a step past him and turned around, my back to the door.

"Nice weather," he said, looking past me at the door.

"Ehrmm, yeah," I managed.

"Good day for rock climbing."

I began to turn around to look at the building. I hadn't considered climbing it.

"No," he said. "Don't turn around. Let's chat."

"Chat?" I asked. "About what?"

"You see that Bears game last night?" he asked. I had no clue what he was talking about or even who the Bears were but he continued. "Man, that was something else. The way that team works together, it's almost as if..." Vince stopped in mid-sentence as the front door opened. An employee pushed the door open, and headed towards the parking lot. "They move as a single unit," he continued. I couldn't help myself. I turned around. The door had already closed.

"Crap," I said. "We could have made it inside."

"Yes, a coat hanger."

Vince said strange stuff sometimes. That was just part of the package. It wasn't crazy-person stuff, it was just stuff that most people were too dense to understand. I had a pretty good idea I had just witnessed his first crazy-person moment. "Let's go," he said. "I need a washcloth. I need to go back to the hotel." I had no idea why he needed a washcloth, but I was relieved to hear he was still a safe crazy person. I had heard of axe murderers, but never washcloth murderers.

We passed the ride back to the hotel in silence; Vince seemed lost in his thoughts. He pulled up in front of the hotel, parked, and told me to wait for him. He emerged a few minutes later with a wire coat hanger and a damp washcloth. He tossed them into the back seat. "This should work," he said, sliding into his seat and closing the doors. I was afraid to ask. Pulling away from the hotel, he continued. "I should be able to get in with these."

I gave him a look. I can't exactly say what the look was, but I imagine it was somewhere between "I've had an unpleasant olfactory encounter" and "There's a tarantula on your head." Either way, I was pretty convinced he'd lost his mind or had it stolen by aliens. I pretended not to hear him. He continued anyhow.

"Every building has to have exits," he said. "Federal law dictates that in the case of an emergency, exit doors must operate from the inside out without the user having any prior knowledge of its operation." I blinked and looked up at the sky through the windshield. I wondered if the aliens were coming for me next. "Furthermore, the exit must not require the use of any key or special token. Exit doors are therefore very easy to get out of."

"This has something to do with that door we were looking at, doesn't it?" I asked. The words surprised me. Vince and I were close to the same operating frequency.

He looked at me, and then I knew what *my look* looked like. I instinctively swatted at the tarantula that I could practically feel on my head. "This has *everything* to do with that door," he said, looking out the front window and hanging a left. We were headed back to the site. "The front door of that facility," he continued, "is formidable. It uses a very heavy-duty magnetic bolting system. My guess is that it would resist the impact of a 40-mile-an-hour vehicle. The doors are very thick, probably shielded, and the prox system is expensive."

"But you have a washcloth," I said. I couldn't resist.

"Exactly. Did you notice the exit mechanism on the door?"

I hadn't, and bluffing was out of the question. "No," I admitted.

"You need to notice *everything*," he said, pausing to glare at me. I nodded and he continued. "The exit mechanism is a silver-colored metal bar about waist-high."

I took my shot. "Oh, right. A push bar." The term sounded technical enough.

"No, not a push bar." Access denied. "The bar on that door is touch-sensitive. It doesn't operate by pressure; it operates when it senses it has been touched. Very handy in a fire." We pulled through the site's gate and parked. Vince unbuckled and grabbed the hanger and the washcloth from the back seat. He had untwisted the hanger, creating one long straight piece of strong, thin wire. He folded it in half, laid the washcloth on one end and folded the end of the hanger around it, then bent the whole thing to form a funny 90-degree-angled white washcloth flag. I smartly avoided any comment about using it to surrender to the guards. "Let's go," he said.

We walked to the front door. It was nearly 6:00 P.M. and very few employees were around. He walked up to the door, jammed the washcloth end of the hangar between the doors at waist height and started twisting the hanger around. I could hear the washcloth flopping around on the other side of the door. Within seconds, I heard a muffled *cla-chunk* and Vince pulled the door open and walked inside. I stood there gawking at the door as it closed behind him. The door reopened, and Vince stuck his head out. "You coming?"

The customer brief was a thing to behold. After the millions of dollars they had spent to secure that building, they learned that the entire system had been defeated with a washcloth and a wire coat hanger, all for want of a $50 gap plate for the door. The executives were incredulous and demanded proof, which Vince provided in the form of a field trip. I never learned what happened as a result of that demonstration, but I will never forget the lesson I learned: the simplest solutions are often the most practical.

Sure we could have messed with the prox system, figured out the magnetic tolerances on the lock or scaled the walls and used our welding torches—just like in the movies—to cut a hole in the ceiling, but we didn't have to. This is the essence of no-tech hacking. It requires technical knowledge to reap the full benefit of a no-tech attack, but technical knowledge is not required to repeat it. Worst of all, despite the simplicity, a no-tech attack is perhaps the most deadly and misunderstood.

Through the years, I've learned to follow Vince's advice. I now notice *everything*, and I try to keep complicated thinking reined in. Now, I'm hardly ever off duty. I constantly see new attack vectors, the most dangerous of which can be executed by anyone possessing the will to do so.

TIP

The Key to No-Tech Hacking The key to no-tech hacking is to think simply, be aware, and to travel eyes open, head up. For example, when I go to a mall or some other socially dense atmosphere, I watch people. To me, strangers are an interesting puzzle and I reflexively try to figure out as much about them as I can. When I pass a businessman in an airport, my mind goes into overdrive as I try to sense his seat number and social status; make out his medical problems; fathom his family situation (or sense his sexual orientation); figure out his financial standing; infer his income level; deduce his dietary habits; and have a guess at his home address. When I go to a restaurant, I drift in and out of conversations around me, siphoning interesting tidbits of information. My attention wanders as I analyze my surroundings, taking it all in. When I walk through the parking lot of a building, I check out the vehicles along the way to determine what goes on inside and who the building's residents might be. I do all this stuff not because of my undiagnosed attention deficit disorder but because it's become a habit as a result of my job. I have personally witnessed the power of perception. When faced with tough security challenges, I don't charge. I hang back and I watch. A good dose of heightened perception levels the playing field every time.

A Word about Social Engineering Jack Wiles talks quite a bit about social engineering in his chapter, so I won't belabor it here. Suffice it to say that a good no-tech hacker is also a good social engineer. As we discuss these techniques, bear in mind that an attacker employing good social engineering skills alongside these attacks makes for a very worthy adversary.

Physical Security

I remember my first physical assessment. I imagined myself picking locks and disabling electronic surveillance systems. I imagined myself as that marine in the movie *Aliens*, frantically noodling with wires in an electronic lock, desperately trying to get my team inside to safety. Although I ended up breaking into all sorts of amazing places in real life—and eventually did bypass a number of electronic surveillance systems—I never had to resort to picking a single lock. Simpler techniques always prevailed. In this section, I'll share some of what worked best for me.

Tailgating

Tailgating describes the act of gaining unauthorized access to a restricted area by following closely behind an authorized individual. When I suggested tailgating into the fortress, Vince opted for the washcloth trick. His idea was better given the situation, but tailgating is still one of the best no-tech methods for gaining access to a facility.

Through the years, I've noticed signs and placards reminding employees to be on the lookout for tailgaters. The fact that "tailgater" has become a common term in the business environment testifies that this is a common problem. Still, it works.

Years ago, I was tasked with a physical assessment against a state government facility. The facility was broken into two distinct areas: an open area to accommodate the general public and a restricted area for state employees. We were tasked with entering the restricted area and gaining access to the closed computer network inside. Our initial reconnaissance revealed that the open and restricted buildings were interconnected, but an armed guard stood watch over the connecting hallway. The restricted building's front door was similarly protected. Swipe card readers—none of which appeared vulnerable to the washcloth trick—protected the side doors. Armed guards in marked vehicles patrolled the parking lots. Somewhat discouraged, we continued monitoring the buildings. Eventually we came upon a cluster of smokers huddled outside near a door. I knew immediately we had found our way in. We headed to the nearest gas station and I bought a pack of cigarettes and a lighter.

I had come prepared to social engineer my way into the building as a phone technician.[2] I was wearing cruddy jeans, work boots, and a white T-shirt with a phone company logo. I had a phone company employee badge clipped to my collar. My bright-yellow toolbox sported phone company logos and the clear top revealed a small stack of branded payphone info-strips. The toolbox was filled with phone test equipment. A battered hardhat completed the look.

The official-looking getup was, of course, a complete fabrication. I downloaded the phone company logo from the Internet. I printed the T-shirt myself using iron-on transfer paper. I printed the badge on my home printer and laminated it with a $2 kit. The payphone strips were liberated from some local payphones. The phone test gear was legitimate; I had collected it for just such an occasion. I found the hardhat abandoned on the side of the road—its battered condition made it more convincing. (See Figure 8.1.)

Figure 8.1 Paraphernalia of a Phony Phone Technician

Approaching the group of smokers would have been a bad idea, regardless of how good an actor I turned out to be. If they watched me wander towards them from the parking lot, they would certainly consider me an outsider. If instead they came out of the building and found me already there, halfway through a smoke, they might assume I had come *out* of the building for a break.

I waited for the smokers to disburse and made my way to the side door. A pair of employees eventually came out for a smoke and talked amongst themselves. I greeted them casually and joined in their small talk. They chattered about company politics and I nodded appropriately, making sure to blow smoke up into the air every now and then to convince them of my familiarity with cigarettes. I grunted about how the phone system was a pain in the rear-end. They laughed and I tried not to gag on the cigarette, wondering the whole time if I was turning as green as I felt. As they put out their smokes, they swiped their badges. I flicked my cigarette into the road and held the door open for them. They thanked me for the kind gesture and I filed in behind them. Once inside I wished them a good day and had my way with the facility.

I made my way through the building and was never challenged. At one point, I even walked through the security office. The receptionist looked surprised to see me until I pointed to an empty desk and told her the phone was broken. She wasn't sure whether the phone was broken or not but she let me in—I was the phone guy after all. I plopped my toolbox on the desk, picked up the phone and heard a dial tone. I shook my head, put the phone back on the cradle and lifted my toolbox off the desk, taking with it a stack of important looking documents. I left the office grumbling about stupid work orders and how they always give me the wrong jack number and how it always made me look like an idiot. The receptionist giggled and told me to come back any time. I think she liked me.

All in all, it was a good day. The facility was simple to gain access to despite the expensive safeguards. I left with hardcopy proof of my presence and I had softcopy proof of my intrusion into their network thanks to the data on my paperback-sized computer. The employees never challenged me because they recognized the logo and knew that it belonged to a phone company. If the logo looked legit, the credentials looked legit. If the credentials looked legit, I looked legit. But I had purposely played the role of a technician from the *wrong* phone company. The company I selected was a recognized data and voice service provider. They did not provide local hardware support. In layman's terms, even if I was an employee of that phone company, I had no business being in the facility, and even if I did, I wouldn't have been testing phone handsets.

It all boiled down to playing a convincing role. I used the age-old technique of tailgating to gain initial access to the building and then threw in a healthy dose of social engineering to schmooze those I met inside. Every step of the way an employee took me at face value, even though any one of them could have put an immediate end to the break-in.

Bear in mind that the phone technician gag isn't the only one at my disposal. Depending on the situation, I could have played the role of a delivery person, an electrician, a plumber, an elevator repairman or any other kind of service personnel. The choices are endless. All I need to do is be in the right place at the right time, present a convincing demeanor, and dress the part. Finding the right place and time takes patience. Schmoozing takes practice. Dressing the part simply requires that I get a decent photo of the person I'm interested in imitating. At first, I found this difficult. I would sneak around trying to get a crisp candid photo to work from, but failed miserably. The pictures would end up blurred or off-centered, and in most cases I couldn't make out the small details that render the outfit convincing. Eventually I learned to follow my own advice and take the simplest approach. Now, I just *ask* for permission to photograph service personnel. I ask in a polite, non-threatening way and most workers are more than happy to oblige me. The guy shown in Figure 8.2 was extremely accommodating, allowing me to photograph his outfit, his truck and even his employee badge.

Figure 8.2

> **NOTE**
>
> You'll certainly tire of hearing this, but it bears repeating. The delivery company is not at fault for allowing their employees to be photographed. The security weakness lies in allowing your employees to remain non-confrontational when something seems off. Employees need to understand that tailgating should never be permitted, and service personnel should not be taken at face value. Challenge their presence, especially if they are unfamiliar or something seems out of place.

Where Are Your Badges?

My phone company getup was convincing, but without the badge I doubt I would have made it inside. The badge identified me as a phone guy. However, the badge was nothing more than a laminated bit of printer paper. To use security jargon, that laminated paper was my *authentication token*. By letting someone visually inspect it, they could draw a conclusion about whether or not I was legitimate. This type of visual identification is a weak authentication mechanism because it is so easily duplicated. Unfortunately, many facilities rely on exactly this type of security, yet it amazes me how many badges I see worn out in public.

I spot at least ten different types of badges a day. If I had a nickel for every time I saw a new badge, I'd have a *whole* lot of nickels. Even though I've seen hundreds or thousands of badges in my lifetime, I still get giddy when I see a new one because I know beyond a shadow of a doubt that I could somehow use it to gain access to that company. Even if they employ some sort of electronic system to validate the card—we'll talk more about those systems later in this section—I could probably use the badge to tailgate or social engineer my way inside. Getting giddy about site badges is admittedly strange, but I've long since given up on the doldrums of normality. These days I go all the way; I carry a camera wherever I go to capture badges I spot in the wild. I spotted the badge shown in Figure 8.3 in a local mall.

Figure 8.3

Badges sometimes appear in packs, as the photo in Figure 8.4 reveals.

Figure 8.4

I captured this next photo (see Figure 8.5) as I sat in a corporate lobby. The walls were lined with all sorts of plaques and awards that the company had earned through the years. Several flat-screen monitors droned through PowerPoint presentations extolling their corporate virtues. I amused myself with a game of "count the buzzwords" until I saw this particular slide and nearly flipped backwards out of the overstuffed leather armchair.

Figure 8.5

This slide was one of several that showed groups of employees—in various stages of corporate bonding—all wearing their badges. After spending a total of two minutes in the building's open lobby, I had no less than ten badge photos. Fortunately for this company, I was "off duty" and never discovered if a laminated bit of printer paper would be enough to work my way inside.

Government agencies have known for years that employee badges should be removed when leaving the workplace. The more secretive agencies are very proactive when it comes to enforcing this policy. I was not surprised to discover so few open-air badges around more secretive government buildings. The keyword here is *few*. While spending some time in the D.C. corridor, I came upon an outdoor barbeque catered by an office leasing company. The event was designed to show appreciation for the various corporate tenants, some of which were government related. As I wandered around the large catering tent, I was amazed at the number of badges I spotted. I was so busy snapping pictures of people that I nearly forgot to take advantage of the free grub.

Although I saw badges belonging to several different companies, some were more surprising than others, like the airfield badge shown in Figure 8.6.

Figure 8.6

I am relatively certain that airport security personnel do not rely solely on visual badge identification as an authentication mechanism, but the photo is interesting nonetheless considering it was taken well away from airport property.

Two women waiting in line caught my eye (not in that way). The taller of the two was very important-looking. She was dressed in a smart black suit and was having an important-sounding conversation on her Blackberry cell phone. It wasn't the geek-chic cell phone that caught my eye, but rather the plethora of badges and paraphernalia dangling from her lanyard. Traveling in tech circles, I've seen my share of lanyard clutter, but this nice lady took the prize for most neck-flair toted by a female. (See Figure 8.7.)

Figure 8.7

As I drew closer, I realized that her badge was decidedly governmental in appearance. I took a few photos—which neither of them seemed to notice—and after reviewing them, I realized I had a horrible angle on the more interesting badges. As she continued chatting into the phone, I swung around to the other side of her and stepped in as close as I could without triggering her (admittedly impaired) stalker detection system. Less than a foot away from her, I snapped the photo shown in Figure 8.8.

Figure 8.8

This particular badge is issued to government employees stationed at the Pentagon. The Post-It note reminds her to "bring a copy of yesterday's all hands to DSS H.Q." Granted, security at the Pentagon is second to none. I know from personal experience that the guards stationed at the Pentagon mean business. They are not to be trifled with. I also know that visual identification of a badge at the Pentagon means absolutely nothing. All badges are electronically verified, and the security of that electronic process is world-class. Still, I had no doubt that Pentagon security personnel would not take kindly to employees exhibiting this kind of careless behavior. I'm not pointing the finger at the Pentagon, but I need to illustrate an important point: even the most die-hard government agencies hire sometimes-careless human beings. The *policies* in place at the Pentagon ensure that careless behavior does not negatively impact the security posture of the facility. Corporate security officers should take this lesson to heart. Visual identification of an employee badge is not a secure authentication mechanism. Do not allow any avenue for social engineers. Establish a secure access mechanism and back it up with sound, enforceable policy that employees understand and are bound to. Employees should understand that security is not someone else's problem.

Electronic Badge Authentication

I think I have successfully established that visual badge identification is inherently insecure. Electronic verification is a much more secure method of authentication. Although electronic systems have security issues as well (see the sidebar) there are some no-tech attacks that are interesting as well. It is not uncommon to see proximity-type cards in plain view, as shown in the photo in Figure 8.9.

Security Alert...

High-Tech Badge Attacks

Many technological differences exist between *swipe* cards and *proximity* or *contactless* cards, but they can be attacked in similar ways. Both can be copied, but thanks to the device developed by Jonathan Westhues (detailed at http://cq.cx/prox.pl) contactless cards can be copied from a distance even when they are carried in a pocket or purse. To prevent this type of attack, consider combining access cards with PIN identification schemes, or deploy a system that relies on encryption, challenge-response systems, or reader access lists, like HiD's *iClass* line.

Figure 8.9

This pair had executed good common sense and removed their site badges. However, their access cards were still in plain view. Although the possibility existed for cloning the cards, in the spirit of no-tech I suggest that an adversary can use visual inspection to learn quite a bit about the card's owner. Consider the typical *Datawatch* card shown in Figure 8.10.

Figure 8.10

The logo on the left-hand side of the photo reveals it was manufactured by HiD Corporation (http://www.hidcorp.com). The physical characteristics and lack of additional logos on the card suggest it is *proximity*-based and is not an *iClass* card. This means the card may be prone to duplication. The toll-free number on the card belongs to Datawatch Systems. An adversary can call this number, speak to a representative, read off the top row of numbers, and learn not only the address and building number the card will work on, but in some cases the suite or room number as well.

Most people would never consider wearing a Post-It note on their forehead revealing their work address, but it's surprising how many people wear these electronic cards in plain sight which reveal essentially the same information. Access cards like these should be removed when leaving a work area.

Lock Bumping

Lock picking is a fairly technical exercise. It requires knowledge of lock mechanics and internals, and perfecting the technique takes quite a bit of practice. *Lock bumping*, on the other hand, falls firmly into the no-tech hacking category. The technique involves the use of *bump keys*, or *999 keys*, which are keys that have been made by cutting a key blank so each cut is made to a maximum depth and the tip and shoulder have been filed down by approximately half a millimeter. To a trained eye, bump keys have a very distinct look—the cuts are too uniform—as shown in Figure 8.11.

Figure 8.11

Permission Granted by Toool—The Open Organization Of Lockpickers

The technique works by inserting a bump key into a lock and tapping the key while turning the key slightly in the lock. The bottom internal pins in the lock are nudged, transferring momentum to the pins sitting above them. As the top pins fly upwards, the bottom pins remain down. When the pins separate, the cylinder can be turned, and if done correctly, the lock will open. Bypassing a lock with a bump key takes much less skill than picking the lock with a traditional lock pick set or electronic pick device. This means that just about anyone can compromise a vulnerable lock. For more information on prevention and identification of vulnerable locks, see the references mentioned in the sidebar, or personally contact a professional locksmith or security provider.

Security Alert...

Treasure Trove of Bumping Info

Lock Bumping has been around for many years, but has gained popularity because of several recent works. Marc Tobias's book *Locks, Safes, and Security* is an excellent reference book for professionals, and includes a great piece on bumping or "rapping" as it is sometimes called. His Web site (http://security.org) and alerts page (http://security.org/dial-90/alerts.htm) is also an excellent resource. If you're looking for more accessible material, I highly recommend the awesome whitepaper *Bumping Locks* (http://www.toool.nl/bumping.pdf) by Barry Wels and Rop Gonggrijp of Toool, The Open Organization of Lockpickers, and their awesome video workshop *What the Bump?* at http://connectmedia.waag.org/toool/whatthe-bump.wmv. The Toool Web site (http://connect.waag.org/toool) has a ton of resources and videos I highly recommend.

Master Lock Brute Forcing

As a kid, I remember seeing the cool Master Lock commercial with the lock that was secure even after being drilled clean through by a rifle round. For me, and for many others, Master Lock became synonymous with security. To this day, I purchase Master Locks based on the brand name alone. However, do not buy just based on the brand name. Always investigate all the product offerings to make sure you're getting a product that suits your needs. For example, the Master Lock model 1500D combination lock is ubiquitous (see Figure 8.12).

Figure 8.12

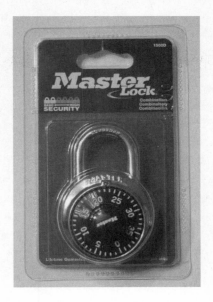

However, as Figure 8.13 shows, the packaging clearly reveals that the lock is meant for only basic security tasks.

Figure 8.13

Still, I see this exact lock used in high-security applications almost daily, despite the fact that a dangerous brute-force attack against it has come to light.

Brute forcing describes a technique in which every possible solution for a problem is checked to see if it is the solution. For example, a hacker could brute force a password by trying every combination of possible passwords until one works. This technique is relatively slow, even when automated, but if every possible combination is tested, it works reliably. Most mechanical combination locks can be brute-forced if an adversary has enough time and patience to complete the attack—and therein lies the rub. Most adversaries have neither the time nor the patience to brute force a combination lock. In the case of the Master Lock, if we assume each of the numbers on the dial is active—which is not the case—we are left with 40^3 or 64,000 possible combinations. If an attacker tries one combination every five seconds—a reasonable speed considering the clearing process and the left-right turns—it could take as long as 88 hours, or nearly four days, to work through every combination. At this rate, the attacker would fall before the combination did.

A shortcut was discovered that reduces the number of combinations to 100. At five seconds per attempt, it would take an attacker a mere eight minutes to brute force one hundred combinations. Since this book is about protecting your own assets, I won't go into all the details required to open a lock using this technique, but rather I will describe how to arrive at the last number in the combination. If you use this technique against your own locks and are able to determine the last number of the combination, you may want to have a professional locksmith evaluate your situation, or choose a higher-security Master Lock.

To begin, you will need to apply tension to the shackle of the lock. A simple way to do this is to hold the lock in one hand and use a finger to apply upward pressure as shown in Figure 8.14. The stylish thumb ring is optional for this exercise.

Next, begin turning the dial. If enough tension is applied, the dial should stick between two numbers. This is called a *sticking point*; 12 sticking points exist on each affected lock. The first goal is to keep a record of the location of each sticking point. For example, the lower boundary of this lock's first sticking point is one. (See Figure 8.15.)

Figure 8.14

Figure 8.15

The high boundary of this same sticking point is the number two as shown in Figure 8.16.

Figure 8.16

The location of the first sticking point rests between these numbers at 1.5, which is obviously not a whole number. To find the next sticking point, release the tension on the shackle, turn the dial past the current sticking point's high boundary and reapply tension. The dial should stick again, revealing the location of the next sticking point. Some sticking points will rest on whole numbers. For example, the low boundary of this sticking point is 7.5. (See Figure 8.17.)

Figure 8.17

The high boundary of this same sticking point is 8.5 as shown in Figure 8.18.

Figure 8.18

This means that the sticking point rests on eight. Keep a record of each sticking point. Table 8.1 shows the sticking points of my test lock.

Table 8.1 The Sticking Points on My Lock

Low Boundary	High Boundary	Sticking Point
1	2	1.5
4	5	4.5
7.5	8.5	8
11	12	11.5
14.5	15.5	15
17.5	18.5	18
21	22	21.5
24	25	24.5
27.5	28.5	28
31	32	31.5
34	35	34.5
37.5	38.5	38

Notice that more than half of the sticking points do not land on whole numbers. These are decoys and should be removed from the list of potential combination digits. In our example, we are left with five numbers: 8, 15, 18, 28, and 38. Notice that each of these numbers end in the same digit—the number eight. These matching numbers should be removed from the list as well, leaving only one number, 15, which is the last digit of my lock's combination.

If this technique works on your lock, there's a good chance the lock is vulnerable to a brute-force attack. If the technique does not work, you may have a newer 1500D Master Lock. It is speculated (on www.wikihow.com/Crack-a-Master-Combination-Lock) that 1500D Master Locks with serial numbers beginning with the number 800 are not vulnerable to this attack, although unverified sources have reported success against these newer locks as well. Either way, don't be quick to throw stones at Master Lock. Do your research, and don't purchase basic security products for high-security tasks. Consider purchasing a higher security Master Lock for your application, or get the advice of a professional locksmith or security professional.

NOTE

Several Web sites—listed at the end of this chapter—discuss this vulnerability in great detail. However, there's a decent amount of math and memorization involved in determining the first and second digits of the combination. Tim "Thor" Mullen presents a shortcut he worked out in his book *Stealing the Network: How to Own A Shadow* by Syngress Publishing. The story, co-authored by Tim, Ryan "Blue boar" Russell, and myself, tells a gripping tale of what hackers are capable of in the real world. By all accounts, the story is fiction, but the techniques, like the Master Lock brute force, are not. Check out the entire *Stealing* series to see what you might be up against when the hackers take the gloves off!

Picking Locks with Toilet Paper?

In 1992, the BBC reported that certain cylindrical axial pin tumbler locks were vulnerable to bypass by unskilled thieves. Twelve years later, in August of 2004, Marc Tobias, author of *Locks, Safes, and Security,* found that Kensington and Targus were using similar cylindrical axial designs in their laptop lock products. His report suggested that the locks could be easily bypassed with a pen or a toilet paper tube. In September of 2004, Chris Brennan described on his forums (www.bikeforums.net) how an expensive Kryptonite bike lock (which used the same cylindrical axial design) could be bypassed with a Bic pen. Chris posted videos to www.bikeforums.net/video and a media frenzy ensued.

Enter Barry Wels of Toool. While presenting at a hacker conference, Barry created a video (http://www.toool.nl/kensington623.wmv) showing how to apply the bypass technique to a specific Kensington laptop lock system. The hacker community found the video interesting, but the public in general was awed by the fact that he accomplished the bypass in mere moments using the cardboard from a toilet paper roll. (See Figure 8.19.)

Figure 8.19

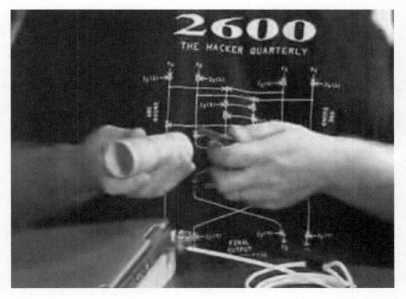

While there is always speculation about who thought of what first, nearly one million people have downloaded the video from Barry's site, and countless others have downloaded it from sites like Youtube.com. I love Barry's video because it is so accessible and it clearly demonstrates what I'm trying to show in this chapter: even the most complex security systems are at risk from simple attacks. If you have sensitive data on a laptop, and you rely on a single locking device to protect that data, you'll probably get burned whether or not the lock is vulnerable to this attack. Whenever you rely on a single layer of security, odds are you'll get burned. A laptop lock isn't a bad idea, but if you're concerned about losing sensitive data on the machine, consider some sort of crypto solution as well. Above all, try to think like a hacker. In that frame of mind, is a spindly cable the best solution?

Electric Flossers: A Low-Tech Classic

Lock picking is a real skill. To do it right, you've got to have a working knowledge of how locks operate and you need to practice. With the advent of newer devices, lock picking seems more accessible than ever. Still, lock-picking guns and electric devices are not foolproof. They require a decent amount of skill to successfully operate. In addition, these electric devices are expensive. Most amateurs would not consider investing a small fortune in a specialized device that's not foolproof.

I can just imagine the look on some hacker's face when he or she strolled down the dental care aisle in the local Wal-Mart and spied this new-fangled electronic flossing device. (See Figure 8.20.)

Figure 8.20

I'm not sure who came up with the idea of hacking this innocent-looking thing, but someone did. The result was a tiny, inexpensive electric lock-picking system. According to Jared Bouck over at Inventgeek.com, this little device, when combined with even a makeshift tension wrench, will open most padlocks in a matter of seconds. (See Figure 8.21.)

Figure 8.21

The Web site demonstrating the technique is located at inventgeek.com/Projects/lockpick/lockpick.aspx, and the video demonstrating the technique in action can be found at inventgeek.com/Projects/lockpick/lockpick.avi. This might be a good time to revisit the no-modified-electric-flossers-in-the-workplace policy.

Information Security

A physical vulnerability can certainly put your information at risk, but there are quite a few no-tech hacks that can place your information at risk directly. In this section, I'll share a few of the more popular no-tech hacks I've relied on over the years.

Shoulder Surfing

Shoulder surfing is a classic no-tech attack in which an adversary peers over the shoulder of a victim with the intention of gleaning sensitive information like usernames or passwords. Although the technique has been around since the invention of the computer itself, the attack is still amazingly effective thanks to the proliferation of portable computers and wireless public access points. (See Figure 8.22.)

Figure 8.22

Although I will primarily focus on information that can be gleaned from simply looking at the screen, I have come to realize that a great deal of information can be determined by looking at the machine itself. (See Figure 8.23.)

Figure 8.23

The business card attached to this machine not only highlights the name of the company this gentleman works for but also his name, job title, address, home phone, and cell phone numbers. As an adversary, I could perform my initial reconnaissance on him without even glancing at his screen. In many cases, I see property stickers, property passes, barcodes, and even stencil paintings on machines. An adversary can use this information to profile and perhaps even target an individual.

Some individuals, like members of the military, are extremely conspicuous when seen in public. I don't need to see a business card to realize that the gentleman in Figure 8.24 is a member of the United States military.

Figure 8.24

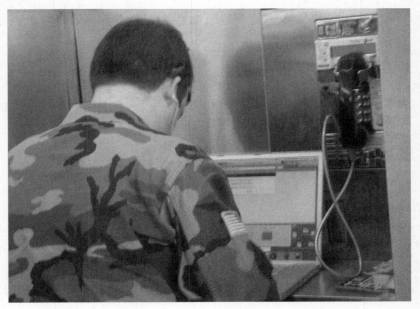

It's not hard to tell that he is a fan of Apple products. The Mac Addict magazine, the Mac laptop, and the iPod headphones all confirm this. If I were to start a conversation with him in order to glean sensitive information, I could use his love (and my knowledge) of Macs to naturally engage him. In this situation though, social engineering was not necessary. With the headphones on and his back turned, he was oblivious to my approach. I was able to take several pictures of him as he worked and I eventually approached to within inches of him. I snapped the photo in Figure 8.25 that revealed in stark detail not only the dermatologic properties of his neck but also his laptop screen.

Figure 8.25

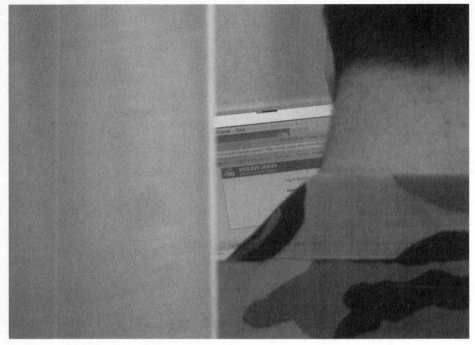

As it turned out, he was not casually surfing the Web, but was logging into the administrative console of a BEA WebLogic server. I watched as he typed in his credentials, made a quick adjustment to my camera and took another photo. The flash fired as I had instructed it to, and he turned around sharply, finally noticing me. I quickly pointed the camera towards myself and rubbed my eyes. He shrugged and returned to his work, convinced, I assume, that I was some kind of digital camera newbie just figuring out the ropes. This is common behavior. Most users of portable computers have grown accustomed to blocking out the world around them. This makes the job of an adversary even easier.

However, there's a bit more to shoulder surfing than simply reading a login page. Often, an adversary can piece together a startling amount of information from what seems like very little. Take, for example, the photo in Figure 8.26 of a temporarily unattended laptop I spotted in a coffee shop.

Figure 8.26

I have altered the image to keep the owner's company name confidential, but by using the information on the screen, an accomplished no-tech hacker can glean an awful lot of information. For starters, the desktop background indicates that the laptop is running Windows XP Professional. Other aesthetic clues such as the Start button configuration back this up. The operating system of a machine is a necessary piece of information a technical attacker can use to determine the type of attack to launch. Generally, an attacker would need to analyze a series of network packet responses to determine this information, but in this case that is probably unnecessary; it is unlikely the laptop's owner has installed another operating system's desktop background. Although they are a bit blurry since they were captured in the field, the desktop icons reveal more information. (See Figure 8.27.)

Figure 8.27

This is obviously some sort of sales software, but a Google search reveals that SalesLogix is the leader in mid-market CRM (customer relationship management) software. The search goes on to say that SalesLogix is "the most powerful sales tool on the Web." Another pair of icons (shown in Figure 8.28) refers to *SAP*, a common business software solution provider.

Figure 8.28

The existence of the SAP logon client indicates the logon credentials for the service may be installed on the laptop as well. Another similarly interesting icon reads *SecuRemote*. (See Figure 8.29.)

Figure 8.29

A Google search reveals that *SecuRemote* is a virtual private network (VPN) client. As with the SAP logon software, all or part of the VPN credentials may reside on the laptop. This could grant an adversary access to services inside the corporate network. At the very least, the mere existence of a particular brand of VPN is valuable information to a technical attacker.

Two more icons on the desktop reveal that *Palm* personal digital assistant (PDA) software has been installed on the machine. (See Figure 8.30.) The existence of this software on the laptop suggests the owner is most likely in possession of a Palm PDA device.

Figure 8.30

These icons also suggest that the Palm device is backed up onto the machine. If an adversary gains access to the laptop, they may also gain access to the data stored on the Palm. Another icon (shown in Figure 8.31) reveals the existence of the AT&T Global Network Client.

Figure 8.31

The icons provide a great deal of information, but a technically savvy attacker can learn even more by looking at other details on the screen. For example, what information can you determine by looking at the taskbar shown in Figure 8.32?

Figure 8.32

The taskbar itself reveals that the operating system of the machine is a modern version of Windows. The battery indicator shows this machine is most likely a laptop, and that there are 58 minutes of battery power remaining. We can tell that the system is currently unplugged from a power source because there is no electrical plug icon next to the battery. The icons reveal a great deal of information about the system as well. Starting from the left, the first icon is for Trillian, an instant messaging aggregator. The color and style of the icon reveal that the application is currently connected. The next icon shows the machine is connected to a wireless access point. The ever-popular AIM (AOL Instant Messaging) icon is next, and the style indicates it is also connected to a server and that the user is logged in. The battery icon is self-explanatory. The MSN instant messenger icon is next. It shows the service is disconnected and thus the user is not logged in. The speakers are muted, as revealed by the next icon. The white rectangular icon belongs to the IBM Hard Drive Active Protection icon, which indicates that an IBM hard drive is installed in the machine and that no shocks have been detected. The last icon, the Microsoft Security Center, is an indicator that the operating system of the machine is Windows XP or later. Last but not least, the system clock is set to 3:08 P.M. This information can be corre-

lated with the current local time to help determine the time zone the owner originated in.

This is a great deal of technical information, but it also reveals quite a bit about
the owner. We know, for example, that he or she is a heavy instant messenger user, as
evidenced by the number of clients installed. It also appears, at first glance, that the
user is non-technical since the running applications are simple in nature—other than
the IBM software, which may have been installed by default.

A busier task bar reveals even more. What can you tell from looking at the
expanded version of the taskbar in Figure 8.32? What judgments can you make
about the user based on the taskbar revealed in Figure 8.33?

Figure 8.33

Many of the icons look the same, but some are different, and they change the
profile of the user slightly, uncovering more specific information about the machine
being used. The icon to the left of the battery indicates the laptop has an Intel
Pro/Wireless 2200BG wireless network adapter. The icon to the right of the battery
icon indicates that Norton Anti-Virus is running and that auto-protect has been
enabled to protect against virus threats. The next icon, the one that looks like a
green onion, would raise a technical user's eyebrows and would make the owner of
the laptop a very interesting target. The onion is an icon for Vidalia, a package that
incorporates Tor (The Onion router) and privoxy, two tools used to anonymize a
user's Internet activity. A user surfing the Web with Tor enabled surfs in complete

and utter anonymity. Remote Web sites can't tell where they are coming from, and anyone sniffing the local network traffic can't see where they are going. The blue envelope icon belongs to the IBM Message Center, which confirms that the laptop was most likely manufactured by IBM. The last icon on the right belongs to the Windows Tablet and Pen Settings Control Panel item. This reveals that the machine is a tablet PC.

Again, this information is very interesting to a technical attacker, but when pulled together it can be used to paint a very clear picture of what type of information the machine might contain and the technical ability of the machine's owner.

So what can you do? The best defense is to remain aware when traveling. Don't put yourself in situations that invite shoulder surfers. Position your back to the wall when using your machine, and never leave your machine unattended. Don't wear company logos and remove extraneous markings and information from your mobile computing devices, especially if your company name might entice an adversary. The tech support folks in your organization can probably provide you a long list of tech things to avoid when traveling. Follow their advice.

Security Alert…

Taskbars?

StankDawg (please don't call him "Mr. Stank") wrote a terrific paper called "The Art of Electronic Deduction," which formed the basis for this section. Many hackers like myself always know to pay attention to the smallest details, but the idea of unpacking a taskbar is quite interesting and unique. His paper can be downloaded from http://www.docdroppers.org/wiki/index.php?title=The_Art_of_Electronic_Deduction, and StankDawg's Web site is located at www.stankdawg.com.

Dumpster Diving

Another favorite hacker sport, *dumpster diving* describes the act of slogging through the trash in search of valuable tidbits of information. This might sound messy, but it doesn't have to be. Many times, interesting stuff is just hanging out there, waiting to be grabbed, as shown in Figure 8.34.

Figure 8.34

Many times, trash is just trash, but in this case, this dumpster dangling document is labeled *for internal use only*. For this particular company, the phrase seems to have lost its meaning. (See Figure 8.35.)

Figure 8.35

I've found similar documents—such as the one in Figure 8.36 revealing proprietary information—lying *outside* of dumpsters.

Figure 8.36

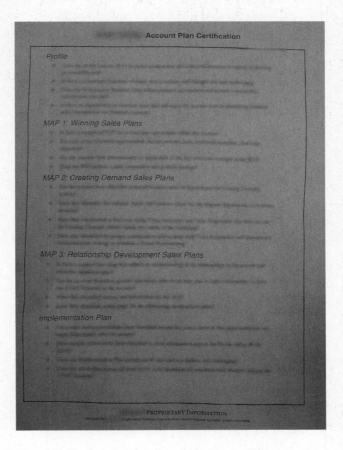

Admittedly, I've only seen a handful of cases that were this blatant. More often, I have to actually stick my head into the dumpster and peer inside. I discovered the document in Figure 8.37 in a dumpster on top of an open box of similar papers. It contains client, sales, and account information along with the Social Security numbers of the sales staff that received incentive payments on a particular contract.

Although this dumpster first appeared empty, the white envelopes littering the bottom of the container caught my eye. This particular health care invoice (See Figure 8.38) appears to have been opened and discarded, as if the recipient were finished with it. If this were my healthcare invoice, I would have certainly shredded it, or at least put it in the cat litter bag to deter even the most dedicated snoop.

Figure 8.37

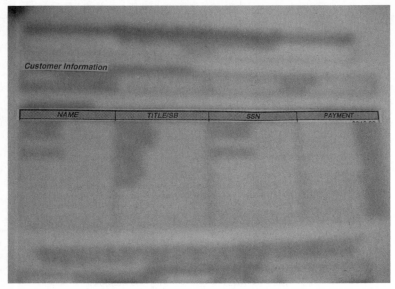

Figure 8.38

The invoice in Figure 8.39, addressed to someone else, was discarded even before it was opened.

Figure 8.39

Further examination of the dumpster revealed other similar unopened envelopes. Examination of the address information on other envelopes in the dumpster revealed that these invoices were not discarded by the patient, but rather by the health care provider. In this case, it appears the patients had no control over how their confidential health information was handled. Obviously, this particular health care provider thought HIPAA had something to do with large thick-skinned semi–aquatic African mammals.

So what's the solution? It's to keep an eye on your trash. If I can grab all this without so much as touching a single piece of refuse, you should be able to get a feel for things by glancing at your dumpster every now and again. Signs like that in Figure 8.40 are a nice idea and serve as a great reminder.

Figure 8.40

Of course a nice sign is no replacement for an actual lock. (See Figure 8.41.)

Figure 8.41

The bottom line is that you should know what's in your trash before the bad guys do. If you find stuff in your trash that doesn't belong, you have a policy problem, or more likely an enforcement problem. If you deal with sensitive data (and who doesn't, really) it's in your best interest to keep a tight reign on what ends up in that big green box outside.

Watching TV, Hacker Style

So far, we've seen some interesting low-tech hacking techniques, but each of them requires some work. Shoulder surfing and dumpster diving takes a bit of walking, and God forbid, sometimes a bit of lifting. I know some of you (particularly the ones sitting on the couch, about ready to put this book down and grab for the remote) are thinking there must be something easier. Well, this section is for you. It's possible to be a full-fledged no-tech hacker from the comfort of a couch. In fact, this technique *requires* that you actually chill out for a while, put your feet up, and watch TV. You heard me right. The catch is that you have to be at a hotel, preferably a nice one. Isn't it amazing the tortuous lengths a dedicated hacker will go to?

After years of playing road warrior as I bounced from gig to gig, the hotel room became my home away from home. I never had cable TV as an adult, so flipping through the channels was a nice treat. Eventually, the thrill wore off and I found myself wanting something more. I knew better than to travel down the road of the $13-an-hour adult channels (don't get hooked, it'll wreck your life) but the technology behind the hotel TV system intrigued me. I began by fiddling with the TV controls, trying to access anything other than channel 3. I used the channel control buttons on the front of the TV as well as the remote, but the result was always the same: the TV had been locked down, allowing access to only seven or eight channels, which were odd channels showing nothing but static. Playing with the pay-per-view buttons on the remote got me nowhere. Everything I did gave me the distinct feeling I was pounding on the front gate of the castle. The system had been designed to deter this kind of fiddling.

I tossed aside the remote and pulled out the TV to check the rear connections. I found a standard coax cable coming from the wall, connecting to a funny box on the back of the TV. Another coax cable ran from the box to the back of the TV. My first thought was to unplug all the cables and bypass the magic box. Closer inspection revealed something I didn't expect. (See Figure 8.42.)

Figure 8.42

Hard plastic sleeves secured the cable ends. Removing the cables required a special tool that slipped inside the sleeve and allowed access to the cable's collar. After considering the problem for a few moments, I rummaged through my bag and found my car keys. I jammed my ignition key down inside one of the protective collars and cranked it counter-clockwise. The cable turned inside the collar. I kept at it, and the cable rotated with each turn of the key. After several full rotations, the cable was a twisted mess, but eventually it came free and untangled, flailing around like an injured snake. I unscrewed each of the remaining cables and connected one of them from the wall directly into the back of the TV. I grabbed the remote and began flipping through the few channels the TV allowed. Each of them came in clearly; the static I had seen previously was gone. This was a sign that the hotel's raw cable feed was displaying cleanly through the TV's tuner, exactly as I had hoped. It was an interesting find, but not nearly as interesting as what I found on channel 75. (See Figure 8.43.)

Figure 8.43

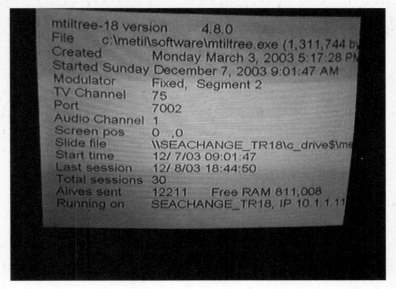

```
mtiltree-18 version       4.8.0
File       c:\metil\software\mtiltree.exe (1,311,744 by
Created           Monday March 3, 2003 5:17:28 PM
Started Sunday December 7, 2003 9:01:47 AM
Modulator         Fixed, Segment 2
TV Channel        75
Port              7002
Audio Channel  1
Screen pos        0  ,0
Slide file        \\SEACHANGE_TR18\c_drive$\me
Start time        12/ 7/03 09:01:47
Last session      12/ 8/03 18:44:50
Total sessions  30
Alives sent       12211      Free RAM 811,008
Running on        SEACHANGE_TR18, IP 10.1.1.11
```

As I read the information on the screen, the geek in me was delighted to see an IP address (10.1.1.11), a port number (7500), a pathname to a Windows or DOS executable (c:\metil\software\mtiltree.exe), and a universal naming convention (UNC) link to a machine share (\\SEACHANGE_TR18\c_drive$). I plopped down on the bed and gawked at the screen. My mind spun with the possibilities. Servers were running on the hotel's cable system, each connected by an IP network. The hacker in me wanted to jump in and start port scanning or sniffing, or *something*, but it was late, and I hadn't exactly been authorized to poke about the hotel's network. I snapped a few photos and reassembled the TV and the black box, silently cursing the TV for not allowing me access to more channels. There was interesting stuff on the blocked TV channels, I was sure of that.

When I returned from my gig, I couldn't get the hotel network out of my mind. I fruitlessly searched the Internet for a way to unlock the channels on the TV[3] and had just about given up on the prospect when I came upon an interesting device in a thrift shop. (See Figure 8.44.)

Figure 8.44

The device was an ancient cable box—a tuner, basically—that connected between a cable feed and a television. I paid less than three dollars for it, and brought it along on my next gig.

The moment I walked into my hotel room, I removed the cables from the back of the TV (making short work of the annoying sleeves) and connected my cable box between the cable feed and the TV. I turned on the TV, set it to channel 3, and began flipping through channels on the cable box. Just as I had suspected, I could view all the standard cable channels. However, as the numbers climbed I hit more of the interesting *Seachange* channels. Then, suddenly, I found one channel that wasn't like the others. (See Figure 8.45.)

I had to read the information on the screen several times before I realized I was looking at someone else's room bill. The screen flashed briefly and the next page displayed. I watched as Mr. Green flipped through his account information. Thanks to a $3 device, I was snooping on the hotel's customers. This technique works because certain channels are unlocked and distributed on an as-needed basis. If I were to use my remote to view my room bill, a channel would be allocated and unlocked, and the requested information would be shown on my TV. The cable box gave me the ability to see every channel, including the channels currently allocated to other customers. If a customer activated a custom feature on the TV, I could see what was happening if I viewed the same channel. Of course, the majority of customers used the system to view on-demand movies. If a customer paid for a movie, I could tune in as well and the hotel wouldn't know I'd watched it without paying. (See Figure 8.46.)

Figure 8.45

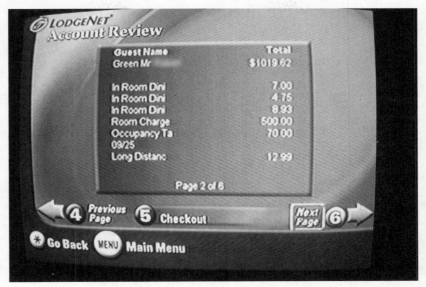

Figure 8.46

Some hotels have adopted more robust systems that allow customers to use the in-room TV as an Internet terminal. A wireless keyboard often accompanies this type of system. (See Figure 8.47.)

Figure 8.47

I've caught customers surfing the Web and checking their e-mail. The e-mail in Figure 8.48 reveals the passcode for a new 800 number. The number itself was sent in the previous e-mail.

The photo in Figure 8.49 shows a customer logging in to their American Express account. If I were an adversary, there's no telling what I could do with this information.

Figure 8.48

Figure 8.49

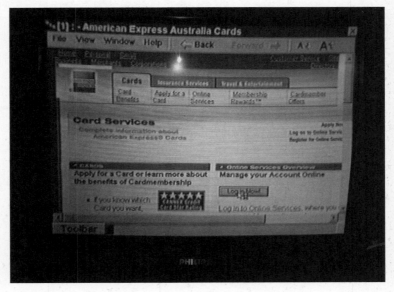

Figure 8.50 shows a customer logging in to their Internet banking site. The balances shown in this account were rather large. An adversary might decide to target this individual based on their income level.

Figure 8.50

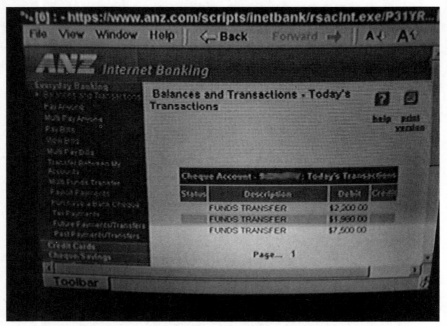

Adam Laurie, a.k.a, Major Malfunction, has discovered that hotel cable systems can be even further abused. By toying around with a PC-controlled IR (infrared) device, Adam found that he could reprogram the hotel television directly to allow him access to all the restricted channels, without a special tuner. Not only was he able to view channels already in use, he could change the ID embedded in his television to appear to be another hotel patron. After changing the code, he found it was possible to review their room charges, order items like room service, change the status of the room, learn who was staying in the room and for how long, and more. Adam even discovered he could take control of the administrative systems like these through the use of the in-room wireless keyboard. (See Figure 8.51.)

Figure 8.51

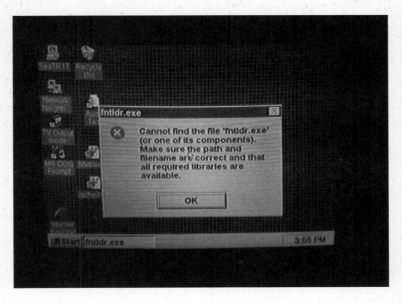

This functionality was made possible by the black box I disconnected to hook up my tuner. For more information about Adam's work, see his presentation at www.alcrypto.co.uk/MMIrDA/mmirda_syscan05.pdf.

Keep these vulnerabilities in mind as you travel, and encourage your employees to do the same. Hotel TV–based Internet systems are never considered safe for any purpose, and your personal information may be at risk if an adversary is staying in the same hotel. And remember, those $13 charges for in-room entertainment that are so anonymous. Anyone in the hotel can see them, and how many $13 in-room entertainment possibilities are there, exactly?

Checklist

Links to sites:

- www.toool.nl/kensington623.wmv

- http://connect.waag.org/toool/:
  Toool—The Open Organization of Lockpickers; barry@toool.nl, rop@toool.nl

- http://connectmedia.waag.org/toool/whatthebump.wmv: Toool's lock bumping video

- www.bikeforums.net/video: One of the founding sites for the U-Lock bypass videos

- http://security.org/dial-90/alerts.htm: Marc Tobias's alerts page

- http://security.org: Marc Tobias's Web site

- www.fusor.us/lockpick.html: Master Lock brute forcing

- www.everything2.com/index.pl?node_id=1304470&lastnode_id=0: Master Lock brute forcing

- www.toool.nl/bumping.pdf: "Bumping Locks" by Barry Wels and Rop Gonggrijp

- http://cq.cx/prox.pl: Jonathan Westhues's Proximity Card cloner

- http://en.wikipedia.org/wiki/Van_Eck_phreaking: Van Eck Phreaking

- www.docdroppers.org/wiki/index.php?title=The_Art_of_Electronic_Deduction: StankDawg's great paper on electronic deduction (used for the shoulder surfing section)

- www.hidcorp.com: HID corporation, world class manufacturer of site security products

- www.toool.nl/bumping.pdf: Toool's great lock bumping whitepaper

- www.toool.nl/kensington623.wmv: Toool's great video showing Kensington Lock picking with a roll of toilet paper

- www.wired.com/news/privacy/0,1848,68370,00.html: A Wired article about Adam Laurie's Hotel TV bypass/snooping work

Summary

Hackers are certainly a technical bunch, but in this day and age, it pays to think simply. No-tech attacks are simple to pull off, but the effects can be devastating to your facility's security posture. Learning to think like a hacker is not necessarily as difficult as it may seem. Pay attention to the little things, and keep a vigilant watch for opportunities you are offering the no-tech hacker.

Notes

1. http://en.wikipedia.org/wiki/Van_Eck_phreaking
2. Of course, the phone company I emulated had no part in this. I have no affiliation with them, and this attack in no way reflects a security problem with that particular phone company. Neither my company nor I endorses this kind of behavior except in conjunction with an authorized security test. And please don't full-body tackle every poor phone technician you spot in the hallway.
3. I didn't know about Adam Laurie's awesome work and talk at www.wired.com/news/privacy/0,1848,68370,00.html. I'm not entirely sure his work was public back when I tried this.

Chapter 9

The Basics of Penetration Testing
by Russ Rodgers

Russ Rogers (CISSP, CISM, IAM, IEM, HonScD) is author of the popular *Hacking a Terror Network* (Syngress Publishing, ISBN: 1928994989); coauthor on multiple other books, including the best selling *Stealing the Network: How to Own a Continent* (Syngress, ISBN: 1931836051); *Network Security Evaluation Using the NSA IEM* (Syngress, ISBN: 1597490350) and Editor in Chief of *The Security Journal*. Russ is Cofounder, Chief Executive Officer, and Chief Technology Officer of Security Horizon, a veteran-owned small business based in Colorado Springs, CO. Russ has been involved in information technology since 1980 and has spent the last 15 years working professionally as both an IT and INFOSEC consultant. Russ has worked with the United States Air Force (USAF), National Security Agency (NSA), and the Defense Information Systems Agency (DISA). He is a globally renowned security expert, speaker, and author who has presented at conferences around the world including Amsterdam, Tokyo, Singapore, Sao Paulo, and cities all around the United States.

Russ has an Honorary Doctorate of Science in Information Technology from the University of Advancing Technology, a Master's Degree in Computer Systems Management from the University of Maryland, a Bachelor of Science in Computer Information Systems from the University of Maryland, and an Associate Degree in Applied Communications Technology from the Community College of the Air Force. He is a member of both ISSA and ISACA and cofounded the Global Security Syndicate (gssyndicate.org), the Security Tribe (securitytribe.com). He acts in the role of professor of network security for the University of Advancing Technology (uat.edu).

Introduction

For the past 10 years, I've spent a lot of time doing penetration tests. Originally, I was working solely from a technical perspective. We did the normal stuff back then, poke around a bit, run some scanners, find vulnerabilities and misconfigurations, exploit holes, and own the network. In the beginning, it was never all that formatted or organized.

But working for the Department of Defense has its perks, and one of those was the continued need to mature the processes we used and create a truly effective and repeatable method. Throughout that time in my career, I learned how to document all those little thought processes that "go on" within the head of most hackers. But documenting was never enough, as I would soon learn.

In 2000, I took a course offered by the National Security Agency (NSA) called the INFOSEC Assessment Methodology, or IAM for short. Being the technical guy I was, I about died in that class. The reason was simple: the course focused on organizational aspects of information security that needed to be in place before all the technical vulnerabilities would stop running rampant through the organization.

In this chapter, we'll address the basic attributes that are common in all successful penetration testers. We're not going to cover the specific tools or include a ton of screenshots. Dozens of books already have that covered. Our goal is to identify those useful attributes so you can better address your own methodologies, as well as determine your weaknesses and areas for improvement.

Know the Security Analysis Life Cycle

Back in the days when we first started doing this type of work, it was all technical. That's all we did. We were the geeks, the freaks behind the keyboard; the ones that could work *around* the system controls. What we did seemed normal enough to us, but to the uninitiated, it was something akin to black magic or voodoo.

What I didn't realize at the time was that there are things that have to occur along all levels of the security life cycle in order for a penetration test to have the greatest value to the customer. The most basic of which is the fact that pen testing is just a piece of the overall security life cycle that must be addressed. As with most life cycles, things need to occur in their proper order (at least the large majority of the time); otherwise, the results could be meaningless or have significantly less value.

The standard security life cycle looks something like this: An organizational/programmatic assessment occurs; a full comprehensive technical evaluation is rendered; findings are presented to the customer; the customer takes appropriate the steps to close technical problems and implement defenses; and then a test of those defenses takes place. This is where the penetration comes into play. If we put this process into a flow chart or image, it would look like Figure 9.1.

Figure 9.1 The Basic Security Analysis Life Cycle

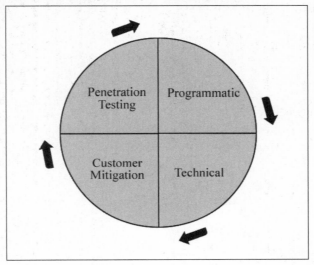

Tools & Traps…

Pay Attention to the Feedback Loop

As you walk through the life cycle we've been discussing, you should understand that, inherently, there are times when a feedback loop occurs and the cycle goes backward a step before continuing on again. For example, the most obvious form of this is the final report. When you provide the report to the customer, you're providing feedback to them. The customer should take the feedback and make certain changes to encourage better security. Another feedback loop (that is not specifically pointed out in Figure 9.1) is right after the penetration testing. Once the test is complete, you will provide your results to the customer yet again in another feedback loop. The customer will step back, address those concerns, and then move forward in the process again.

The truth of the matter is that this flow of activities and information is most advantageous to the customer. In other words, they can expect the absolute best possible results from a process similar to this one. Let's examine why that is.

Programmatic Testing

As a security professional, you understand that technical vulnerabilities can be found and fixed. But you also know that an organization that has not fixed the root cause of the issue will continue to have technical problems later on down the road. The findings may be different (in some cases they're the same, just on different systems), but technical vulnerabilities will continue to rear their ugly heads.

The root cause of those vulnerabilities is undefined, immature, or undocumented processes for areas of control within the organization. For example, a good deal of the vulnerabilities we find in technical evaluations or pen tests can be directly attributed to a lack of proper patching of applications and operating systems. Sure, we can find all the current technical issues and help the customer remedy those, but if the organization fails to address the actual patch process within the organization, they're going to continue having these findings in the future. The organizational, or programmatic, assessment locates these areas of procedural weakness in the organization and allows them to fix those issues. Once proper controls are in place, the number of findings in that area will lessen over time. The process is a bit more complex than the paragraph I've devoted to it here, but for more information, I recommend you check out *Security Assessment: Case Studies for Implementing the NSA IAM* (Syngress Publishing, 2004).

TIP

It's important to understand the entire security life cycle, even if you only work in a single area. By understanding how your area of expertise relates to the other areas in the life cycle, you'll be better prepared to answer customer questions, create useful output from your processes, and mature in your own professional experiences.

Technical Testing

But we all know that organizational findings aren't all there is when examining a customer. The technical piece is extremely important. A comprehensive technical evaluation will provide the customer with a clear picture of where those vulnerabilities lie and what the potential impact could be on their organization if those systems are compromised. The goal here is to allow the organization to understand what technical vulnerabilities currently exist, so they can close those while they're still working on creating a mature organizational security program.

Customer Responsibilities

Now that we've done the work, we want to provide the customer with a final report that details our findings, clearly and precisely. A poorly written report, or one that doesn't communicate with the intended managerial or executive audience, will seldom be of much use. But once the customer has received your well written report, they have to step up to the plate and roll up their sleeves.

This is where the rubber really meets the road, from a customer perspective. For each finding we've detailed, they need to implement a fix: a defense or mitigation. Think along the lines of fortifying a castle with a variety of defenses that will help stop an invading army. They'll implement moats, drawbridges, and towers. They'll employ guards, archers, and watchmen. Iron bars will be integrated into the stonework around all the sewer and water avenues in and out of the area. This analogy explains, basically, what the customer should be working on, based on your final report.

Penetration Testing

Finally, we're at the fun part (and the focus of this chapter), the penetration test. Once the customer has a full understanding of their security posture, both organizationally and technically, and they've had the opportunity to defend against their weaknesses, they'll need someone to test their defenses. This is similar to the television show where families hire a former burglar to try and break into their homes and prove whether it's possible or not. The thief doesn't need to find *every* way into the home, only one. Proving he/she can get into the home is the goal of the show, and that's also the goal of a penetration test.

Optimally, this life cycle will repeat itself every year or two. The shorter the time lapse from one life cycle to the next, the more secure and mature an organization has the opportunity to be. If the time between one full life cycle to the next is too long, the organization is likely to slip back into old habits and insecurity.

Know When to Deviate

This might sound a bit counterintuitive initially, but first I'm going to show you why you shouldn't normally deviate from the security analysis life cycle before I tell you why you should. As with all good rules, there are exceptions and we'll point those out here. But let's first look at why you shouldn't.

Stick to the Life Cycle

Going back to our castle analogy, let's suppose that the owner of the castle comes to you one day and says, "Reader, I'd like you to perform a penetration test on my castle and see if you can get in. My dear friend, the Baron of Castle Malarky, has recently used similar services and found them to be quite entertaining and useful." Okay, stop. Let's look at this request. It sounds like fun, doesn't it, the chance to try to break in to a castle? But let's get more information first.

You ask the owner of this castle whether he has done any work to put up defenses or protect his home. He answers with a resounding "No." Don't laugh! You know this happens all the time, don't you? The situation is a bit clearer now, isn't it? So what do you do?

Breaking into a castle with no defenses sounds like a really dumb idea. First off, it's not likely to be very challenging at all. Secondly, what is the owner actually going to walk away with once the work is through? What will you tell him that he doesn't already know? "Sir, you have no defenses in place and it was quite easy to get in through the front door." And remember, he's paying for this.

Ethically speaking, if you're a security professional you have certain obligations in situations such as these. It reinforces your good reputation if you explain the security analysis life cycle to the customer. They need to understand that the penetration test is the final step in security analysis, not the first. If they've done no work at all to secure the organization, then it's quite likely to be an easy paycheck for you and not very informational to the customer. The goal of a penetration test is to break in, not find all the problems that may lurk within the organizational and technical structures of the company.

Break Out of the Life Cycle

With all that said, let's look at an example of why it may make some sense to deviate from the norm. In the past six years alone, I've run into two organizations that had a legitimate reason to step outside the normal running of the security analysis life cycle and go directly to the penetration test. Both organizations had similar reasons for the deviations.

Remember when the big "DotCom" boom hit and then tanked just a few years later? During that time, companies built up huge infrastructures, teaming with workers delivering ideas and products to the market with astounding speed. But the bubble burst, leaving those companies bloated and unable to react. Due to these circumstances, companies were forced to cut back dramatically. Organizations and work forces were scaled down to give the companies a fighting chance in the now brutally competitive markets. One side effect of these cuts was the reduction of security budgets.

Executives think in dollars, revenue; it's what they get paid to do. Initially, security professionals were unable to prove a *return on investment* for all those dollars spent on securing the organization. If you can't prove ROI, you tend to get cut. At the time, very few organizations were comparing information security expenditures to the costs of an insurance policy.

The organizations I dealt with, in particular, needed a penetration test in order to take those security vulnerabilities and prove to their executive boards that the security budget needed to be bolstered, or the organization was headed toward disaster. In both cases, the board relented that there were obvious concerns that were not being addressed because the security departments had been laid off, en masse, or the security budget had been severed.

This is just an example, but keep it locked away in the back of your mind. You may not run into a case exactly like this one, but there's a good chance you'll encounter a situation that requires you to think outside the box. Besides, that's what hackers do; think outside the box.

The Penetration Tester Mentality

The most important tool in any penetration tester's toolkit (more important than any application, script, or exploit) is his/her mind. Good pen testers have an uncanny ability to locate issues on-the-fly. And since every customer and situation is different, this is a "must have" attribute. Let's look at some of those attributes that make up a good penetration tester.

Know the Core Processes

There are certain things that every penetration tester does, with every client. We'll cover them in more detail in the next section, but as a quick prelude; we look at what information we can get publicly, we find out what components and services exist on the network, we locate all the known vulnerabilities, we break in to a target system, we escalate our privileges, we expand our reach, and we ensure our ability to get back into those systems later by installing backdoor applications.

It seems silly to think that hackers are that organized, but we are. We might not document all of these processes, but they are the basics used nearly every time. Understanding the methodology used provides a reliable structure for the successful penetration of customer systems. If you roll in to a customer site and just "wing it," things aren't likely to turn out so well. I've had dozens of customers call up concerned about a "prior engagement" with a security firm that lacked processes and had poor results.

TIP

Never underestimate the importance of following a standardized and mature process. Mature and repeatable processes allow for someone else to step into your shoes if you get hurt or are unable to complete your work.

Think for Yourself

Whereas core processes provide a foundation that can be taught to nearly everyone, creativity is the hallmark of all great penetration testers and is a much less tangible trait. Teaching people to *think* like a hacker is much more difficult; thus, this trait is normally what separates the wheat from the chaff. Every customer and situation you encounter as a penetration tester will be different. That's not to say there won't be similarities, but as a whole, each job is different.

When we discuss the difference, consider them in terms of different management, network architecture, applications, patch levels, policies, and employees. Each of these will impact your ability to have a successful penetration test. Penetration testers view each new organization as a puzzle. Imagine, if you will, that you're doing one of those maze puzzles found on the kids menu of the local hamburger joint. In the center of the maze you normally have the objective you must reach. Your starting point lies somewhere just outside the perimeter of the maze. Penetration testing is similar in that you come into the organization from an outside perspective and must find your way to the critical information that lies at the heart of that organization (the maze).

The real trick here is that each pathway to the data is littered with obstacles. To be successful, you'll need the ability to break through obstacles, or simply bypass them altogether. This is where creativity will really help. Remember, try to be flexible in your thought processes so every possible option will be available to you as you attempt to reach your goal.

Ethical Conduct

Over the years, I've seen any number of people try to differentiate between malicious hackers (often referred to as crackers) and penetration testers. The truth is that knowledge-wise and mentally, they're nearly identical. The big differentiator is the ethical constraints that professional penetration testers apply to their conduct. Because they are employed by professional organizations, both commercially or for the federal government, there are ethical standards that need to be constantly monitored.

Don't get me wrong. The desire to solve the puzzle, and the burn to be successful, still exists in the penetration tester, as it does in most hackers. We still enjoy the thrill of victory, as it were, but we also understand that the work we do could potentially put the customer at risk and should be performed with caution. When performed correctly, a penetration test can be used to improve the customer's defenses and improve their overall security posture.

Know When to Fold

Knowing when to fold your cards is a classic poker strategy that has paid off for smart card players for years. The same holds true when considering a penetration test. There will be times when you want to spend more time on a particular area that looks vulnerable. Sometimes this will pay off by providing you with a pathway into the network. Other times, it may be a complete waste of effort. Knowing when to back off from one area of examination and move on is a critical skill to have. The sooner you can come to terms with the idea that you can't compromise every vulnerability that exists, the sooner you can move on to more promising opportunities.

This is important to understand. I've seen folks get completely sucked into the process of compromising a single, potential vulnerability, all the while ignoring more promising issues elsewhere. Remember, the objective is to gain control of the customer network and get at its critical information; it's not to find *every* vulnerability. We're just trying to work our way through the vulnerabilities with the most likelihood of compromise; sometimes referred to as the low-hanging fruit. If you get too absorbed in one area, you may miss something that could be the difference between success and failure.

Use the Right Tools

Regardless of your skill level or how long you've been a penetration tester, you will always need the right tools. It's hard to argue with a jury of your peers, so the best place to look for the most popular and useful tools publicly available right now is at www.sectools.org. Fyodor, author of the legendary Nmap port scanning tool, compiles this list based on votes from professionals and hackers around the world. This top 100 list of applications is a must see for anyone in this line of business.

Build Your Own

Scripting and programming are your friends. That large majority of penetration testers that I know, who are actually quite successful at what they do, have a knack for creating scripts and programs that do a lot of the manual labor for them. For instance, resolving a complete IP address block through a domain name server using reverse lookups could provide a lot of useful information, but doing that type of work manually would be time consuming. The creation of script might take an hour, but the time it would save in the long run would more than compensate for that. By building your own tools, you can be assured you understand what the tool is doing, create more efficient methods for performing your tests, and put the information into a format that works for your own penetration processes.

The Penetration Methodology

We mentioned it briefly earlier, but let's look at a standard methodology often used by hackers and professionals alike. The methodology is intended to start with a high level overview of the organization and slowly work itself into the details. As we move our way down the methodology, we gain a better understanding of how the organization processes, stores, transmits, and protects its critical information. We have eight steps in this penetration methodology that we'll discuss in more detail. You can see these steps in Figure 9.2.

NOTE

As you step through this process, it's important to take lots of notes. Make sure you detail which computers and accounts you've compromised, where you've installed backdoor software, and the avenues you took for each compromise. This information will be useful to the customer later when they need to implement defenses and clean up after your work.

Figure 9.2 An Example Penetration Methodology

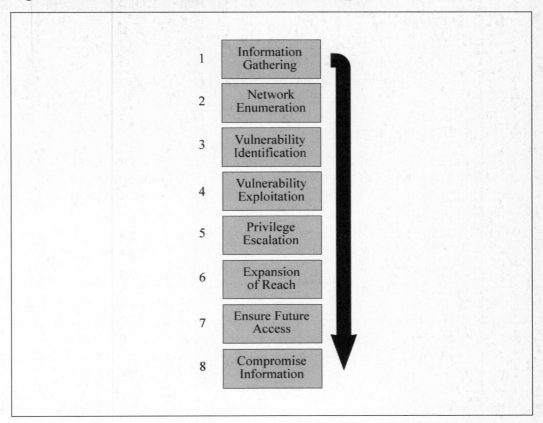

Information Gathering

The first task on any penetration test is identifying what information you can glean from public resources. The most notable, and most used, medium for this work is the Internet. It's amazing the information you can get simply by using search engines like Google, scouring newsgroup archives, perusing mailing list archives, and looking at public records that the company has willingly released into the wild.

Search Engines

We won't go into too much detail on search engines since Johnny Long already covered that, but suffice to say that this will be one of your first tasks. Looking through search engines using the correct syntax can reveal a plethora of very useful information to a penetration tester. Most search engines will do queries based on postings to newsgroups, mailing lists, forums, and other forms of communication. They'll also search through information found on publicly available Web pages for your target, or their partner organizations. The most popular search engine used by penetration testers is undoubtedly Google. Regardless of what you use, though, make sure you understand the full list of options available to you in your search. For instance, Google comes with dozens and dozens of different search options that aren't commonly known and may help you in your searches.

Newsgroup Searches

Newsgroups have been a huge part of the Internet for decades now. The most well known is the USENET newsgroups. They were around before the Web was graphically based. These groups are basically huge message lists that users can subscribe to in order to watch for conversations or information on particular topics.

For those of us that have been in the online world for the past 20 years or more, we've most certainly used these groups in the past to communicate with other professionals or hobbyists. For instance, if you're having issues with your router configuration, you might decide to post your question to a newsgroup. This allows hundreds, if not thousands, of other readers to view your question and respond to it. The cool part is that these messages are all archived on the Internet in a variety of places and can be located later by doing search queries.

The following are some hints for performing these searches:

- Search for the company name
- Search for the company domain (for example, customer.org)
- Search for the name of individuals you know work there (say, Joe Schmo)
- Search for the company phone number
- Search for the public IP address space of the customer

Forums and Blogs

Forums and blogs have started to slowly replace newsgroups in the public eye. All sorts of useful information can be found on public blogs or technical support forums. Administrators will often post messages to these types of communities in order to get feedback on particular technical issues that might be causing them headaches. They're also known to post in response to posts from other people around the world. Posts such as these might contain valuable information about the architecture in use at the customer site. For instance, an administrator might post a response to a query on the forums stating something like, "In our organization, we use product X and I've found that if you configure it like this, the problem will go away." This information could help you focus your initial attacks on the organization

Normal users and employees are oftentimes another way to find out what's in use at the organization. And because they're less likely to be educated in information security, they tend to provide more sensitive information in their posts. For example, let's say a user is having issues with a Web application in the organization. Instead of turning to their own administrators, which on multiple occasions have explained in clear, precise terms to the user how it's not really a problem, users will often post messages on forums instead. We've seen examples of information given out publicly to include application type, version number, patch level, configuration information, and, on occasion, actual code from the application. All of this information can be used to expand your attack.

DNS / WHOIS / ARIN

A number of protocols and services exist that operate on the Internet to keep the traffic moving back and forth. They're publicly available resources that, when used correctly, can provide the foundation of knowledge needed to map out the target organization. All of these protocols have been around for decades and provide vital information required to keep the Internet available and functioning. Using these services, we can create our target list, verify it, and check for errors or mistakes in our current target list.

Domain Name Service (DNS)

The first of these is called Domain Name Service, or DNS. DNS translated those hardware Internet addresses (such as 192.168.1.1) to names that are easier to remember. Each organization that has an Internet presence will have corresponding entries in a DNS server. If the server is privately held and operated, it may contain information on a good deal more computers than should be public knowledge. The DNS enumeration should be performed on the target customers' DNS servers in order to locate any unknown ways into the network. It's not unusual to find network administrators have created DNS entries to their home boxes to make connections between home and work easier. That home computer may be the ticket into the corporate network.

WHOIS

The WHOIS provides information on the actual domain name(s) registered to a company or organization. For example, the simple command *whois customertarget.com* will review information about the registration contact for the domain, the billing contact for the domain, and the technical or administrative contacts for it. It could also include phone numbers, e-mail addresses, physical addresses, and full names.

ARIN

The American Registry of Internet Numbers (ARIN) controls the dissemination and use of IP addresses employed by entities within the United States. The Web site, www.arin.net, provides a valuable resource to help verify the scope of a given project, or to determine if other addresses should be within scope. The information provided to the user at this site looks quite similar to that of the WHOIS output, with the exception that the information provided relates to the organization that registered the block of IP address space, versus the domain names.

Web Site Mirroring

Mirroring Web sites is a great way to get the files back on to your local machine for a closer look. For larger organizations, it's simply too big a task to go through each page online. Some mirroring tools, like wget under Linux, allow you to mirror just the information you want. Other tools, such as Sam Spade or Black Widow, will go a step further by parsing the information as it's downloaded, making it much quicker to spot hidden usernames, e-mail addresses, or passwords.

Aside from hidden information, you can gain a plethora of useful tidbits about how the organization operates, important points of contact (useful for social engineering), important partners that may be linked from the pages, and other information that has made it into the public domain. We've even had some clients that posted their network architecture maps on their Web site for their customers to see. Talk about making things easier.

Financial Web Sites

Regardless of their line of business or the industry in which they operate, companies make money through interactions with customers and investors. Some of these companies are publicly traded on stock markets, while others may be privately held. Both entities, however, can be listed on financial news Web sites.

This information is useful because it provides data on how the company operates financially, who it has acquired (or sold itself to) in recent history, and where important financial partnerships exist that may indicate a trusted technical relationship as well. Recent acquisitions for your target company can often provide an easy way into the customer network. It's often difficult to pull multiple organizations, which were previously autonomous, together into a single, cohesive, and standardized entity.

Because of this, vulnerabilities may exist within the trust relationships that were developed to enable interaction between these entities.

Network Enumeration

Network enumeration is one of the most recognized hacker activities on the Internet. Because of its high-profile nature, dozens of tools and applications exist for performing these activities. The basic goal of network enumeration is to find out what components exist on the network, such as firewalls, computers, routers, switches, and printers. The port scan is the most familiar activity in this area. Port scans can be performed using any number of protocols, such as TCP, UDP, and ICMP. The most popular port scan tool is by far Nmap, but you can find many other similar tools at www.sectools.org.

Aside from finding out what components make up the target network, we also want to know what services, applications, and shared file systems are out there. Available services or applications may provide an avenue of attack, whereas shared file systems or printers could potentially allow an avenue of attack and access to sensitive information. Having this information will help you focus your attacks, saving time and effort on the penetration test.

Vulnerability Identification

Vulnerability scanning automates the process of determining what well-known vulnerabilities exist on the network. Imagine having to look at every computer manually, across the network, and trying to figure out what vulnerabilities existed. Some of these tools are freeware, such as Nessus (www.nessus.org), while others are commercial in nature, such as Saint (www.saintcorporation.com). The goal of this process is to collect as much useful information as we can in the shortest amount of time.

The two tools listed in the previous paragraph are general vulnerability scanners and will attempt to find issues in a large number of services and host types across an organization's network. Other tools, such as SPI Dynamic's WebInspect (www.spidynamics.com) or NGS's NGSSQuirrel (www.nextgenss.com), specialize in vulnerabilities on specific applications. For example, the NGS application is written by some of the world's foremost experts in database security and will help locate issues in databases that could provide an avenue into the network.

Vulnerability Exploitation

Exploiting the vulnerabilities is what separates the professionals from the script kiddies. The truth hurts, but a good many professionals in the security world depend wholly on the use of scripts and exploits written by other people. While this may be useful in some circumstances, the sole use of these exploits indicates the lack of maturity in the tester's knowledge and processes. A high quality tester will often have their own methods and scripts to help them break into a customer network.

The painful truth, however, is that we can't all know everything. So, based on that, there will be times when everyone will need to use someone else's work. The thing to understand is that you need to be absolutely certain that the code is safe to use on the customer's network. Although we're trying to break into the network to get a foothold in as many boxes as possible, we're still there to help the customer, not bring them down. In this case, it's really helpful if you already know how to program and read code.

The exploitation of vulnerabilities, whether taking advantage of a configuration issue or a software bug, provides us with the door into a single computer. This is the important first step that provides us with a normal user account. Everything else from here on out is based on this simple step.

Privilege Escalation

Once you find yourself in a target computer with a normal user account, you'll want to find a way to escalate your privilege to that of a root or Administrator user. In most cases, we'll concentrate on local Administrator or root access first, and then move on to the domain level access. The normal progression of access escalation is depicted in Figure 9.3.

Figure 9.3 The Access Escalation Process

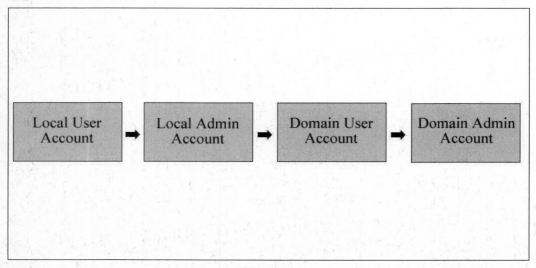

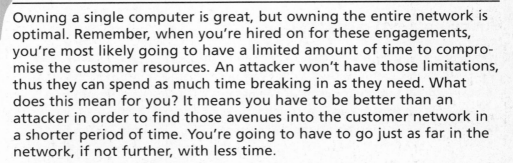

Tools & Traps...

Instant Domain Administrator

You should know that when you do penetration testing on a consistent basis, you'll naturally become familiar with some vulnerabilities or configuration errors that represent the opportunity for immediate acquisition of a domain administrator account. Although we provide Figure 9.3 as a basis, there are exceptions, as in most cases. Sticking to a process just for the sake of sticking to it doesn't make much sense if you can own the crown jewels in less time and with less effort. Be on the lookout for those items that could present such an opportunity and take advantage of those as they crop up.

Expansion of Reach

Let's expand on the concept of access escalation a bit. In Figure 9.3, we kept things pretty simple by talking strictly about the access level of the accounts we were trying to compromise. If we take that one step further, we'll take the full network into account as well, versus a single host. Look at Figure 9.4 for an example.

TIP

Owning a single computer is great, but owning the entire network is optimal. Remember, when you're hired on for these engagements, you're most likely going to have a limited amount of time to compromise the customer resources. An attacker won't have those limitations, thus they can spend as much time breaking in as they need. What does this mean for you? It means you have to be better than an attacker in order to find those avenues into the customer network in a shorter period of time. You're going to have to go just as far in the network, if not further, with less time.

Figure 9.4 The Access Escalation Process for a Full Network

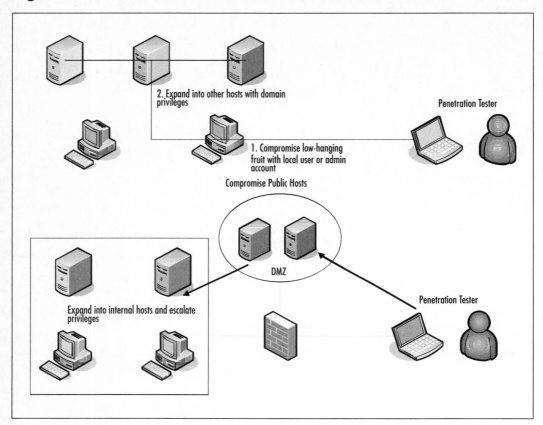

Ensure Future Access

Once you've gained the access to key systems in the customer network, you don't want that access removed right when you need it. Some customers may notice odd things occurring on their network. For instance, Bill Morrison from the accounting office doesn't normally log in to the server at 11 P.M., or maybe there has been an unusually high level of Web traffic occurring during off hours.

When this type of activity is noticed, the customer may cut off your access, either intentionally or unintentionally. To avoid this, you'll need to secure your future access to these systems through a number of possible means. These could include backdoor applications and/or additional privileged accounts.

Backdoor applications often run in the background on a compromised system, allowing access back into the system at a later date. They often run on nonpopular ports and require a username and/or password to access the application. In instances of remote compromises, the backdoor will likely use a port that is allowed in and out through the firewall. Regardless of the port being utilized or the actual application in use, the goal is always the same: maintain and control access to compromised targets. In some cases, you may be able to simply create alternative administrative or root accounts. On systems that have hundreds of users, the new account isn't likely to ever be detected.

> ### WARNING
>
> The use of some backdoor applications could cause more issues for your customer than good. For instance, there are a lot of these applications in the public space, but if you don't have access to the source code, you can never be sure of how they really operate. What if the application leaves the customer vulnerable beyond what you believe? How will you ever be able to ensure the customer is secured from that point forward? The same holds true with root kits. Always make sure you're using only approved backdoor applications that you know for sure can't be hijacked by a real attacker.

Compromise Information

At the core of any organization is certain information that is used on a daily basis to keep it profitable and in business. This could include customer data, such as credit card information, or it could include something much more sensitive, such as proprietary research and development data. This information is the actual goal of any penetration test. After all, it doesn't matter if you can get into the network if you can't compromise the information, does it?

You've gained account access, escalated that to administrative access, and expanded your access throughout the entire network. At this point, start looking for the treasure. Can you find those financial documents, research information, or patient health records?

WARNING

Always remember that you're here to help the customer, not actually cause damage. If you download information, it needs to be stored securely on encrypted drive partitions. Never disseminate this information to third parties or outside entities. Protect all access and information at the highest level of sensitivity possible.

The Cleanup

Once the job is done, present your findings to the customer and get ready for the cleanup. What? Surely you didn't think you were done. You've taken over user accounts, created your own administrative accounts, installed backdoors, changed passwords, and taken sensitive information from the customer network. You need to set everything right now.

The first step is to go back through your notes and undo everything you've done. Let the customer know about all user accounts you had access to. They'll need to change passwords on all those accounts. Help the customer remove any backdoor applications you may have installed. Return all information you have obtained during your work and delete all soft copy information from your encrypted storage medium.

And finally, answer any and all questions the customer may have concerning how you achieved such resounding success on their network. Part of your ethical duty to the customer is to perform a knowledge transfer, ensuring that the customer has a better understanding of the thought processes and techniques that an attacker would use to compromise their network. Understanding this will help the customer better protect themselves and their customers.

Summary

Most people who work in the field of penetration testing will tell you that it's a lot of fun. You're challenged with each new customer. But to be the most successful and helpful security professional you can be, you need to understand the entire security analysis life cycle and how you fit into it.

The security analysis life cycle begins with a thorough look at the customer's programmatic and organizational processes. What policies are in place to protect the organization? Are those policies enforced? Are they focused on protecting those critical pieces of information that the business relies on? What is the impact if the customer loses confidentiality, integrity, or availability of those information types? How is that information protected at a policy and human level?

The next step is the technical evaluation that provides a comprehensive analysis of technical vulnerabilities at the customer organization. This piece of the life cycle looks at the network and the hosts. All applications and operating systems are taken into account. The goal is to find as many vulnerabilities as possible, and to allow the customer adequate opportunity to fix or mitigate those vulnerabilities. This is called customer mitigation and is the time when a customer builds their defenses. Finally, the customer tests their defense through the use of penetration testing. This is where you come in.

Every good penetration tester has a hacker mentality. They use standard processes with each job, but also know when to step outside those lines and do things a bit differently. There is no shortage of good tools for performing this type of work, but having programming and scripting skills will only make your work better.

A standard methodology for penetration testing includes the following steps: Information Gathering, Network Enumeration, Vulnerability Identification, Vulnerability Exploitation, Privilege Escalation, Expansion of Reach, Future Access, and Information Compromise. Finally, once all these steps are complete, the professional penetration tester will help the customer clean up their network and provide the customer with a full knowledge transfer. During the penetration testing process, copious notes should be taken to log each account or computer that has been modified. These notes will be used during the cleanup phase.

It should be noted that privilege escalation starts with obtaining a local user account and then trying to escalate that to a local administrator account. From this point, we'll try to escalate to a domain level user or administrative account. Another important note is that escalation also consists of expanding your access across the network. For instance, you may initially compromise a single computer, but you're goal is to expand that access to as many other hosts and network components as possible.

Chapter 10

What Is Steganography?

by Greg Kipper

Greg Kipper (CISSP) is a Senior Security Engineer with Tenacity Solutions Incorporated. Tenacity is a woman-owned, small business that is headquartered in Reston, VA, that specializes in information security and information assurance. Greg has been involved in the field of security and information assurance over the past 13 years. Through his experiences in the security sector as a systems engineer, security analyst, and consultant, he moved into the emerging field of digital forensics. The last seven years of his career have been spent on working on forensic investigations studying the future of technologies and their forensic impact of that data to the process of evidence. Some of his notable works include the books *Investigator's Guide to Steganography, Wireless Crime and Forensic Investigation*, and the upcoming *Proactive Forensics* as well as a Congressional report outlining technical methods of reducing the risk of Insider Threat. Greg continues to actively contribute to the fields of security and digital forensics giving lectures annually at DoD Cybercrime, TechnoSecurity, and TechnoForensics.

Introduction

[Syngress Publishing, along with Greg Kipper, would like to thank Auerbach Publications for letting us use a portion of Greg's book, *Investigator's Guide to Steganography*, as a starting point for this chapter.]

When I was approached to contribute a chapter to this book, I was excited to have the chance to revisit steganography again since finishing my first book *Investigator's Guide to Steganography* in 2002. This chapter will follow much the same model as my book did by approaching steganography in the context of how it fits into the real world. This chapter has no code and is meant for everyone from forensic investigators to security managers. It is my goal here to give you a solid understanding of the basics of steganography, what it can and can't do, and to arm you with enough information to determine where it fits into the particulars of your specific career path.

Defining Steganography

Steganography, in its most basic definition, is a type of hidden communication that literally means "covered writing." Another excellent definition for steganography is "hiding in plain sight." Steganography is where the message is out in the open, often for all to see, but goes undetected because the very *existence* of the message is a secret. In short, the communication is taking place right in front of someone's eyes, but unless they're in the know (meaning the sender or recipient), the message goes unnoticed. In contrast, *cryptography* is where the message is scrambled, and unreadable, but the existence of a message is often known, or at the very least easy to identify because of its unreadable nature. Often times throughout history, encrypted messages have been intercepted but have not been decoded. While this protects the information hidden in the cipher, the interception of the message can be just as damaging because it tells an opponent or enemy that someone is communicating with someone else. Steganography takes the opposite approach and attempts to hide all evidence that communication is even taking place.

Some Useful Definitions

- **Cover Medium** The medium in which we want to hide data. It can be an innocent looking piece of information for steganography, or an important medium that must be protected for copyright or integrity reasons.

- **Stego Medium** The resulting combination of a cover medium and an embedded message and a stego key.

- **Payload** The amount of information that can be stored in the cover media. Typically, the greater the payload, the greater the risk of detection.

The following is a side-by-side comparison of some of the characteristic differences between steganography and cryptography:

- **Steganography** Hides a message within another message, so it appears and functions like a picture, video, or sound file.
- **Cryptography** The message is encrypted; looks like a meaningless jumble of characters.
- **Steganography** A collection of graphic images, video files, or sound files on a disk that may not look suspicious—in fact, this is often quite normal, especially on a personal computer.
- **Cryptography** A collection of random characters on a disk may look suspicious and is almost always a red flag during a forensic analysis.
- **Steganography** A smart eavesdropper can detect something suspicious from a sudden change of message format. For example, a user suddenly stops sending pictures and starts sending sound files.
- **Cryptography** Most eavesdroppers can detect a secret communication from a message that has been cryptographically encoded; also called traffic analysis.
- **Steganography** Requires caution when reusing pictures or sound files.
- **Cryptography** Requires caution when reusing keys.
- **Steganography** No laws are currently associated with steganography.
- **Cryptography** Some laws ban cryptography.

The Differences between Steganography and Watermarking

Watermarking and steganography differ in an important way. Steganographic information, in order to be effective, must never be apparent to a viewer unaware of its presence. This feature is optional when it comes to watermarking since there are both visible and invisible watermarks.

The Prisoners' Problem

To illustrate how steganography works in practice, let's look at the most commonly used example, which was described by G. Simmons in what he called "The Prisoners' Problem." It goes like this: Alice and Bob (our two fictional characters) have been arrested and placed in different cells. Their goal is to develop an escape plan and bust out of jail. The snag is that their only way to communicate is through the warden, Wendy. Wendy being an alert and able warden will definitely not allow Alice and Bob to communicate in code (encryption) and if she should notice anything suspicious, one or both will immediately be put in solitary confinement. So Alice and Bob must communicate in a manner that will not arouse suspicion. Thus, they must communicate invisibly, using steganography.

The scenario goes on to explain that a smart way of doing this would be to hide the information in an innocuous looking message or picture. Bob could draw a picture of a blue cow in a green pasture, and then ask Wendy to pass it along to Alice. Wendy would of course look at it before passing it on, and thinking it just a piece of abstract art, would hand it to Alice not knowing that the colors in the picture conveyed a message to her.

While this method can work in theory, some problems could stop the escape. Wendy may accidentally or purposely alter the picture and therefore change or destroy the message. If Wendy did purposely alter the picture, thereby destroying the message, it would be considered an active steganographic attack. We'll talk about this method of attack and others later in the chapter. The Prisoner's Problem model can be applied to a lot of situations where steganography might be used for communication. Alice and Bob are the two parties who want to communicate, and Wendy is the eavesdropper, and while this model can be an effective means of communication if used properly, it's also important to recognize and consider the potential of passive, active, or malicious attacks.

History and Steganography

In recent years, I've noticed that the general public's awareness of steganography has grown significantly. The reasons for this are varied. Some of the awareness came from the terrorist attacks on the United States on September 11, 2001, where speculation swirled around steganography as one method the terrorists used to communicate attack plans. The success of Dan Brown's bestseller *The DaVinci Code*, whose storyline is loaded with steganography, and the growing awareness of security (and privacy) in home and work environments (and everything in between) have helped this issue seep into the public consciousness as well. To drag out the tired cliché that "those who don't study history are doomed to repeat it," this next section will give you some interesting insights and context into steganography by showcasing some of the prominent people, events, and methods used throughout history.

The Greeks

In *The Histories*, Herodotus documented several instances where steganography was used. One such case involved a Greek named Histaiaeus, who wanted to encourage Aristagoras of Miletus to revolt against the Persian king, and managed to do so in a rather inventive way. In order to pass these instructions securely, Histaiaeus shaved the head of his messenger, wrote the message on his bare scalp, and then waited for the hair to grow back. When the messenger reached his destination—and Aristagoras—his head was shaved and the message read. While this certainly isn't the quickest method of communication, it was very effective since the messenger was able to pass guard inspections without harassment since he was carrying nothing suspicious.

A more modern variant of this same idea was used in the William Gibson story, and later movie, called *Johnny Mnemonic*. In the story, Johnny, an information courier played by Keanu Reeves, has 80GB of data storage implanted in his head where clients upload sensitive information that he then physically and covertly carries to its intended recipient, bypassing traditional communication channels.

The Chinese

The Chinese used steganography during the Yuan dynasty to revolt when China was ruled by the Mongolian people. The leaders of the time, unhappy at having to submit to foreign rule, created an inventive method of coordinating the rebellion without being discovered. The rebel leaders, knowing that the Moon Festival was drawing near, ordered the making of special cakes called "moon cakes." Baked into each moon cake was a message with the outline of the attack. On the night of the Moon Festival, the cakes were dispersed, the messages read, and the rebels successfully attacked and overthrew the government. What followed was the establishment of the Ming dynasty. Today, moon cakes are eaten to commemorate this legend.

Gaspar Schott

Gaspar Schott in his book *Schola Steganographica* described a method of encoding secret information by matching letters to specific musical notes. This "music" would never be pleasant to listen to if played, but to the untrained eye it would appear to be normal sheets of music when, in fact, it was an encoded message.

Giovanni Porta

Italian scientist Giovanni Porta, born in 1535, made contributions both to steganography and cryptography. Porta described a method of how to conceal a message within a hard-boiled egg by making a type of ink from a mixture of alum and vinegar and then using it to write on the shell. The solution would penetrate the porous shell, and leave a message on the surface of the hardened egg albumen, which can be read only when the shell is removed.

Girolamo Cardano

The Cardano Grille system may be something you're already familiar with, although you may never have heard the name Cardano. The basics are that each recipient has a piece of paper with several holes cut it. When the "*grille*" (the piece of paper with holes) is placed over an innocuous looking message, the holes in the grille line up with words in the larger message and reveal the hidden message. Anyone intercepting the message would be nescient to the fact, because the words the grille sees have been hidden in a larger message that takes up the entire page. Providing that the sender is a decent wordsmith with a good imagination, even difficult messages can be sent with the grille while the larger message will still be literate and also sound meaningful.

   Another way to use the grille method is to take a page from a book and employ certain letters within the words on the page to create the grille. Once the grille is passed to the intended recipient, that person only has to have the book, or the page of the book, that corresponds to the grille to retrieve the message.

The Culpers

Steganography played a role in the Revolutionary War and helped George Washington on many occasions. The code ring consisted of five people and used the codename Samuel Culper. Several trial and error attempts at secret communication prompted The Culpers to adopt invisible ink as one of their security precautions. The invisible ink was used on a blank piece of paper, and after the message was written, was reinserted into a ream of new, blank paper. Washington knew that by counting from the top down to a specific sheet how to find the hidden message. He would then apply a second solution to make the ink appear. A concern of Washington's was that carrying around blank sheets of paper would create suspicion, so he ordered that the invisible ink also be used on regular messages, and that the secret message be written between the lines or under the message.

Civil War Rugs

A form of steganography was used prior to the Civil War to aid slaves in escaping to freedom. In the 1800s, the underground railroad was one of the main escape routes used by slaves. Quilts, which were hung outside to dry, became an ideal way to display information inconspicuously. The quilts would have special patterns sewn into them which would convey messages to prepare or provide direction to escaping slaves who knew what to look for.

World War I

During World War I there were several periods and instances where steganography was used with success. One method was called a Turning Grille; this took Cardano's Grille method and enhanced it. The Turning Grille looked like a normal grille (a square sheet of cardboard) divided into cells, with some of the cells punched out. To use the Turning Grille, the encoder would write the first sequence of letters, and then rotate the grille 90 degrees, write the second sequence of letters, and so on, rotating the grille after each sequence.

There was also a record during the war of a cable censor who received the message "Father is dead." The censor changed the message to "Father is deceased." A reply came back: "Is Father dead or deceased?"

World War II

Steganography, and its prevention, were also prevalent in World War II. After the attack on Pearl Harbor the United States enacted a censorship organization. This organization worked to think of ways that coded messages could be passed in the open and took steps to stop them or, if there was a message, destroy the code.

Chess games were banned by mail, crossword puzzles were examined or removed from correspondence, newspaper clippings and student's grades were removed.

Stamps were removed and replaced with ones of equal value but different denominations or numbers. Children's pictures were replaced, Xs and Os from love letters were removed, and of course blank paper was replaced and tested for invisible ink. Mass media was censored, too. Telephone and telegraph requests for special songs were not allowed and mail-in song requests would be held for a random amount of time before being played.

The Vietnam War

Another, and well-publicized, example of steganography happened during the height of the Vietnam War. Commander Jeremiah Denton, a naval pilot who had been shot down and captured, was paraded around by the North Vietnamese in front of the news as part of a propaganda event. Knowing that he was under the proverbial microscope and unable to say anything openly critical about his captors, he blinked his eyes in Morse code, spelling out **T-O-R-T-U-R-E**, as he spoke to the media.

Analog Steganography

In the previous section, we covered some of the very basics of what steganography is and isn't, along with some creative uses of it throughout history. In this section, I will flush out some of the specific techniques of "analog" steganography—meaning no computers are used in the creation or transmission of the message—to further your knowledge and provide some contrast for the next section, which delves into the realm of digital steganography.

Microdots

The microdot is a page-sized photograph that has been reduced to 1 mm in diameter. The microdot became a popular and commonly used form of steganography during WWII. The process of creating a microdot is pretty straightforward, but requires a few specialized pieces of equipment. First, a photograph of the message is taken, which reduces it to roughly the size of a postage stamp. Next, the image is shrunk further with a reverse microscope, bringing it down to 1 millimeter. The negative is then developed and the image is punched out of the film. A common way to do this was with a syringe needle whose point had been filed down. Once the needle separated the dot from the rest of the film, it was placed on the cover text, over a period or under a stamp, and cemented in place. Professor Walter Zapp, a German, is credited with creating a device that could perform most of these processes mechanically.

One-Time Pads

A one-time pad is a method of encoding a message with a random key once, and only once. This type of encoding is an unbreakable system, because no matter how much time or sample text a cryptanalyst had available, breaking the code would be impossible. The cipher would never be the same twice.

Semagrams

A semagram is essentially nothing more than a symbol. Its literal meaning is, in fact, semantic symbol. Semagrams are associated with a concept and do not use writing to hide a message. Remember our example in the Prisoners' problem. Bob sent a picture to Alice, where the picture, or more specifically, characteristics about the picture, conveyed secret information. A semagram can be almost anything that doesn't use words to hide a message.

Null Ciphers

A null cipher is an unencrypted message crafted in such a way that the real message is "camouflaged" in a larger, innocent-sounding message. A null cipher is also sometimes referred to as an open code. Null ciphers have one big drawback: sometimes they don't always "sound" quite right. The message may read clumsily, and because of this, suspected messages were detected my mail filters, although many innocent-sounding messages often went undetected.

An example of a message containing null ciphers is

Fishing freshwater bends and saltwater coasts rewards anyone feeling stressed. Resourceful anglers usually find masterful leapers fun and admit swordfish rank overwhelming anyday.

Taking the third letter in every word, the following message emerges:

Send lawyers guns and money

Type Spacing and Offsetting

Type spacing or type offsetting is a subtle way of distorting the text in a message to hide additional data. Type spacing was created as a way to discourage illegal copying of textual material. While this makes its invented purpose technically a form of watermarking, type spacing can also be used to send a message in secret. To encode a secret message using type spacing, all one would have to do is adjust specific letters ever so slightly from their normal position. The letters that are out of position indicate the secret message.

Invisible Ink

Invisible inks are colorless liquids that require heat, light, or a special chemical to change its color and make it visible. The basics behind reactions that don't use heat involve an acid or a base, and a PH indicator. The colorless liquid, which is either an acid or base, is applied to paper and dries, making it invisible. When a PH indicator is introduced, it reacts with the acid or base properties of the dried liquid and changes color. Several types of liquids that work well as invisible inks have been used throughout history. Some of them are milk, vinegar, lemon juice, and even urine.

Newspaper Code

During the Victorian era, newspapers could be sent without charge. As a result, the poorer classes of the time made use of this and invented the newspaper code. The process couldn't be more straightforward. Holes were poked just above the letters in the newspaper so that when the dots were transcribed off the newspaper and written together, the secret message would be revealed. While this method of steganography took a fair amount of time, it did allow people to communicate freely.

Jargon Code

A jargon coded message changes words instead of replacing individual letters. Jargon code is word-crafting at its finest, and usually requires a good bit of imagination on the part of the sender. A number of years ago, I worked a summer job at Disneyland as one of the boat drivers on "The Jungle Cruise." After being there for a couple of weeks, I was introduced to the local jargon code that the male employees would use to tell other male employees an attractive woman was in the vicinity. The word was "Alp," and it was surprisingly effective for those of us who knew what to listen for. This one word allowed a few young men to effectively communicate in crowds of several hundred people at a time without drawing undue attention. This example is certainly one of the simplest forms of jargon code. Normally it is something more than just one word, but it illustrates the point of communicating out in the open quite well without anyone noticing.

Digital Steganography

Around 1996, digital steganography really started coming into its own. It became something more and more people were talking about and experimenting with. Today, when most people think of steganography, they think of "digital steganography"—hiding secret messages in pictures, on public Web sites, and so on. With the history lesson behind us, let's dive into the details of the types, techniques, and tools of digital steganography.

Steganography Techniques

When it's all said and done, there are really only three ways to hide a digital message in a digital cover. The basic three are the injection, substitution, and generation of new files.

Injection

Data injection takes the secret message and directly embeds it in the host medium (picture, sound file, or video clip). The problem with this kind of embedding is that it usually makes the host file larger; therefore, the alteration is easier to detect.

Substitution

Normal data is replaced, or substituted, with the secret data. This usually results in very little size changes to the host file. However, depending on the type of host file and/or the amount of hidden data, the substitution method can degrade the quality of the original host file.

Generation of New Files

A cover file is *generated* for the sole purpose of concealing a secret message. As illustrated in the Prisoners' Problem, Bob creates a picture of something innocent that can be passed to Alice. The innocent picture is the cover that provides the mechanism for conveying the message, which in that example was the particular color of a cow.

A more modern form of generation of new files is the program Spam Mimic. Spam Mimic embeds a text message within a rather daunting piece of spam that can be e-mailed to an intended recipient. While this generated spam doesn't make a whole lot of sense, it makes enough sense to be believable, and that's all that's needed.

The Six Categories of Steganography

In all methods of steganography, something is being done to conceal a message. Naturally, these actions or techniques can be separated and analyzed to learn what's happening during the whole process. The six categories of steganography are substitution system techniques, transform domain techniques, spread spectrum techniques, statistical method techniques, distortion techniques, and cover generation techniques. We'll look at each of these, one at a time.

Substitution System

Substitution system steganography replaces redundant or unneeded bits of a cover with the bits from the secret message. Several available steganography tools use the Least Significant Bit (LSB) method of encoding the secret message. LSB works like this. In a digital cover file, there is a tremendous amount of wasted or redundant space. It is this space that the steganography program will take advantage of and use to hide another message (on the bit level) within the digital cover.

Transform Domain Techniques

The transform domain technique is also very effective, but is a little trickier to explain. Basically, transform domain techniques hide message data in the "transform space" of a signal. If you're saying to yourself, "Huh?," hold on and I'll explain. Every day on the Internet, people send pictures back and forth, and most often they use a JPEG format. JPEGs are interesting in that they compress themselves when they close. In order for this to take place, they have to get rid of excess data (excess bits) that would otherwise prevent them from compressing. During compression, a JPEG will make an approximation of itself to become smaller. This change transforms space; thus, it can be used to hide information.

Spread Spectrum Techniques

In this section we briefly define two types of spread spectrum techniques: direct sequence and frequency hopping.

In direct sequence spread spectrum, the stream of information to be transmitted is divided into small pieces, each of which is allocated to a frequency channel spread across the spectrum. A data signal at the point of transmission is combined with a higher data-rate bit sequence (also known as a chipping code) that divides the data according to a spreading ratio. The redundant chipping code helps the signal resist interference and also enables the original data to be recovered if data bits are damaged during transmission.

Frequency hopping is when a broad slice of the bandwidth spectrum is divided into many possible broadcast frequencies. In general, frequency-hopping devices use less power and are cheaper, but the performance of direct sequence spread spectrum systems is usually better and more reliable.

Statistical Methods

Statistical methods use what's called a "1-bit" steganographic scheme. This scheme embeds one bit of information only in a digital carrier and thus creates a statistical change, even if it's only a slight one. A statistical change in the cover indicates a 1, while a cover left unchanged indicates a 0. This system works based on the receiver's ability to distinguish between modified and unmodified covers.

Distortion Techniques

The distortion method of steganography creates a change in a cover object to hide information. The secret message is recovered when the algorithm compares the changed and/or distorted cover with the original.

Cover Generation Methods

Cover generation methods are probably the most unique of the six types. Typically, a cover object is chosen to hide a message in, but that's not the case here. A cover generation method actually creates a cover for the sole purpose of hiding information. Spam Mimic is an excellent example of a cover generation method.

Types of Steganography

Now that we've looked at the categories of stego, let's look at the two types of stego: linguistic and technical.

Linguistic Steganography

Linguistic steganography can be described quite simply as any form of steganography that uses language in the cover. A number of forms of linguistic steganography are covered in the next sections, but the two most basic categories are open codes and text semagrams.

A program that takes advantage of linguistic steganography is NICETEXT, which uses the technique of linguistic steganography in a very inventive way. The goal of NICETEXT is to provide a program that can transform cipher text (encrypted text) into text that looks like natural language, while still providing a cover for the original cipher text. An added benefit of this type of program is that it can be applied to many different languages.

Text Semagrams

Text Semagrams work with graphical modifications of the text, such as type-spacing and offsetting. They concern details that are tiny, but nonetheless visible. Certain methods work without text as well. These are called real semagrams.

Technical Steganography

Technical steganography is a little broader in scope since it doesn't necessarily deal with the written word, even though it communicates information. Technical steganography is the method of steganography where a tool, device, or method is used to conceal the message. Let's have a look at some technical steganography methods.

Embedding Methods

The technical challenges of data hiding are formidable. Any "holes" to fill with data in a host file, either statistical or perceptual, are likely targets for removal by lossy compression. The key to successful data hiding is the finding of holes that are not suitable for exploitation by compression algorithms.

Least Significant Bit (LSB)

Least Significant Bit (LSB) is the substitution method of steganography where the right-most bit in a binary notation, the bit with the least impact on the binary data, is replaced with a bit from the embedded message. This method provides "security through obscurity," a technique that can be rendered useless if an attacker knows the technique is being used.

Transform Techniques

Three main types of transform techniques can be used when embedding a message in steganography. They are the Discrete Cosine Transform (DCT), the Discrete Fourier Transform, and the Wavelet Transform, which simply embeds the secret data in the cover during the *transformation* process in various ways.

Spread-Spectrum Encoding

Spread-spectrum encoding is the method of hiding a small or narrow-band signal (a message) in a large or wide band cover. The foundation of this process begins with a spread spectrum encoder. The encoder works by modulating a narrow band signal over a carrier. The carrier's signal is continually shifted using a noise generator and a secret key that makes the noise seem random. The message is embedded in the existing noise of the carrier signal. This spreads the narrow signal over a wide area, decreasing the density of the hidden signal and making it much more difficult to detect within the overall carrier signal.

Perceptual Masking

This form of steganography occurs when one signal, or sound, becomes impercep-tible to the observer because of the presence of another signal. This method also exploits the weaknesses of the human visual and auditory systems. A common example that almost everyone has seen is in spy films where someone is trying to communicate with someone else in a room they know is bugged. Usually the secret agent will turn up the stereo, run the shower, or do some other innocent (but noisy) task that allows a whispered conversation to take place without being heard.

Steganography Applied to Different Media

When you get right down to it, digital steganography is really just the digital manipulation of 1s and 0s. This fact allows for several choices of cover media since we know that whether it is a document, picture, video, or even a file system, in the end it's all just binary. In this next section, we'll look at how stego manipulation can be applied to a wide variety of digital media.

Still Images: Pictures

The methods of steganography are quite varied. With still images, LSB insertion and spread spectrum techniques are commonly used. Texture block is another method. Texture block uses low bit-rate data hiding and is accomplished by copying a region from a random texture pattern in a picture to an area of similar texture resulting in a pair of identically "*textured*" regions in a picture.

Moving Images: Video

Steganography, when applied to a video file such as an .avi or .mpg, typically uses Discrete Cosine Transform (DCT) manipulation, meaning that as the video is compressed and/or decompressed, secret data can be added during the transformation process.

Audio Files

The following are various audio file methods:

- **LSB insertion** The bit with the least impact on the binary data is replaced with a bit from the embedded message.

- **Differential phase variation** The sound file is divided into blocks, and the initial phase of the sound file is modified with the secret message, preserving the following relative phase shifts. This is an effective method given it has a low signal-to-noise ratio.

- **Spread spectrum schemes** The method of hiding a small- or narrow-band signal, the secret message, in a large- or wide-band cover.

- **Adding echo to the audio signal** A slight echo is added to the signal using two different delays to encode the 1 and 0 bits. The echo is too slight to be perceived by the human ear.

Text Files

Three methods exist for text files:

- **Open-space** The use of white space between words or sentences to hide data.

- **Syntactic** Uses modification of the word order or punctuation to hide a message.

- **Semantic** Uses synonyms to encode a secret message. See the example in the section titled "World War I" ("Is Father dead or deceased?").

Steganographic File Systems

This is another particularly interesting way of applying steganography. Let's take a closer look. A steganographic file system is a method of storing files in such a way that it encrypts data and hides it so well that it can't be proven it's there.

A steganographic file system can

- Hide users' documents in other seemingly random files.

- Allow the owner to give names and passwords for some files while keeping others secret.

- Behave like a second layer of secrecy. Encrypted files are out in the open and visible, but not understandable. Stego files aren't even visible, and an outsider can't look for files that "aren't there."

Hiding in Disk Space

Three main methods exist for hiding data in disk space: unused sectors, hidden partitions, and slack space. In this section, we'll take a closer look at how each is carried out.

Unused Sectors

Similar to the method used in the "Steganographic File Systems" section, tools that hide data in unused sectors, such as S-tools, will take the file and spread the bits out throughout the free space on the floppy. Though undetectable in the normal Windows viewer, the file is still there.

Hidden Partitions

A hidden partition on a hard drive is another way of hiding information, sometimes large amounts, in plain sight. This method isn't terribly robust since a close examination of the hard drive, independent of the operating system, will usually reveal that the drive is bigger than the OS is letting on.

Slack Space

Slack space is a type of unused space in a disk. Even if the actual data being stored requires less storage than the cluster size, an entire cluster is reserved for the file. The unused space is called the *slack space*. If minimum space allocated is 32kb and the file is 6kb, then 26kb is left unused and considered unavailable by the operating system. This unused space (slack space) could be used to hide information without showing up in any directory or file system.

Hiding in Network Packets

A covert channel is described as "any communication channel that can be exploited by a process to transfer information in a manner that violates the systems security policy." Essentially, it is a method of communication, referred to as Internet Steganography, that is not part of an actual computer system design, but can still be used to transfer information to users or system processes that normally would not have access to the information. Hiding information within network packets can be accomplished a couple of ways. One is Packet Header Manipulation, which hides data in empty fields of the packet header, and Packet "sorting," which re-sorts packets in such a way that their sequence carries with it a meaning of either 1 or 0, which will ultimately yield a hidden message.

Issues in Information Hiding

Most things in life require trade-offs of some sort. Something for nothing isn't the way the universe works, and information hiding is no exception. The following is a list of limitations associated with trying to hide information steganographically.

Levels of Visibility

When you are looking at the first issue in information hiding, determining levels of visibility can be done by asking one question. Does the embedding process distort the cover to the point where it is visually noticeable? If the image is unacceptably distorted, the carrier isn't sufficient for the payload; if it isn't distorted, the carrier is adequate.

Robustness vs. Payload

To have a robust method of embedding the message, you must have redundancy to resist changes made to the cover. This redundancy subsequently lowers the payload.

The exact opposite is also true. With little or no redundancy (robustness), the payload of the secret message can be larger.

more robust = lower payload

less robust = higher payload

File Format Dependence

Some image and sound files are either lossy or lossless. The conversion of lossless information to the compressed "lossy" information can destroy the hidden information in the cover. A good example is to think of the conversion of an uncompressed bitmap to a compressed, estimated jpeg. The compression and estimation change the bits to include the bits that might be the embedded message.

Watermarking

The definition of *watermarking* is "a form of marking that embeds copyright information about the artist or owner." In the traditional manufacture of paper, wet fiber is subjected to high pressure to expel the moisture. If the press's mold has a slight pattern, this pattern leaves an imprint in the paper—a watermark—which is best viewed under transmitted light. Today, the word "watermark" has been borrowed by high technology. Digital watermarks are imperceptible (or barely perceptible) transformations of digital data. Often, the digital data set is a digital multimedia object. While digital images are most often mentioned in the same breath as digital watermarking, we note that watermarks can be applied to other forms of digital data, such as pictures, videos, and music.

Classification of Watermarks

In this section we briefly discuss two types of watermarks: fragile and robust.

Fragile

The fragile watermark is one of the watermarking methods for authentication that has a low robustness towards modifications, where even a small change of the content will destroy embedded information, showing an attack attempt was made. In short, fragile watermarks are *supposed* to break. Think of it as a digital version of the foil put under the cap of an aspirin bottle. It's pretty hard to get by that without it looking like it's been tampered with.

Robust

A robust watermark is almost exactly the opposite of a fragile watermark. A robust watermark can be either visible or invisible, depending on its purpose. Robust watermarks are very difficult to remove or damage. The easiest example of a robust watermark can be seen any time you turn on the television. CNN, ESPN, and the Sci-Fi Channel all have a watermark in the lower right-hand corner, not only to let you know what station you're on, but also to let you know that what you're watching is their content. Removing a visible watermark, especially in the television example, would be very difficult to do without someone noticing after the fact.

Steganography Tools

There are literally hundreds of steganography tools available on the Internet, and new ones are being released all the time. Using the same list I outlined in the earlier section "Steganography Applied to Different Media," I've listed some tools that will allow you to use steganography on a variety of digital media.

Still Images: Pictures

Blindside is an application that allows you to conceal a file, or set of files, within a single digital image. The resulting image appears identical to the human eye, but can typically contain around 50k of secret data. The concealed files can also be password protected. Blindside operates by creating slight color inflections in an image which, although invisible to the human eye, can free up a great deal of space in which to store information. A proprietary cryptographic algorithm can also be used to scramble the data with a secret pass phrase.

Moving Images: ideo

Info Stego (see Figure 10.1) is a steganography and watermarking tool that lets you protect your private information, secret communications, and legal copyright using information watermark and data encryption technology. Info Stego can hide your important information or copyright mark inside another file, which can be picture, sound, or video. Also, as with any steganography or watermarking program, other people can't notice the file change.

Figure 10.1 The Info Stego Interface

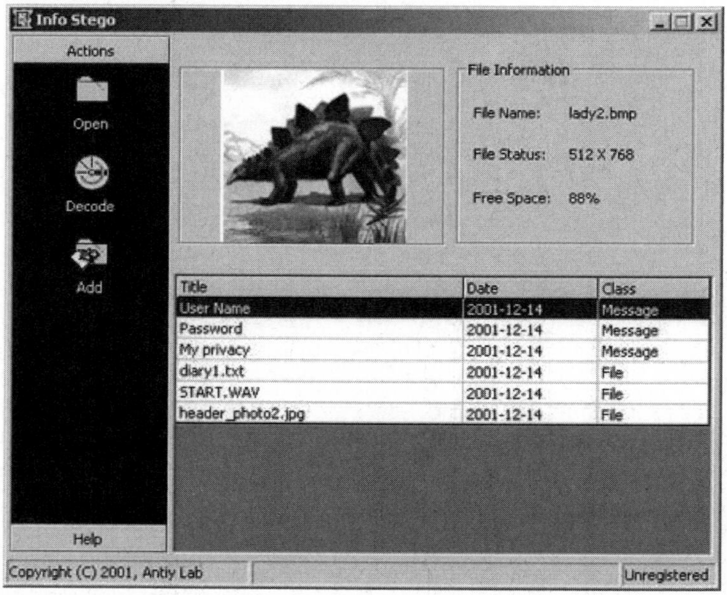

Audio Files

MASKER is a steganography and encryption program that supports several high-performance coding algorithms, including Cast-256, Blowfish-256, Rijndael-256, and Twofish-256. The cover image can be an audio file, a program, or a video file. Even after the hidden information is embedded, the file will still be fully functional. Additionally, files can be compressed for network transmission.

Text Files

KPKFile provides security for your sensitive files by encrypting and hiding them. It has a steganography option, allowing the user to bury an encrypted file within another still working file, such as a Microsoft Word document or a bitmap image. KPKFile can also create secret folders that are impossible to access without the proper password.

Steganographic File Systems

BackYard is just one example of a steganographic file system program that can completely hide and protect your files, folders, and drives by making them completely inaccessible, meaning completely hidden from the Windows operating system, and rendering them write protected. You can use any other protection scheme you specify. Different protection profiles can be created with different files and directories, and be activated with a single hotkey. bProtected, Bury Bury, Dark Files, Disk Hide, and Drive Hider are some other examples of stego file systems.

Real-World Uses

In the grand scheme, it is fair to say there are very few legitimate uses for steganography. While it is often common to consider an invisible watermark and steganography synonymous, there are actually a couple significant differences between the two, mainly intent and the type of information encoded in the cover medium.

In today's workplace, the strained balance between computer security and employee privacy is growing more and more unstable. This instability creates an environment where steganography could be used as a very effective way of bypassing normal communication channels. Web mail or other Internet-based meeting places are being used as ways of communicating outside and around the firewall. With security and privacy policies on everyone's mind, both employees and employers alike, steganography may become the next big obstacle security officers have to face when it comes to controlling communication within their networks.

As to other darker activities such as terrorism, espionage, insider threats, and criminal activities, analog forms of steganography have been used in the past with great success, and there is nothing to suggest that digital steganography isn't being used now, and won't continue to be in the future. Often, the argument arises that "we're just not seeing any evidence of steganography being used," which unfortunately for the people charged with investigating these matters is exactly the point. One isn't supposed to see any evidence, since that's steganography's invented purpose.

Detection and Attacks

Steganography detection is usually a very difficult task, especially in instances of low payloads, since fewer bits are replaced, altered, or inserted. However, there are some ways to tell. The following is a list of methods, and a partial list of tools, used for detecting steganography.

Detection

Statistical Tests

Statistical tests can reveal that an image has been modified by determining that its statistical properties deviate from the norm. Some tests are independent of the data format and just measure the entropy of the redundant data. Expect images with hidden data to have a higher entropy than those without.

Stegdetect

Stegdetect is an automated tool for detecting steganographic content in images. It is capable of detecting several different steganographic methods to embed hidden information in JPEG images.

Stegbreak

Stegbreak is a program that uses dictionary guessing to break the encoding password. It is used to launch dictionary attacks against JSteg-Shell, JPHide, and OutGuess.

Visible Noise

Attacks and analysis on hidden information may take several forms: detecting, extracting, and disabling or destroying hidden information. Images with too large a payload may display distortions from hidden information. Selecting the proper combination of steganography tools and carriers is important to successful information hiding.

Appended Spaces and "Invisible" Characters

Appended spaces and "invisible" characters refers back to the technique of hiding data in spaces within text.

This form of text semagram uses the white space in a document to denote binary values. The white space can be between individual words, sentences, or even between paragraphs. Almost any combination is possible, but to a point, if the text appears to have too much white space, it can be subject to scrutiny. While this form of steganography can work effectively, it has a few big drawbacks. First, if the document is digital, any modern word processor would be able to show the spacing irregularities or, worse, reformat the document and destroy the hidden information. The other drawback is that this method doesn't transmit a large amount of information easily, which can limit its practicality.

Color Palettes

Some tools have characteristics that are unique among stego-tools. In some steganography programs the color palettes have unique characteristics that don't appear anywhere else. For example, the program Hide and Seek creates color palette entries that are divisible by 4 for all bit values. The palette modification creates a detectable steganography signature.

Attack Types

It is usually easier to destroy than to create, and in the case of attacking steganographic files, this remains true. Since steganography is for the most part relatively fragile, a number of methods exist for attacking stegged files or suspected stegged files. A couple of these may actually yield the hidden message after considerable work, but most simply destroy the message, making its recovery by anyone impossible.

Stego Only Attack

The stego only attack is one where we only have the stego-medium, and we want to detect and/or extract the embedded message.

Known Cover Attack

The known cover attack is used when we have both the stego-medium and the cover medium, so we can make comparisons between the two.

Known Message Attack

The known message attack assumes we know the message and the stego-medium, and that we want to find the method used for embedding the message.

Chosen Stego Attack

The chosen stego attack is used when we have both the stego-medium and the steganography tool or algorithm.

Chosen Message Attack

The chosen message attack is one where the steganalyst generates a stego-medium from a message using some particular tool, and looks for signatures that will enable the detection of other stego-media.

Disabling or Active Attacks

Blur

Smoothes transitions and decreases contrast by averaging the pixels next to the hard edges of defined lines and areas where there are significant color transitions.

Noise

Random noise inserts random colored pixels to an image, while uniform noise inserts pixels and colors that closely resemble the original pixels.

Noise Reduction

Reduces noise in the image by adjusting the colors and averaging pixel values.

Sharpen

Sharpening is the opposite of blur. It increases contrast between adjacent pixels where there are significant color contrasts, usually at the edge of objects.

Rotate

Rotation moves an image around its center point in a given plane.

Resample

Resampling involves an interpolation process to minimize the "raggedness" normally associated with expanding an image.

Soften

Soften applies a uniform blur to an image to smooth edges and reduce contrasts. It causes less distortion than blurring.

Summary

The first, and best, strategy is to stay educated. As everyone reading this knows, volumes of information about almost every variant of steganography are just a few Google searches away. And the information contained in this chapter should give you the ability to ask some very specific questions depending on your needs at the time.

With the continuing increase in computing power, data storage, and the increase in the size and complexity of the files themselves, the ability for greater payloads will increase as well. I suspect this will make steganography even more difficult to detect as time goes on since there is nothing to say that the payload size has to increase along with the file size. For example, let's say I wanted to send a stegged message in an image to a friend via e-mail five years ago through Yahoo! or Hotmail. With the most basic of tools, I could have embedded a few kilobytes worth of ASCII text data into a 1MB JPEG and e-mailed it with no problems. Today, I could take those same few kilobytes of text and embed them in a 10MB JPEG, or MPEG, or MP3. My point is this, with the commonplace high-speed bandwidth and the natural progression of increasing file sizes, along with the ability to move them across the Internet, this will give someone wishing to use steganography much larger cover mediums to choose from, without necessarily having to increase the size of the hidden message; thus, making detection just that much more difficult.

Steganography in digital form is not a young technology anymore, and I suspect it will continue to increase in importance in the security community as time goes on. Since I still don't have that crystal ball I've been wanting, I can at least offer you some guidelines on being as prepared as possible regarding upcoming changes.

1. Again, keep yourself informed.

2. If you have to create a defensive strategy, consider the time factor; 80 percent today is better than 100 percent tomorrow.

3. Apply offensive weaponry in defensive ways. Be creative; your adversaries will be.

4. Keep the community informed if you discover a new threat.

5. Do not consider any form of protection you might want to add as too extreme. It is *your* network and information, after all.

Chapter 11

Insider Threat
by Dr. Eric Cole

Dr. Eric Cole is currently chief scientist for Lockheed Martin Information Technology (LMIT), specializing in advanced technology research. Eric is a highly sought-after network security consultant and speaker. Eric has consulted for international banks and Fortune 500 companies. He also has advised venture capitalist firms on what start-ups should be funded. He has in-depth knowledge of network security and has come up with creative ways to secure his clients' assets. He is the author of several books, including *Insider Threat: Protecting the Enterprise from Sabotage, Spying, and Theft* (Syngress Publishing, ISBN: 1597490482); *Cyber Spying: Tracking Your Family's (Sometimes) Secret Online Lives* (Syngress Publishing, ISBN: 1-931836-41-8); *Hackers Beware: Defending Your Network from the Wiley Hacker; Hiding in Plain Sight*; and the *Network Security Bible*. Eric holds several patents and has written numerous magazine and journal articles. Eric worked for the CIA for more than seven years and has created several successful network security practices. Eric is an invited keynote speaker at government and international conferences and has appeared in interviews on CBS News, "60 Minutes," and CNN.

Introduction

I was sitting at my desk when my phone rang. I answered the phone and it was a large pharmaceutical company who was interested in consulting services. They started off the conversation stating that they had some problems and thought that my company might be able to help. They had noticed a trend with one of their foreign competitors. Every time they went to release a new product (in this case a new drug), one of their competitors would release a similar drug with a similar name several weeks before them and would beat them to market. If you understand the drug industry, you'll know that this is a serious problem. The first company to get a product to market usually is able to obtain a higher market share and higher demand than its competitors. Therefore, this represented a huge monetary loss to the company and the executives were concerned.

This initially sounded like a potential problem but I needed more details. My follow-up question was how often had this occurred and over what time period. The executive I was talking with said it had happened eight times over the prior 12 months. I was sitting there thinking: You *think* there is a problem? My next question was, "Why did you wait so long to call someone?" Their answer was, "We figured it was just a coincidence, because the only way this could have happened was if an insider was giving the information to a competitor and we trust all of the employees so this could not be the case." Over the next several months they were going to realize how wrong that previous statement was.

I led an internal assessment team and over the course of several months found three different groups of people (each consisting of 2-4 people), working for two different competitors. Actually, one group was working for a foreign competitor and the other two groups were working for a foreign government.

The fact that this story is true is scary, but what makes it even more troubling is that this happened more than 18 months ago and I have worked on and am aware of at least 15 other similar cases. The average monetary loss of the case I worked on was estimated at $350 million annually.

The Devil Inside

"I trust everyone, it is the devil inside that I do not trust," is a great line from the movie *The Italian Job*. Everyone has the potential do to harm, including your employees. If you look at the minimal background checks that most companies perform on their employees, you have to wonder what that trust is based on. Why is it that once a total stranger is hired at your company, you now completely trust that person? Just because they are now called an employee does not mean they have loyalty to your organization and would do nothing to hurt the company. We do not want you to be so paranoid that your company cannot function, but a healthy dose of paranoia is good.

Aldrich Ames, Robert Hanssen, and other spies had one thing in common: they passed the polygraph (lie detector test) with almost a perfect score. How could a machine that tests whether people are lying not catch the biggest liars that cost so many people their lives? The reason is a polygraph does not detect lies, it detects guilt. In these cases, either the people felt justified by their actions and did not feel guilty about them or they were trained to be able to bypass and deceive people. Only by closely watching people over time will you start to understand that there are certain people who cannot be trusted.

Insider threat and corporate espionage rely on the fact that it is sometimes better to live in denial and be happy than to know the truth and have to deal with it. One of my associates recently found out his wife was cheating on him and was very annoyed with the person who told him. The person who told him said, "Why are you mad at me? Didn't you want to know?" And the person's response was, "No." It was easier to live with a lie than deal with the truth. While most executives might not be bold enough to admit this, it is very true in corporations and governments around the world. It is easier to trust your employees and keep life simple, than to suspect everyone and deal with the complexities it creates. However, if it will put your company out of business, cause hundreds of millions of dollars' worth of loss, or cause people to die, you might think differently about the answer.

Nobody wants to believe the truth, but corporate espionage via the insider threat is causing huge problems. Many companies either do not have the proper monitoring to realize or do not want to admit that it is happening to them. For some reason, with many crimes, including insider threat, victims feel embarrassed and ashamed. They are the victims, they did nothing wrong, but for some reason these criminals turn the tables on who is at fault. I have heard rape victims say that it was their own fault they were raped. I have also heard numerous times that it is a company's fault if they are stupid enough to be a victim to insider threat. With that mentality, who is going to admit that this happened to their company? The only person at fault is the attacker—not the victim.

The Importance of Insider Threat

Organizations tend to think that once they hire an employee or a contractor that that person is now part of a trusted group of people. Although an organization might give an employee additional access that an ordinary person would not have, why should they trust that person? Many organizations perform no background checks and no reference checks and as long as the hiring manager likes them, they will hire them. Many people might not be who you think they are and not properly validating them can be an expensive, if not a fatal, mistake. Because many organizations, in essence, hire complete strangers who are really unknown entities and give them access to sensitive data, the insider threat is something that all organizations must worry about.

If a competitor or similar entity wants to cause damage to your organization, steal critical secrets, or put you out of business, they just have to find a job opening, prep someone to ace the interview, have that person get hired, and they are in. The fact that it is that easy should scare you. Many companies have jobs open for several weeks and it could take a couple of weeks to set up an interview. That gives a competitor focused on your company a four-week period to prep someone to ace an interview. This is what foreign governments do when they plant a spy against the U.S. They know that a key criterion for that person is passing the polygraph, so they will put that person through intensive training so that he or she can pass the polygraph with no problem. This points out a key disadvantage that organizations have. The attacker knows what process you are going to follow to hire someone and all they have to do is prep someone so they ace that part of the process.

In terms of the importance, I often hear people say that it is only hype and that it cannot happen to us. This is synonymous to thinking that bad things only happen to others, they never happen to you; until they happen to you and then you have a different view of the world. I remember several years ago when my father got diagnosed with having a cancerous brain tumor. It shocked me, devastated me, and changed my views forever. Prior to that I knew that people had brain cancer but it was something that I could not relate to or understand because I never thought it could really happen to me or someone I love. Bad things happened to others, not to me. This is the denial that many of us live in, but the unfortunate truth is bad things do happen and they could be occurring right now and you just do not know about it.

Insider threat is occurring all the time, but since it is happening within a company, it is a private attack. Public attacks like defacing a Web site are hard for a company to deny. Private attacks are much easier to conceal.

Because these attacks are being perpetrated by trusted insiders, you need to understand the damage they can cause; how to build proper measures to prevent the attack; how to minimize the damage; and, at a minimum, how to detect the attacks in a timely manner. Many of the measures companies deploy today are ineffective against the insider. When companies talk about security and securing their enterprise, they are concerned with the external attack, forgetting about the damage that an insider can cause. Many people debate about what percent of attacks come from insiders and what percent of attacks come from outsiders. The short answer is who cares? The real answer is this:

- Can attacks come from external sources?
- Can an external attack cause damage to your company?
- Can an external attack put you out of business?
- Can attacks come from internal sources?
- Can an internal attack cause damage to your company?
- Can an internal attack put you out of business?

Since the answer to all of these questions is YES, who cares what the percent is? Both have to be addressed and both have to be dealt with. I would argue that since the insider has access already, the amount of damage they can cause is much greater than an external attacker and the chances of getting caught are much lower. If an attacker comes in from the outside, he has access only to systems that are publicly accessible and he has to break through security devices. If an attacker comes from the inside, she has full access and minimal if any security devices to deal with. As our digital economy continues to grow and the stakes increase, anyone who wants serious access to an organization is not even going to waste his time with an external attack, he is going to go right for the trusted insider.

Finally, to highlight the importance of insider threat, everyone is getting on the bandwagon. The Unites States Secret Service is conducting a series of studies on the insider; conferences are popping up on the subject. Why? Because billions of dollars are being lost and something has to be done to stop the bleeding. You will never be able to completely remove the insider threat because companies need to be able to function. If you fire all your employees, you might have prevented the insider attack, but you will also go out of business. The key is to strike a balance between what access people need and what access people have.

Insider Threat Defined

Since everyone uses different terminology, it is important to define what we mean by insider threat. The easiest way to get a base definition is to break the two words apart. According to *www.dictionary.com*, insider is defined as "one who has special knowledge or access to confidential information" and threat is defined as "an expression of an intention to inflict pain, injury, evil, or punishment; an indication of impending danger or harm; or one that is regarded as a possible danger." Putting this together, an insider threat is anyone who has special access or knowledge with the intent to cause harm or danger.

There is a reason that the insider threat is so powerful and most companies are not aware of it; it is because all the standard security devices that organizations deploy do little if anything to prevent the insider threat.

However, as much as we do not want to admit it, this is no longer true (if it ever was). The problem with insider threat is that it takes only one person who is disgruntled and looking for a quick payoff or revenge and your company is compromised. Unfortunately, it is really that easy and one of the many reasons that the problem has gotten so out of hand.

The world is also a different place than it once was. Most people today, by the time they are at the age of 30, have had more jobs than both their parents combined across their entire careers. In the past, people worked for one company for 30 years and retired. Having worked for one company for an entire career builds loyalty. However, today people switch companies fairly often and while most people are not intentionally out to perform corporate espionage, there is a high chance they can inadvertently perform it. When you switch companies, you most likely are going to stay within the same industry, unless you are making a complete career change, which is unlikely. Therefore, the chance that you are going to work for a competitor is very high. This means some of your knowledge from your previous employer, despite your best efforts, will leak over into this new company.

People do not like to hear it and employers do not like to admit it, but the biggest threat to a company is their internal employees. Your employees or anyone with special access (like a contractor) have more access than an outsider and therefore can cause a lot more damage. However, most organizations and media still focus on the external threat and pay little attention to the insider threat. Why? The short answer is the external threat is easier to see and easier to defend against. If an external attacker defaces your Web site, it is easy to detect and defend against. It is also difficult to deny because everyone can tell that it happened. However, if an employee makes copies of all of the customer credit cards and walks out with it on a USB drive that fits in his or her wallet, it is very difficult to detect and defend against.

Authorized versus Unauthorized Insider

An insider is anyone with special or additional access and an insider attack is someone using that access against the company in some way. The key question to ask is why does that person have the access they have and how did they get that access? One of the best ways to defend against the insider threat is to institute a principle of least privilege. Principle of least privilege states that you give an entity the least amount of access they need to do their job. There are two key pieces to this. First, you are giving your employees additional access. For employees to be able to perform their job at a company, it is obvious that they will need to be given special access that a normal person does not have. This means that every employee, contractor, or anyone else performing work at your organization has the potential to cause harm. The second key piece is needed to do their job. This focuses in on how critical access is to an organization. You know that every employee is going to be given special access; you just want to limit and control that access to the minimum possible subset.

The problem with most organizations is that employees are given a lot more access than what they actually need to do their jobs. Although the risk of insider threat is present with every employee, giving them additional access just increases the damage and increases the number of people that could cause harm. If only five people out of 3000 have access to a sensitive database within your organization, one of those five people would have to be motivated for an insider threat problem to arise. However, if 300 out of 3000 people have access to that information, the odds of finding or motivating someone is much higher. Therefore, the more people that have access to a piece of information, the greater the chance it could cause harm to your organization.

In addition, the more access that a single person has, the greater the damage that person can cause. If 10 different managers each have access to only 10 different pieces of sensitive data, for all 10 pieces of data to be compromised, 10 people would have to be involved. However, if one person had access to all 10 pieces of data, then it would take only one person to cause a grave amount of damage to the organization.

Based on this analysis, two criteria are critical for analyzing the potential for insider threat: number of people with access to a piece of information and number of pieces of data a single individual has. Carefully tracking and controlling critical data and people with critical access can minimize the potential for insider threat.

We have clearly shown that access is the avenue in which insider threat is manifested. The question is how did they get that access? If they were given the access then they are authorized to access the information. If they were not given the access, but stole, borrowed, or acquired it without permission, then it is unauthorized access. The reason the distinction is important is that it helps determine the countermeasures that could be put in place. Security devices like firewalls, passwords, and encryption protect against unauthorized access. If an unprotected wireless access point is set up, people who are unauthorized to connect to the corporate network can still connect and access sensitive data. Someone who is unauthorized to access the file server can walk up to an unlocked computer and access sensitive data. However, if proper security is put in place with firewalls, encryption, and passwords, an unauthorized person should no longer be able to connect to an unprotected wireless access point or to sit down in front of an unlocked system. So the security measures that are present today can prevent unauthorized insider threat.

However, all the current security measures today will not prevent the authorized insider. You can set up all the security you want on a network, but that will not stop someone with proper authorization. An authorized insider is someone with a valid reason for accessing the data but who uses that access in a way that was not intended by the company. The NOC manager is given access to customer passwords, because he needs that access to do his job. However, it is very hard to stop him from giving that information to an attacker or a competitor. When talking about authorized insider threat, intent plays a key role. People need access to do their jobs, but what are their intentions once they get access? Luckily, as the case studies in the later chapters will demonstrate, negative intentions rarely go without warning.

Categories of Insider Threat

Depending on the levels of access someone has, there are different categories of insider:

- Pure insider
- Insider associate
- Insider affiliate
- Outside affiliate

Each type has different levels of access and different motives.

Pure Insider

A pure insider is an employee with all the rights and access associated with being employed by the company. Typically, they have keys or a badge to get access to the facility, a logon to get access to the network, and can walk around the building unescorted. They can cause the most damage because they already have most of the access they need.

Elevated pure insider is an insider who has additional privileged access. This usually includes system administrators who have root or administrator access on the network. These people were given the additional access to do their jobs; however, in many cases, they are given more access than what they need. Very often when companies try to mitigate the risk of an insider threat, the best area to focus on is limiting the access of the elevated pure insider. This is also called the "principle of least privilege," or giving someone the least amount of access they need to do their job. Notice the key factors in this definition: you are not stopping people from doing their jobs; you are just taking away the extra access that they do not need.

With the pure insider, the key areas to focus in on to detect or prevent damage are access, behavior, and money. Throughout this book you will see that an underlying factor of insider threat is access. If someone does not have proper access, it makes their job much harder. Limiting and controlling access is key.

The second factor that comes into play is behavior. In many cases, when someone commits an insider attack, there have usually been personal behavior patterns that were predictive of such behavior. Usually they openly talked bad about the company or management. They tended to be unhappy and angry at work and might even have stated that one of these days they were going to get back at the company.

A third driving factor with the pure insider is money. Many of the people who perform these attacks have financial issues. A normal employee would not commit insider threat. However, if you add in stress and financial issues and someone comes along and offers a large sum of money to make all of their problems go away, there is a chance that person might be tempted. Therefore, tying this in with the second point, good managers should understand and watch for unusual behavior patterns. If a certain employee is complaining about financial issues and child support and three months later is driving a new Lexus, you might want to be concerned.

Insider Associate

Insider associates are people who have limited authorized access. Contractors, guards, and cleaning and plant services all fit under this category. They are not employees of the company and do not need full access, but they need limited access. Limited access usually takes the form of having physical access to the facility but not access to the network. This is best illustrated by a scene in the movie *Wall Street*. Charlie Sheen needed access to stock trading information. The easiest way he found to obtain it was to get a job at the company that provided the janitorial services for the company who he needed information on. He was given access to all of the offices after hours and as he was cleaning the offices he looked at and made copies of sensitive information that was left on people's desks. We tend to forget that in an office building, locking a door really does little to protect the security of the information in your office. With one company I worked for, everyone left sensitive data on their desks and locked their doors. The problem was that a master key was kept in a central location that anyone could use to gain access to an office. We have to remember that there are other people who can gain access to our offices and therefore sensitive data must always be properly secured.

To minimize the damage an insider associate can cause requires user awareness and controlling access. Raising awareness is meant to change someone's behavior as compared to training that is meant to teach someone a new skill. Many employees feel that their building, floor, and office are properly secure and leave systems logged in and information out that they shouldn't. User-awareness sessions can help change behaviors patterns, as people understand that locks do little to protect information. They must understand that a lot of people have potential access and that they should always properly secure sensitive data and lock systems before they walk away from them. In addition, you should carefully examine any activity that requires access to a facility. For example, why does the cleaning staff need access to everyone's office every night? I recommend that the cleaning staff not have a master key to each office. Instead, when people leave at the end of the day, they can put their trash can in the hallway. If they want their office vacuumed, they can leave their door open; if they do not want someone to have access, they can lock it. If employees leave their doors open, they know others can gain access and therefore will make sure that all sensitive date is properly secured.

Insider Affiliate

Pure insiders and insider associates have a legitimate reason to access the building. The next two categories of insider do not. An insider affiliate is a spouse, friend, or even client of an employee who uses the employee's credentials to gain access. This can be as simple as a friend coming to visit you, so you get them a badge for the building. When you take a phone call they go to use the rest room and on the way back they wander around looking at what is on people's computers and on their desks. While this can cause some problems it can usually be controlled.

The more damaging insider affiliate is someone who directly acts as an employee using the employee's credentials. The most common is remote access. Your spouse wants to sit on the couch and surf the Web and wants to borrow your laptop. You give him your user ID and password so he can log on and access the Internet. But what else is he accessing either deliberately or on purpose? I have also seen cases where a spouse is running out for the day and hands over his access card for the building and PIN number and says, "Can you swing by the office and pick up a few papers for me?" Once again, people think this is harmless, but if you stop and think about it, you'll realize the results can be very damaging.

To prevent insider affiliates, the best measure is to implement policies and procedures. You should never take for granted that employees will do the right thing. I have seen people say, "Well, of course everyone should know that they should not let someone borrow their user ID and password." But then I see others saying, "Why can't I, I am not doing any harm and I did not know that I wasn't suppose to."

The short answer is to never make assumptions. You should have clearly written policies and procedures, explain them to all employees, and require that they sign off that they understand them. Then, any deviation from the policy can be taken as a deliberate action on the part of an employee.

Outside Affiliate

Outside affiliates are non-trusted outsiders who use open access to gain access to an organization's resources. Today, one of the best examples is wireless access. If a company sets up an unprotected wireless access point, what stops an outsider from connecting? Nothing. Therefore, if an outsider is sitting at a Starbucks across from your office building and connects to your wireless network, are they breaking into your network? No. You are leaving the door wide open and they are wandering in. This is the same as leaving the front door unlocked with no access controls or guards, allowing anyone to walk in off the street.

Although the outside affiliate seems obvious, it is often overlooked by many companies. Protecting against the outside affiliate requires proper access controls in place for all types of access, including virtual and physical access.

Key Aspects of Insider Threat

The key thing to remember when dealing with insiders is that they have access and in most cases will exploit the weakest link that gives them the greatest chance of access, while minimizing the chances that they get caught. Why try to break through a firewall and gain access to a system with a private address, when you can find someone behind the firewall with full access to the system? I know it has been emphasized many times, but taking advantage of access is a driving force in the insider attack.

Most people, when they think of attackers, think of someone with a huge amount of technical sophistication that can walk through virtual cyber walls and gain access to anything that they want. However, insiders take advantage of the fact that they already have access, so many of the attack methods tend to be very low in technical sophistication. In some cases, if a pure insider or insider associate has partial access, they will sometimes use additional techniques to increase their access. However, since they are typically not dealing with any security devices, most of the methods tend to be fairly straightforward.

It is also important to remember that to launch an effective attack, attackers need knowledge of the organization they are trying to attack. External attackers could spend weeks, if not longer, trying to acquire the information they need to launch a successful attack. In some cases, if they cannot gain enough knowledge, they might decide to go against a different target. However, in the case of the insider, they have full knowledge of your operations. They know what is checked and what is not checked and can even test the system. For example, when they are trying to access their private shares, they could click on someone else's and see if anyone says anything. If they do this multiple times and nothing ever happens, they have now gained valuable knowledge that either access information is not being logged or not being watched. Because they have access to the operations, they either have detailed knowledge of how things operate or they can gain it quickly by testing the system.

> **NOTE**
>
> A private share is a folder on a file server that is only accessible by that individual and meant to hold personal or sensitive information. For example at most companies each person has his or her own private share to store files.

Acceptable Level of Loss

Everyone has heard the phrase no pain no gain or no risk no reward. Every company in business has to take some level of risk; otherwise, the company will not be able to survive. If you say that your company will have no risk of insider threat, then do not hire any employees. However, the second you hire one employee your chances of having an insider attack increase; as you hire more employees the risk keeps increasing. From a naïve standpoint, you might ask, if your risk keeps increasing why would you keep hiring people? The short answer is so that the company can grow and revenues and profits can increase and most companies are willing to take that risk.

This is also true of external attacks. As soon as you provide e-mail and Web services to the Internet, your chances of being attacked from the outside increase. However, your level of service and revenues also increase so it is a risk worth taking.

The bottom line is you have to figure out what your acceptable level of loss is and then build in proper measures to protect against it. Many companies do not do this, throw caution to the wind, lose large amounts of money, and potentially go out of business due to insider attacks. It is much better to realize that there will be some level of loss but build in measures to minimize it to an acceptable level.

For example, hiring and giving everyone administrator access would be a huge potential for loss and not one that I would be willing to accept. On the other hand, if you require that anyone needing administrator access has to justify why they need it, get sign off by two executives, and go through a series of additional background checks before he or she is given the access, this will help reduce the risk. You might also put measures in place to rotate out key positions so it would be harder for a person to cause damage over a long period of time. In the chapters that follow, you will see how rotation in particular could have drastically shortened damage in many insider threat cases, such as when Mel Spillman stole nearly five million dollars over 15 years. In addition, you might set up separation of duties in which two people are required to perform a certain function, which prevents a single person from causing damage. This could have been monumental in reducing some of the visa fraud cases we will discuss, such as when Hsin Hui Hsu sent fraudulent letters inviting potentially hundreds of unauthorized Chinese nationals into the United States for "discussions" that were never meant to take place.

None of these measures mentioned would stop a determined attacker, but they enable you to properly manage risk to an acceptable level.

Insider attacks are likely to occur against your organization; the questions is whether you will be able to prevent most of them and in cases where you cannot prevent them, can you detect them in a timely manner?

Prevention versus Detection

One saying that I use a lot is, "Prevention is ideal but detection is a must." You always try to prevent attacks as much as possible and in cases where you cannot prevent an attack, you try to detect it in a timely manner and minimize the damage. The problem with insider threat is that prevention does not scale very well. If someone wants to compromise a piece of data he is going to do it. Therefore, while prevention measures should be put in place, they must always be teamed with detective measures. You have to assume that someone with inside knowledge and access will be able to work around the prevention measures; the key is, can you detect them and then take follow-up action to control the damage?

When I work with many companies on insider threat, they tell me that they want to put measures in place to detect attackers, not prevent them. Their logic is: if we prevent someone from doing something, they will just get more sophisticated and those more-sophisticated measures we might not know about. On the other hand, if we detect that someone is doing something, we have the proof and can take follow-up action to stop them by prosecuting or taking other measures against them.

In reality, what we are striving for is covert detection with reactive prevention. The reason this is the case is that there is so much going on in a network it is very difficult to find the malicious behavior. Many people say it is like finding a needle in a haystack. I think it is a lot worse than that and is like finding a single grain of sand among all the beaches in the world.

The problem with insider threat is finding enough information or having a high-enough level of confidence to know that someone is committing an insider attack. Most of us would agree that if we are 99 percent sure that someone is committing an insider attack, we would take action against them; if we were one percent sure, we would not take action. It is always easy to define the extremes, but what about the area in the middle that is gray? What is the burden of proof for your organization in which you have enough information to take action?

I want you to re-read the preceding paragraph. At first you might wonder what it has to do with prevention versus detection, but as you read it closely, you'll see it is talking about behavior: having enough indication that someone is up to no good. To gain the proper level of confidence, you must gather information, which is a category of detection. With detective measures you are monitoring and gathering information; when you have enough data points, you take action.

I am not saying that prevention should never be used against insider threats; I am just saying that you need a fine balance between prevention and detection. Preventive measures will stop a basic insider, which is what you want. A low-grade attacker you just want to stop and make go away, they are not worth additional effort. However, when it comes to high-end attackers who will put in whatever measure is necessary to accomplish a task, prevention will not stop them. It will just cause them to dig deeper and make it harder for you to find them the next time they come back. In these cases, detective measures will be key for finding and stopping them.

The bottom line is, to stop the insider threat problem, an organization has to put together a comprehensive and integrated solution of preventive and detective measures that encompass both host- and network-based solutions.

Insider versus External Threat

Arguing over whether insider versus external threat causes the most damage is what I categorize across the industry as a holy war. A holy war is a situation where you have smart people on both sides who disagree and the disagreement has gone on for so long that a stalemate has occurred. Regardless what the other side says, the group in disagreement will not listen. This is a no-win situation. The short answer that I stated previously in this chapter is: they both can cause damage and they both have to be addressed.

The problem to date is that most security efforts and focus have been on the external threat. At most organizations more energy and effort have been put against the external threat than the internal threat. The reason is simple: it is easier to stop, easier to control, and more visible. If you have system x you can state that it should not be accessible from the Internet and put measures in place to prevent it. Then if someone accesses it externally, it sets off a flag. The problem with the insider threat is, people are suppose to access server x but only for legitimate purposes. Now you have to measure intent when someone accesses data, which is almost impossible to do.

In addition, the outsider threat is more understood. We understand the means and methods and exploit scripts that are utilized to attack systems because we have a lot of case study. With insider threat we know it is occurring and it is damaging, but we have less factual data to base conclusions on.

Companies that are going to survive and thrive in the coming century are going to have to turn their focus to the insider and take action against these types of threats. Otherwise, by the time they do, there will not be much of their company left to save.

Why the Insider Threat Has Been Ignored

At this point you might be saying that if the insider threat is so damaging, why has it been ignored and why haven't people been focusing on it early? There are many reasons for this. First, it is not an easy problem. It is very hard to understand and almost impossible to get your arms around. Both the CIA and FBI knew of the damages of insider threat and took many measures to prevent it. However, over the past ten years they have still been severely impacted by it.

There are three key reasons that the insider threat has been ignored:

- Organizations do not know it is happening.
- It is easy to be in denial.
- Organizations fear bad publicity.

Each of these three areas will be examined in the following sections.

Organizations Do Not Know It Is Happening

Many companies do not even realize it is happening to them. Companies have good quarters and they have bad quarters; they have times where revenue is high and they have times when revenue is low. When the bad times occur, there are usually reasonable explanations for them. If a company had poor earnings in a given quarter because a new product they released did not do as well as they thought because a competitor came out with a similar product two months earlier, it is easy to write this off to poor market analysis. Because insider threat is a relatively new area for companies, their first thought is not going to be that it was because of an insider attack.

As insiders keep increasing in sophistication, it is going to be harder and harder for companies to know it is happening to them and are going to find other explanations for why the damage occurred.

We are not trying to turn companies into Chicken Little, where they run around saying the sky is falling, but we are trying to raise companies' awareness of what is happening and potentially give them an alternative explanation to what is happening when none of the conventional explanations seem to make sense. It is a hard problem and difficult to investigate, but the key thing to remember is: it will not go away. If you ignore it, it will only get worse. Therefore, if you think there is the potential that your organization is the victim of an insider attack, the sooner you start working the problem, the easier it will be and the less energy you will have to put in down the road. Insider threat is like a fire. The sooner you can detect a fire, the easier it is to deal with it. Ignoring a fire will not cause it to go out; it will keep getting worse and worse over time.

I would argue that if your company has been in existence for a while and has employees, the internal attack is occurring at some level. It might be a frustrated employee deleting some files, or someone bringing supplies home for the children, or people leaving sensitive documents at another location. While these might not seem damaging, think of the fire example. Do you want to put the fire out now while it is small or wait until it becomes a big problem?

It Is Easy to Be in Denial

After you admit you have a problem, you have to deal with it. One of my friends had a drinking problem and he would never admit to it. Everyone around him kept saying that they do not understand how he cannot recognize he has this problem. It turned out that it was twofold. First, he always justified it in his mind and down-played it so he thought it was not as bad as it really was. Second, he knew that once he admitted he had a problem, he would have to do something about it, which he did not want to do.

These things are true with any problem that a company or person faces. It is sometimes easier to live in denial than to accept the truth and have to deal with it. Also, some companies write it off saying that they are willing to accept a certain level of loss to insider threat. That would be okay if they could answer these two questions: How much are you losing to insider threat? And what is your level of tolerance? If companies knew the answers to these questions and could live with them, that would be acceptable. The problem is that most companies have no idea how much money they are losing.

When it comes to insider threat, you are going to have to pay now or pay later and the sooner you pay, the less you will have to pay. While it is easier to live in denial for a short period of time, it is easier to identify and deal with the problem now than allow it to grow worse over time.

Fear of Bad Publicity

In some cases, companies are acknowledging they have a problem and dealing with it but not telling anyone because of the fear of bad publicity.

If a financial institution had three large clients compromised because of an insider attack and they publicly announced it, how many other clients would change banks because they fear that it could happen to them? The funny thing is a bank admitting they had a problem and fixed it is more secure than a bank who claims they never had any problems. However, when it comes to bad publicity, logic does not always hold up. Therefore, many places would rather keep their dirty secrets inside than expose them to the public. The real question that most executives ask is: what benefit or good will come of publicly announcing we had a problem? Except for raising awareness across the industry, little direct benefit will come to the company.

Why the Insider Threat Is Worse Than the External Threat

We have talked about the difference between the insider and external threat and why the insider threat has been ignored. In this section we are going to look at why the insider threat is potentially worse and what action must be taken to prevent and detect these types of attacks.

Although any type of attack can cause damage, the insider threat is usually worse for the following reasons:

- It's easier to implement.
- Current solutions do not scale.
- There's a high chance of success.
- There's less chance of being caught.

Easier

In many cases the insider attack is fairly easy because the person committing the act either has all or most of the access she needs. In addition, she has the knowledge to pull off the attack with less chance of being caught. A person committing an external attack has no idea what is going on at the other end. Fifteen people could be watching and ready to take legal action against him or they could be ignoring him. He could be very close to success or very far from it. He receives little knowledge and information and because the details of the site he is attacking are unknown, he is executing a blind attack, which is very difficult.

While some inside attacks are sophisticated, many of them are very straightforward because the attacker has the knowledge and access needed to commit the attack in a seamless manner.

Current Solutions Do Not Scale

Most security devices that are deployed at organizations are meant to stop the external attack. Firewalls, intrusion detection systems (IDS), and intrusion prevention systems (IPS) are based off some attack vector that they are trying to prevent. Firewalls block access to certain ports, which stops an attacker but does not stop an insider. If an insider needs access to certain information to do his job, a firewall will allow it. If that person uploads data to an external site or e-mails it to an unauthorized party, it is almost impossible for a firewall to prevent. IDS and IPS work off known signatures of attack. Most external attacks have known signatures, most internal attacks do not. In addition, most security devices are deployed at the perimeter. Once you get past the perimeter there are minimal internal protection measures.

As we have talked about, limiting access and implementing policies and procedures are key to preventing the insider threat. It should not be surprising that most organizations do a terrible job at controlling access and an even worse job at having clear, consistent policies. While companies claim they are doing this, they are not doing a good job. The analogy I like to use with security policies is that of sex when I went to high school. When I was in high school, everyone talked about sex and said they were having sex, but in reality, very few people were having sex and those that were having it were doing it incorrectly. Sorry for the bluntness, but that perfectly describes the state of security policies today.

Security measures that are in place are mainly for the perimeter and do not scale to the insider. Measures that will protect against the insider are hard to implement at a large organization and do not scale very well.

High Chance of Success

If someone gives you all the details and gives you the access you need, success is almost guaranteed. Now, I want to be careful not to over hype how easy the insider threat is, but I would at least argue that it is going to be easier than the external threat. One of the reasons there are more case studies on external threat in this book is because more people get caught. Particularly in the chapter on commercial threats you will notice that more than half the insiders were caught when the competing company they offered their proprietary information to contacted the authorities. What about the companies that are not so honest and ethical? How many other cases are out there that we are not aware of? The more people that get caught, the better you can understand a given problem.

Even if companies have proper access control in place and solid policies, the insider threat will be easier than the external threat for the foreseeable future.

Less Chance of Being Caught

If you know the environment and have access, you are technically not breaking in. If you are not breaking in, the chances of being caught are much lower. If an attacker has to maliciously compromise a firewall and use a zero-day exploit to break into a system and is doing things that are not suppose to be done, he has a higher chance of being detected. However, if he is accessing data that he is allowed to access but using it a manner that he is not supposed to, it is much harder for that action to be detected.

The Effect of Insider Threats on a Company

We have spent a lot of time laying the foundation for the insider threat and why an organization needs to be concerned with it. This section is where the rubber hits the road and we start to show how it can really impact your company and potentially put you out of business. It is one thing to know that the insider threat exists; it is completely different to see how it can affect your company's bottom line.

The obvious types of insider activity focus on disgruntled employees and usually revolve around destroying data or modifying data to cause harm to an organization (sabotage). Although these attacks cause monetary loss, they usually are easy to detect after the fact because the insider wants to take credit for his actions. Based on that, these are usually one-time attacks, where once the attacker performs his actions, he either disappears or is caught.

Other types of attacks are more damaging because they are done for different reasons, mainly financial gain, and therefore are much harder to stop or detect. The first area is fraud. According to *www.dictionary.com*, fraud is defined as:

"Deception carried out for the purpose of achieving personal gain while causing injury to another party. For example, selling a new security issue while intentionally concealing important facts related to the issue is fraud."

Releasing false information to outsiders or intentionally misrepresenting a product internally, all fall under the category of fraud. The more knowledge that you have, the easier it is to present false information to obtain the desired results that you are after.

One of the most damaging forms of insider threat is theft of intellectual property (IP). Although some companies do not recognize or admit to it, every organization that is in business has IP that must be protected. If this IP is compromised or given to the wrong person it could undermine the financial stability of the company. If a company understands, recognizes, and protects its IP, it can still be compromised, but it will be much harder. What is devastating is situations were a large percent of internal employees have access to sensitive IP. It only takes one person to cross the line and cause damage to the organization. In many cases, IP cases revolve around theft or breach of confidentiality of IP.

A twist on this is sabotage or modification of critical IP. One way to damage a company is to take sensitive IP and give it to a competitor. Another method is to modify the IP so it does not work or causes harm, which would cause the company to discontinue the use of that IP, which in some cases can be even more damaging. Would you rather have a viable product that has strong competition or no viable product regardless of the competition?

Fraud, theft of IP, and sabotage can all lead to the following:

- Monetary loss to the organization
- Financial instability
- Decrease in competitive advantage
- Loss of customers
- Loss of consumer confidence

There are many indicators that insider threat is happening at your company but companies have to be looking in the right area to see them. If your eyes are closed or you are looking the wrong direction, you might never realize that there is a problem.

What you have to remember is that insider attackers rarely think about the consequences of their actions or when they do, they obscure the facts to justify them in their minds.

How Bad Is It—Statistics on What Is Happening

I can talk all day about the damage insider threat is causing companies and the cases that I have seen, but I thought it would be helpful to list some statistics across the industry and from recent reports. This section will show statistic, charts, and information from external sources, to validate the damage insider threat is causing across the world.

Insider Threat Study

The first set of findings is from a recent report titled "Insider Threat Study: Illicit Cyber Activity in the Banking and Finance Sector" that was written by the National Threat Assessment Center of the United States Secret Service and the CERT Coordination Center. The full report can be found at: www.sei.cmu.edu/publications/documents/04.reports/04tr021/04tr021.html

The following are some critical points from the study. Each conclusive point from the study will be listed followed by brief analysis:

Conclusion

In 87 percent of the cases studied, the insiders employed simple, legitimate user commands to carry out the incidents. Only a small number of cases required technical knowledge of network security. For example, very few cases were carried out via a script or program (nine percent), and only slightly more involved spoofing or flooding (13 percent). There was no evidence that any insider scanned computer systems to discover vulnerabilities prior to the incident.

Analysis

This report highlights that this is not a technical problem but predominately an access problem. For external threat it is mainly a technical problem that can be solved with security devices like firewalls, IPS, and IDS. The insider already has access and is just using the access they have in an unauthorized manner.

Conclusion

In 70 percent of cases studied, the insiders exploited or attempted to exploit systemic vulnerabilities in applications, processes, or procedures (for example, business rule checks, authorized overrides) to carry out the incidents. In 61 percent of the cases, the insiders exploited vulnerabilities inherent in the design of the hardware, software, or network.

Analysis

One of the big problems with insiders is that they have knowledge. External attackers cannot exploit something they do not know about. An insider knows your organization's deepest, darkest secrets and will utilize them to her advantage. A trusted insider might know about a security hole and purposely not fix it so she can use it to gain access later. She might also create security holes that no one else will find, so she can get back in later. In most organizations, if a security engineer or system administrator wanted to create a back door that no one else knew about and that was virtually undetectable, he could. The reason is that most organizations do not have enough people to implement full checks and balances and they trust that their employees and contractors will always do the right thing.

Conclusion

In 78 percent of the incidents, the insiders were authorized users with active computer accounts at the time of the incident. In 43 percent of the cases, the insider used his or her own username and password to carry out the incident.

Analysis

In most cases, insiders are not really breaking into a system. They are just taking advantage of access they already have. What is also interesting is that they are using their actual accounts, so they are not trying to hide anything. Either they know the organization's security is so bad that they are not even looking at the logs; they do not care if they get caught; or they are so unsophisticated about technology that they do not even realize that someone could be watching them. With regards to the first item, in most cases insiders will test the waters. They will try something minor and see if anyone notices. If no one notices they will be a little more aggressive. If after several times no one notices, they figure they are in the clear. This is typically how an insider is caught because over time they let their guard down and push the limits (they get greedy) and someone notices.

Conclusion

There were some cases in which the insider used other means beyond his or her user account to perpetrate the harm. Twenty-six percent of the cases involved the use of someone else's computer account, physical use of an unattended terminal with an open user account, or social engineering (that is, gaining access through manipulation of a person or persons who can permit or facilitate access to a system or data).

Analysis

When performing an insider attack, even if the company is fairly secure, the weakest link in any organization is the human link. One person leaving his terminal unlocked for one hour on one day when he goes to a meeting provides the opportunity for an insider attack. In cases where an insider cannot find an unlocked terminal, she can usually obtain some level of access through social engineering attempts (just asking).

Conclusion

Only 23 percent of the insiders were employed in technical positions, with 17 percent of the insiders possessing system administrator or root access.

Analysis

This is no longer a revenge of the nerds situation. When insider threat is mentioned, most people think it is perpetrated by the technical staff. On the contrary, it can be anyone with a computer across your entire organization. Anyone who has access to the physical building that houses your organization has the potential to commit insider threat. This is why the problem is so difficult to detect and prevent: any one of your employees or contractors has the potential, means, and methods to cause harm.

Conclusion

Thirty-nine percent of the insiders were unaware of the organizations' technical security measures.

Analysis

This is one of my favorite statistics. A little less than half of the people committing insider threat did not know and did not care about any technical security measures that were in place. Reading deeper into this, the technical measures did nothing to detect or stop the attack. Reading even deeper, the reason technical measures were ineffective is because almost 40 percent of the attacks were non-technical.

Conclusion

In 81 percent of the incidents, the insiders planned their actions in advance.

Analysis

Initially, insider attacks were mostly reactive attacks by disgruntled employees. Now it is turning into a pre-meditated crime. People are carefully thinking about what they want to do, learning the environment, and carefully planning the crime so they do not get caught. Pre-meditation also implies that there is more to gain, for example monetary rewards. If an attacker just wants to cause loss to the company, he doesn't have to plan too much and it is usually a one-time event. If he wants to increase compensation to himself, it takes longer to plan it so he does not get caught, because he wants the crime to be a recurring event.

Conclusion

In 85 percent of the incidents, someone other than the insider had full or partial knowledge of the insider's intentions, plans, or activities. These included:

- Individuals involved in the incident and/or potential beneficiaries of the insider activity (74 percent)

- Coworkers (22 percent)

- Friends (13 percent)

- Family members (9 percent)

Analysis

No matter how good you think you are, there are always going to be others who know about what you are doing. You see this all the time in the media after someone is caught committing a crime and they interview their friends. There is always a friend or co-worker who says, "We always knew Johnny was suspicious and was up to no good; this does not surprise me at all." The question is: why didn't they say anything? If you want to catch an insider, you must raise awareness among co-workers to report suspicious activity.

Conclusion

In 31 percent of the incidents, there was some indication that the insider's planning behavior was noticeable. Planning behaviors included stealing administrative-level passwords, copying information from a home computer onto the organization's system, and approaching a former coworker for help in changing financial data.

Analysis

A crime is never composed of a single incident. There are many sub-components that have to occur before the actual crime is committed. In this case, the sub-components of insider threat are usually obvious actions that can be detected, prevented, and acted upon before the actual crime is committed.

Conclusion

Sixty-five percent of the insiders did not consider the possible negative consequences associated with carrying out the incident.

Analysis

There are many things that make an insider tick, but most of them are selfish reasons related to the individual. Financial gain, frustration, anger, and payback are all examples. In many cases the insider fails to look at the negative actions that could occur to them or the organization. This also ties in with the previous conclusion that other people, including family members, knew something was going on. Clearly letting people know the consequences of their actions and what could happen is often a solid deterrent against insider threat.

Conclusion

The motive and goal for most insiders studied were the prospects of financial gain (both 81 percent). Twenty-seven percent of the insiders studied were experiencing financial difficulty at the time of the incident.

Analysis

Money is a drug that entices almost everyone to become its prisoner. Money is a strong motivator and most people think if they had more money, that all their problems would go away. Therefore, it should be no surprise that one of the strongest motivators of committing an insider crime is money. There is a reason that government agencies that handle classified information require their employees and contractors to fill out financial disclosure forms. Money problems can be a big indicator of someone who might commit espionage attacks against an organization. It means they are highly susceptible to bribes when approached with an opportunity to earn fast money. When foreign governments are trying to recruit spies, money is usually the number one incentive and is usually a factor they look at to determine who they should recruit.

Conclusion

In 27 percent of the incidents, insiders had multiple motives for engaging in the incident.

Analysis

Although money is a primary motivator, there are usually secondary motivators. This is the straw-that-broke-the-camel's-back syndrome. In many cases there is usually a seemingly minor event that tips the scales to someone committing corporate espi-onage. During analysis, many people ask how Johnny not receiving a three-percent raise would cause him to try to destroy the company. What these analysts fail to realize is that that was just the last straw. If you go back two years, what caused Johnny to do this was his divorce, financial trouble, sick parent, not getting promoted three times, and working longer hours than anyone else. Not getting the three-per-cent raise just pushed him over the edge.

Conclusion

Insiders ranged from 18 to 59 years of age. Forty-two percent of the insiders were female. Insiders came from a variety of racial and ethnic backgrounds and were in a range of family situations, with 54 percent single and 31 percent married.

Analysis

For every crime, people like to put together demographics of the people who are most likely to commit the crime. For different types of robberies, law enforcement can tell you the demographic profile of someone likely to commit the crime. This helps law enforcement in preventing and investigating the crime because they can focus in on a smaller group. However, with the insider, there is no demographic pro-file. The people committing these crimes are all across the board. Therefore, anyone at your organization could be committing corporate espionage. From the summer intern to the 30-year-tenured executive, they all have the potential of committing internal espionage.

Conclusion

Insiders were employed in a variety of positions within their organizations, including:

- Service (31 percent)
- Administrative/clerical (23 percent)
- Professional (19 percent)
- Technical (23 percent)

Analysis

This conclusion drives home our previous point that there is no profile that can be generated of someone who will commit insider threat. Almost every position in your organization has sensitive information and access is all that is needed to commit this crime. In cases where a given position does not have access, it is usually fairly easy to obtain that access.

Conclusion

As reported earlier, only 17 percent of the insiders had system administrator/root access prior to the incident.

Analysis

The reason the insider threat is so devastating to an organization is that almost every position has more access than they need to do their job. So when someone decides to turn to the dark side, they already have access to the information they need. If organizations did a better job of controlling access to sensitive data, it would make the insider threat more difficult, easier to detect and easier to control.

Conclusion

Twenty-seven percent of insiders had come to the attention of either a supervisor or coworker for some concerning behavior prior to the incident. Examples of these behaviors include increasing complaints to supervisors regarding salary dissatisfaction, increased cell phone use at the office, refusal to work with new supervisors, increased outbursts directed at coworkers, and isolation from coworkers.

Analysis

Many organizations say that they wish there were indicators of people who will commit insider-threat activities. The answer is: there are. Insiders that cause harm to the organization have visible showed behavioral and professional problems at the office. In many cases, organizations never tie these people back to causing damage, but this conclusion shows that those people need to be isolated and removed from the organization.

Conclusion

Twenty-seven percent of the insiders had prior arrests.

Analysis

What makes this conclusion even scarier is that most of the employers probably had no idea that their employees had prior arrests. Most employers don't perform background or financial checks during the hiring process. If someone aces an interview, she is hired. However, validating the background and knowing the individual you are dealing with are critical.

Conclusion

In 61 percent of the cases, the insiders were detected by persons who were not responsible for security, including

- Customers (35 percent)
- Supervisors (13 percent)
- Other non-security personnel (13 percent)

Analysis

Firefighters are responsible for putting out the fires not for detecting the fires. The population is responsible for detecting the fires and calling them in so the experts can do their jobs. While this makes perfect sense, many companies don't follow it. Many companies say it is the security department's responsible for finding security breaches. That is one of the reasons the problem is so bad today. It is the security department who is responsible for dealing with the problems, but it is the entire company that is responsible for calling in the problems. Everyone must be trained to notify the appropriate people if they see suspicious behavior.

Conclusion

In at least 61 percent of the cases, insiders were caught through manual (that is, non-automated) procedures, including an inability to log in, customer complaints, manual account audits, and notification by outsiders.

Analysis

Because many of these attacks are low-tech crimes, in many cases they are detected with low-tech methods. Automated devices will help, but nothing can replace the analytical capability of a human. Humans must be involved and must perform the analysis to determine if there is a problem.

Conclusion

Eighty-three percent of the insider threat cases involved attacks that took place physically from within the insider's organization. In 70 percent of the cases, the incidents took place during normal working hours.

Analysis

Your organization is going to be the crime scene of the attack. Many people think that these attacks are done covertly in the middle of the night and therefore they look for anomalies in access time. However, many attacks are committed during normal works hours as part of a person's job.

These conclusions should help to lay the groundwork that many of the ways that people look at insider crime and who is committing these crimes are different from what was originally thought. While this section focused on a specific report, CERT also tracks computer crimes across the Internet.

The attacks are increasing exponentially and will continue to get worse. What is interesting is that because there are so many attacks occurring and it is getting so out of hand, CERT no longer tracks this information.

Beware of Insider Threats to Your Security

The next set of information on insider threat is from an article titled, "Beware of insider threats to your security." The full article can be found at www.viack.com/_download/200408_cdm.pdf.

The following are some of the key findings from the article:

Conclusion

The Gartner Group estimates that 70 percent of security incidents that cause monetary loss to enterprises involve insiders.

Analysis

When executives ask why they should be concerned about internal threat, this statistic is the driving theme. The reason is, it could cost your organization a significant amount of money and potentially put you out of business.

Conclusion

Credit reporting agency TransUnion recently stated the top cause of identity theft, which the FTC reported as generating business losses of nearly $48 billion in 2003, is now theft of records from employers that maintain records on many individuals.

Analysis

This is starting to show that the inroads of insider threat are deep and wide. Identify theft is being traced back to the trusted insider that is using and compromising information that they should not have access to. For any organization that maintains sensitive information about their clients, this is a huge concern. If client information is compromised because your organization did not properly protect it, your organization could have liability issues. Also, many states and the federal government are looking at making it a requirement that if you think that personal information might have been compromised, you must report it to the individual and potentially to the government.

Conclusion

Recent FBI statistics show that 59 percent of computer hackings are done internally (based only on what is reported).

Analysis

A long-debated issue is what percent of attacks occur from within the organization. Although the number can be debated, the recent CSI/FBI Computer Crime Report states that more than half of all attacks and monetary damage to an organization is done by a trusted insider. Regardless of whether you believe the statistic or not, insider threat is a huge problem and will only continue to get worse.

Conclusion

A source inside the United States intelligence community stated that more then 85 percent of all incidents involving the attempted theft or corruption of classified data involved an individual who had already been thoroughly vetted and been given legal access to that data.

Analysis

Controlling access is critical, but producing granularity of controls is even more important. For classified information to be publicly revealed, it almost has to be an inside job, because only insiders have access to the information. Therefore, the only way this information can be compromised is if someone trusted either deliberately or accidentally reveals it to someone who should not have access. Now if the US government, which takes extensive measures to protect classified information, still has internal compromises, is there any hope for small, non-governmental organizations?

Espionage: A Real Threat

Many companies do not even realize they are being attacked and victims of corporate espionage; and in cases where they do realize it, they are not reporting it. This is the basis for the next article we are going to cover, "Espionage: A Real Threat," which can be found at: www.optimizemag.com/article/showArticle.jhtml?articleId=17700988&pgno=3

This article shows that economic espionage is on the rise.

Preliminary System Dynamics Maps of the Insider Cyber-Threat Problem

The next report is an exercise that was undertaken as part of CERT. The report displays the results of what is to be deemed a work in progress. It is important to note that it is not a complete report or a finished product. In addition, many of the findings are based on expert opinion and not factual data. Nonetheless, I though that several of the key diagrams from the study were worth inclusion in this section with some additional explanation. The full report can be found at: www.cert.org/archive/pdf/InsiderThreatSystemDynamics.pdf

What is important to note is that all of the attacks included both high and low-tech attack methods. In addition, the motivation of the attacks covered the broad range. Nonetheless, you can see that the coverage of insider threat and the potential damage is very broad.

Do You Really Know What Your Programmers Are Doing?

Anyone with any access to critical data could represent a threat to your organization. A key group of people who have a large amount of control in an organization are the programmers. Programmers implement applications that are either used internally or sold externally to a large number of customers. Backdoors and other problems in code could represent a large threat to intellectual property of an organization

The article "Do You Really Know What Your Programmers Are Doing?" which can be found at www.mintaka.com/whitepaper/White%20Paper%20-%20Security.pdf, talks about the impact of insider threat.

What is of interest is the breakdown of human threats. Although human threats can be non-malicious and can come from outsiders, many of the threats come from insiders.

How Much Is Too Much Data Loss?

Finishing up this section, we are going to look at the article "How Much Is Too Much Data Loss?" which can be found at http://internetnews.com/security/print.php/3503331.

This article highlights some of the similar points that we have seen, but it is also a good summary of the problem insider threat represents to an organization.

The following are some of the key points:

Conclusion

According to the Gartner Group, 70 percent of security incidents that occur are inside jobs, making the insider threat arguably the most critical one facing enterprises.

Analysis

Although the insider threat is one of the most critical risks facing an organization, very few organizations either recognize it or know that it exists. Many organizations that I have worked with on insider threat recognize it as a major problem only after there is a problem or huge monetary risk to the organization.

Conclusion

One out of every 500 e-mail messages contains confidential information, customer data, employee data, financial information, intellectual property, or competitive information," said Kelly. She offered another way to look at it: a company with 50,000 employees, each sending 10 e-mail messages outside the company per day, would incur nearly 1,000 potential data security violations per day.

Analysis

This emphasizes that the problem is occurring on a regular basis and is a part of normal business. One of the reasons so many companies suffer from insider threat is because it is so difficult to solve. If it were an isolated problem or one that infrequently occurred, it would be easy to solve. However, since it is ingrained in how people normally operate, it would require an entire paradigm shift to solve.

Conclusion

The Ponemon Institute, a private research company, recently released its 2004 Data Security Tracking Study with alarming results. Of the 163 companies participating, 75 percent, or 122 companies, reported a data-security breach within the past 12 months. The majority of the companies were Fortune 1000.

Analysis

What is scary about this is that only a small percent of companies actually know about and detect security breaches. If 75 percent admitted having a breach, the actually number of breaches and monetary loss is much higher.

Conclusion

A recent survey by the FBI and Computer Security Institute found that between 2000 and 2003, about 40 percent of all companies confronted an attempted information snatch each year.

Analysis

The good news is that organizations are starting to crack down on internal threat. The problem is that in many cases, it is too little to late.

Targets of Attack

If you do not know what someone is trying to do or target it is hard to stop them. Therefore in order to build appropriate protection measures and to understand the real threat, you need to understand what is being targeted. After you understand what the attacker's end objective is, you can not only build appropriate defense measures, but you can also test those measures to make sure they are effective.

If someone is committing insider threat, he is targeting your company; more specifically, he is targeting your IP. At the center of the bulls-eye is your organization's IP. That is what ultimately differentiates your organization from the competition; it is what makes your organization unique and is the financial engine behind its success.

There are different levels and types of IP that can be a target of attack. The obvious types of IP that would represent the greatest loss to your organization fall along the lines of formulas, source code, customer lists, and marketing plans. This obvious, or primary, IP is what forms the core of your business line. If someone asks you what your organization does, the primary IP is most likely highlighted in that description. For example, if you ask someone what Pepsi does, they would say they produce soda. Even in that brief description, their primary IP is identified: the recipe and methods for producing their brand of soda. Microsoft produces software. Once again, even in a two-word description the organization's IP is quickly identified. Therefore, the first step in the protection of your organization is to create a list of the primary IP in your organization, minimize and control who has access to it, and focus your attention on protecting that information.

Although primary IP is often the main focus, you cannot lose sight of the non-obvious, or secondary, IP for your organization. While it might not be as critical as the primary IP, it can still cause damage and has to be identified and tracked. Secondary IP is the street address of your building, system configurations, routers, access to critical areas, etc. These do not represent the core business line, like primary IP does, but they support the primary IP and could still be targeted by an insider.

To illustrate the difference between primary and secondary IP, let's look at two examples. If a pharmaceutical employee takes the recipe for a new drug and gives it to a competitor, she is clearly attacking the company's primary IP. However, if a disgruntled employee of an Internet sales company disconnects the primary Internet connection so customers cannot get to the company's e-commerce site, he is targeting the secondary IP.

In both cases, it is critical to know what your primary and secondary IP are because they will be the targets of attack. The more you can do to protect them, the better off you will be. Although this seems easy, correctly identifying IP is often the hardest and most-overlooked area of most companies. I guarantee you if you go up to any key stakeholders in the company and ask them what the primary and secondary IP are for your organization, they will either miss items or be incorrect on what those items are. Sometimes things that seem obvious and straightforward are very difficult to identify. Therefore, do not take the task of identifying IP lightly. Spend the time and energy to do it correctly because the better job you do in iden-

tifying the prospect of attack, the easier your job will be in protecting and preventing those attacks.

Just to show you how bad the problem is, let's assume that you have correctly
identified the IP for your organization. Now ask yourself who has access to that
information. If you are not scared enough, ask yourself the follow-up question of
even if you knew who had access, would you know who is accessing the data, when
they are accessing it, and what they are doing with it. What seemed like an easy
question is growing rapidly in complexity as you start to develop a plan of attack. In
reality, the problem of dealing with insider threat is not easy. I often compare it to
accounting for each grain of sand on a beach and making sure they do not move.
However, it is worthwhile to make the investment because if you do not, since the
threat is growing rapidly, there might not be any part of your company left once the
attacker is done. You have to always remember that the ultimate goal of an attack is
to cause harm to your company.

Now that we have looked at the main target, let's briefly examine what an
attacker could do to your primary or secondary IP. In dealing with what they can
do, we can map it back to the core areas of security: confidentiality, integrity, and
availability. After you identify the IP, you have to ask yourself what the primary
attack vector is going to be. Would they try to reveal the information to someone
who should not have access (confidentiality), modify it to reduce the value
(integrity), or destroy it (availability)? Typically, the high-end insider primarily
focuses on confidentiality with integrity as a secondary goal. The lower-end attacker,
for example, a disgruntled employee, will usually focus on availability with integrity
as a secondary goal.

The Threat Is Real

Insider threat is no longer a fictitious concept that people write about and that you
see in movies. It is real and it is happening all the time and those who do not take it
seriously may be hurt by its results.

Think of the damage that viruses and worms cause to organizations. These are
attacks that start on the Internet and manage to get through organizations' firewalls,
perimeters, and security devices and cause severe loss. If an external worm can penetrate an organization with ease, what can someone who is behind the firewall and
security perimeter do? The short answer is: almost anything they want. Although
people can argue over the validity and strength of firewalls, IDS, and perimeter security, at least there are some measures in place. When it comes to insiders, there is
little stopping them because they are a trusted entity. What is even worse than not
preventing them is not trying to detect their actions. This means that not only is

nothing stopping an insider but nothing is watching or recording their actions to even tell something is happening.

As we talked about earlier, many organizations would rather live in denial than fix the problem. Unfortunately with a real threat, denial will only cause more harm. The insider threat is like a tumor; if you realize there is a problem and address it, you will have short-term suffering but a good chance of recovery. If you ignore it, it will keep getting worse and while you might have short-term enjoyment, it will most likely kill you.

You might be saying that you acknowledge that the threat is real, but that your company is not vulnerable. The reality is that almost every organization is vulnerable because almost every organization has minimal if any controls in place and they do not carefully control access to data. Some organizations might have some basic access controls in place, but that is not good enough. If even one person has more access than what they need to do their job, that is too much access. Giving everyone the least access they need to do their job is critical, plus putting auditing measures in place to track behavior, even if you know that access is strictly controlled. What stops someone who has legitimate access from e-mailing it to someone who should not have access? Not only do you have to strictly control access, you must also monitor it. Since too-much access it what leads to ultimate compromise and too-little monitoring is what leads to someone not being caught or controlled, both play a critical role in your insider threat arsenal.

More and more organizations are starting to recognize that insider threat is important; the problem is it is after the fact. I know of a ton of companies that have been victims to insider threat; I do not know of any that have successful stopped an insider threat initially. All of our case studies, histories, and knowledge of insider threat are after the problem occurs and a company gets compromised. The real problem is we are finding out about the problem because of the damage not because the insiders are being caught. At least if we caught the insider after the fact we could stop that person from doing it again. Unfortunately, we know it is happening but we do not know who did it. This creates a double-edged sword. Most executives do not believe what they cannot see, so they initially do not take insider threat seriously. Then, after it happens and there is critical damage, they ask why no one warned them or told them it was a problem so they could have fixed it.

So far in 2005 it is estimated that more than 10 million identities have been stolen, with a loss of more than $50 million resulting from it. What more proof do we want that this is a real threat? You might ask what stolen identities have to do with insider threat. The answer is: there is a direct correlation. How is personal information taken to steal someone's identity? Through an insider who has access to that information for the company they work for. Credit card fraud and identity theft are both caused by insiders stealing information they should not have access to.

The Bali bomber wrote a manifesto from jail urging terrorists to take terrorism to cyberspace. Why? Because he knows that is a weak link that can easily be exploited. Organizations and countries have critical infrastructures all stored in computers. If that information is compromised, it could have the same impact as an actual bomb.

The book *Unrestricted Warfare*, by Qiao Liang and Wang Xiangsui (Beijing: PLA Literature and Arts Publishing House, February 1999), which can be downloaded at www.terrorism.com/documents/TRC-Analysis/unrestricted.pdf, talks about how cyber weapons will become the weapons of the future. The key fact is that this levels the playing field across all countries. Who can compete with the nuclear arsenal of the U.S.? However, with cyber weapons, all the barriers to entry and monitoring are gone. Just think if you put together two or three of the cyber weapons together in a coordinated fashion, you would have the cyber version of the perfect storm.

Insider threat needs to be moved up in importance and discussed in boardrooms prior to attacks, not after significant monetary loss. Proactive measures need to be to taken to stop insider attacks from occurring, not reactive measures to clean up the mess.

What is scary is there is really minimal skill needed to launch these attacks. You really do not need to know anything if you have access. You just drag and drop information you should not be sending outside the company and you e-mail it to a competitor or a Hotmail account. Years of company IP can be extracted in minutes. Even if you do not have access, there are tools you can download and run to get access. If you can install MS Office, you can install and run these tools. Unfortunately, they are really that easy to use. The days of knowing how to write, compile, build, and exploit are gone. These tools are publicly available, free for the taking.

The sale of stolen IP makes the stolen car industry look small time. It is happening constantly and is such a norm, that people do not even realize it. An unprotected computer is an insider threat even if the user of the system is the most ethical employee on the planet. The computer and account has trusted access, not the person, and if someone can compromise the system because the person went to lunch and left his system unlocked, that is a huge source of insider threat and loss for a company.

We can predict with high reliability snowstorms and severe weather before they occur. This early-warning system enables people to prepare and take action to help minimize the damage. The reason we can predict weather is because we look for indicators using radar and other advanced techniques. We need to develop cyber indicators. Some initial indicators that could show a company is vulnerable are: no or weak policies, weak passwords, and no list of critical assets. If we can better iden-tify and track these cyber indicators, we will have a better chance of reacting to the problem.

Profiling the Insider

One problem with the insider threat is there is no single profile that can be used to help identify who might be committing these crimes. With other crimes there are clear profiles you can look for. There is a set profile for the person who would rob a gas station or commit rape. However, with insider threat there is no demographic profile. People who have been caught vary in age, sex, social background, and educa-tion and cover the entire range of categories of people.

There was one report that had a profile for the person most likely to commit insider threat. The profile was someone in their mid 30s, works long hours, logs into the company at night, sometimes works weekends, drinks, smokes, and is divorced. I laugh because that covers almost everyone I know. Therefore rash attempts like this never really generate anything meaningful in terms of a demographic profile.

One of the biggest indicators of an attacker is someone who is highly frustrated with his company and/or boss and who openly admits to his frustration and dissatis-faction with his job. You unfortunately see this all the time, when someone goes into work and shoots someone and they interview their co-workers and they say, "Johnny always talked about doing this, we knew it would happen someday and was only a matter of time." You think, why didn't anybody say anything or the boss do anything about it. The problem is in the past people never took this very seriously. Management and co-workers have to realize that these verbal outbreaks could be a pre-cursor to additional actions and if acted upon early, the crime could be prevented.

Most of the attacks were never very technical in nature. Based on the wide range of access most people have, it is fairly easy for people to commit these crimes. Many people committing the crimes have been at the company for 3-5 years, so they are viewed as trusted entities. Finally, many of the people committing the crimes justify the crimes in their minds and do not fully understand the repercussions of their actions. In one case a spouse said, "I knew my husband was doing this but I never thought he would get arrested and be put in jail. I wish I had said something sooner." In another case, the person blamed the company because he had to get an expensive operation and since the company would not give him a bonus he felt it was his right to commit the crime.

The motives for committing the crimes cover a broad spectrum, but the main areas are financial gain, revenge, and retaliation for a negative work environment. In addition, most of the insiders that were caught got caught because they were greedy, they bragged, or they got sloppy. Unfortunately, this means that the good criminals rarely get caught.

Preventing Insider Threat

There is no single thing that you can do to prevent an insider threat. The concept of defense in depth applies here as it does to all areas of security. No single solution is going to make you secure. Only by putting many defense measures together will you be secure and those measures must encompass both preventive and detective measures.

Some of the key things that can be done to prevent or minimize the damage of the insider threat are the following:

- **Security awareness** Employees, contractors, and any other insiders need to be educated on how to protect corporate assets. They need to under-stand the dangers and methods of social engineering and be careful what information they give out. They also have to be cognizant that insiders could exist at their company and not only do their part to protect corpo-rate assets (for example, locking their workstations), but they also have to look for indications of insider threat and report them to the correct parties.

- **Separation of duties** Any critical job function or access to critical infor-mation should involve two or more people. This prevents a single person from committing an inside attack.

- **Rotation of duties** All critical jobs should have multiple people who perform the roles and those people should be rotated through periodically. If a person knows that someone else is going to be performing a given role in two months, it will be much harder for them to commit fraud or other insider attacks, because there is a good chance someone might catch it later.

- **Least privilege** Any additional access that someone has can be used against the company. Although access is needed for people to perform their jobs, this access should be carefully controlled. People should be given only the access they need to do their jobs and nothing else.

- **Controlled access** Access is what someone is going to use to compro-mise an organization. The more a company knows what access people have, the better they can control it.

- **Logging and auditing** Organizations must know what is happening on their network and this information must be reviewed on a regular basis. If someone's actions are not logged, a company will have no idea who did what and will not be able to detect the insider. Even if this information is logged, if it is not reviewed on a regular basis, an organization will not be able to catch an attacker in a timely manner.

- **Policies** A policy states what a company's stance is on security and what is expected of anyone with inside access. A policy is a mandatory document that is clear and concise and that everyone must follow. If a policy does not exist, how do insiders know what is expected of them? I once knew an employee that bragged about making copies of software when he left a company. When I questioned his concern of legality and theft, he replied simply by saying, "I never signed anything." This information must be presented to them in a way that they understand and it must be made clear that they have to follow it.

- **Defense in depth** When it comes to network security, there is no silver bullet. No single solution is going to make you sure. Organizations must deploy a layered security model, with checks and balances across each layer.

- **Look beyond technology** Many inside attacks are not technology driven. Organizations must realize that non-technology-based solutions need to be implemented across the company.

- **Archive critical data** Any critical information must be properly archived and protected. This way all the IP is not in one place if a system gets destroyed or compromised.

- **Complete solution** Any solution that is implemented must include all aspects of the company: people, data, technology, procedures, and policies.

New World Order

The world is a different place than it used to be. Insider threat is occurring and it is increasing at a rapid pace. Organizations that do not understand it or are not willing to get on the bandwagon are going to suffer damage and loss. Organizations that are going to survive have to realize the threat is real and take action immediately, because most likely the damage has already begun beneath the surface.

Organizations must understand that security is an ongoing task that must constantly be done and readjusted. Security goes way beyond technology and is never complete. There is no such thing as 100 percent security. Which means you will never get it right but you have to keep trying to get it close enough. In order to properly implement security you must understand the organization's structure, mission, and politics so security can be seamlessly integrated. Security is a means to an end but it is not an end state.

There are some insiders who will do anything they have to in order to compromise your organization. However, there are a lot of insiders who just take advantage of opportunity. They are working on a system, they find a problem, no one is watching and they take advantage of it. The determined insider will always be a problem, but the opportunistic insider can be stopped by organizations with comprehensive, integrated security solutions.

Many people, who have been at companies for several years and have been caught committing insider threat, were found to have less-than-perfect backgrounds when they were investigated. They had criminal records that the company never new about. Think of the damage that could have been saved if the company did the proper checks prior to the incident as opposed to after.

If you want to find where the hole is in a tire, you put it under water and see where the bubbles come out. Now, we are not suggesting that you hold your employees' heads under water until they confess, but we are saying that if you tighten down security you will quickly see the problem areas emerging.

Future Trends

We have covered a lot of ground in this chapter and felt that an appropriate summary would be necessary to cover the future trends that we see occurring in the industry.

Policies and Procedures

Many companies, from a cyber perspective, lack clear control and direction in terms of protecting and controlling access to their critical assets. While companies are focusing on long-term strategic plans for their organizations, they need to address the critical IP and put together clear guidelines for what is expected of their insiders. As we move forward, the lack of solid policies is going to manifest itself more and more in companies. Companies that are serious about the insider threat are going to realize that the old style of inefficient policies is no longer going to work. Therefore, instead of trying to re-work existing policies, companies are going to realize that they are going to have to re-write their policies from scratch.

It is critical with any organization that everyone is on the same page with regards to protection of information. Just because you have a policy does not mean people will follow it; however, without the policy as the starting point, there is no way you can perform consistent enforcement across an organization. While it is difficult, and executives never want to put things in writing, it is critical that a clear, concise policy with appropriate repercussions be put in place.

Access Controls

Access is the gateway in which the insider threat is manifested. Typically, in most organizations, access control is poorly implemented and poorly understood. Moving forward, companies are going to have to change this. Those that have been burnt in the past by insider threat or those that want to make sure they do not get burnt moving forward, will have to take the time to properly control access to critical data. This is a multi-staged process, involving identifying critical IP, determining who should have access to it, and controlling and tracking that access.

Miniaturization

Data and critical IP is at the heart of any organization and extracting and compromising that information is at the heart of insider threat. As technology continues to advance, storage devices are going to become smaller and smaller and embedded in other devices. Storage devices that fit in watches or pens and that are the size of pennies will make it much harder to be able to track and control this information. Attackers are always going to take the easiest path or exploit the weakest link when they are compromising an organization, and with storage technology getting smaller and smaller, the physical attack will become that much easier.

Even with guards and other physical security measures, it is too easy for someone to walk out with large amounts of information. Therefore companies are going to have to do a better job of locking down computers. In reality, do most individuals at a company need access to USB, serial, and parallel ports on their computers? The short answer is no. They have backup and storage across the network, there is not a legitimate reason we should be handing out laptops and desktop computers that make it trivial for this information to be extracted. Through software and hardware, these devices can be disabled and locked down to stop someone from using them in an inappropriate manner. As storage devices become so tiny that they can pass through any guard, companies will have to react by implementing a principle of least privilege at the hardware level.

Moles

As perimeters continue to be tightened down and new security devices get added to the perimeter arsenal, external attacks are going to become more and more difficult. As external attacks become more difficult it is not going to be worth the attackers' efforts. They are going to rely more on the use of moles to extract the data and cause damage to organizations. Planting an insider as a mole is as trivial as putting together a résumé, acing an interview and getting hired. Taking an insider and converting them to a mole is as easy as finding a weakness and exploiting it. Two common weaknesses are money and blackmail. It is usually easy to find someone who has some financial trouble. Offering them money to help them out is a temptation some people cannot resist. In addition, most people have deep, dark secrets. Finding out those secrets and threatening to reveal them is another way to convince people to cooperate.

Since moles are so easy and extremely effective, attackers are going to rely more and more on this method to accomplish their goals. This is why performing thorough background checks and validating employees and monitoring them is going to be even more critical.

Outsourcing

Outsourcing is becoming a norm for companies of all sizes. The cost-benefit analysis not only points to the fact that it is here to stay but that it is going to increase in popularity moving forward. This section is not implying in any way that outsourcing is bad, it is just pointing out that with outsourcing comes new challenges and concerns that a company has to be aware of.

With outsourcing, you are taking the zone of insiders and increasing it to the outsourcing company. In most situations, any source code that would be outsourced is considered IP for the company. Therefore, there is now a whole new group of people that will not only have access to the source code but could also make inadvertent changes to the code or create backdoors. Confidentiality can be controlled thought NDA, contractual agreements, background checks, and internal isolation by the outsourcing company. Integrity checks require that any code, whether it is outsourced or not, be validated by a separate party. Whether code is developed inside your company or outside there is the potential that an insider can create back doors to cause problems at a later point in time. Therefore third-party testing and code review must be performed to minimize the potential damage.

Porous Networks and Systems

As new functionality and enhancements are added to networks, they are and will continue to become more porous. A more porous network means the number and chances of having outside affiliates increase. As more holes are punched through the firewalls and wireless and extranet connections are set up, the exposure of the critical infrastructure increases and the number of potential people who can access critical IP also increases.

Therefore, organizations need to understand that these phenomena are happening and build in appropriate controls at the host and server level.

Ease of Use of Tools

Attack tools are not only increasing in ease of use but also increasing in capability and functionality. In the past, manual methods were required to use tools to gain access. In the future, the tools will become completely automated. Now, an insider who does not have proper access can gain access through the use of one of these tools. Because the landscape is going to continue to increase in complexity from a defense standpoint, the sooner that companies can start to defend against the insider threat the easier it will be.

Relays on the Rise

Attackers do not want to spend money on expensive resources or attack from their own systems because it is traceable. Instead, attackers use relays. A relay is a site that has weak security; the attacker breaks into the site and sets up a safe haven. From this site she can load all her tools and launch attacks. Now she is using someone else's resources and if a victim traces back the address it will go to the relay site and not the real attacker. This concept is not new, but moving forward it is going to be taken to a new level.

Attackers are going to start to compromise and infiltrate entire companies and use them as massive control centers for insider attacks. In essence, corporations will inadvertently be sub-funding illicit activity because they have poor security. If I am going to launch a massive insider attack, I need resources, I need Internet connectivity, and what better place to find it than a large company that has redundant T1 or T3s and extra servers? In essence, attackers are finding that organizations provide them "free" collocation services.

You might ask, while a company would prefer this does not happen, what is the big concern? The biggest concern with this happening to an organization is downstream liability. This means that if your company has such weak security that they allow themselves to be a launching-off platform, they could potentially be held liability for being grossly negligent in securing their enterprise. Not only could this cause serious monetary issues for a company, but if legal action is taken, the case is public and that could result in bad reputation, loss of customer confidence, and loss of customers.

Social Engineering

The weakest link in any organization is the people. Since most insiders had full access it has always been easy to just compromise an insider. However, as companies start to tighten controls, full access is going to be limited and taken away. Therefore, attackers need other ways to get the information or access they need; the solution: social engineering.

Social engineering is human manipulation where you pretend to be someone you're not with the sole goal of gaining access or information you otherwise would not have.

Social engineering is a very powerful, yet easy tool at the attacker's disposal. As social engineering attacks increase, organizations need to do a better job at education, making people aware, and defending against these types of attacks.

Plants

When many people think of insider threat they think that as soon as someone has access, they will commit the act immediately. While this would seem logical, it is easy to trace and the person is usually limited in access and capability. A good insider knows that patience is the key.

More and more governments are putting plants in competing companies in foreign countries. They view this as a long-term investment, so they will give you a fully qualified candidate to work at your company. This person will work their butt off for many years, learning the process, gaining trust, getting promoted, and then eventually will slowly start to extract sensitive information from the company.

This model is highly effective and very hard to detect and trace. No one thinks that someone would get hired at a company and work very hard so that in five years he could compromise data. To many of us it does not make sense, but to the skilled attacker or government organization it is a worthwhile investment.

Tolerance Increasing

As attacks increase, people's tolerance for pain increases. There are worm outbreaks and other attacks that three years ago would have made the front page of every paper, but today they do not even get a mention because people's tolerance for this type of behavior is increasing. Instead of doing something about it, we are accepting it as a norm.

This model is very dangerous because as soon as you get in the acceptance mode, the problem will keep getting worse and worse and no one will notice.

Something has to change; otherwise, the impact of the insider will cause such financial loss that it will impact the entire economic infrastructure.

Framing

As attackers get more sophisticated, they are looking for ways not to get caught. Especially in the case of the plant, if you worked three years in an organization you would want to get a lot of mileage out of it and not commit one act of insider threat and get caught. The easiest way to not get caught is to frame someone else. Instead of using your own identity, more and more attackers are compromising and using someone else's identity so that person gets blamed for the attack. If a skilled attacker does this properly, he can build up so much evidence against the person he is framing that there is no questioning or doubt in anyone's mind who committed the insider attack.

This trend is very scary because now you have innocent people becoming victims, in addition to the company. Therefore it is very critical that companies carefully examine the facts to make sure they are not punishing the wrong person.

Lack of Cyber Respect

It is amazing, but we are raising a generation today that has minimal respect for the cyber world. The total lack of appreciation and understanding of cyber ethics is downright scary. Many people would never think of stealing someone's wallet, but they have no problem reading people's e-mail or compromising their user ID and password.

As organizations put together new policies and procedures, they have to realize that they have a long road ahead of them in changing how people perceive and act towards information that exists in a digital format. By covering the future trends, you will help your organization properly build defensive measures against the insider threat that will not only work today but scale tomorrow.

Summary

This chapter was meant to serve as an introduction to how bad the problem is and why you should be concerned about it. Some problems if you ignore them they will go away, this problem will only continue to get worse. It is important that organizations understand the risks that insider threat can have, realize it is occurring today and take action to minimize or prevent the damage that it can cause.

Index

3Gs rule of personal protection, 48–50
802.11
    authentication, 225
    security (encryption), 228–230
    standard, 205–206, 209
999 keys, 250–251

A

access
    controlling, 367, 378
    employee, problems with, 342–344
    unauthorized wireless, 206–207
access points (APs)
    attacks, 208
    physically securing, 215
    spoofing, 232
active handheld devices, 127
Active Memory Image, 129
active RFID systems, 155–156
ad-hoc mode, wireless, 217–218
affiliates, insider, 346–347
agency phonebooks, 15–16
Air Force One, and RFID technology, 146
American Registry of Internet Numbers (ARIN),
    302
American Society for Industrial Security (ASIS),
    172
analog steganography, 318–320
AOL (America On-Line), 80
appended spaces, and steganography, 332–333
Appert, Nicolas, 55
ARIN (American Registry of Internet Numbers),
    302
Art of Deception, The (Mitnick and Simon), 6
ASIS (American Society for Industrial Security),
    172
assessing
    advocacy sources, 180–181
    information content, 179–180
    information sources, 185–186
associates, insider, 345–346
attacks
    See also specific attack
    detecting and disabling steganography attacks,
        332–333
    on hidden information, 332–334
    steganographic, 333–335
    targets of insider attacks, 369–371
audio files
    MASKER program and, 330
    steganography and, 325–326
auditing, 375–376

authentication
    802.11, 225
    badges, employee, 243–250
    Kerberos, 228
    open system, 225–226
    RADIUS, 219–221
    shared key, 226–227
    two-part, 16
authorized insiders, 342–344, 358
Autopsy Browser, 111
availability, and wireless, 210–211
awareness programs
    employee, 10, 16–17, 31, 33–35
    keystroke readers, 21–23

B

badges
    conference, 159
    employee, 12–13, 243–250
Bali bomber, 373
bandwidth, RFID frequencies, 152–154
Basic Service Set (BSS), 218
batteries
    backup, 69
    for emergency lighting, 62–65
bit stream copy, 108
BITS banking consortium, 172–173
Black's Law Dictionary, 79
Blindside application, 329–330
blogs, forums, 300–301
Bluetooth connections, 139
bomb recognition training, 17, 19
Bouck, Jared, 260
Boy Scouts of America Field Book, The, 57
Brennan, Chris, 259
Brown, Dan, 314
browsers, cleaning system, 190–191
BSS (Basic Service Set), 218
building operations
    alerting system, 47
    drop ceilings, 20
    phone closets, 23
    security, 17, 235–251
bump keys, 250–251
business materials assessment, 181–183
business continuity plans (BCPs), 47
business defense plan, 46

C

cadaver RFID chips, 159
candles, 61

canned food, 54–55
carbon monoxide poisoning, 66–67
Cardano Grill system, 316, 317
CCIPS (Computer Crime and Intellectual
    Property Section), 170–171
CDs, and seizure of digital information, 86, 87,
    104–105
cellular devices, handheld forensics, 135–137
cellular phones, 71
CERT CC, 171
chain of custody, 115
Challenge-Handshake Authentication Protocol,
    226
chemical light sticks, 62
child pornography, 109
Chinese, and steganography, 315
chosen stego, message steganographic attacks, 334
Cole, Eric, 337
Coleman lanterns, 61, 65
collection of evidence, 129–130
color palettes, steganography tool, 332
communication, importance of, during
    emergencies, 70–72
Communications ISAC, 173
community shelters, 52
Computer Crime and Intellectual Property
    Section (CCIPS), 170–171
computers
    authorized seizure. *See* seizure of digital
        information
    discarded, 26–30
    obtaining information from running, 105–107
    pulling the plug on, 88–89
conference badges, 159
confidentiality, and wireless, 209–210
consumer value tags, 151
contactless cards, 249
contingency plans, 46–47
control points, evacuation, 48–49
cooking in emergencies, 57–58
copying vs. imaging and hashes, 107–108
countermeasures, social engineering, 5
cover generation steganographic methods, 323
crackers, 2
crime
    civil vs. criminal events, 78–79
    potential RFID, 161–162
    scene procedures, 85–88, 113–115
    seizure of digital information. *See* seizure of
        digital information
cryptography
    See also encryption, steganography
    described, 312
    vs. steganography, 313
CSI/RBI Computer Crime Report, 366
Culpur, Samuel, 316
Cyber Crime Investigations (Syngress), 78
cyberthreats

CERT report on, 367
information sources about, 169–172
cylindrical axial pin tumbler locks, 258–260

D

data injection, 320
data objects and digital information seizure,
    76–77, 80, 107–110
Datawatch cards, 250
DaVinci Code, The (Brown), 314
deep Web search utilities, 176–177
DefendAir paint, 216
demilitarized zones (DMZs), 217
denial-of-service attacks, 210
Denton, Jeremiah, 317
Department of Homeland Security, US-CERT
    (United States Computer Emergency
    Readiness Team), 171–172
Department of Justice, Computer Crime and
    Intellectual Property Section (CCIPS),
    170–171
detecting
    and disabling steganography attacks, 332–333
    insider threats, 349–350
devices
    cellular, handheld forensics, 135–137
    PDAs. *See* PDAs
    storage, seizure of, 87–88
dial-up modems, 5–6
digital evidence
    collection, 111–112, 129–131
    defining, 79–82
    preservation, 128, 137–139
    seizure methodology, 82–86
    seizure procedures, 112–115
digital forensics, 124, 125–129
digital information seizure. *See* seizure of digital
    information
digital steganography, 320–321
Direct-sequence spread spectrum (DSSS),
    204–205
directories, corporate, 15–16
disabling steganography attacks, 332–335
discovery phase, OSINT, 169–178
disease, impact of pandemics, 39
disk space, hiding information in, 326–327
distilled water, 56
distortion steganographic techniques, 323
DMZs (demilitarized zones), 217
DNS (Domain Name Service), 301
documenting
    penetration tests, 298
    seizure of digital information, 113
Domain Name Service (DNS), 301
door signs, 23
Drake, Phil, 37
drinking water, 56–57

drop cords, electric, 68
dumpster diving, 10–12, 271–277
Durrand, Peter, 55
DVDs, and seizure of digital information, 104–105
dynamo flashlights, 63–64
dynamo radios, 72

E

e-mail and seizure of digital information, 80
E-ZPass RFID system, 158
EAP point, 227
EAS (Electronic Article Surveillance), 145
eavesdropping, 207
electric flossers (lock picking), 260–261
electric generators, 66–68
Electricity Sector (ESISAC), 173
Electronic Article Surveillance (EAS), 145
electronic badges, 248–250
Electronic Crime Force, 169
electronic locks, 150
Electronic Product Code (EPC) and RFID, 152
emergencies
    building exits, 42
    cooking in, 57–58
    lighting, 61
Emergency Management and Response ISAC, 173
emergency power, 66–70
employee
    access, issues with, 342–344
    awareness programs, 10, 16–17, 31, 33–34
    badges, 12–13, 243–250
Encase, 111
encryption
    imaging vs. copying and hashing, 107–108
    and keystroke readers, 21
    watermarking, 328–329
    as wholesale seizure limitation, 91
    WEP, 228–230
    WPA, 230–231
EPC (Electronic Product Code) and RFID, 152
escape pack for emergencies, 43–45
ESISAC (Electricity Sector ISAC), 173
espionage, 367
ethical conduct, penetration testing, 297
ethical war driver, 200
evacuation
    personal bags, 52–53
    workplace plans, 48–50
evidence, digital
    collection, handheld forensics, 129–131
    defining, 79–82
    preservation, 128, 137–139
    seizure of digital information. See seizure of digital information
exits, emergency, 42
Exxon Mobil SpeedPass, 159

F

Family Education Rights and Privacy Act, 209
family preparedness
    generally, 38–41
    personal plans, 41–45
    plans, 50–53, 58–59
    ready kits, 59–61
Faraday devices, 135, 138
FasTrak RFID system, 158
Federal Bureau of Investigation, InfraGard and, 170
Federal Information Security Management Act, 209
Federal Rules of Criminal Procedure (FRCP), search and seizure provisions, 80–81
Federal Rules of Evidence (FRE), evidence presentation, 80–81
fee-based information services, 177–178
file systems
    handheld devices, 126–127
    steganographic, 326, 331
filters, water, 56–57
Financial Services/Information Sharing and Analysis Center (FS/ISAC), 172
financial services sector, information about threats, 172–173
fire drills, 49
fire plans, family, 50–51
firewalls, 217, 354, 355, 357
first aid kit, 49–50
FIRST (Forum for Incident Response Security Teams), 171
first responders
    and handheld forensics, 131–133
    and seizure of digital information, 96–102, 100
flashlights, floodlights, 63–66
food
    cooking in emergencies, 57–58
    for preparedness pantry, 53–56
Force Field Wireless, 216
forensic handhelds. See handheld forensics
Forensic Examination of Digital Evidence (NIJ), 105, 116
forensic laboratory backlogs, 93–94
Forensic Toolkit, 111
Forum for Incident Response Security Teams (FIRST), 171
forums, blogs, 300–301
fragile watermarks, 329
freeze-dried foods, 55
frequencies
    RFID (radio frequency identification), 152–154
    wireless, 204–205
Frequency-hopping spread spectrum (FHSS), 204–205
FRS (Family Radio Service) radios, 73

FS/ISAC (Financial Services/Information Sharing and Analysis Center), 172
fuel for emergency cooking, 57–58

G

garage door openers, 26
gas appliances, 58, 63
generators, electric, 66–68
global source tagging, 145
Green, Ron, 165
Grunwald, Lucas, 156

H

hacking, no-tech. *See* no-tech hacking
ham radios, 73
handheld devices
   forensics. *See* handheld forensics
   PDAs. *See* PDAs
handheld forensics
   analysis and reporting, 141
   cellular handling, 135–137
   evidence collection, 129–131
   evidence preservation, 137–139
   first responders, collection and PDA handling, 133–135
   introduction to, 124–129
   maintaining forensic data connections, 139–141
handheld lights, 63–64
hard drives
   destroying old, 29–30
   imaging, 107
hardware
   computers. *See* computers
   and MAC addresses, 224
   seizure, limitations on, 90–98
hashes vs. copying, imaging, 107–108
headlamps, 64–65
Health Insurance Portability and Accountability Act (HIPAA), 209
Helix tool, 111
HiD badges, 249–250
hiding information. *See* steganography
high frequency (HF) band, 153
High Tech Crime Consortium, 170
Highway Information Sharing and Analysis Center (Highway ISAC), 173–174
HIPAA (Health Insurance Portability and Accountability Act), 209
Histiaeus, 315
history, steganography's use throughout, 314–317
Hurricane Katrina, 39
Hurricane Wilma, 50

I

IBSS, wireless mode, 217–218

identification
   employee badges, 12–13, 243–250
   radio frequency. *See* RFID
identity theft and dumpster diving, 11–12
IDS (intrusion detection systems), 231, 354, 357
illumination lamps, 65
iLook, 111
ImageMasster, 111
imaging
   information, data objects on-scene, 107–110
   techniques, handheld devices, 129
imaging information, data objects on-scene, 117–118
Info Stego tool, 330
information
   analysis support, 192–193
   digital. *See* digital information
   discovery, sources for, 169–178
   hiding. *See* steganography
   imaging on-scene, 107–110
   online contacts. *See specific organization*
   security programs, 212
   seizure of digital information. *See* seizure of digital information
Information Technology ISAC, 174
InfraGard, 170
infrastructure modes, wireless, 217–218
injection, data, 320
insider threats
   acceptable level of loss, 348–349
   authorized vs. unauthorized insiders, 342–344
   categories of, 344–347
   defined, 35, 341–342
   effects on organization, 355–357
   future trends, 377–382
   impacts of, 371–374
   insider vs. external threats, 350–351, 353–355
   introduction to, 338–341
   key aspects of, 347–348
   preventing, 375–376
   preventing vs. detecting, 349–350
   profiling insiders, 374–375
   reasons that organizations ignore, 351–353
   statistics about, 357–369
   targets of attack, 369–371
integrity, and wireless, 210
intelligence, open source. *See* Open Source Intelligence
interference, wireless, 207–208
internal auditors, 31
International High Crime Investigation Association, 170
Internet
   anonymous surfing, fee-based services, 190
   capacity during emergencies, 40
   emergency information on, 71
   news, assessing, 183–184

Internet Crimes Against Children (ICAC) Task Forces, 109
intrusion detection systems (IDS), 231, 354, 357
intrusion prevention systems (IPS), 354, 357
inventories, and RFID technology, 145
invisible ink, 319
'invisible' Web, 176–177
IPS (intrusion prevention systems), 354, 357
IPv6 (Internet Protocol version 6), 94
IrDA connections, 139
irradiated foods, 56
ISPs, and seizure of digital information, 108
Italian Job, The (movie), 338

J

jamming, wireless, 207–208
janitors and key control, 10
jargon code, 320
Johnny Mnemonic (movie), 315

K

Katrina (hurricane), 39
Kensington laptop lock systems, 258–260
Kerberos authentication method, 228
kerosene lamps, 61
key control, 8–10
Key Ghost hardware loggers, 20
keystroke readers, loggers, 20–23
Kipper, Greg, 311
kits
    family ready, 59–61
    first aid, 49
    personal evacuation bags, 52–53
known cover, message steganographic attacks, 333–334
KPKFile program, 331

L

laboratory analysis, factors limiting wholesale seizure of digital information, 93–94
Laurie, Adam, 284, 285
LEAP (Lightweight Extensible Authentication Protocol) point, 227
least privilege principle, 342, 375
Least Significant Bit (LSB), 321, 324
LED (light-emitting diode) lights, 63–64
legal framework for seizure of digital information, 77, 109–110
legal liability and wireless access points (APs), 223
Liang, Qiao, 373
lie detector tests, 339
life cycle, security analysis, 290–293
light sticks, 62–63
lighting
    motion-sensing lights, 25
    types of, 61–66

Lightweight Extensible Authentication Protocol (LEAP) point, 227
linguistic steganography, 323
locks
    electronic, 150
    high-security, 24
    and key control, 8–10
    lock picking equipment, 27–28
    picking, bumping, 250–261
    testing, 25–26
Locks, Safes, and Security (Tobias), 252
loggers, keystroke, 20–23
logging, 375–376
logon, SAP logon software, 267
logs, reviewing video security, 24–25
Long, Johnny, 233
low frequency (LF) band, 153
LSB (Least Significant Bit), 321, 324

M

MAC addresses, 224, 232
maglites, 63, 64
man-in-the-middle attacks, 207
marketing materials, assessing, 181–183
MASKER program, 330
master keys, 8–10, 150
Master Lock brute forcing, 252–258
MD5 hash, 108, 128
Medeco locks, 9–10
media
    hardware seizures, limitations on, 90–98
    identification of digital, 86
    storage. *See* storage media
meeting points, family, 51
meta search engines, 176
microdots, 318
microwave band, 154
miniaturization, 378
mirroring Web sites, 302
Mitnick, Kevin, 6, 7
modems, dial-up, 5–6
moles, 378–379
motion-sensing lights, 25
MRE (Meals Ready to Eat), 54
Mullen, Tim, 258
Multi-State ISAC, 174

N

Napoleon, 55
National Institute for Standards and Technology (NIST), 112
National Vulnerability Database (NVD), 171
network packets, hiding information in, 327
network security, goals of, 211–212
networks
    enumerating, 303
    porous, 379–380

virtual private networks (VPNs), 219
news, assessing Internet, 183–184
newsgroup searches, 300
newspaper code, 319–320
NIST (National Institute for Standards and Technology), 112
Nmap port scan tool, 303
no-tech hacking
    information security, 261–285
    introduction to, 234–239
    lockpickers, 251–252
    physical security, 235–251
NOAA (National Oceanic and Atmospheric Administration), radio emergency information, 71–72
null ciphers, 319
NVD (National Vulnerability Database), 171

O

O'Brien, Dennis F., 143
one-time pads, 318
online contacts information. *See specific organization*
Open Source Intelligence (OSINT)
    collection trade craft, 189–191
    direction, 166–169
    discovery phase, 169–178
    discrimination phase, 178–191
    dissemination phase, 194
    distillation phase, 191–193
    introduction to, 166
Open System Authentication, 225–226
operating systems, PDAs, 126–127
Operational Security (OPSEC), 189
optical media, 87
Orwell, George, 144
OSAC (Overseas Security Advisory Council), 172
OSI model, and RFID, 147, 157
OSINT. *See* Open Source Intelligence
outside affiliates, 346–347
outsider-insider threats, 5–6
outsourcing, 379
Overseas Security Advisory Council (OSAC), 172

P

Palm PDAs, 127, 267–269
pandemics, impacts of, 39
pantry, preparedness, 53–58
partitions, hidden, 327
passive RFID systems, 155–156
passports, U.S., 158
passwords
    insecure wireless, 221
    storing safely, 15–16
PDAs (personal digital assistants)
    digital forensic foundations, 125–129
    and digital forensics, 124

first response cards, 131–133
penetration testing, 25–26
    deviations from procedure, 293–295
    methodology for, 298–308
    security analysis life cycle, 290–293
    tester mentality, 295–298, 309
perceptual masking, steganographic technique, 324–325
perimeter security, 215–216
personal digital assistants. *See* PDAs
personal emergency plans, 42–45
personal evacuation bags, 52–53
personal information, assessing, 186–187, 193
pet food, medications, 59
phone closets, 23
phonebooks, corporate or agency, 15–16
phones, cell, 71
physical media vs. digital media, 86–88
piggybacking, 13
plans
    business defense, 46
    personal emergency, 42–43
    workplace evacuation, 48–50
plants (insiders), 381
policies, security, 376
polygraphs, 339
port scans, 303
Porta, Giovanni, 315–316
portable 12-volt inverters, 69–70
portable electric generators, 66–68
POTS (Plain Old Telephone Service) line, 73
power, emergency, 66–70
power outages, 62
PPA (Privacy Protection Act), 92
preparedness
    family plans. *See* family preparedness
    general need for, 38–41
    pantry in home, 53–58
    workforce, 45–48
preservation of evidence, 128, 137–139
preventing insider threats, 349–350, 375–376
principle of least privilege, 342, 375
Prisoner's Problem, 313–314, 321
privacy, and wholesale seizure of digital information, 92–93
Privacy Protection Act (PPA), 92
private share on folders, 348
privilege escalation, 304–305
procedures, security, 377–378
profiling insiders, 374–375
programmatic penetration testing, 290
programmers and insider threats, 368
protocols. *See specific protocol*
proximity cards, 249
Public Transportation ISAC, 174
pulling the plug on computers, 88–89
pure insiders, 344–345

R

radio frequency identification. *See* RFID
radios
    SAME alert, 71–72
    types of, 72–73
RADIUS (Remote Authentication Dial-In User
       Service) servers, 219–221
RAID arrays, 90–91
RAM (random access memory)
    capacity of PDAs, 133
    and seizure of digital information, 105–107,
       114, 117–118
Red Cross
    first aid kits, training, 50
    local shelter information, 52
Reeves, Keanu, 315
relays, security of, 380
Remote Authentication Dial-In User Service
       (RADIUS) servers, 219–221
reporting, handheld forensics, 141
reports, information assessment, 194
resources
    cyberthreat information sources, 169–172
    espionage, 367
    insider threat information, 365
    tracking and monitoring with RFID, 147
RFDump tool, 156
RFID (radio frequency identification)
    active vs. passive systems, 155–156
    applications of, 157–163
    EPC and, 152
    frequencies, 152–154
    introduction and background, 144–146
    purposes of, 146–147
    security from functional perspective, 150–151
    software tools, 156–157
    technology explained, 147–150
risk assessments, performing mini, 3–5
robust watermarks, 329
Rogers, Russ, 289

S

sabotage, 355
SalesLogix, 266
SAME alert radios, 71–72
SAP logon software, 267
Sarbanes Oxley, 209
SC0ISAC (Supply Chain), 174
scanning, vulnerability, 303
Schola Stenanographica (Schott), 315
schools, early dismissal from, 51–52
Schott, Gaspar, 315
search engines, 175–176, 299–300
SEARCH organization, 106–107

*Searching and Seizing Computers and Obtaining
      Electronic Evidence in Criminal Investigations*
      (Dept. of Justice), 80–81, 99
Secure Socket Layer/Transport Security Layer
      (SSL/TLS) protocol, 227–228
security
    802.11 (encryption), 228–230
    analysis life cycle, 290–293
    building operations, 17
    configuration weaknesses, 221–222
    information, 261–285
    logs, video, 24–25
    network. *See* wireless
    physical, 235–251
    policies, 377–378
    preventing insider threats, 375–376
    RFID (radio frequency identification), 150–151,
       159–161
Security Assessment: Case Studies (Syngress), 290
seizure of digital information
    common issues within, 112–115
    determining most appropriate method, 115–117
    digital evidence, defining, 79–82
    hardware seizures, limitations on, 90–98
    introduction to, 76–79
    methodology for, 82–89
    options for, 98–112
semagrams, 318, 323
servers, RADIUS, 219–221
Service Set Identifier (SSID), 218–219, 232
SHA1 hash, 128
shared key authentication, 226–227
shelf-stable foods, 54
shelters, community, 52
shoplifting tags, 145
shoulder surfing, 261–271
shredders, 13–14
Simon, William, 6
slack space, steganographic technique, 327
SMART tool, 111
social engineering
    awareness programs, 31–35
    countermeasures, 8–31
    described, 2–3, 381
    mini risk assessment, 3–5
    motivations of perpetrators, victims, 6–7
    outsider-insider threats, 5–6
soft pack canning, MRE (Meals Ready to Eat), 54
solid-state inverter generators, 69–70
Spectacular Computer Crimes (Bloombecker), 100
spoofing
    access points, 232
    MAC addresses, 224
spotlights, 65–66
spread spectrum
    steganographic encoding, 324
    steganographic technique, 322

and wireless, 204–205
spy chips, 151
SSID (Service Set Identifier), 201, 218–219, 232
SSL/TLS (Secure Socket Layer/Transport Security
    Layer) protocol, 227–228
StankDawg, 271
States v. Gawrysiak, 81
static handheld devices, 127
statistical steganographic methods, 322–323
Stealing the Network (Mullen), 258
steganography
    analog, 318–320
    applied to different media, 325–327
    detection and attacks, 332–334
    digital, 320–321
    distortion techniques, 323–325
    hiding in network packets, 327
    introduction to, 312–317
    issues in information hiding, 328
    real-world uses of, 331
    six categories of, 321–323
    tools for, 329–331
    watermarking, 328–329
Stegbreak, Stegdetect tools, 332
stego only attacks, 333
Steve Jackson Games, Inc. v. Secret Service, 92–93
storage media
    data objects and digital information seizure,
        76–77
    identification of digital media, 85–88
    PDA capacities, 128–129
    seizure of, 87–88
stoves, cooking, 58
substitution system steganography, 321
supplies
    escape pack for emergencies, 43–45
    preparedness pantry, 53–58
Supply Chain ISAC, 174
Surface Transportation ISAC, 174
swipe cards, 249

T

tags
    consumer value, 151
    RFID (radio frequency identification), 148–149
tailgating, 13, 16–17, 240–243
targets of insider attacks, 369–371
technical penetration testing, 290–291
technical steganography, 323–324
televisions, hacking hotel, 277–284
terrorism and preparedness, 38–41
testing
    home preparedness plans, 58–59

penetration. *See* penetration testing
text files
    KPKFile program for, 331
    and steganographic techniques, 326
text semagrams, 323
texture block steganographic method, 325
threats
    See also specific threat
    financial services sector, information about,
        172–173
    to home wireless users, 213
    insider. *See* insider threats
    outsider-insider, 5–6
    physical, from wireless attacks, 208–209
    physical, information about, 172
    preparedness and, 38–41
Tobias, Marc, 252
Todd, Raymond, 197
tools
    for digital evidence collection, 111–112
    handheld forensic, 140–141
    penetration testing, 297–298
    steganography, 329–331
training
    employee awareness, 10
    first aid, 49
transfer domain steganographic technique, 322
transfer switches, electric generators, 67–68
transform steganographic techniques, 324
Turning Grille, 317
type spacing, offsetting, 319

U

ultra high frequency (UHF) band, 153–154
unauthorized insiders, 342–344
unauthorized wireless, 206–207
United States Computer Emergency Readiness
    Team (US-CERT), 171–172
United States Secret Service, 169
UNIX systems, 144
Unrestricted Warfare (Liang and Xiangsui), 373
UPS power supply, 69
US-CERT (United States Computer Emergency
    Readiness Team), 171–172
USA Patriot Act, 169
U.S. v. Stephenson, 115
USSS ECTFs, 170

V

validating information, 192
victims of social engineering, 7
video

Blindside application and, 330
security logs, reviewing, 24–25
steganography and, 325
virtual private networks (VPNs), 219
visible noise, and steganography, 332
VPNs (virtual private networks), 219
vulnerabilities
  assessing, 4–5
  National Vulnerability Database (NVD), 171
  scanning, exploiting, 303–304

W

Wal-Mart, 147
war driving kits, 199–203
water in preparedness pantry, 56–57
Water Information Sharing and Analysis Center
    (WaterISAC), 175
watermarking, 313, 328–329
Web sites
  about lock security, 285–286
  financial, 302–303
  mirroring, 302
Wels, Barry, 259
WEP (Wired Equivalent Privacy), 228–230
Westhues, Jonathan, 249
WHOIS service, 301–302
Wiles, Jack, 1, 235
Windows Encrypted File System, 103
Wired Equivalent Privacy (WEP), 228–230
wireless
  802.11 standard, 205–206
  awareness, introduction to, 198–203
  eavesdropping, 207

FHSS and DSSS, 204–205
interference and jamming, 207–208
legal liability, 223
network security, 211–223
protection bags, 135–136
technology weaknesses, 224
unauthorized access, 206–207
workforce
  continuity, 40
  preparedness, 45–48
workplace evacuation plans, 48–50
WPA encryption, 230–231
WPA-Enterprise, 231

X

Xiangsui, Wang, 373

Z

zero-day exploits, 355

Buy a Syngress book and attend either one of the Techno Conferences for 50% off current price

To take advantage of this offer, simply visit the TheTrainingCo website at www.TheTrainingCo.com and select the conference you would like to attend.

Once you have navigated to the conference registration page online, select the appropriate (Industry, Government or Law Enforcement) **Payment Type** and deduct 50% of that price for the **Payment Amount** that you enter. And finally, enter "Syngress Publishing Special Offer" in the comments section of the form.

That's all you need to do. You will be sent a confirmation notice as well as regular Techno Briefs with information about upcoming training events, how you can get lots of free stuff as well as important information you will need as you get closer to the event you have chosen.

If you have any questions, call 410.703.0332 for more details...